THE MONARCH OF MYSORE
HIS HIGHNESS SRI NALWADI KRISHNARAJA WODEYAR - A BIOGRAPHY

Author : **Rajasevasaktha Padmashri C K Venkataramaiah**

Translator: **S Naganath**

INDIA • SINGAPORE • MALAYSIA

Copyright © S Naganath 2024
All Rights Reserved.

ISBN
Hardcase   979-8-89322-295-1
Paperback 979-8-89067-807-2

This book has been published with all efforts taken to make the material error-free after the consent of the author. However, the author and the publisher do not assume and hereby disclaim any liability to any party for any loss, damage, or disruption caused by errors or omissions, whether such errors or omissions result from negligence, accident, or any other cause.

While every effort has been made to avoid any mistake or omission, this publication is being sold on the condition and understanding that neither the author nor the publishers or printers would be liable in any manner to any person by reason of any mistake or omission in this publication or for any action taken or omitted to be taken or advice rendered or accepted on the basis of this work. For any defect in printing or binding the publishers will be liable only to replace the defective copy by another copy of this work then available.

Maharaja of Mysore Sri Nalwadi Sri Krishnaraja Wodeyar

Late Yuvaraja Sri Kanteerava Narasimharaja Wodeyar

Present Ruler Maharaja Sri Jayachamarajendra Wodeyar Bahadur

DEDICATION

This small token of the author's humble offering to the Maharaja Sri Jayachamarajendra Wodeyar Bahadur is made on this day to him with his prior approval. This book is dedicated to His Highness the Maharaja of Mysore by a loyal subject and a time-honoured Royalist with all reverence.

श्रीः
नाल्वडि श्रीकृष्णराज - नवरत्नमाला

1. श्रीमत्कृष्णमहाप्रभो! तव मही राजन्वती सत्यस-।
   ङ्कल्पतां प्रतिपद्य पूर्ववदियं संशोभते सम्पदा ।
   लोके सदणभूषितं सुचतुरं रूपाधिकं वल्लभं
   सम्प्राप्यातितरां यथा कुलवधूस्तद्वज्जगच्छ्रेयस्ते ॥

२. श्रीमत्कृष्णमहाप्रभो! तव यशः कान्ता दिगन्तेषु चो-
   क्षुष्णन्ती भवदीय सद्गुणकथागीतमृतेनादरात् ।
   इण्डचामण्डलसार्वभौममणिहृद्रङ्गस्थले सौहृदा
   नृत्यन्ती बिरुदानन्य .... चिरं मोदते ॥

३. श्रीमत्कृष्णमहाप्रभो! तव मनः कासारसीम्पन्तरे
   सरि-तोषामृतसेवनादनुपमानन्दात्सुखं प्राणिनः ।
   जीव्यन्ति स्म किरातभीतिरहित सज्जीवनोत्कर्षता -
   क्षान्योन्याधिगतोत्सुकात्सुचरितास्ताम्राज्यलाभाद्द्रुवम् ॥

४. श्रीमत्कृष्णमहाप्रभो! तव महीराज्यं स्वराज्यं क्षितौ
   सौध्यं भव्यकलावचोऽतीतम्पर्नेशं श्रीसुन्दरं मन्दिरम् ।
   कोशं मङ्गलदेवतास्थितिसमावेशं च यद्भाषितम्
   सर्वानन्दविभूषितं सुरुचिरस्वान्तं नितान्तं धृतम् ॥

५. श्रीमत्कृष्णमहाप्रभो! तव कृपास्रोतस्विनी वेदिता
   प्रागदेशापरपश्चिमोत्तर दिशामन्तेव क्रमात् ॥
   प्राज्ञेषूत्तमपण्डितेषु कविषु प्रौढेषु दीनेषु च
   सद्भिदां वचस्सु गायकेषु परं व्याप्तं जगन्मण्डलम् ॥

६. श्रीमत्कृष्णनृपकुञ्जरमणे! त्वद्दानधारासरित्क -
   ल्लोकान्तरवेल्लदम्बुधिलसन्म्परम्भसारोद्गता ।
   सङ्गीतोत्सुकरङ्गदं गजचमूश्रृङ्गारभङ्गीलसत्
   भृङ्गस्सर्वदिगन्तरेषु च परं गायन्ति दद्रैभवम् ॥

೭. दानेनार्कसुतं धनेन धनदं क्षान्त्या क्षितिं देजसा
पद्माप्तं यशसा सुरेन्द्रमपिं यद्बुद्ध्ना च वाचस्पतिमं ।
धैर्येणाचलराजमम्बुधिमगाधेनान्तरङ्गेण स-
द्रूपेणात्मभवं निराकृतमिति प्राहुर्जगत्थां स्फुटम् ॥
೮. श्रीमत्कृष्णनिभो! भवन्नगरसामीत्याद्रि श‍ृङ्गाग्रसत्
रत्नौधादिविचितकूटविलसत्प्रासाद मध्ये स्थिता ।
चामुण्डा सुतवत्सला स्वसुतलोलाधार्यगाम्भीर्य
सद्धैर्यादि प्रसमिक्ष्य विस्मितमना शौले बभूवेप्सया ॥

೯. श्रीमत्कृष्णविभो! त्वदीयपुरकल्याणाधिकं वीक्ष्य च-
च्छक्रस्यामरवतिमपि तथा कर्तुं सयन्तो भवेत् ।
विद्यद्दीपविधान धूमशकट प्रस्थानतन्त्रीप्रवृ -
त्याख्याम्ररयानमुख्यविषयाण्यालोकय संलज्जिता ॥
श्रीकृष्णराजनृपते! नवरत्नमाला-
मम्लानसौरभगुणोज्ज्वलवर्णलीलाम्
उल्लसितार्थविलसत्सुमनोमतुलां
मालामिवान्तरगळेऽर्प्य प्रलोभात् ॥

|| Nalwadi Krishnaraja - Navaratnamala ||
by Vidwan Motaganahalli Mahadeva Sastri

An English Summary

To Srimath Krishnaraja Mahaprabhugale, [the motto of Yadu Dynasty of Mysore is "I shall uphold the Truth"] your ancestors adhered to the truth and remained loyal to the truth during their reign.

All the previous rulers were virtuous, wise and handsome. The state has enjoyed prosperity from time memorial, because of their just rule.

Hail, Maharaja! Your fame has spread in all the four directions. Your citizens are singing ballads praising your noble qualities. Your fame and honour have found echo in the hearts of other rulers of India. All living creatures in your state are enjoying and living in harmony and happiness. Your citizens are safe and they are not afraid of evil-doers, thieves and highwaymen. The citizens of the state help each other, they love each other and live in peace. Your cities have grand buildings, which are proud monuments to your vision. In your shrines and treasury, Sri Mangala Devi (Goddess of auspiciousness) resides and looks after the welfare of everybody. Your compassion for subjects knows no bounds and it is known in the east and the west. The Royal Court of Mysore has given refuge to scholars, poets, artists, actors and musicians. Your charitable acts have flown down like a gentle stream and merged with the ocean.

You are so generous that you have not turned back anyone to go empty-handed. The music soirees and the cavalry, elephant and camel regiments are famous all over the world. His Highness could be compared to Karna in charitable acts, Kubera in possession of wealth, Mother Earth in tolerance, Sun God in effulgence, Devendra - God of Gods in fame, Bruhaspati in wisdom, Himavanta in courage, Samudra in dignity and Manmatha in good looks. The Goddess Chamundeshwari on top of the hill protects the members of the Royal Family and the subjects from misfortunes. The Goddess Chamundeshwari is pleased with the rule of Sri Nalwadi Krishnaraja Wodeyar and so, she has decided to preside over the Mysore State forever.

Your Highness has made every possible effort to convert Mysore city into the famed city of Amaravati (heavenly city) of Lord Devendra. Our kind *ruler has introduced railways, electricity, telephones and air travel to make this state into a modern state, thereby making Mysore more beautiful than Amaravati.*

I have composed this "Navaratnamala" with the sole intention that it should be an ornament, which adorns the neck of our beloved Maharaja forever.

By Vid. Motaganahalli Mahadeva Sastri (Great grandfather of Translator Prof. S. Naganath. From the family archives - read before His Highness during the Silver Jubilee function in Bangalore in September 1927)

Sir Mirza M. Ismail
Dewan of Mysore (1926-1941)

Contents

Foreword... *19*
Prologue... *21*
Biographer's Biography: Rajaseva saktha Padmasri C.K. Venkataramaiah...... *33*
The Tale of the Translator..................................... *41*
Acknowledgements... *45*
1. Unveiling of Momentous Events............................. 47
2. Childhood 59
3. The Death of the Patriarch 85
4. Regent's Appointment.................................... 95
5. Education 103
6. Background... 171
7. The Investiture Ceremony of Maharaja Sri Krishnaraja Wodeyar IV .. 195
8. The First 25 Years of Nalwadi's Reign (1902–1927) 217
9. The post-Silver Jubilee Reign of the Maharaja.................. 269
10. Maharaja as a Game Hunter 321
11. Patron of Arts and Music 367
12. The Torch Bearer of Dharma 397
13. Recent Developments in the State........................... 447
14. Praiseworthy Noble Qualities of the Maharaja Sri Nalwadi Krishnaraja Wodeyar.. 511
15. The Present Ruler Sri Jayachamarajendra Wodeyar 555

Foreword

In the following pages of his book, Mr. C. K. Venkataramaiah, a gifted scholar in Kannada and Sanskrit has attempted a biographical memoir of His Highness Sri Krishnaraja Wadiyar, Maharaja of Mysore, who after a most successful and eventful reign for nearly four decades, passed away in August last. I feel it is a proper privilege to write a foreword to this book.

Our late Sovereign was a Ruler of Exceptional Character and capacity, who, by his wise, progressive and benevolent reign and his unfaltering devotion to the good of his State, had conquered the hearts of his people and won the esteem and regard not only of his own countrymen in India but even those across the seas. The death of a few rulers has caused such deep and universal sorrow among the people of their States as the passing of His late Highness.

In the annals of modern kingship there are to be found few instances of a Prince, who was so genuinely loved and respected by the people during his lifetime as His late Highness was, and so universally mourned and missed when he was gone. In regard to fewer rulers, perhaps one could venture to prophesy, as one can safely do in the case of the late Maharaja of Mysore, that the results of their constructive statesmanship will endure to posterity and that the memory of their kindly human deeds will linger through the corridor of time.

Of the statesmanship, the personality and the numerous acts of benevolence of His late Highness, Mr. Venkataramaiah has written with a rare felicity and brilliance. It is altogether eminently readable and a very worthy biography of our noble Ruler, which he has produced. Mr. Venkataramaiah has brought to bear upon his task literary gifts of a very high order. He is the master of a style and diction, which have won him a place of honour among contemporary Kannada men of letters. Above all, he possesses, in a more than adequate degree, the quality of true admiration for the subject and the element of deep understanding without which a really successful biography is hardly ever written.

It has been truly said that the greatest monument for our great Maharaja is the very State that he left behind him. In every phase of Mysore's activity today and in the history of the growth and development of every branch of the Administration is revealed the quiet, conscientious working of the mind of a Ruler who was incessantly thinking of the welfare of the millions, whom Providence had entrusted to his care and who inspired by a constant and unwearying endeavour to promote their highest good. Mr. Venkataramaiah may well feel gratified that he has produced a biography of intense and abiding human interest. His book can be read for the sheer delight of a brilliant study, but it is also of special value as it affords an intimate glimpse into the life of a great man and his real personality.

And not the least of the merits of this biography is the wealth of authentic anecdotes which the author has, through his personal contact with His late Highness, been able to bring together to illustrate what has often been said in regard to him – that he was verily "a Prince among men and a man among Princes." In a word, Mr. Venkataramaiah has given us a living and vivid picture of our late Ruler.

It is superfluous for me to commend to the public a work of this kind. For the subject constitutes its own recommendation. The appeal of a true biography of His late Highness is bound to be as wide as the respect and adoration which he inspired, when he was alive, and in the case of this book, one can confidently say that it will be warmly welcomed and read in all parts, where Kannada is understood and appreciated. By reason of its literary excellence and of the greatness of the hero of the biography the success of Mr. Venkataramaiah's effort is doubly assured.

Bangalore
18th April 1941

Mirza M Ismail
Dewan of Mysore
[Original in English]

Prologue

I appealed to His Highness Sri Nalwadi Krishnaraja Wodeyar some three years ago to grant me permission to write an official biography of our ruler. The Maharaja graciously gave his consent for writing this biographical work. I did extensive research and collected material over a long period of time. I also approached Yuvaraja Sri Kanteerava Narasimharaja Wodeyar for his permission to include many incidents connected with his life in this book. He was equally magnanimous in giving his permission to include many incidents connected with his life. My greatest regret in life is that I could not complete this biography and give it as a humble offering to Maharaja and Yuvaraja during their lifetime. Alas! They are not with us anymore.

Our Monarch is a great *"chetana"* (Sentient force); he led a supremely pure and noble life of an ascetic (Rishi). If his life achievements are enumerated leaving out all flowery descriptions of language, it will still run to several volumes. In general, the citizens of our state and those people living in the neighbouring states know our Maharaja as a remarkable administrator. It is globally known how much the princely state of Mysore has made great strides in economic development through political reforms under Maharaja's rule of 38 years and earned the Sobriquet of "Modern State." This is a historical achievement of our ruler. Even if you leave this out of biography, he still comes out as a great charismatic personality.

Viceroy of India Lord Linlithgow (1936-1943) in his tribute to the Maharaja said on 17th March 1941, "The Maharaja of Mysore Sri Nalwadi Krishnaraja Wodeyar would have made his mark in any field of work. He was an exceptional person blessed with great competence and genius." In fact, many of his subjects are not aware of his noble qualities such as humility, exceptional musical talent, cultured behaviour and inherited traditional values.

Nalwadi lost his father, Maharaja Sri Chamarajendra Wodeyar, at a young age and at the investiture ceremony, he was only ten years old. The future ruler was moulded and shaped by his mother Queen-Regent Sri Vanivilasa Sannidhana and by his gurus and mentors. He put all his efforts into earning the intellectual acumen required to rule the state in an ideal manner. He developed, with great effort, a refined speech and good conduct. He spent eight years in the Royal school honing his skills and acquiring immense knowledge. During his youth, he worked hard to improve his physical strength and intellectual abilities. This remarkable achievement in his school days alone deserves great respect.

When Nalwadi took the reins of power at eighteen years of age, he personified all the hopes and aspirations of the people of Mysore State. It is no exaggeration if I say he became the focus of attention and expectations of all Indians. During those difficult times, the Maharaja shouldered enormous responsibility and executed various projects with great dignity and honour. The Maharaja loved his subjects immensely. He demonstrated his love for them by big deeds and by small deeds.

Once Nalwadi was walking through Dariabaugh garden in Srirangapattanam and he noticed a large-sized red rose in a bush. The gardener, noticing this, plucked this big rose and presented it to His Highness. Instead of being pleased with the rose, he exclaimed, "How could you do this? You have denied others an opportunity to admire the beauty of this rose."

The people of Mysore have cultivated a love and loyalty for the Wodeyar ruling family for centuries. Nalwadi had carved for himself a lofty niche in the hearts of his subjects. During the last few years of his life, Nalwadi ceased to be a ruler but had become a patriarchal figure to his subjects. His highness suffered several bereavements during his lifetime. But the death of his mother Queen-regent, death of his sisters and the untimely death of his younger brother the Yuvaraja Sri Kanteerava Narasimharaja Wodeyar cast a heavy shadow of sorrow upon him. He tried to overcome this deep sorrow by spending a lot of time with Yuvaraja's son and daughters. But until the end, he was concerned with the welfare of his subjects. When he died, the subjects cried inconsolably. Those people who had interacted with His Highness on a personal level mourned his death much more intensely. The vernacular press brought out special editions to express their condolence on the eve of the Maharaja's death. The chief editors of *"Thayinadu," "Deshabandhu," "Prajamata," "Vishwa Karnataka," "Swatantra Karnataka"* and other papers wrote lead articles praising the contribution of the Maharaja and expressed deep felt sorrow at his untimely demise. The love and loyalty to the departed soul of everyone was a universal phenomenon. All over the state, in every town, condolence meetings were conducted by various organizations over several weeks.

I am fortunate enough to enjoy the patronage of the Maharaja and the Yuvaraja with regard to my creative writing work. When Prince Sri Jayachamaraja Wodeyar was studying in the Royal School, his father Yuvaraja asked me to write a play for these students, so that they could stage it. I had, until then, written only one play called *"Our Society"* in Kannada. I wrote a historical play called *"Ranadhira,"* which was staged by Royal School students before the Maharaja and Yuvaraja. This play was very much appreciated by the royal family members. This encouraged me to write several plays. The "Amateur Dramatic Association" of Bangalore staged my plays *"Mandodhari"* and *"Nachiketa"* at Sri Jaganmohana Palace auditorium for Mysore public.

This drama troupe was scheduled to stage my play *"Nachiketa"* on the next day at Sri Rangacharulu Town Hall before the Yuvaraja. But the Maharaja, who had returned to Mysore from an official trip, also joined the Yuvaraja to watch the play. The author had personally presented His Highness a copy of the play *"Nachiketa."* The Maharaja, despite exhaustion, was keen on watching this play. In the auditorium, he told this author, "I have read your play. Now, I am keen on watching the play today." During the play, the author was called by the Maharaja and was asked many questions pertaining to the play. This author managed to give him satisfactory explanations. At the end, before leaving for the palace, the Maharaja said, "Your play is very interesting. I enjoyed it very much. I congratulate you. I am very glad that such a clean and interesting play has come from your pen. I congratulate you on the great success of the play and I hope many more plays like the one in question will come from your pen, depicting Indian ideals and Indian life in pristine purity."

Later, the Maharaja gave an audience to me on three occasions. He spared a lot of time and spoke to me affectionately. He received my books with great grace. He also gave his consent to dedicate my next work *"Basa Mahakavi"* (Great Poet Basa) to His Highness in a formal manner. I feel my humble work attained a greater stature through this dedication.

The Maharaja began to invite me to deliver several lectures at Bangalore Palace after 1937. While delivering my lectures, the Maharaja sat in the front row with a pleasant smiling face. His effable manners endeared him to us. He was undoubtedly a great personification of kindness and love. Whenever I stood in the proximity of His Highness, I felt he was a father figure to me. I never felt that he was a ruler and I am a mere subject. Nalwadi always treated me with great affection and genuine love. Those were the days when I felt doubly blessed to enjoy his benevolent patronage. These are the days of regret, sorrow and dejection as he is not amidst us in flesh and blood. His sweet memory haunts me and moves me to tears from time to time.

During my first lecture, I was not told how much time was allotted to me. Hence, I kept looking at the clock frequently during my lecture. After 45 minutes, I resolved to conclude my lecture after another 15 minutes. The Maharaja generously complemented me on my lecture. During my second lecture, I noticed to my consternation that the clock had disappeared from the table. Later, the Maharaja informed me that he got the culprit removed because he did not want the speaker to be constrained by time. After one hour and forty-five minutes, the speaker was asked to conclude his lecture. At the time of leave-taking, the Maharaja told the author, "There are two types of lecturers, one kind chooses a topic and begins to explore it in detail, he chases the subject matter with all his vigour, acumen and intellect. The second kind compresses the matter and delivers the lecture within the given time frame. When we noticed your concern with the clock, it was removed from the table so that you would be free to expound your subject at leisure." It is like a swimmer who is swimming in the sea being diverted to a narrow canal to swim. I felt elated by the Maharaja's compliments. But still, I made a submission to His Highness that I did not want to prolong my lecture because his time was precious. But he replied that he would ask the speaker to conclude his lecture if he had other official engagements. The Maharaja invited me to lecture in the Bangalore palace for twenty days. He also gave me ample time to expand my subject matter. He encouraged me with words of appreciation. One day, my lecture lasted two and a half hours. After my last lecture, he said, "We want this lecture series to continue for some more time. I am going on a tour from tomorrow. After my return, I will send for you." These were his famous last words to me. Because Nalwadi made two trips from Mysore to Bangalore after my last lecture. His highness made a trip on 30th June 1940 to Bangalore and returned to Mysore on the same day. His second trip was in July 1940. That is when he developed a heart problem and finally succumbed to it.

I want to narrate this particular incident to show his extraordinary powers of forgiveness. His highness wanted to see my play "*Brahmavadini*" on stage. It was a lengthy play consuming a good three hours. His Highness requested me to reduce the play to two and a half hours as he was slightly indisposed.

So, I requested my players to omit certain scenes in the play to reduce its duration. But before His Highness, the players forgot their instructions and stretched the duration of the play to three and a half hours. This happened due to their enthusiasm and various other reasons. I was overcome by guilt and remorse because I could not keep up my end of the bargain. I was full of trepidation until the next meeting. When I went to Bangalore palace for my next lecture, I was overcome by a feeling of shame and embarrassment. I decided to offer an apology on behalf of my drama troupe. I told His Highness that I was ashamed to show my face to him. He asked me smilingly, "Why?" I replied that the play "*Brahmavadini*" did not end after two and a half hours. Because of the over-enthusiasm of actors, it was stretched to three and a half hours. But the Maharaja smiled and said, "Our regret is the play ended after three and a half hours. It should have continued for one more hour." I replied, "Your Excellency, you are a figure of forgiveness. I bow before you with utmost reverence. Your love for me overwhelms me. I am blessed, blessed." Nalwadi replied, "Why do you talk like this? I was not under any obligation to watch the play until the end. I could have easily walked out of the theatre. But the play was very interesting. Hence, I stayed back. Now resume your lecture." Once, he also watched my play "*Tenali Ramakrishna.*"

I am greatly indebted to the present ruler, Maharaja Sri Jayachamaraja Wodeyar Bahadur, for his patronage and encouragement. His Highness has kindly permitted me to dedicate Nalwadi's Biography to him. When I expressed a desire to present my complete works to His Highness, he readily granted me a special interview. I could not present this book to the Maharaja and Yuvaraja during their lifetime because of their untimely death. I am greatly consoled by the fact that at least I could present it to the present ruler of Mysore State. I am much obliged to him for his kind words and encouragement to pursue my creative writing. I could complete this book because of the encouragement received by me from Dewan Mirza M. Ismail, Huzoor Secretary Rajasabha Bhushana T. Thumboo Chetty, Rajamantra Praveena Dewan Bahadur Poorna Raghavendra Rao, Rajasevasaktha M. Rama Rao and Siddiq-ul-Mulk Sadeg Sad Shaw. They have also provided me with rich information about the deceased Maharaja. Huzoor Secretary T. Thumboo Chetty has been kind enough to provide me with numerous black and white photographs from the private collection of the palace. I am grateful to Dewan Sir Mirza M Ismail for the beautiful foreword written by him for my work. It has contributed to the enrichment of my humble work. It is my good fortune to have received such gracious help from these two gentlemen. I once again thank them from the bottom of my heart.

The following eminent men have provided me with generous information about His Highness Sri Nalwadi Krishnaraja Wodeyar. They have shared their experiences, feelings and emotions with me. They have provided me with reliable and truthful accounts of various episodes. I am extremely indebted and grateful to these gentlemen and ladies for providing me with valuable historical material.

Acknowledgements:
1. Rajasevasaktha S. Hiriyannayya
2. Surgeon Extraordinary Dr. S. Subba Rao
3. Sri Sri. Vasananda Swamy
4. Rajasevasaktha Dr. N. Rangacharya
5. Brahmasri Guru Seva Praveena Nanjangud Srikanta Sastri
6. Brahmasri Dharmadhikari Vidya Visharada Kunigal Ramasastri
7. Brahmasri panditaratnam Kankanahalli Narayana Sastri
8. Brahmasri Pouranika Ratnam Holavanahalli Seshacharya
9. Brahmasri Thiruvallur Sinivasa Raghavacharya
10. Rajasena Bhushana Lt. Col A.V. Subramanyaraja Urs.
11. Rajasena Tilaka Lt. Col S. Gopal Rao
12. Sri. K. Basavaraja Urs
13. Sri D. Srikanta Lakshmi Kantharaja Urs
14. Sri H.L. Devaraja Urs.
15. Sri M.P Subramanyaraja Urs
16. Sri. H. Muddaraja Urs
17. Sri D. Ramaiah
18. Sri D.N. Nilakanta Rao
19. Sri. A. Venkata Subbiah
20. Sri C.V. Subramanyaraja Urs
21. Sri. F.C. Devaraja Urs
22. Maj. M.C. Subbaraja Urs
23. Sri H. Siddaraja Urs
24. Janab M.G. Mekhri
25. Sri S. Garalapuri Sastri
26. Sri V. Subramanya Iyer
27. Dr. M.H. Krishna

28. Sri. A. C. Lingaraja Urs
29. Sri H. Nanjaraja Urs
30. Sri D.C. Nanjaraja Bahadur
31. Janab Humayun Mirza
32. Sri T. Subramanyaraja Urs
33. Sri T. Ramaiah
34. Sri Rao Bahadur N.S. Nanjundiah
35. Sri G. Devaji Rao
36. Janab T. S. Alikhan
37. Sri T. M. Jeevanna Rao
38. Sri C. Nanjaraja Iyengar
39. Sri P.G. Sacchidananda Pillai
40. Sri K. Narasimha Iyengar
41. Sri D. Venkatnanjappa
42. Sri T.G. Doreswami Iyer
43. Sri C. Ananda Rao
44. Brahmarishi Purohit Sri Nanjunda Sastri
45. Brahmasri Mahavidwan Sahityaratnam Gopala Krishna Sastri
46. Brahmasri Ritwik Ramasastry
47. Sri K. Subba Rao
48. Sri N. Narasimhamurthy
49. Brahmasri Mahavidwan Sahityaratnam Bettahalasur Venkatarama Sastri
50. Brahmasri Mahavidwan Panditaratnam Kashi Subramanya Sastri
51. Brahmasri Sosale Krishnaswamy Sastri
52. Sri S. Gopalaswamy
53. Brahmasri Vishveshwara Bhat
54. Gayaka Shikamani L. Muthaiah Bhagvathar
55. Vynika Praveena Venkatagiriappa
56. Sri S. RamaRao
57. Sri Venkatanarayan Rao
58. Sri M.S. Subramanya Sastri
59. Sri L. Raja Rao
60. Smt. Pandita Sundaramma
61. Lokasevaparayane Smt. K. D. Rukminiamma
62. Sri Byranna
63. Sri Gurikar Basaavalingiah

Many more people have provided me with additional information. I am equally grateful to them. I can never forget these five men who are not alive today giving me very valuable and firsthand eye witness accounts of their encounters with the Maharaja and Yuvaraja. They are:
1. Rajakaryaprasaktha Rao Bahadur M. Shayam Rao
2. Lt. col. B.P. Krishne Urs
3. Sri P. F. Bowring
4. Sri P.S. Govinda Rao
5. Sri Vynika Praveena Subbanna

It is my bounden duty to thank the following officials and various departments, who have given valuable black and white photographs for publication:
1. The portrait of Sir Mirza M. Ismail from Dewan's office.
2. The following photographs were received from the publicity office and Government printing press
   a. First Cabinet minister Rajamantra Praveena N. Madhava Rao
   b. Second Cabinet minister Rajamantra Praveena K.V. Anantharaman
   c. Photos of Khedda enclosure
   d. Sri Krishnaraja Sagar and Brindavan Gardens
   e. Silver Jubilee Technological Institute
   f. 5 photos of the Khedda operation were obtained from the Secretary Dasara Exhibition committee.
   g. The remaining photos and printing blocks were provided by
      (i) Maj. M.C. Subbaraja Urs
      (ii) Janab T.S. Alikhan
      (iii) Sri D.N. Nilakanta Rao
      (iv) Palace officials

I offer my heartfelt thanks to all the above-mentioned individuals and official departments for sparing to me all these rare photos. I am also indebted to the Bangalore press officials for printing this biography in record time.

During the writing of this book, I referred to a number of books. I have not given a separate list of books referred to under the section of Bibliography. I referred to several well-known books while writing on the history of Mysore State. I have relied on Palace publications for information on pilgrimages to holy towns. As far as legislative reforms are concerned, I have gathered my material from government gazettes and reports published from time to time.

I have mentioned titles of books and authors in the footnotes. I have drawn inspiration from my study of famous biographies and historical works written by famous international writers while writing this biography. I have done meticulous research work so as to collect reliable data, facts and information on the Maharaja and Yuvaraja in the process of writing this biography. I seek the forgiveness of my readers if there are any lapses on my part. I have only lighted a small lamp before the extraordinary ruler's portrait of His Highness Sri Nalwadi Krishnaraja Wodeyar, whose fame and reputation will be an everlasting and enduring phenomenon of our times. This small work is my humble offering of love, devotion and dedication to my idol.

Bangalore
18-04-1941

C.K. Venkataramaiah

Rajasevasaktha Padmasri C.K. Venkataramaiah

Biographer's Biography: Rajaseva Saktha Padmasri C.K. Venkataramaiah

The author of this biography was born in a middle-class Brahmin family on 10th December 1896 at Patlu village in Channapatna Taluk, Bangalore District. His father, Krishnappa, was a "*Shanubhog*" (Village Accountant) a petty government official liable for frequent transfers. His mother's name was Nanjamma. His family was made up of two elder brothers, one elder sister and one younger brother. His grandparents were Puttaniah and Rangamma and the family belonged to *Kashyapasa Gothra* (clan).

C.K. Venkataramiah attended a local village elementary school called "*Coolie mata.*" He had to walk a few kilometres to Channapatna every day to attend middle school and high school. Once on the way to school C.K. Venkataramiah fell unconscious on the road as he had not eaten his breakfast. He was rescued and his life was saved by a cartman. His father, Krishnappa, died suddenly when C.K. Venkataramiah was twelve years old.

Despite many privations, he decided to study the intermediate course in Bangalore. He gave private tuition to some school students and earned some money to sustain himself in Bangalore. He also earned some money by writing articles for "*Sadhvi*" (a Kannada newspaper) and "*Swarajya*" (an English journal edited by Annie Besant)

When he passed his intermediate course, the family arranged his marriage with Smt. Venkata Subbamma, the daughter of Sri Krishna Rao and Sitamma residents of Javagal, Banavara Taluk, Bangalore District.

He joined B.A. Course at Central College and came under the influence of Prof. A.R. Krishna Sastry and Professor Bellave Venkatanarayanappa. Prof. A.R. Krishna Sastry founded his literary journal "*Prabhudda Karnataka*" during this period. C.K. Venkataramiah began to contribute articles to this journal.

His Kannada novel "*Samyuktapaharana*" was serialized in ten instalments and later published as a novel. C.K. Venkataramaiah's talented classmates were S.V. Ranganna and N. Neelakantappa in Central College. Prof. A.R. Krishna Sastry had set a question on "*Nala Charitra*." C.K. Venkataramaiah wrote an elaborate critique of "*Nala Charitra*" in a notebook in fine handwriting, which impressed his professor immensely. His mentor in Central College started a "*Kannada Sangha*" for the propagation of Kannada language and literature.

At that time, in Mysore State, "Devaraja Bahadur Paritoshaka" was a prestigious literary award for budding writers. C. K. Venkatramiah sent a monograph on "Constitutional History" (English) and a Kannada novel called "*Argala Kumari*" for the state-level literary competition. He won first prizes in both categories of Kannada and English competitions. He received a handsome cash award of Rs. 500 for his English book and Rs. 100 for his Kannada novel. These two award-winning works are not available to us. After graduation, he decided to go to Bombay to pursue an M.A. Kannada course and an L.L.B course simultaneously at Bombay University. He managed to acquire an M.A. Kannada degree and a law degree in a two-year period from Bombay University. It was a hectic schedule of attending classes from morning until night.

In Bombay, a rich Muslim businessman had started a project of translating the Koran and other Islamic texts into various Indian languages. C. K. Venkataramiah agreed to translate many of those works into Kannada. He earned some money in this manner during his student days in Bombay.

He began his legal practice under a famous advocate called Sri Devojirao in Srirangapattana. Although he made a great impression on the bench and bar, his heart was not in the legal profession.

C.K. Venkataramaiah came across a Mysore State Gazette notification advertising the post of chief translator. He applied for the job and took the selection examination. When results were announced, his name had topped the list. He joined the state government service as a chief translator.

In those days, the Mysore Legislative council and Mysore Legislative assembly had adopted the English language as an official language to conduct business in the Houses. Sri Nalwadi Krishnaraja Wodeyar had made a decision to translate the speeches of the Maharaja, Dewan, British Resident, visiting dignitaries and the debates inside the two houses into Kannada. He wanted ordinary literate Kannadigas to read and understand the proceedings of the government. He came to translate the speeches of Dewan Sir Mirza M. Ismail.

In the official circles, he came to be called "Kannada Dewan." Later in his career, he was offered a Magistrate's post, but he refused to abandon his chosen profession. He worked as a chief translator for some thirty years.

Throughout his life, C.K. Venkataramaiah championed the cause of the Kannada language. He worked as a Secretary of Kannada Sahitya Parishat from 1930 to 1940. When he was secretary of Kannada Sahitya Parishat, he served faithfully these vice-presidents Karpur Srinivasa Rao, Dr. D.V. Gundappa and Prof. B.M. Srikantaiah. He travelled across Mysore State and Kannada-speaking regions of Bombay, Hyderabad and Madras States. He travelled at his own cost. He did not claim travelling and boarding expenditure from Kannada Sahitya Parishat. In fact, he became a popular speaker on the lecture circuit. Nalwadi invited him to Bangalore palace 26 times to deliver lectures on various topics.

In 1934, C.K. Venkataramaiah started "*Vasanthothsava*" (Spring Literary festival) at Kannada Sahitya Parishat, Bangalore. He was also accorded the honour of officiating as president of Kannada Sahitya Sammelan (Annual literary conference) in 1947 in Harpanahalli, Bellary district.

C.K. Venkataramaiah worked tirelessly for the new Karnataka state re-organization. He enlisted the support of other eminent Kannada litterateurs and sent them on lecture tours. They were paid their remuneration for delivering lectures. But he never claimed any money from the organization for his own lecture tours.

His critical acumen came to be expressed through such essays as "The Poetic style of the Poet Ranna – A study of "*Gadayuddha*" and a critical analysis of Sri Aurobindo's Epic poem "*Savithri*." The first essay exhibits C.K. Venkataramaiah's in-depth scholarship of ancient Kannada classics and the second essay explores the philosophy of Sri Aurobindo through "*Savitri*," which is written in English.

The government of Karnataka requested C.K. Venkataramaiah to write a scholarly book on "Mahakavi Kalidasa." Throughout his life, he had delivered hundreds of lectures on Kalidasa. Now, he wrote a 700-page book delineating the whole oeuvre of the great Kalidasa, which eventually became a classic in its own right.

C.K. Venkataramaiah's critical trilogy deals with Basa, Kalidasa and Bhavabuti. He wrote the book "*Bhavabuti Mahakavi*" with equal expertise and insight. This is what C.K. Venkataramaiah wrote about Bhavabuti, "This great poet was well acquainted with Valmiki, Vyasa, Basa, Kalidasa,

Bana and Subhandhu. But Bhavabuti employed cliché-ridden words and often employed an abstruse style of writing in Sanskrit. Perhaps, this did not endear him to the readers. But the great poet was confident that in the coming years, a discerning audience for his plays will be available to appreciate him."

In his younger days, he tried to learn Carnatic classical music, but he could not pursue it seriously. But later in life, he encouraged his first son, Vid C.V. Nagaraja, to learn Carnatic classical music. He eventually became an established and reputed performing artist in Karnataka. C.K. Venkataramaiah developed a good friendship with eminent musicians such as Vid Vasudevacharya and violinist T. Chowdaiah. Whenever he visited Mysore in the company of Dr. D.V. Gundappa, he invariably visited Sri Ralapalli Anantha Krishna Sharma at his residence, which would always result in an impromptu concert.

His only daughter, Smt. C.V. Ratnamma was encouraged to pursue higher education. At that time, girls were getting married in adolescence without obtaining the benefits of higher education. He sent his daughter to high school and college much against the practice of the conservative society of that time. The orthodox Brahmin clergy threatened to socially boycott his family if Ratnamma was not withdrawn from the educational institution. He did not budge even an inch because of their threats. Later, C.V. Ratnamma wrote a biography of the lady scientist Madame Curie in Kannada language. His second son, C.V. Chandrashekar, was the CEO of "Spun Silk Mill" in Channapatna.

The third son C.V. Vishweshwara earned national and international fame as a reputed Astro-physicist. After graduating from Central College, he went to the U.S. for his higher studies. He obtained a Ph.D. from the University of Maryland. He taught at New York University and at the University of Pittsburg. He was a Director of Raman Research Institute and the Indian Institute of Astro-physics. He was also the founder Director of Jawaharlal Nehru planetarium in Bangalore. He is famously known as the "Black hole man of India."

Dr. Saraswathi Vishveshwara, wife of C.V. Vishveshwara, is a reputed Indian Bio-physicist with specialization in the area of Molecular Biophysics. She is a platinum jubilee scientist, who has worked on computational biology. She is a former Head of the Department of Biophysics at the Indian Institute of Science, Bangalore. Her daughter, Smitha Vishveshwara, is also a physicist doing research in the U.S.A.

"*Aalida Mahaswamigalu*" (The monarch who reigned) and Rajasevasaktha padmasri C. K. Venkataramaiah

As the chief translator of Mysore State, C.K. Venkataramaiah had the added advantage of being in the proximity of His Highness, the Dewan, the cabinet ministers and other high-ranking officials of Mysore administration. He also became a close confidante of the Maharaja and Yuvaraja. He was a firsthand eye witness to the history being made. He also enjoyed the confidence of the "who's who" of Mysore State.

This biography of Nalwadi is 82 years old. It is a historically important document. C.K. Venkataramaiah worships his heroes – the Maharaja and the Yuvaraja. His first Royal honour came to him in the form of the "Rajasevasaktha" title from the Maharaja Sri Jayachamaraja Wodeyar. In retrospection, we may call him a "Royalist." One feels after 75 years of Independence, the Indian democracy deserves the epithet of former USA Ambassador Kenneth Galbraith's comment, "India is a functioning Anarchy." Our parliamentary system of democracy is plagued by casteism, regionalism, and corruption and our elected representatives are proud of their criminal record. Our parliamentary practices are an embarrassment to educated citizens.

At times, I feel we could have retained our Maharajas and Nawabs like in Malaysia. The head of the state of Malaysia is an elected monarch chosen from among the nine state sultans every five years. India could have dispensed with the present system of nominated governors and elected vice-president and president for a term of five years.

C.K. Venkataramaiah does not find any flaws or short comings in his heroes. He does not dwell on the private lives of Maharaja and Yuvaraja. There is no information on the relationship between Maharaja Sri Nalwadi Krishnaraja Wodeyar and Maharani Kumari Pratap Devi, who were married for forty years. The Maharani was rarely seen in public functions. The royal couple did not have any children.

While reading C.K. Venkataramaiah's biography of Nalwadi, we are reminded of Thomas Carlyle's book, "*On Heroes, Hero-worship and Heroic in History*" (1841). Thomas Carlyle held that "Great men should rule and others should revere them." This opinion is endorsed by our author C.K. Venkataramaiah.

In English literature, the "*Life of Samuel Johnson L.L.D*" (1791) by James Boswell occupies pride of place. This is considered as the father of all biographies. The quotation of Thomas Carlyle sums up C.K. Venkataramaiah's approach to his hero, "Boswell wrote a good book because he had a heart and an eye to discern wisdom, and an utterance to render it forth; because of his free insight, his lively talent, above all his love and childlike open-mindedness'... Towards Johnson, however, his feeling was not sycophancy, which is lowest, but reverence, which is the highest of human feelings."

"*Aalida Mahaswamigalu*" (Kannada version) is a hardbound volume with 84 rare black and white photographs. According to my guess estimate, it has taken the author 6 to 7 years of laborious research work. The 1941 edition does not carry a price tag. According to the author, he obtained the consent of the Maharaja and the Yuvaraja before embarking on this biographical project. So, this biography came to be written with the prior approval of His Highness. Hence, it becomes an official biography of the Maharaja and Yuvaraja.

C.K. Venkataramaiah's biggest regret was that the book was published after the demise of his heroes, the Maharaja (3rd August 1940) and Yuvaraja (11th March 1940). He could not present copies of the biography to them during their lifetime. So, he has dedicated this book to his successor, Maharaja Sri Jayachamaraja Wodeyar, with his prior permission. During the making of this masterpiece, various government agencies and palace officials have collaborated with the author.

This book in the Kannada version runs to 587 pages, the foreword by Dewan Sir Mirza M. Ismail is in English and a prologue by the author in Kannada runs to another 22 pages and the total number of pages in the first edition is 609 pages.

"*Aalida Mahaswamigalu*" deals with the dynastic history of Mysore Wodeyars albeit briefly, the restoration of power to Sri Chamarajendra Wodeyar and after the monarch's death the queen regent was empowered to rule for eight years, as the scion of the royal family, Sri Nalwadi Krishnaraja Wodeyar, was a minor aged only 10 years. The author describes in detail 38 years of Nalwadi's rule of Mysore State, which is a glorious golden period. He also heralds the rule of Maharaja Sri Jayachamaraja Wodeyar after the passing away of Sri Nalwadi Krishnaraja Wodeyar. He predicts another glorious chapter in the history of Mysore. Sri Jayachamaraja Wodeyar ruled from 1940-1950 as Maharaja and Rajapramukh (1950-1956) of the state and later was Governor of Mysore state (1956-1964) and Governor of Madras (1964-1966).

C.K. Venkataramaiah deals in this biography with the Legislative reforms, economic reforms, and infrastructure projects like Bhadravathi

Iron and Steel Industry, Shivana Samudra Hydro-Electric project, Mysore Sandal Soap Factory and Silk factory. Nalwadi brought about many reforms in the educational field. He invested a lot of money in women's education and established Mysore University in 1919. The Maharaja also initiated various programs to bring about social change in the lives of the scheduled caste and scheduled tribe population. C.K. Venkataramaiah discusses the obsession of the Maharaja and the Dewan with the architectural splendour of Mysore and Bangalore. Although the Maharaja killed rogue elephants and man-eating tigers, he had immense compassion for animals and birds.

C.K. Venkataramaiah also deals with Nalwadi's passion for Carnatic, Hindustani and Western classical music. He was a generous patron of fine arts like music, drama, dance, painting and sculpture. One can say Nalwadi was generous to a fault. He helped poor people and sick people without any hesitation.

The Maharaja loved game hunting, polo, squash, horse-riding, trekking in the Himalayas during pilgrimages and long-distance motoring. His spirit of adventure and courage in the face of adversity is narrated in detail.

The saying Caesar's wife must be above suspicion was implicitly followed by Nalwadi. The Maharaja was a very religious Hindu with proven secular credentials. His personal life was guided by Hindu Dharma Sastra, the epics, the Vedas, Upanishads and Bhagavad Gita. Even during the European tour, he observed all the religious rituals and festivals.

His life was a life of moderation, abstinence and dedication to higher spiritual goals. The monarch who was called *"Raja Rishi"* by the whole world died at a comparatively young age of 56 years (1884-1940). Can any other ruler in any part of the world and in any other age replicate the "Dharmic Rule" of Nalwadi Sri Krishnaraja Wodeyar? The Maharaja only received Rs. 13 lakhs as his privy purse for maintaining palace staff, etc. He often donated money to charitable causes from his private funds. His Spartan lifestyle, religious austerities and genuine love for his subjects knew no bounds. His patriotism was not only directed at Mysore State, he loved the whole of India as a nation-state. After reading this biography written before India gained Independence, the reader swings between the Comparative World between "then" and "now" like a pendulum.

The sensitive and sensible reader is overwhelmed by the sordid present and he can only slip into depression, despondency, pessimism, vulnerability and disgust. The present-day political leaders (there may be some exceptions) are not very promising. Today, our Indian society is plagued by corruption, casteism, nepotism, dishonesty and immorality. The lives of Maharaja and the Yuvaraja can be an eternal inspiration for creating a better Indian society, where people live in harmony and peace. Sri. C. K. Venkataramaiah passed away on 03rd April 1973 after a brief illness in Bangalore.

Bangalore
26/05/2023   S. Naganath

References
(1) Padmasri Rajaseva Saktha C.K.Venkataramaiah by C.V.Vishveshwara – Hoysala Male- 21 published by Hoysala Karnataka Sangha, Bangalore
(2) "Basa Mahakavi" by C.K. Venkataramaiah published by Kuvempu Bhasha Bharathi. Biographical sketch of Padmasri C.K. Venkataramaiah by Sri. Vigneshwar Bhat
(3) C.K. Venkataramaiah by H.S. Krishnaswamy Iyengar- "Varada Vyakthi" in Sudha Magazine, 1971.
(4) "Sirikannada Saraswatharu" by Prof. G. Venkatasubbaiah

The Tale of the Translator

I love Mysore as it is my place of birth. We lived on Dewan Sir Sheshadri Iyer Road. Often, we passed in front of Dewan's official residence. It was a big colonial mansion and now, it houses the Government Commercial Tax Commissioner's office. The citizens of Mysore looked forward to 9 days of Navaratri celebration culminating in the Vijayadashmi royal procession in full pageantry. The added attraction was the Dasara exhibition and the amusement arcade at Jeevanarayana Kere grounds.

Our family had its own royal links for over 150 years. My great grand uncle, a renowned Sanskrit scholar, was in the court of Sri Chamarajendra Wodeyar and Sri Nalwadi Krishnaraja Wodeyar. His name was Asthan Maha Vidwan Motaganalli Ramasesha Sastri, who is remembered for his "Magnum Opus" translation of *"Bhagavatha Mahapurana"* available in Sanskrit to Kannada in eight volumes. His two other works are *"Karnataka Mudra Rakshasa Natakam"* and *"Karnataka Mukundananda Bana."*

His nephew, Asthan Vidwan Motaganahalli Subramanya Sastri, graced the royal court of Sri Nalwadi Krishnaraja Wodeyar. His creative output is phenomenal. He translated Valmiki's Ramayana from Sanskrit to Kannada with co-author Veda Brahma Pattabhirama Sastry in eight volumes. He also translated from Sanskrit to Kannada 32 volumes of *Sri Skanda Puranam*. He translated several Sanskrit plays and *"Lalithapokyana"* (2 volumes) into Kannada. Sri Jayachamaraja Wodeyar had allocated a monthly pension to him until the end of his life. He was a personal friend of C.K. Venkataramaiah and he also edited Kannada Sahitya Parishat's literary journal *"Parishad Patrike."*

My own father Dr. S. Srikanta Sastri was a faculty member of the History Department when Prince Jayachamaraja Wodyar was pursuing an intermediate course and B.A course in Yuvaraja College and Maharaja College during 1935-1938. Prof. M.H. Krishna, HOD of the History Department requested

Dr. S. Srikanta Sastri to engage in history classes of Prince Sri Jayachamaraja Wodeyar in 1937.

Later, the translator of this biography had the good fortune of being a classmate and friend of Prince Srikantadatta Narasimharaja Wodeyar between 1969 and 1974 at Mysore University. One unforgettable incident in my memory is being invited to attend the birthday party of Prince Sri Srikantadatta Narasimharaja Wodeyar on 20th February 1970 at Mysore Palace. It was a memorable occasion because some of us were formally introduced to His Highness Sri Jayachamaraja Wodeyar on that evening.

Later, I was a professor of English at The National College Jayanagar, Bangalore and another happy coincidence occurred. Prince Varchus Urs, son of Princess Meenakshi Devi Avaru became my student and he passed out of our college after completing the Pre-University course to study Law elsewhere.

It is an unforgettable coincidence that Rajamata Dr. Promoda Devi, wife of Maharaja Sri Srikantadatta Wodeyar, lived in a mansion on the corner of Dewan's Road and Sri Vanivilasa Sannidhana Road. Some of us cannot forget our childhood association with the Rajamata during that period.

When I first read *"Aalida Mahaswamigalu,"* what struck me was that the modern-day left historians had completely ignored the contribution of the rulers of Wodeyar's Dynasty in the making of modern Mysore. How can one ignore the contribution of Sri Chamarajendra Wodeyar (Reign 1868-1894), the rule of Regent Sri Vanivilasa Sannidhana (Reign 1895-1902) and the rule of Nalwadi Sri Krishnaraja Wodeyar (Reign 1902-1940) and Maharaja Sri Jayachamaraja Wodeyar (Reign 1940-1950) amounting to a total of 82 years? Many modern-day historians began to give credit to the Dewans for the modernization of Mysore State. Let us not forget that the ruler's vision, dream and the will to implement big projects for the benefit of the common man alone were responsible for the far-reaching changes that miraculously took place in Mysore State. During the war years, when food and petrol rationing affected millions of citizens, they raised the question of why we should pamper University teachers with such high salaries. The Mysore Government took up adult literacy programmes with the help of these scholars. The University professors were sent to cities and small towns to deliver lectures on various topics of interest to the general public. This came to be called "The Mysore Experiment." The principal Prof. J.C. Rollo of the Maharaja College attended an International Conference on higher education in London, where he presented a paper on "The Mysore Experiment," which was acclaimed by the delegates and by the London press.

    C.K. Venkataramaiah has done a yeoman service to the Mysore Royal family by recording these historical facts for the future. His meticulous scholarly research work and collection of vast material for writing this biography is a super human triumph. I have endeavoured to remain faithful to the original Kannada version of the biography. C.K. Venkataramaiah's Kannada language is lucid, smooth-flowing and direct, and he does not tax the reader by making it a long-winded and boring read. His style of writing is crisp and succinct. The translator hopes that the biography finds its rightful place in the annals of Indian History and now is the propitious time.

28.05.2023　　　　　　　　　　　　　　　　　　　　　　　　S. Naganath

Acknowledgements

The translator is indebted to the following individuals, who have contributed in various ways to the success of this project. They have taken immense trouble to contribute their expertise and skill.
1. Dr. S. N. Bhagirath has helped me by typing the first few chapters of the book during the Covid epidemic from the U.K.
2. Smt. Poornima Ramakrishna of Mysore has patiently and diligently typed (D.T.P) the remaining chapters of the book and also revised it after a round of proofreading.
3. I have taken the help of Sanskrit scholar Dr. K. L. Prasannakshi, who has translated all the Sanskrit quotations into Kannada. In turn, I have rendered it into English. She has also transcribed *"Navarathnamala"* into the Devanagri script and given me a summary of this poem written by Pandit Motaganahalli Mahadeva Sastri.
4. I am greatly indebted to the Mysore Royal family, whose head Rajamata Srimathi Pramoda Devi has encouraged me in this endeavour through kind words. I have also received enthusiastic backing from my former student, Sri. M. L. Varchuswee Raje Urs, (son of Rajakumari Late Meenakshi Deviavaru) and, in fact, he has helped me by giving the correct meaning of the word *"Dustina Bokkasa."* The word has not found its way into the Kannada dictionary yet.
5. The original black and white photos in the book have been digitally processed by the staff of G.K. Vale and Co, R.T. Nagar Bangalore to the optimal conditions. Many thanks to them.
6. I am equally grateful to the editorial staff of Notionpress, Chennai for bringing out this biography in a very pleasing manner.
7. Last but not least, my wife Smt. Padma Naganath who has helped me with reference work taking copies of documents from the computer and in editing work of this biography. My grateful thanks to her.

8. I thank Sri. S.L. Ravishankar for designing the coverpage and back cover of the page in an aesthetically appealing manner.
9. I thank Prof. D. A. Shankar for his valuable suggestions given to me after reading my manuscript in the initial stages which have helped me make the necessary proof corrections.

Chapter 1
Unveiling of Momentous Events

******

OM Bhadram Karne Bishrunayama Devah
Bhadram pashyemaksha Biryajatrah
Stirairangiah Sthustavagham Sastnobih
Vyshema devahitam yadayuh||
(*Rig Veda – Mandala 1 – Sukta 89 – Mantra 8*)

Let us hear only auspicious tidings from our ears,
Let us live a life of supreme sacrifice (Yagna) with vigour and competence,
Let us see auspicious and pleasant sights,
Let us serve God through strong and sturdy physical body.
Let us dedicate our longevity and energy to please Gods with our humble service for the reminder of lifetime.

******

Sri Nalwadi Krishnaraja Wodeyar (1884 – 1940), the Maharaja of Mysore enjoyed a reputation at home and abroad as a morally upright and honest ruler. Because of this visionary ruler, the Princely State of Mysore came to be reckoned as a progressive state in India. The various political scientists from different continents have showered encomiums and praise upon this modern ruler for holding up a mirror to the British rulers, who were administering 75% of the Indian sub-continent.

Sri Nalwadi Krishnaraja Wodeyar's untimely death on 3rd August 1940 at Bangalore has left a void in the Princely state, but he is missed by several thousands of people at the national and international level. A British aristocrat by the name Lord Walter Horace Samuel second viscount Bearsted wrote in his condolence letter to the then Dewan of Mysore State – Sir Mirza M. Ismail, "Those of us, who had reposed great admiration and respect in the Maharaja cannot help but grieve greatly for his sudden passing away. Those who had developed an intimacy with him could not restrain their grief and sorrow. Amongst the rulers of the world, one does not come across a king, who made the best use of his opportunities wisely and appropriately or for that matter, one who helped to improve the quality of life of his subjects as he did with utmost care and dedication is rarely seen by the discerning historians, either at present or in the past." (Not a verbatim reproduction.)

Major General A. M. Mills, in his condolence message to the Dewan, says, "Whenever I paid an official visit to Mysore State, I noticed with great astonishment the Maharaja Nalwadi Krishnaraja Wodeyar conducting himself with such charming dignity and expressing boundless compassion towards one and all. He was a good Samaritan and an unblemished pure soul. The untimely demise of the Maharaja is a great loss to the British Empire." (Not a verbatim reproduction.)

It is a well-known fact that the Maharaja was a generous patron of poets, painters and musicians. Until the end, he remained an ardent worshipper of Goddess Saraswathi. He did not neglect to improve his intellectual abilities throughout his life. He was an avid reader of books and often enjoyed playing the violin and flute.

Sri Nalwadi Krishnaraja Wodeyar embodied the best qualities of Indian Culture. His love and compassion for animals and birds had become proverbial. Like the great kings of the yore, the Maharaja was guided by the dharmic values. His spartan and simple life style earned him the sobriquet of "Raja Rishi" (A Sage-Emperor). The Maharaja was not oblivious to the best virtues of Western civilisation. His Western style of education made him aware of the beneficial and humane values of Western culture. The welfare of his subjects was closest to his heart. He was ever willing to go the extra mile to better the lives of the plebians.

All the great achievements of man are expressed only in the form of universal love. The Maharaja loved one and all equally and had immense concern for animals and birds. All religions of the world preach compassion and love for living things. The great poet Valmiki rishi was moved by the death of the *Kruancha* bird. The plaintive cry of the female Kruancha bird, when the hunter killed its male partner inspired him to compose the Ramayana epic. [The noble teachings of Gautama Buddha, which gave him a divine status are great compassion for living things and his concern for the welfare of one and all]. When we apply this criterion to the deceased ruler, he automatically qualifies for the title of man of the century.

Once, the Maharaja was on an official visit to Kolar district. They were travelling in a cart (coach) drawn by an Oxen towards Bagepali town. The Maharaja was accompanied by the district deputy commissioner. It began to rain heavily. The Maharaja had an umbrella in his hand. But he did not unfurl it. The deputy district commissioner also carried an umbrella with him. The bemused official volunteered to open it, as he noticed the Maharaja getting drenched in the rain. But the Maharaja requested the official not to open the umbrella. Because he had not opened his own umbrella, so as not to scare the oxen. If two black umbrellas had been opened on the cart, it would have caused panic in animals. The Maharaja did not want them to run amok and break their legs in confusion.

The Maharaja with his entourage was making his progress towards the travellers' bungalow. He noticed on his way a poor old woman's dilapidated hut with a damaged roof and a broken door. Later in the evening, he set out of his traveller's bungalow on foot, of course, followed by his entourage. He carried a bag full of fruits in his hands and made his way through slush and mud to the hut of the old woman. When he arrived at the poor woman's cottage door, he saw the old woman in tattered clothes, sitting in a corner, hungry and shivering on that day. She had not earned even a few paise to afford a few morsels of rice. She was overwhelmed to see the Maharaja at her door with a bag full of fruits. He enquired about her health and gave her enough money to get the cottage roof and door repaired for the coming monsoon (rainy) season. This was yet again another act of charity done by the ruler instinctively without seeking any publicity. Even the well-heeled gentry of the town had not taken note of this unfortunate old woman's plight.

When the Maharaja went on a pilgrimage tour to Kailash and Manas-Sarovar, the accompanying staff witnessed an unforgettable incident. The Maharaja wanted to take a dip in the Manasa Sarovar Lake for the well-being of his subjects. Unfortunately, on that morning, the weather was nippy, cold and misty. His personal physician advised him not to take a bath in the freezing waters. But the Maharaja would not heed the advice. He told everyone that by taking a bath in the holy lake, he would be earning God's grace for his subjects. He took a bath in the cold lake and when he emerged out of water, he was blue and unconscious. He was given first aid and his body was massaged by his bodyguards. All these efforts revived him and he told the astonished bystanders that he wanted to take a second dip much to the chagrin of his physician. This time, he was taking a bath in the holy waters for the redemption of the souls of his ancestors. The history repeated Itself for the second time. After the revival, the Maharaja announced quite vociferously that he wanted to take a dip in the waters for the third time. The royal attendants tried to prevent the third suicidal bathing by their ruler but to no avail. This time, he was taking a bath in the sacred waters for the redemption of his own soul. Once again, the Maharaja's condition after the bath was critical. Perhaps Lord Shiva's grace helped him to survive this near-death experience once again.

On another occasion, the Maharaja visited the scenic waterfall at Jog in Shimoga district. Here, the Sharavati river plunges down in four different streams of waterfalls called by the names of Raja, Rani, Rocket and Roarer. The height of the waterfall is 833 feet and it is a sight to behold during the monsoon season. During the reign of the Maharaja, there was a government guest house on a hill, opposite to the waterfall. The poor people could not afford to stay in this state guest house. The Maharaja passed an order for the construction of a *dharma chatra* (a free government guest house with food and accommodation) for his subjects. In a short while, this building came up and it was visited by ordinary folks. This kind of concern for the less fortunate subjects of his state endeared him greatly to them.

The Maharaja endorsed noble human values from his early childhood. Those rare virtues like love and adherence to truth and dharma distinguished him from other rulers. He upheld moral values and practised charity. He was religious by nature and loved his subjects as if they were his own children. He loved all the beasts and birds with great fervour. The greatest virtue of the Maharaja was that he practised round the clock what he preached in an unfailing manner. There were no contradictions between his private life and public life. His life was as transparent as the life of Mahatma Gandhi. [That is why Gandhi described Mysore State as *Ramarajya*. – Ed. Note.]

More than One's Expectations

The Maharaja, during his early years, was educated in a private royal school, whose headmaster was Sir S. M. Fraser (I.C.S. Retd.). This is the personal evaluation of Maharaja's character by his mentor. "His highness has understood me very well. But I have not been able to understand his highness at all." This shows the early maturity of the Maharaja's intellect. Another Britisher by name Sir Evan Maconochie, K. C. I. E., C. S. I., who succeeded as Private Secretary to the Maharaja after Sir S. M. Fraser (Retd.) writes about the Maharaja, "His parting assurance to me was that in any contingency, His Highness could be trusted to go 'four annas better (a quarter of a rupee – a colloquial expression)' that could be expected, an assurance that was to be most fully complied with." The analogy of four annas is to reiterate the fact that the Maharaja was trustworthy, reliable and dependable. He could be expected to tread the extra mile to fulfil a promise given to a person.

On the first day in royal school, the young prince aged only ten years noticed he was requested to sit on an ornate chair with a cushion covered with velvet and lace. The remaining eight or ten students had ordinary wooden benches and writing tables. The young prince refused to sit on this special chair and declined any preferential treatment or privileges. So, he occupied the ordinary wooden bench along with his classmates to the surprise of the teachers.

The school had a unique system of recognising the calibre of a student. The class teacher would ask a question to a front bench pupil. If he did not answer the question correctly, then the same question would be posed to the rest of the class. Any student who answered the question correctly would be promoted to the front bench. The first student, who failed to answer the question correctly would be sent back to the place vacated by the second student. Some students in the class were given to lying and cheating. If the prince had to occupy such a student's place, he would take out a wet sponge and wipe the seat clean, before occupying it. He did not appreciate deceit and falsehood in others. He wanted to avoid any contamination and pollution.

The young prince studying in the school also received instructions in the political administration of the state. Once the school head invited some village headmen and accountants to come to the school with their records, files and ledgers. One of the village headmen explained how they kept records of local farmers with regard to ownership of farms, animals and houses. The village accountant explained to the young prince the intricacies of tax collection from the farmers. At the end of the interview, the village headmen showed the ledger entries with regard to births and deaths in the village. The young prince went through the records meticulously for a long time. He also asked several questions pertaining to the records. The headmaster S. M. Fraser and other teaching staff members thought this was a mere waste of time to enquire about these records. The prince asked the village headman about his children. The headman replied his eldest child was two years old and his youngest child was three months old. He got their names and date of birth from the headman. The prince asked whether their birthdays were celebrated every year. The headman replied that they celebrated the birthdays of these children in a modest way since the circumstances did not permit any extravaganza. The prince laughed loudly and told the by-standards that the names and date of birth of these two children could not be found in the records. If the village headman did not record the births of his own children, how can you expect him to record the births of others' children? The prince had exposed the incompetence of the village record keeper.

A Repository of Indian Culture

The Maharaja was blessed by Gods to inherit the best qualities and values of a Hindu ruler. He was an embodiment of all that is exemplary in the Eastern and Western civilisation. Even the best aristocratic family members of the blue-blooded royal families of Europe were no match to the cultured personae of His Highness Sri Nalwadi Krishnaraja Wodeyar. He was well-mannered, gentle and a strict disciplinarian to the core. Legions of foreign dignitaries have praised the Maharaja for his sagacity, courtesy, benevolence and generosity. He practised the Vedic *Dharmasastra sutras* in everyday life. The Dharma gurus of different sects and religions had high praise for this exceptional individual. His sole aim in life was to keep his subjects happy and contented. He worked day and night to make the state of Mysore a model state in the country.

A Great Sacrifice

There were many instances in the life of the Maharaja when he risked his own life to save the lives of others. Once, the Maharaja was travelling in his Rolls Royce, on a mountainous road. It was late in the evening and darkness had enveloped the hills and valleys. The chauffeur was driving the car on the edge of a precipice with the headlights switched on. On either side of the road lay deep gorges of several thousands of feet deep. The Maharaja noticed suddenly a row of ox-driven carts with farm produce making progress towards them. The bright glare of the head lamps of the car and the chauffeur honking repeatedly added to the confusion. The ox drawing the first cart became nervous and fidgety. It began to pull the cart to the edge of the precipice. The Maharaja ordered the chauffeur not to honk and to park the car on the extreme left side of the road. He made the car driver switch off the headlights. The Maharaja told his two companions not to get out of the car. But he jumped on to the road in a jiffy and ran to the rescue of the first cart. He caught the bridle ropes which bound the oxen to the cart. He managed to drag the oxen back to the centre of the road. He ordered the cart driver to hold the reigns tight, as animals were dragging the cart to the right side of the road. The driver realised that the doomsday had arrived for him and his animals. The Maharaja's palms were profusely bleeding as he was dragging the animals and the cart to safety. He escorted the first cart personally by pulling the animals to march forward bypassing the parked car. There were 21 oxen carts behind the first cart laden with goods. The Maharaja, unmindful of his bleeding palms, escorted the remaining 21 carts to safety. The villagers who escaped a terrible disaster and sure death expressed their immense gratitude to the saviour of the day. The Maharaja advised the cartmen to have a few extra hands to navigate the carts on such dangerous mountainous roads. He returned to the car nonchalantly, while all along ignoring his bleeding palms.

The chauffeur switched on the headlamps and started the engines of the car. The other two companions of the Maharaja, apologetically informed him that they would have joined the rescue operation if not for the royal injunction. The Maharaja placidly told them that he had been bestowed with long life and strength by his parents. Similarly, they had been bestowed with these gifts by their parents. Moreover, their lives were equally precious. He was prepared to risk his life in an emergency. He did not want to endanger the lives of his companions unnecessarily.

Once in the deep jungles of Mysore State near Bandipur, a huge rogue elephant began to give a lot of trouble to the *Soliga* tribesman. This big male elephant with impressive tusks would attack forest dwellers and kill them. It did not spare motor cars and buses. During night time, the glare of the headlamps of speeding vehicles usually scare elephants. But this particular elephant went after these vehicles at night time. This rogue elephant had already killed several people in the most violent manner. Even the *Kadu Kurubas* who lived deep inside the forest were afraid of this elephant. This was reported to the Maharaja and his help was sought in this matter as he was a good *shikar* (marksman). The Maharaja ventured into the deep forest on a tamed elephant carrying a howdah. Only a handful of persons accompanied him. They were led by a Soliga tracker. He intuitively led them to the deepest part of the forest. There was a thicket of thorny bushes and a dark interior filled with thick bamboo stalks and huge trees. The tribesmen crawled on all fours and reached the centre of the forest. He noticed the lone tusker sulking in the dense jungle. He returned with great difficulty all bruised up and with bleeding hands and legs. He whispered to the Maharaja that the rogue elephant had taken refuge there in a secluded spot. He could not go any further because of the thorny bushes. The Maharaja, with his double-barrelled gun, jumped from the Elephant's howdah. He did not bother about the lurking danger at the distance nor the thorny bramble bushes, which caused injuries to him. He ventured into the interior hideout without any fear. When he rushed into the forest interior, he was staking his life. But he could approach the rogue elephant unnoticed and unseen, he took aim with his gun and pumped bullets into the body of the elephant. The elephant fell down in one swoop with a loud thud and the companions and the Soligas cheered the Maharaja heartily.

Once, the Maharaja was vacationing in the hill town of Ooty. He owned a European manor house called Fern Hill Imperial Palace, which was his summer residence. The Maharaja loved horse riding greatly and whenever an opportunity afforded, he took off on his horse. One early morning, he began his horse ride on the hills and dales of Ooty. Some of the areas of Ooty were off-limits for safe riding on horses. These trails traversed the mountain paths skirting deep gorges with Nilgiri shola forest. On this morning, he noticed a British rider who had fallen off his horse, and his unconscious body was lying on some bushes down the slope. The injured horse was lying on the ground, bleeding. The Maharaja got down from his horse and scrambled down the cliff to the rescue of the Britisher. He did not mind the risk that he was taking during this rescue mission. He hauled the unconscious body of the Britisher on his shoulder and climbed the steep cliff with great difficulty. He carried the injured and unconscious Britisher to the town hospital for medical aid. This brave act of the Maharaja received all-round praise from Indians and Europeans alike. The Englishmen and women admired the bravery of the Maharaja because a native prince had gone all out to save a member of the ruling class.

The Maharaja of Mysore decided to conduct a Khedda operation in 1917 to trap wild elephants and tame them later. This kind of Khedda operation was conducted once in four years to augment the working elephant population. In 1917, it was going to be conducted at a place called Budhipadaga in Chamaraja Nagar taluk. The Maharaja of Mysore invited His Highness Maharaja Sri Gaikwad of Baroda state. The Soliga tribals would dig up a circular pit of enormous proportion. This pit was surrounded by a series of tall tree trunks forming a first layer of wall. These tall tree trunks were installed in the ground to a depth of four feet. These tree trunks were tied to each other by thick strong ropes. The stockade pit had three tree trunk circular walls. This circular theatre of Khedda operation had an entrance with tree trunks measuring at least 30 feet in height and a circumference of at least 30" or 40." This large pit could at least accommodate 50 or 60 Elephants in an area measuring 20 – 50 yards. Around the circular stockade pit, the forest department officials would construct a gallery for VIPs. The Soliga tribesmen would drive wild Elephants and young ones from a distance of 5 or 6 miles. They would encircle groups of wild Elephants and herd them towards the Khedda pit. They created a din with the help of drums and horns. They carried flaming torches, which scared wild elephants. They burst fire crackers to instil fear in the animals. They would drive forty or fifty elephants with their young ones into the stockade. The mahouts on tamed elephants called *"Khumkis"* would assist in this operation. The two Khumki elephants would box in a wild elephant and bring it under control. The Soligas tied the legs and neck of the Elephant to pin it down to one place. It was an arduous and risky task to tame wild elephants. They were often tortured with sharp implements to subdue them.

In the 1917 Khedda operation, a huge male elephant with big tusks was also trapped. But this furious elephant began to behave wildly. The Khumki elephants could not subjugate the wild tusker. These scenes were being watched by the Maharaja of Baroda and his family members. The Mysore royal family led by Sri Nalwadi Krishnaraja Wodeyar were also present in the gallery. Many Europeans and Indian officials were watching this spectacle. The ferocious and violent wild elephant began to ram its head against the first ring of the barricade. It managed to cause a breach and entered the second ring. It began to attack the second circle barricade of tree trunks. Even the makeshift gallery with visitors began to shake and swing wildly. Many spectators jumped from a height of 10 feet to the ground and made a hasty run to safety. The Maharaja of Baroda and his family members were shaken to the core. They were requested to scramble down in a hurry to safety by Nalwadi Krishnaraja Wodeyar.

Meanwhile, the Soligas had lit a huge bonfire outside the third circle of the barricade. The elephants are scared of fire and fire crackers. The Maharaja saw that the elephant was about to bring down the third barricade. He ordered the Khumki elephants to surround it from four sides. The brave Soligas managed to tie ropes to its legs, trunk and neck and tied it to stakes. Slowly, the wild elephant came to be subdued. Because of the Maharaja's presence of mind, the terrible situation was brought under control. He avoided the certain death of many spectators.

Equanimity of Mind

The Maharaja had an innate ability to control his temper, even when the situation did not warrant it. Once, a palace attendant was entrusted with the duty of giving the Maharaja warm water for washing his face and hands. The poor attendant did not notice that the jug of water given to him was scalding hot. The jug of hot water slipped from his hands and fell upon the feet of the Maharaja. The Maharaja bore the excruciating pain with great difficulty. The situation demanded a proper dressing down of the attendant. The attendant was trembling with fear and profusely apologised for the lapse in his behaviour. Instead of scolding the humble servant, the Maharaja consoled him and pardoned his mistake.

Britannica Glorifies Mysore State

The Encyclopaedia Britannica (1938) edition contains a report on the Princely State of Mysore in the British-Indian dominion. I quote here a part of the content on this Princely State of Mysore in the British-ruled Indian dominion, "Mysore, a Hindu State with just claims to be the most progressive in India…" This unique distinction was achieved only because the late Maharaja strived hard with patriotic fervour to make it a progressive state. This lone incident demonstrates his egalitarian outlook, which occurred in the month of October 1936. The Mysore State, nee the whole of Hindu India celebrates on a grand scale the ten days Dasara festival.

During the first nine days, the Maharaja of Mysore conducted in the evenings a royal durbar for his courtiers. The eminent classical musicians performed in the evenings. On one of the days, during the Europeans only durbar, the palace's western band performed Western classical compositions. It is needless to state that invitees were VIPs hailing from India and abroad. They were attending the Maharaja's durbar wearing either Indian formal dress or western formal dress of black tail coat and white shirts with bow neck ties and cravats. They were surprised to hear well-known Western classical compositions rendered with such finesse by the palace orchestra.

India had a large population of poor and downtrodden people belonging to the caste of untouchables (Panchama). These people were underprivileged and did not belong to the *"Chaturvarna"* caste system. They were beyond the pale of four prominent castes, the *Kshatriyas* (the warrior caste), the *Brahmins* (the twice-born elite), the *Vyshyas* (the rich businessmen) and the *Shudras* (the farmers and the working class). The untouchables of India were barred from entering Hindu temples and they could not socialise with the upper caste gentry. Gandhi started the temple entry movement all over India. But the enlightened monarch of Mysore on a particular day in the 1936 Dasara celebration invited the untouchables of Mysore State to attend the evening palace durbar. This was hailed as a revolutionary move by a progressive monarch. The Maharaja also introduced reservation of seats in educational institutions and a certain percentage of government jobs were also reserved for untouchable Hindus and tribal people.

One of the British invitees to the royal durbar has recorded in his observation, "A remarkable instance of the enlightened character of the administration occurred in October 1936, when the Maharaja, though a strictly orthodox Hindu, admitted (for the first time) members of the depressed classes to participate in ceremonials connected with the celebrations of the Dasara festival at the palace." *"How striking a breach this affected the age-long caste traditions can be appreciated only by those who had seen its rigidity on the spot."* - These words of an English journalist sum up the revolutionary nature of the monarch's all-inclusive move to welcome untouchables into the palace.

Chapter 2

Childhood

******

Maathru Devo Bhava
Pithru Devo Bhava
Acharya Devo Bhava
Athithi Devo Bhava.
Mother is a divine being
Father is a divine being
Teacher is a divine being
Guest is a divine being
(***Taitteriya Upanishad***)

******

Victorious *Vikramanama namasamvathsara* (year)

The month of March in 1881 was a special month for the members of the Royal family and to the citizens of the Mysore State. After the defeat and death of Tipu Sultan, the East India Company restored the rule of Wodeyars in the Mysore State. The five-year-old Prince Sri Krishnaraja Wodeyar III was empowered to sit on the throne by the Britishers. In 1831, close on the heels of the Nagara revolt (a civil insurrection) and citing maladministration, the British took direct control of the princely state later. For the next fifty years, successive British commissioners administered the state. In 1881, the British reinstated the Maharaja Chamarajendra Wodeyar X, educated in the British system as the ruler of Mysore state. The Queen Sri Vanivilas Sannidhana Srimati Kempananjammani delivered a female child on 11th March 1881. The birth of a daughter heralded a new chapter in the history of the Mysore state. Sri Chamarajendra Wodeyar X was installed by the Britishers as the Maharaja of Mysore. His coronation ceremony took place on 25th March 1881. The

Viceroy of India, Lord Rippon, could not personally attend the coronation ceremony. The Governor of Madras, Sir William Patrick Adam, attended the coronation ceremony as an official representative of the Viceroy of India. It was a grand, colourful and glittering ceremony conducted in the palace. The secretary to the Governor of Madras State read out a proclamation sent by the Queen Empress of India Victoria declaring Maharaja Chamarajendra Wodeyar as the new ruler of the Mysore State. The new born daughter of the Maharaja was looked upon as a harbinger of good luck and she was named Princess Jayalakshammani. The Maharaja appointed S. V. Rangacharlu as the Dewan of the Mysore State, equivalent to the post of present-day Chief Minister.

Two Important Decisions

In 1881, two revolutionary decisions of the Maharaja Chamarajendra Wodeyar came to be implemented. The first decision was to set up a people's representative legislature to conduct state business. This institution was created even before the founding of the Indian National Congress. This democratic movement was the brain child of the Maharaja and the Dewan.

The second revolutionary decision was mooted by the Queen to start a girls' high school in the state capital in 1881. The girls' school was named after the Maharani and it was called Maharani Vani Vilas girls' high school. There was stiff resistance to impart education to girls in India. All over India, child marriages were the norm and imparting Western types of education to girls was a taboo. Later on, this girls' school became a college to impart University level degree education in Science and Humanities subjects.

In June 1883, the Queen delivered another daughter, who came to be named Princess Krishnajammani. Exactly one year later, on 4th June 1884, the Queen gave birth to a male child, the future successor to the throne of Mysore State. The young male child was named Sri Nalwadi Krishnaraja Wodeyar, who is the protagonist of this biography.

Birth of a Male Heir

Some twenty days prior to the birth of the male child, Queen Victoria had conferred the tittle upon the Maharaja Chamarajendra Wodeyar "G. C. S. I." (The most exalted order of the Star of India – G. C. S. I. – Knight Grand Commander of the Star of India) in recognition for his excellent administration of the Princely State of Mysore. The birth of the future scion was announced to the world by the firing of cannons. All the major Hindu temples of the state performed special *pujas* (rituals) for Gods and Goddesses. The palace officials distributed sugar and fruits to the citizens of Mysore freely. The lady relatives of the royal family came to see the new born prince. They offered as *"Nazar"* gold coins in a bamboo tray to the Queen (*Marada Honnu* – Kannada). During this ritual, the Queen would touch the gold coins and return them to the donors. Many prisoners languishing in state prisons were granted their liberty and set free. The poorest of the poor people received new clothes, money and food from the royal treasury. On the seventh day after the birth of the child, the baby boy was given an auspicious name. On that day, special pujas were performed in important temples. The citizens were served with sumptuous grand lunch and gift money was given to each person. The school children sang in a chorus a specially composed song for the occasion titled "Come, O! Ye everyone to see the royal new prince at the palace."

Maharaja Sri Chamarajendra Wodeyar with his children –
R to L Princess Sri Jayalakshammani, Prince Sri Nalwadi Krishnaraja Wodeyar
on lap and Princess Cheluvajammani

Cradle Rocking Ceremony

The rulers of Yaduvamsha, from time immemorial, worshipped Goddess Chamundeshwari, whose temple is situated on top of the lone hill in Mysore. Goddess Chamundeshwari is none other than Parvati, the consort of Lord Shiva. She took the avatar of Chamundeshwari to vanquish the terrible demon (Asura) Mahishasura. The fiery Goddess appeared on a lion and fought a violent battle with Mahishasura and killed him. The popular myth recalls that the body of the demon eventually became the lone hill on the Cauvery plains. The temple of the Goddess stands on a protuberance shaped like the head of the temple. The Maharaja of Mysore rules as a representative of the Goddess Chamundeshwari (one who severed the head of the demon). The future scion, Sri Krishnaraja Wodeyar, after his naming ceremony had to undergo the "cradle rocking ceremony." The Maharaja Sri Chamarajendra Wodeyar decided to conduct this ritual on the Chamundi hill. All the members of the royal family travelled to the top of the hill on the appointed auspicious day.

In the temple premises, there stands a Champak tree. The palace attendants hung the golden cradle studded with precious stones. It was hung from the tree by four golden chains decorated with flowers. After performing puja to Goddess Chamundeshwari, the King and the Queen lowered the baby into the cradle. The royal princesses rocked the cradle by swinging it to and fro. Melodious lullabies were sung to soothe the royal child.

Birth Anniversary

When the young scion completed one year, there was a gala celebration all over the state. On that day, the royal child was given a holy bath in the morning. Later, the birthday celebration took place in the Amba Vilas Darbar hall attended by the dignitaries with their wives. The royal child was taken out in the evening on a silver palanquin in a procession through the important streets of the fortified town. The young scion visited the important temples within the fort city, such as Threenayaneshwara, Varahaswamy, Prasanna Krishnaswamy and Laxmi Ramana Swamy temples to receive the blessing of Gods and received *Prasadam* (sanctified food).

Until the Age of Five

The little prince was taken around in a perambulator by the two elder sisters and by the servants inside the palace, where there was an open-air quadrangle called "*Madana Vilasa Thotti.*" The large courtyard had several parrots hung there in cages. These talking parrots welcomed the Prince with the words, "Hail to the Young Prince." The two older sisters addressed the prince as "*Thammaiah*" (little younger brother). The palace servants often took the prince on a palanquin in the evenings through the streets of Mysore. The ordinary folks loved the royal child and they had a great reverence for the royal family. This evening exercise was called in the native tongue "*Gali Sevane*" (an outing for a breath of fresh air).

When the prince was aged two years, he was presented with a colourful wooden hobby horse. The child sat on the wooden horse and it was wheeled around the courtyard. The little boy showed curiosity in illustrated books and gazed at them intently. At three years of age, the prince could walk and talk with ease. The Maharaja took the young boy on a midget horse carefully to *Kariyakallu Thotti* (another open-air courtyard paved with black stone slabs).

Childhood days Prince Nalwadi Sri Krishnaraja Wodeyar (Standing) and younger brother Sri Kanteerava Narasimharaja Wodeyar

His Highness Sri Chamarajendra Wodeyar with
Prince Nalwadi Sri Krishnaraja Wodeyar on a pony

Sisters and Brothers

The young boy wore white pyjamas and his top coat was of Damascus velvet with gold decoration. Instead of metallic buttons on the coat, a gold chain held the lapels of the coat together. The young boy sported a silk turban on his head. He wore around the neck a double row of a string of pearls with a gold and diamond pendant. As they had pierced holes in the ear, he could wear diamond studs embedded in gold. Whenever any individual did a namaste, the young boy reciprocated with a namaste from the age of two. The royal couple had one more daughter on 22nd December 1886 and the female child was named Sri Chaluvajammani. Two years later, on 5th June 1888 one more son was born and he was named Sri Kanteerava Narasimharaja Wodeyar. In the later years, the royal couple got two more sons, but they did not survive their infancy.

Childhood

The young scion grew up with his sisters and brother in a cheerful environment. The well-known court poet, Kavitilaka Sosale Ayya Sastri, specially composed a nursery rhyme in Kannada on a parrot. Everyone enjoyed the little prince lisping this nursery rhyme much to the enjoyment of the bystanders. The young prince showed an extraordinary interest in horse riding. The Maharaja Sri Chamarajendra Wodeyar made the older two daughters take riding lessons dressed in male attire. The young prince wanted to ride the horse independently like his older sisters. But he was always escorted by the King holding with his right hand the reins of the horse and he held the boy on the saddle with his left hand. The boy wept and cried saying he wanted to ride the horse on his own. The Maharaja was an amateur photographer and he loved to capture the childhood scenes of his daughters and sons.

The Maharaja Sri Chamarajendra Wodeyar with his children
L to R – Princess Sri Jayalakshammani (standing), Princess Sri Chalujammani (seated), Prince Sri Nalwadi Krishnaraja Wodeyar, Prince Sri Kanteerava Narasimharaja Wodeyar on the lap – Princess Krishnajammani

Royal Children: standing L - R: Princess Sri Chaluvajammani, Prince Nalwadi Krishnaraja Wodeyar; Sitting L - R: Princess Krishnajammani, Prince Sri Kanteerava Narasimharaja Wodeyar and Princess Jayalakshammani

Tonsure of the Head and Initiation Ritual for School Learning

During the month of March in 1889 the Maharaja conducted the "*Aksharabyasa*" and "*Chudakarma*" rituals before the prince attained the age of five. A Hindu boy had to undergo 16 ritualistic Karmas (Shodasha samskara) during his lifetime. The tonsuring of the head of the child and allowing a tuft at the back of the head is called "*Chudakarma*." Every child begins the process of education on an auspicious day after the age of three years and it is called "*Akshara* (imperishable alphabet) *Abhyasa* (exercise)." The ordinary boys and girls began their schooling with a slate and white chalk stylus. But prince Sri Krishnaraja Wodeyar was presented with a silver slate. The small sized expensive pearls had been spread on the slate. The young prince was given a gold stylus to write on the silver slate. The royal priest, after performing Puja to Goddess Saraswathi (Goddess of learning in Hindu pantheons like St. Cecilia) made the young prince write the letter "Sri" in Sanskrit and Kannada. The Brahmin priests received the silver slate, pearls, gold stylus and silver coins as their remuneration.

The Prince joined his two elder sisters, who were students in the royal private school. A few Urs girl students were also studying with the royal princesses. These students were taught by erudite pundits such as Rao Bahadur Ambil Narasimha Iyengar, the former Darbar Bakshi (protocol officer of the palace), the poet scholar Kavi Tilaka Sosale Ayya Sastri and Sri Nanjanagud Subba Sastri, etc. Every morning, the school session began with the school prayer, a Sanskrit hymn. Sri Nanjanagud Subba Sastri was a very old gentleman, who often fell asleep in the classroom. The young Prince played truant by lifting the turban of the Pundit with a stick and toppling it to the ground. The old teacher would suddenly wake up startled by the sudden commotion caused by this practical joke. This old teacher was fond of inhaling snuff, occasionally resulting in a loud sneezing. The young prince imitated the actions of the old pundit by sniffing camphor powder and pretending to sneeze in a similar manner. These pranks of the young prince produced a lot of mirth among his classmates. The royal couple provided their children with garden plots. The children were encouraged to grow flowers and vegetables so that they could develop a love towards nature. This gardening activity instilled healthy competition among them to grow better flowers and vegetables.

Once a week, the children were made to watch the magic lantern slide projection show. They saw pictures of foreign cities, the seven wonders of the world, the solar system, the wild animals and birds and high mountains and forests. They also had wooden building blocks set called "Kindergarten." The children could assemble homes, churches and buildings out of them as a creative activity.

Guru Sri Poorna Raghavendra Rao

The Maharaja appointed Rajamantra Praveena Dewan Bahadur Sri Poorna Raghavendra Rao – a retired first member of the council (minister in King's cabinet) – as a teacher to his children in June 1890. He was a B. A. (Bachelor of Arts) graduate from the University of Madras. The children addressed him as "New Sir" in the Kannada language. Formerly, Princess Jayalakshammani was taught English by Sri Rangacharya. The new teacher was affectionate, kind, loving and wise. He became more of a friend than a disciplinarian strict teacher. But sometimes, Princess Jayalakshammani would entice her classmates to outdoor games. She wanted to skip Poorna Raghavendra Rao's classes. But the teacher would have none of it. He would tell them to learn the lessons by rote and to recite them back to him. The young Prince showered a greater inclination towards outdoor games. They played hide and seek game in the huge palace. The young prince was outsmarted by his older classmates, which left him often in tears. His elder sister consoled him by various stratagems, such as if he was discovered by the search party three times, it was equal to one discovery made in the case of others.

Once Sri Ambil Narasimha Iyengar had asked palace attendants to bring in small cups of various cereals and corn. One cup contained castor seeds, which are bitter and its oil is used as a purgative. Some classmates lied to the prince that castor seeds were as tasty as almonds and he could consume them. The innocent prince ate some castor seeds, which were bitter. This news reached the Maharani and she rushed to the classroom in a panic. The teacher was absent and the queen wanted to punish the mischievous student, who misled the young prince. The young prince took the blame upon himself and told his mother that he ate them of his own volition. He wanted to protect his classmates from the wrath of the Queen.

Once, the young prince expressed his desire to visit the homes of his classmates. They informed him that as a Maharaja, he could not visit the house of the commoners. He replied to them that his father was a Maharaja and as far as he was concerned, he was a commoner.

Princess Jayalakshammani was a reluctant student. She was more fond of outdoor sports. She would often beg Sri Poorna Raghavendra Rao to let off the classes for the day. But he was not lenient with the royal students. He was known to have remarked to the students, that too much cramming would make a student a jackass. Hence, the Princess wanted an unscheduled holiday for the school. But the teacher Rao pointed out that they had not taxed their brains with heavy inputs and where is the question of relaxation. He told the Princess that she should be an example to other students and he did not want to punish her for any lassitude in her behaviour.

Sringeri Pontiff's Benediction

The Princess turned a new leaf and later took a lot of interest in the development of the girls' school started by her mother. When Krishnaraja Wodeyar was seven years old in 1891, the Chief Pontiff of Sringeri Shankara Mutt (Monastery) Sri Sachidananda Shivanubhava Nrusimha Bharati Swamy visited the palace on the King's invitation. The head of the Mutt was considered a Chief Guru to the Mysore Royal household. The Sringeri Mutt was founded in the 8th century A. D. by Sri. Adi Shankaracharya. It was a tradition amongst disciples to invite the chief Guru of Sringeri to their homes for a "Padapuja." The Swamiji usually arrived at the destination on a silver palanquin, wearing a bejewelled gold crown and an expensive cashmere shawl. "Padapuja" literally means washing the feet of the Guru by the disciple with holy Ganges water. This act demonstrates the adoration and reverence of a disciple for his Guru. Later, the holy water collected on a silver plate is sprinkled on the heads of the assembled devotees. Later, the King would offer gold and silver coins as a tribute to the Guru. The whole entourage would be treated to a grand vegetarian lunch. All the members of the retinue and the Guru would receive coconuts, pan leaves and fruits as gifts.

On this morning, everyone witnessed a strange spectacle. The Maharaja requested the pontiff to bless his children. The four children prostrated before the Swamiji and received his blessings. The young Prince, Nalwadi Krishnaraja Wodeyar, was missing. The Maharaja ordered a palace official to fetch the young Prince, who had left the Queen's quarters.

Sosale Ayya Sastri had taught the young Prince the Vedic mantras, which lauds a Guru as,

"*Guru Brahma*
Guru Vishnu,
Guru Devo Maheshwara

Guru Sakshat Parabrahma
Thasmaishri Guruve Namaha."

[Meaning: A true Guru is equal to triumvirates Brahma (creator), Vishnu (the protector) and Maheshwara (the destroyer) – A Guru is a living Supreme Brahma – I salute such a noble Guru reverentially.]

Sosale Ayya Sastri had told the young Prince that the word "Guru" also includes one's parents. The court official ordered by the King to fetch the young Prince found a strange sight. The seven-year-old boy was standing at the door, holding the wooden Sandals of the Sringeri Pontiff close to his chest. His eyes were closed and he was chanting the Vedic mantra of guru worship. The official went back and reported this act of devotion of the young Prince to the Maharaja and the Pontiff. The elderly Sage, who was an *avadhoota* (enlightened one with spiritual powers) blessed the young Prince with tears of happiness in his eyes. The young scion was blessed in the name of God Chandra Mouleshwara and Goddess Sharada Devi. The guru blessed him with the qualities of *Shraddha* (devotion), *Bhakti* (dedication), *Viveka* (discrimination) and *Vairagya* (renunciation), so as to enable him to become an able ruler of the state.

The Maharaja requested the teacher Poorna Raghavendra Rao to teach the English language to the Princes in the year 1891. This teacher taught the Princes basic English Grammar and conversational English. In 1892, Prof. J. Vere joined the English department of Maharaja College, Mysore. He was requested to be the tutor to the princes. This Englishman was surprised by the proficiency of the English language exhibited by the young Prince Nalwadi and he also praised the teaching skills of the Poorna Raghavendra Rao.

The Royal School

The Maharaja Sri Chamarajendra Wodeyar made a decision to start a royal school for his children in Lokaranjan Mahal Palace, also called "Summer Palace" by the people. This school was founded in 1892 with some twenty students. They belonged to Ursu and Brahmin communities. The three princesses Sri Jayalakshammani, Sri Krishnajammani and Sri Chaluvajammani attended an exclusive school in the summer palace, where purdah was observed. The youngest Prince, Sri Kanteerava Narasimharaja Wodeyar, did not attend any school as he was only four years old. He had not undergone "Chudakarma" (the head being shorn of hair) and *"Aksharabyasa"* – the initiation ceremony to start schooling.

The Maharaja appointed Sri Ambil Narasimha Iyengar as Headmaster of the Royal School. The other members of the teaching staff were:
i. *Kavitilaka Sosale Ayya Sastri – Kannada and Sanskrit*
ii. *Janab Hassan Ali – Urdu*
iii. *Sri B. Bhima Rao – Mathematics*
iv. *Sri Hatti Krishna Iyengar – Geography*
v. *Risaldar Mohammad Ali – Horse Riding*
vi. *Jamadar Varadarajalu Naidu –* Military *marching and physical drill exercises*
vii. *Sri Armugham Pillai – Drawing and Painting*
viii. *Sri Viranna – Gymnastics*

This Special Royal School in Mysore was in existence until 1901 A.D. The classmates of Prince Nalwadi Krishnaraja Wodeyar in their own right became successful bureaucrats and officials in the Mysore State Government.
i. *Amin-ul-Mulk Sir Mirza. M. Ismail. K. C. I. E., O. B. E. – Former Dewan of Princely State of Mysore, Hyderabad and Jaipur.*
ii. *Sardar M. Lakshmikanth Raje Urs – Former Dewan of Mysore State*
iii. *Major M. C. Subbaraj Urs*
iv. *Sri M. S. Ramachandra Rao*
v. *Sri H. Siddaraja Urs*
vi. *Sri S. Narasingha Rao*
vii. *Sri Badami Shankar Rao*
viii. *Sri A. C. Basavaraj Urs*
ix. *Sri K. Lingopant Badami, etc.*

Some of my classmates like Sir Mirza. M. Ismail and Janab T. S. Ali Khan joined the school after a year or two of its founding. The three students, who joined the school Raja Seva Nipuna Sri S. Shamanna, Sri. T. Gundappa and Sri B. Venkata Subba Rao were older than the Prince in age. Hence, they were asked to attend a higher class in the school. The prince and his three sisters came to school from the palace in a horse-drawn coach. The other students came to school from their homes in a transportation provided by the palace. All the students received their mid-day meal from the palace. The Royal school was visited by such dignitaries as Maharaja Sri Chamarajendra Wodeyar, Dewan

Sir K. Seshadri Iyer, Huzoor Secretary Raja Sabha Bhushana Sri T. Thumboo Chetty's father Sri T. R. A. Thumboo Chetty and many others visited the Royal School to inspect the progress of students. The visiting dignitaries posed questions and evaluated their learning skills.

Nalwadi's Mature Behaviour

Once, the young Prince was injured during a sports activity. One of the palace attendants accidentally tripped the young Prince, his lips received an injury and led to bleeding. He had hurt a tooth as well in this accident. The report of this accident reached the ears of the Queen. She wanted to reprimand the negligent servant. But the young Prince took the blame upon himself and absolved the servant from any misdemeanour.

Passion for Learning

Once the young Prince fell sick in 1892. He was suffering from typhoid fever. His fever lasted several days. Although he received the best medical attention, occasionally, he would slip into delirium. Throughout his illness, he reposed absolute faith in the family Goddess Chamundeshwari. He often lamented in a delirious state about his absence from the school. He missed classes and his learning curve dived to poor levels. He was worried about losing his first place in academic ranking. When he recovered from a bout of Typhoid fever, he requested his parents to gift a golden crown studded with diamonds and gems to Goddess Chamundeshwari as he had taken a religious vow. The parents complied with his request. The King also served one thousand invitees with a sumptuous lunch to celebrate the Prince's recovery from typhoid fever.

One morning, the Maharaja was riding his horse and he came across a student of the Royal School riding a horse. The young student wanted to show his respect to the King. He dropped the reins from his hands and brought his two palms together to do a namaste. At that moment, the horse reared on its hind legs. The young rider was about to fall off the horse but managed to hold on. The Maharaja scolded the boy for this indulgence and warned him that next time, he would suffer a fall and break his teeth. He also told the young man, that he was like his son Nalwadi Krishnaraja Wodeyar and hence, should not salute him. Similarly, his other classmates were exempted from making salutations to the Maharaja. He always instructed his servants to treat the other boys with due deference. The queen-mother instructed the cooks to serve the same food to all the children.

The students of the Royal School were playing the game of *"Lagge Chendu."* The game involved an Indian rubber ball, which was thrown at the opponent as a target. If the ball hit the opponent, the boy scored a point in the game. The opponent made every attempt to dodge the ball aimed at him. The punishment for the loser was to carry the victor on his back and trudge a distance of 100 yards. Once, the Maharaja was astonished to see a lanky looser carrying the hefty Prince on his back. The Maharaja admonished the Prince for his conduct and asked him not to tax his lean classmate in this fashion.

A Trip to Bombay

In August 1893, the Queen Empress of India Victoria conferred on the Maharaja Sri. Chamarajendra Wodeyar the title of Colonel of the British Indian Army. He had already been awarded the title of "G. C. S. I." The Maharani of Mysore State Sri Vani Vilasa Sannidhana had been awarded the title of "C. I. E." (Commander of the Indian Empire) in June 1892 by Queen Empress Victoria. In 1893, the Maharaja of Mysore with his family decided to visit Bombay City. The Governor of the Bombay presidency had made elaborate arrangements for their stay in the State Guest house. But the Maharaja of Mysore and his family members conducted themselves in such a humble manner that they were often mistaken for commoners. They spent two months in Bombay, visiting all the historical places and museums.

The younger Prince, Sri Kanteerava Narasimharaja Wodeyar, after the initiation ceremony of "Akshara Abhyasa", joined the Royal School as a student. Some of his classmates were lieutenant colonel Late B. P. Krishne Urs, Late Sri. M. Channa Raje Urs, Janab M. G. Mekhri, Sri F. C. Devaraja Urs, Sri K. Subba Rao, Sri H. Mudda Raja Urs, Sri B. Dasappa, Janab Abdul Basith, etc. The Maharaja felt that the young Prince ought to be educated by some Englishmen. The native speakers of English from the British Isles would impart proper etiquette and oratorial skills to the future King, who would be interacting with the Britishers. One Englishman called Major Martin was private secretary to the Maharaja. He had argued before the Royal Commission that the adopted son of Mummadi Krishnaraja Wodeyar had a legal claim to the throne of Mysore. The British had dis-enfranchised the previous ruler on the grounds of maladministration of the state. The British regents ruled the state for fifty years. Major Martin had strongly argued before the Viceroy for the restoration of Monarchy in the Princely State of Mysore.

His son-in-law, Sri J. J. Whitley, M. I. C. E., who was working as an Executive Engineer in Madras Presidency was invited to Mysore to become Head of the Royal School.

The Musical Interlude

The Maharaja Sri. Chamarajendra Wodeyar was an aficionado of Indian and Western Classical Music. He had learnt to play Carnatic Classical Music on the Violin. He was a generous patron of fine arts. Princess Jayalakshammani had not only learnt Carnatic Classical Vocal music, she was also a trained pianist. Her Majesty Srimati Vani Vilasa Sannidhana was a skilled Veena player. The young Prince Nalwadi Krishnaraja Wodeyar had a natural ear for music. He was especially fond of the wind instrument *Nadaswara*. He was provided with a good teacher of music to learn classical Eastern and Western music. Later, Nalwadi was declared by critiques as a true connoisseur of music. The great musicians from all over the country flocked to his court seeking patronage.

Veena Vidwan Shamanna

The first music teacher of the Prince was Veena Maestro Shamanna. After his untimely demise, another great musician, Veena Sheshanna, became his Guru. Sri Veena Shamanna belonged to the Bruhadcharana Iyer community. He had a superb knowledge of "*Tala*" (rhythm). He trained the children of the Royal household to become discerning critics of music. Later, the performing artists were afraid of performing a concert before Nalwadi. They all had a sound theoretical knowledge of Carnatic Classical Music. The other eminent musicians like Sri Chikka Ramappa, father of Veena Maestro Sheshanna, Sri Veena Subbanna's father, Sri Sheshanna, Veena Sri Venkata Giriyappa's father, Sri Dodda (elder) Subba Rao had a great regard for Sri Veena Shamanna as an artist.

Once during the reign of Sri Krishnaraja Wodeyar III (1794 – 1868) – a famous musician from a North Indian state visited Mysore. He was a *Jalataranga* player. The musician kept several water-filled China bowls of different sizes before him. He held with his two hands wooden sticks and struck upon these bowls to produce melodious instrumental music. This artist presented himself before the Maharaja and made a tall claim about his musical skills. He wanted a certificate of appreciation from the Maharaja because he could play *Pallavi* (In Carnatic Classical Music a Pallavi is the main line of a song rendered usually in one cycle and repeated twice in order to give the percussionist the idea of a chosen *taalam*. Sometimes, it is repeated a few more times using different phrases of the *Ragam* to which the song is set. The word "Pallavi" is defined in this manner - "pa" is derived from *padam*, which means a phrase; "lla" comes from *layam* which means tempo; "Vi" is from *vinayasam*, which means variation. Pallavi also forms a part of a special type of rendition called Ragam-Thanam-Pallavi.[1])

The monarch told the musician to come to his court the next day and face the palace musicians in a contest. On the next day, three Veena players of the Mysore court played Pallavi of a Raga in three different time scales. Afterwards, Veena Shamanna presented a composition in Natakuranji Raga *"Anni Tikki Nive Adhikarai"* in three different time scales. In Carnatic classical music, the musicians have a rare genius to sing the Pallavi in one tempo, they keep rhythm with one hand in another tempo and play the Veena instrument in a third tempo. This extraordinary feat requires a very high degree of mental concentration. After this unique performance, Veena Shamanna addressed the visiting artist and requested him to present a Pallavi in Raga Pantuvarali in eight-time scales. He was requested to play the two identical ragas *Kamavardhani* and *Pantuvarali*. He was asked to highlight the *Gandhara Swara* in Raga Pantuvarali and its place in ascending or descending scale. After presenting these two ragas in three time scales, he should perform the raga in the fourth time scale. The visiting artist failed miserably in this test and accepted his defeat. Veena Shamanna exclaimed in exasperation, "Oh Goddess of Music, Saraswathi, these egoistical, puny musicians want to ride piggy back on you. This petty musician wants a certificate of appreciation from the Maharaja. If Goddess Saraswathi were to come down from heaven to play before us, where would she be placed in the musical hierarchy? Tush! the demand for a certificate of appreciation from the Maharaja was only meant for one's satisfaction of ego." Later, the musician Veena Shamanna apologised for his critical comments made against a rival musician.

Field Marshal Sir George Wolseley (later Viscount) visited Mysore City in 1894, soon after Dasara festivities. He wrote an article on the Princely State of Mysore and it was published in a London newspaper. The day after the arrival he visited the new race course in Mysore in a horse-drawn coach. He met Maharaja Chamarajendra Wodeyar's three daughters and two sons. These well-dressed children wearing expensive gold and diamond jewellery like

---

[1.] courtesy Wikipedia

chains, necklaces, cumberbands, ear studs and pearl necklaces were involved in an animated conversation with the European nanny in fluent English. They kept chatting freely until the races began. The two boys wore bejewelled turbans, silk coats and pants. The turbans were adorned with feathers, pearls, emeralds, rubies and diamonds. The visiting military official was very much impressed by their impeccable grooming.

***English Extract**:
"The day after I reached Mysore, I drove with His Highness round the lake (or properly speaking, the tank) to the new race course and it was on the occasion that I first saw his five children – three daughters and two sons. The eldest princess is of marriageable age according to Eastern etiquette being nearly fourteen......Just before the race began, the children joined the father and kept up a brisk conversation all the time with their English governess by whom they were accompanied......The young princess had strings of pearls and other precious stones twisted in their dark silky hair. The two little boys both of whom speak English very pretty wore coats of richly brocaded silk and trousers to match, together with turbans thickly sprinkled with pearls and emeralds which glittered and sparkled brightly as the Sun's rays flashed upon them. Both they and their sisters looked bright and intelligent and they all seemed to be healthy and happy."
*- **Field Marshal Sir George Wolseley (later Viscount)***
*(**Vide pp. 153 – 154, Modern Mysore** by **Rajakaryaprasaktha Rao***
***Bahadur M. Shama Rao, M. A.**)*

Chapter 3

The Death of the Patriarch

******

*"Om Namo Bhagavathe Vyvaswathaaya
Mruthyave Brahma Vidyacharyaya...."*

Om Namo the God of Death Mrutyu, Son of Acharya Vivasvantha, the knower of Brahmavidya we pay our obeisance to you

******

A Trip to Calcutta

Sri Chamarajendra Wodeyar, along with his family members, embarked on a railway journey to Calcutta in December 1894. Everyone began to make enthusiastic preparations for the forth coming trip to Calcutta. But unfortunately, these preparations were marred by signs of ill omen. Some elders in the family were perturbed by these elements. The Maharaja performed several pujas to the family deity Sri Chamundeshwari like the procession of Goddess around the temple on a lion statue, before his departure.

The royal entourage left Mysore by a special train on 9th December 1894 for Poona. They reached Poona on 11th December 1894 and went around the district visiting temples, and forts and climbed Parvathi hill to see the shrine. Later, they travelled to Jabbalpore by train. They visited sacred places of worship on the banks of the river Narmada near Mirganj railway station. Here, the river Narmada flows through narrow gorges of white marble stone. It is a great scenic spectacle to watch in the evening sunset from this location. When Maharaja left Mysore, he already had a cough, cold and fever. He was also suffering from exhaustion. Despite this inopportuneness, he continued his journey to Prayag, Allahabad. Here, the three rivers Ganga, Yamuna and the mythical underground river Saraswathi's confluence has a special significance for Hindus. The Hindus visit Prayag for a holy dip to wash away their sins and they also immerse the ashes and bones of their dear departed. After completing different religious rituals here, the royal family left for Calcutta.

When the royal train reached Calcutta on 21st December 1894, the Viceroy of India, Sir Victor Alexander Bruce, 9th Earl of Elgin was there to welcome the Maharaja and his family members. They were taken to a special guest house belonging to Maharaja of Vijayanagaram at Sealdha. The Viceroy hosted a special dinner in the evening for the Maharaja's family. The family members enjoyed their sightseeing trips around Calcutta city.

Indisposition of the Maharaj

But on 24th December 1894, the Maharaja developed a high fever. On that very day, all India Medical Conference was taking place in Calcutta. One thousand doctors and consultants had come from all over India. This medical conference was inaugurated by the Viceroy of India, Lord Elgin. On 25th December 1894, the Dewan Seshadri Iyer visited the ailing Maharaja. He instructed the Durbar surgeon, Colonel Benson, Assistant surgeon Dr. Hanuman Singh and headquarters surgeon Dr. Krishnaswamy Iyer to look after the Maharaja carefully. As the fever had subsided, the Maharaja decided to visit the Calcutta race club early in the morning to see the thoroughbreds. He ignored the advice of the doctors to desist from venturing out. He returned to his guest house at 09:00 AM and his temperature was high. He was shivering badly and he had become breathless. Sri Poorna Raghavendra Rao requested the compounder to prepare a mustard poultice for the Maharaja. It was applied on the chest and around the throat to ease breathing.

The Maharani was very much distraught by the serious condition of Chamarajendra Wodeyar. She brought to him a hot glass of milk thinking that it would help him to breath easily. He took a few gulps of milk, but it did not improve his breathing. Sri Poorna Raghavendra Rao went in a horse-drawn coach to fetch Dr. Benson from the medical conference. In that huge gathering of doctors, he managed to locate the doctor with great difficulty and he was rushed back to the Royal guest house. He tried his best to treat the suffering Maharaja, but in vain. On 26th December 1894, the condition of the Maharaja further deteriorated. Dewan Sir Seshadri Iyer went to the Government Medical College, Calcutta to fetch the best surgeon in the whole of Calcutta city. Dr. Mac Donald was a professor of surgery at the said institution. He was brought to the guest house in a Chaise post haste. Dr. MacDonald in consultation with Dr. Benson examined the patient. He concluded that the Maharaja had contracted Diphtheria, a dangerous throat infection. But taking into account the Maharaja's young age and physical condition, they thought he would pull through his illness. At that time, the Pasteur Institute of Paris had prepared an antidote for Diphtheria. It was to be administered through an injection. They were exporting this medicine to several countries of the world. The hunt for these anti-toxin capsules began in right earnest on 27th December 1894 in Calcutta city. Diphtheria was a rare occurrence in those days. They searched in hospitals, nursing homes, pharmacies and drug stores. The anti-toxin was not available in any shop and one shop keeper said he sold his last stock only on the previous day to a patient's relative. The poor soul, Sri Poorna Raghavendra Rao, returned empty-handed. Even the experienced doctors became dispirited by the turn of events. They began to discuss among themselves the alternative mode of treatment. Even during the grave crisis, the Maharaja retained an equanimity of mind and a wry sense of humour. He joked with Sri Poorna Raghavendra Rao and Sri Ambil Narasimha Iyengar about whether the doctors had prepared an exit pass for him to go to the next world. The two gentlemen turned pale at this colourless joke.

Severe Decline in Health and the Death of a Ruler

The health of Sri Chamarajendra Wodeyar worsened and he could not perform Sri Chamundeshwari Puja. The Queen was inconsolably weeping at the prospect of losing her husband. Dr. Benson had an invitation that evening for dinner. He went to the Maharaja to obtain permission to attend the dinner party. The Maharaja readily acquiesced to the physicians' request. He did not mind his own suffering and felt that the doctor must honour his invitation. But when the doctor approached Dewan Seshadri Iyer for his consent, the Dewan told Dr. Benson in no uncertain terms that his presence was very much required at the bedside of the Maharaja. He was asked to decline the dinner invitation. On that evening, the Maharaja's health deteriorated very badly. Dr. Benson realised the wisdom of declining the dinner invitation on a day like this. Both Dr. MacDonald and Dr. Benson put in their best efforts to save the life of the Maharaja. But alas! Fate willed it otherwise. The last words of the Maharaja were, "Oh! Mother Goddess Chamundeshwari," and then he closed his eyes. His breathing became more and more difficult and on 28th December 1894 at 05:00 AM he breathed his last. The Queen, stricken with grief, collapsed to the ground, unconscious.

She woke up after some time and began to weep profusely. The news of the Maharaja's death was conveyed to Dewan Sir Seshadri Iyer by Sri Poorna Raghavendra Rao. They both began to weep like young children. They could not bear the sight of the Maharani and her five children crying without any respite.

The Maharaja was admired and respected in other Indian states and also in foreign countries. His able administration aided by noble qualities like universal love and generosity had endeared him to people. In the obituary notice, the Editor of "The Pioneer" newspaper published from Allahabad wrote, "Well educated, amiable, genial, a good sportsman and high-minded gentlemen, Maharaja Chamarajendra Wodeyar gained affection and esteem far beyond the limits of his own territories." The well-known scholar, historian, archaeologist and educationist Benjamin Lewis Rice, C. I. E. had this to say about the Late Maharaja, "The Maharaja Sri Chamarajendra Wodeyar carried himself with great dignity and was completely devoid of arrogance. In every respect, he behaved like an aristocrat of a European noble family. He was a skilled horse rider and knew how to drive a coach. He was fond of sports and a generous patron of horse racing."

The Maharaja was a generous host and treated his guests magnanimously while entertaining them. But as a true practising Hindu, he never forgot to perform religious rituals. He was loved and respected equally by both Indians and Europeans. The Royal Court of Great Britain at Buckingham Palace led by Queen Empress of India Victoria was not a notch above the royal court of Mysore state. The dignity, decorum, and good manners were on par with any royal court in Europe.

The Maharaja loved his family members immensely. He exposed his children to the best of oriental and western culture like classical music, theatre, sculpture, painting and literature. In the matter of State administration, he abided by his conscience and conducted it in a professional manner. During the rainy season, he divided his time between Mysore and Bangalore. During the winter months, he travelled all over India. He spent the hot summer months in the cool environs of the Fern Hill Imperial Palace at Ooty. He had earned the friendships of great many people, because of his extensive travels. He had impressed numerous men and women through his noble conduct and behaviour." (Not a verbatim report, but translated from Kannada).

Tributes to the Maharaja

The Viceroy of India, Lord Elgin, sent his foreign secretary and his personal bodyguards to convey the condolence message on behalf of the British Government to the Maharani Sri Vani Vilasa Sannidhi who cried inconsolably and told the emissary that they came to Calcutta, only to become orphans by losing their head of the State. She wanted to entrust her five children to the care of the Viceroy.

On that morning, the Maharaja of Kapurthala was the visiting dignitary at the Viceroy's house. The guest of honour would have been welcomed with a gun salute depending on his ranking in the hierarchy of Indian Maharajas and Nawabs. But Lord Elgin called off the gun salute as a mark of honour to the departed Mysore Maharaja.

The Maharani, the Dewan and the Darbar Bakshi wanted to conduct the funeral at Benaras. But it would have meant a delay of a day or two. The five children would have suffered privations.

One of the judges of the High Court of Calcutta Sri Gurudas Bannerjee, an authority on Hindu *Dharma Shastra* (Canonical Law) told them that they must conduct the funeral in Calcutta on that very evening. The officials of the Mysore State could not procure a palanquin to carry the dead body to the cremation grounds on the bank of the Hooghly River. The Maharaja of Mysore had a military title of colonel from the British government. Hence, the Viceroy Lord Elgin extended all the military honours to the departed soul. The British army personnel lined on either side of the street. The funeral procession was led by a military contingent. The Viceroy's foreign secretary and personal bodyguards along with the Dewan of Mysore State and Darbar Bakshi marched in front of the cortege. The servants had converted a cot in the guest house into a bier and it was placed on a horse-drawn carriage. Many European dignitaries wearing black dress accompanied the cortege. The Royal family of Kapurthala was represented by Dewan Sri Daulat Ram and Capt. Sundar Singh. Sri Poorna Raghavendra Rao was asked to stay behind so as to take care of the grieving Maharani and five children. The funeral carriage was drawn by four magnificent horses and it was escorted by a cavalry of soldiers.

The funeral procession left the guest house at 2:00 PM and it winded through the major thoroughfares of Calcutta city and reached the cremation ground at 7:00 PM. A large crowd of mourners had gathered on either side of the road. The people of Calcutta respected this reformist ruler, who had started the first legislative assembly even before the British Raj implemented such a scheme in Delhi and this political reform happened before the founding of the Indian National Congress in 1905. The Maharaja had started a girls' school and college before anyone else had taken up the cause of women's education. The Maharaja's military commandant, Bakshi Raja Sena Bhushana Sri Basappaji Urs lit the funeral pyre on the banks of the Hooghly River at Kali Ghat and later, a memorial was erected on the spot. The funeral party returned to the guest house in a dejected mood late in the night.

The Viceroy Lord Elgin sent a condolence letter to the Maharani on 29th December 1894. He also mentioned in that letter that the next successor to the throne of Mysore would be Sri Nalwadi Krishnaraja Wodeyar, son of Sri Chamarajendra Wodeyar. Until further arrangements are made, Dewan Sir Seshadri Iyer will be looking after the administration of the state in consultation with the British Regent and Maharani Sri Vani Vilas Sannidhana.

The Foreign secretary of the Viceroy sent a telegram to the British resident colonel Henderson at Bangalore informing him about the sad demise of Maharaja Chamarajendra Wodeyar. The British resident ordered the sealing of state rooms, treasury and safe guarding the valuables belonging to the state. The resident left for Mysore along with in charge Dewan Sri T. R. A. Thumboo Chetty. Thousands of grief-stricken citizens of Mysore city gathered in front of the palace to mourn the death of the Maharaja. They were also concerned with the future of the princely state. They were worried whether the direct rule would be imposed or monarchy would continue with Nalwadi Krishnaraja Wodeyar as the next successor to the throne. In his condolence speech, the British Regent praised the services of the Maharaja and informed the public after the period of mourning was over, the scion of the royal family would be enthroned. He declared that there was no change in British policy as far as the princely state of Mysore was concerned. The Mysore State observed thirteen days of mourning. The Govt. offices, schools and colleges were closed during this period. The state flag and the Union Jack flew at half-mast over all the buildings.

After completing the funeral rites for the Maharaja, the Royal family members left for Mysore on 30th December 1894. The foreign secretary and Capt. Pollen bid farewell to the Maharani and her children. They reached Mysore city by special train on 3rd January 1895. The Royal family members travelled through the streets of Mysore from the Railway Station to the palace in *purdah* (covered) coaches. The citizens of Mysore stood on either side of the streets on pavements weeping profusely and pitying the young queen and the five little children. When some citizens blocked the street to express their sorrow personally, the police wanted to use force to disperse them. The young Prince Nalwadi ordered the Police not to ill-treat the grieving citizens. They gave way to these coaches after expressing their unsurmountable sorrow.

During this period, in Madras, the "All India National Conference" (a predecessor to the Indian National Congress) was conducting its annual conference. When the news of Mysore Maharaja's death in Calcutta reached the conference venue, a condolence meeting was conducted immediately. After two minutes of silence, a few delegates made speeches praising the Maharaja's contribution towards democratic reforms. The day's proceedings were cancelled and the delegates retired to their quarters. Former Justice of the Bombay High Court Sri Mahadev Govinda Ranade, M. A. L. L. B., C. I. E. told "The Hindu" newspaper correspondent that the sudden demise of the Maharaja Sri Chamarajendra Wodeyar has retarded the political developments in India by two decades.

The progressive monarch was working towards constitutional reforms in British India. Most of the newspapers in India and many in foreign countries including "The Times" London published obituary notices and articles. The Rajaguru Sri Brahma Tantra Swamiji of Parakala Mutt called on the royal family and offered words of comfort and consolation to the Maharani and children. The prominent citizens of Mysore conducted a condolence meeting and passed an appropriate resolution, mourning the death of a noble ruler and they requested through a memorandum to the Maharani that she must guide the young Prince until he comes of age to resume political powers.

The benevolent rule of Sri Chamarajendra Wodeyar of Mysore State lasted only fourteen years. During this period, Mysore State acquired the sobriquet of the modern state.

Lord Dufferin described the growth in Mysore state during 1881 – 1884 in these words, "Maharaja has given the people a good administration, all-round cultural development, peace and order ensured by a stable government and implementation of universal education for boys and girls, which has made it a progressive state. The policy of the British government to allow princely states to co-exist along with presidency states is a prudent policy.

The best example of this policy can be seen in the administration of Mysore State." (Not a verbatim reproduction, only a translation). Frederick Temple Hamilton Blackwood, 1st Marquess of Dufferin and Ava (1826 – 1902).

Another viceroy, Henry Petty – Fitz Maurice, 5th Marquess of Lansdowne (1845 – 1927) expressed in these words the administrative reforms accomplished in Mysore state, "In no other princely state in India, we see the harmonious rapport that prevails in Mysore State between the Maharaja and his subjects. The objective of the Mysore government is to ensure the safety and the well-being of the subjects. The Maharaja has only one goal; that is to promote the welfare of his subjects."

The State Government of Mysore in its Gazette notification dated 30th December 1894 announced the sad demise of Sri Chamarajendra Wodeyar at Calcutta and also the official communication of Queen-Empress Victoria that the next successor to the throne in Mysore State will be Sri Nalwadi Krishnaraja Wodeyar.

Regent of Mysore State Maharani Sri Vanivilasa Sannidhana. (C.I.)

Chapter 4
Regent's Appointment

******

"Prajanam bawasi maata
Ayushmantam Karothu mam"

"Oh! Goddess, you are mother to all our subjects,
Bless me mother with a long healthy life"

******

Coronation Ceremony

It was decreed that Sri Nalwadi Krishna Raja Wodeyar's coronation must be conducted on 1st February 1895. The Maharani was in deep mourning. Nevertheless, she involved herself in making proper arrangements for the coronation ceremony. The invitations were sent to the V. V. I. P.'s in India and abroad. The various royal family members in India were cordially invited to this function. Mysore city was decorated with colourful flags, buntings and green decorations consisting of plantain stalks and mango leaves.

The young prince was going to ascend the throne in Balakane Darbar Hall, where his father, Late Sri Chamarajendra Wodeyar, and his grandfather, Mummadi Sri Krishnaraja Wodeyar had undergone coronation ceremonies. The golden throne was placed on tiger skins facing east as per the Hindu custom. The European guests were seated on the right side of the throne. The royal family relatives, the Maharajas, the Hindu priests and palace officials were seated on the left side of the throne. In front of this hall the bodyguards, soldiers, cavalrymen, the Carnatic classical nadaswara musicians, the English band (Western music band) and designated King's elephant fully caparisoned, the King's personal horse and the sacred cow of the royal family had assembled in the open ground in an orderly fashion. At a little distance away from this cavalcade, the citizens of Mysore had gathered to witness this grand formal ceremony.

Prince Nalwadi Krishnaraja Wodeyar performed the Devapuja and other allied religious rituals before ascending the royal throne. He was formally dressed in a silk coat and sherwani and wore gold and diamond jewellery on his person. At that moment, colonel Henderson, the British resident of the princely state arrived on the scene. He read loudly the official letter of the Viceroy of India to the assembled august gathering. The Viceroy's letter stated that the young prince could become a full-fledged monarch only after coming of age. Until that time the state administration will be looked after by his mother – Queen Sri Vani Vilasa Sannidhana C. I. as regent appointed by the British Raj. She was also expected to consult the Viceroy and the British Regent, before taking important decisions. Col. Henderson shook hands with the young prince and wished him good luck. The prince ascended the throne at 12 o'clock in the afternoon (*Vrishaba lagna*) to the accompaniment of nandhaswara and the twenty-one-gun salute to which the Mysore royalty was entitled. The Brahmin priests recited vedic hymns, seeking blessings of Gods and Goddesses. The Darbar Bakshi Sri Ambil Narasimha Iyengar read out the state government gazette notification about the coronation and the list of names of the previous royal predecessors of the Wodeyar family was read out.

The British resident Col. Henderson presented various expensive gifts sent by the Viceroy of India to the young prince in 21 silver plates. He gave the young Prince expensive jewellery – a string of big-sized pearls to be worn around the neck. The royal family reciprocated this gesture with a gift of 21 silver plates with valuable gifts and 101 plates of "*Tamboola*" (pan leaves, areca nuts, fruits and flowers). Afterwards, the courtiers, officials and relatives came before the prince with "Nazar." Some silver and gold coins would be carried in a handkerchief and the prince would touch it and return it to the owner. Sri Bakshi Basappaji Urs felicitated all the European guests with garlands and "Tamboola."

The British resident and the British officials also presented "Nazar" to the young prince. The representatives of various religious mutts recited mantras and blessed the young prince. They gave gifts, *prasadam* and fruits to the young Maharaja. The coronation was celebrated all over the state. People organised grand luncheon parties for guests. The poor, indigent, and destitute were not forgotten and they were also fed with good food.

Regent's Rule
The most astonishing development was noticed by the British administrators and Indian political pandits that the regent Sri Vani Vilasa Sannidhana ruled Mysore State with great efficiency, foresight and vision. During her brief rule from 1895 – 1902, there was all-round development in Mysore State in the educational sphere, business and commerce and science and technology.

The Chief Guru's blessings
The pontiff of Sringeri Mutt arrived in Mysore in 1895 to meet the bereaved Maharani and her five children. When he entered the palace, he was overcome with sadness, because Maharaja Sri Chamarajendra Wodeyar had passed away. During his previous visit, the pontiff had been received by the Maharaja most warmly. When he returned to Sringeri, he had composed a Sanskrit hymn of benediction wishing the family good health, long life, success and wealth. In the poem, the Guru had mentioned that they should enjoy fame, longevity, humility and riches.

> *"Sri Rama lakshmanaviva sauhardam praapya sustiram suchiram|*
> *Sri Chamarajaputhrau Jiyastham Sharadamba tawa Kripayaa||*
> *Bharathi Sampadbarithou Buddhya Chaiva Tittikashanaya poorna|*
> *Ayushmanta Sukinau booyastham Chamaraja sukumarau||*
> *Deva Dwijaguru Bhaktim Sudhrudaam Dattavacha Vinaya Sampatthim|*
> *Palaya padmajmaanini Satatam Sri Chamaraja Sukumarau"||*

But alas! Now, the family had lost the head of the royal family under tragic circumstances. The Swamiji consoled the Queen and her children with words of strength and fortitude to face this adversity in life.

Brothers
L to R: Prince Sri Kanteerava Narasimharaja Wodeyar,
Prince Nalwadi Krishnaraja Wodeyar

His Highness Sri Nalwadi Krishnaraja Wodeyar's Coronation Ceremony

Chapter 5

Education

******

"Sahana vavathu saha nau boonaktu
Sahaviryam Karavavahai|
Tejasvi Navaditamastu ma
Vidwishavahai||

******

"May the teacher and student pursue studies jointly
May the teacher and the student relish their studies
May they pursue studies with vigour and concentration
May our studies fill us with knowledge, good understanding and intuitive intelligence
Let it not breed hostility and misunderstanding between us
Peace, peace, peace"

After the royal family's return from Calcutta, the obsequies were performed in Mysore for the departed soul. On the 13th day (Vaikunta Samaradhane) the designated male relative of the family gave gifts and donations to Brahmin priests, who recited vedic hymns for the emancipation of the soul of the dead person. The Hindus believe that on the 13th day, the departed soul makes its way to heaven (*Vaikunta*), where Maha Vishnu resides.

Nalwadi and his younger brother Sri Kanteerava Narasimharaja Wodeyar went back to the royal school to pursue higher education. Mr. J. J. Whitley the head of the royal school looked after the administration until 1896 and then, soon after, got repatriated to his old job of executive engineer in the public works department. But during his tenure, he had planned a well-thought-out curriculum for these students. Poorna Raghavendra Rao taught English language and Science. He was an assistant tutor and he demonstrated

Physics and Chemistry experiments to the students in the classroom. The school started in the morning at 11:00 AM and continued until 2:00 PM. After a lunch break of one hour, classes resumed at 3:00 PM. The afternoon session concluded at 5:00 PM. The school head, Mr. J. J. Whitley gave equal importance to sports culture. Sometimes, the students either participated in a parade or in gymnastics. The headmaster ensured that every student took part in games and athletics. The palace chefs served some tasty snacks to the students after games in the evening.

Every day, in the school calligraphy was taught and students had to copy passages in very good handwriting. The drawing and painting classes by an art teacher honed their skills. Whenever the students misbehaved in the school, corporal punishment was meted out to them by an attender called Puttanna. The lone exception to this rule was Prince Nalwadi, who was known for his exemplary behaviour at school. On rainy evenings, Nalwadi's classmate T. Gundappa told interesting Indian tales from epics and history to all the other students. They were very much appreciated by Nalwadi Krishna Raja Wodeyar, who listened to them with rapt attention.

Janab T. S. Ali Khan joined the royal school in 1894 and Sir Mirza M. Ismail joined the school in 1896 in his thirteenth year. Mirza M. Ismail's father Janab Agha Jaan was a bodyguard to Maharaja Sri Chamarajendra Wodeyar. After the death of the Maharaja, he became a personal bodyguard of Nalwadi. During the hot summer months of India, the school was shifted to the Nilgiris hill station of Ooty. The classes were conducted in Fern Hill Imperial Palace. The school also moved to Bangalore Palace for a few months in a year. Prince Nalwadi learnt horseriding, swimming and shooting at Lokaranjan Mahal, Mysore.

Talented Essayist

One day in the classroom, the teacher asked the students to write an impromptu English essay on the topic "Compare and contrast the two cities Mysore and Bangalore." Nalwadi's essay was the best one in the class. The extract of the essay is given below, which shows his felicity with a foreign tongue – English language.

"Bangalore is a nice place for horseriding as there is plain ground for us to ride fast. But at Mysore, there is no such place as in Bangalore for riding. The Bangalore riding school is much bigger one than that of Mysore. There is a big bandstand at Bangalore; but at Mysore, there is not one so big. At Mysore, there are lots of

animals; but at Bangalore there are not so many. The climate at Mysore is a bit hot; but at Bangalore it is very nice and cool. At Bangalore, there are many English men. But at Mysore there are not so many. The Bangalore roads are very nice and not stony. But at Mysore, the roads are not so nice and smooth; they are very hard and stony. At Bangalore, the Lalbaugh gardens are very nice, but the animals are in poor health. At Mysore, the gardens are of poor quality and the animals are of good quality; but we hope we will have the gardens as good as they are there. The crops there were bad; but here they are good. The Palace at Bangalore is after the English fashion (Tudor Revival architecture), but the Palace at Mysore is old fashioned. At Bangalore, there are English Regiments, but there are none at Mysore."

On another occasion, the students were asked to write an impromptu Kannada essay on Chamundi Hill. The ten-year-old Nalwadi wrote in this manner, "Goddess Chamundeshwari sits atop the hill. She is the protectress of Mysore city and its citizens. She is ever vigilant and observes our conduct and behaviour. Hence, we must express our devotion to the Goddess and must perform acts of goodwill." The court poet, Sosale Ayya Sastri read this essay and praised it for its noble sentiments.

Some two years later, Nalwadi was taught in the Kannada class by a teacher, such literary devices as analogy, imagery, exaggeration or hyperbole and excessive praise of a subject. This had an impact on the mind of Nalwadi. The young students had gone to Chamundi Hill on a picnic. The next day, the Kannada teacher asked them to write a brief essay on Chamundi Hill. The other students wrote about the scenic beauty, the one thousand stone steps, which helped a climber to reach the top and view the city from the top of the hill. But Nalwadi used literary devices to describe the hill.

"The Chamundi Hill is an ornament to Mysore city. Goddess Chamundeshwari sits on her resplendent throne, in other words, the very hill itself. Goddess is proclaiming that after she vanquished the demon Mahishasura, his dead body became the lone hill adjacent to the city of Mysore. She is sitting astride on the dead body of the demon. The Goddess Chamundi is assuring the citizens of Mysore city that she is their guardian angel."

The teachers of the royal school took notice that Nalwadi had a natural talent. They considered him as an uncut diamond, who required only further polishing and cutting. They brought this to the notice of the Queen mother. They were only watering a growing plant to become a huge teak tree.

The teaching faculty of the royal school admired the diligence and dedication of Nalwadi towards his studies. He stood first for the whole class because of his hard work. In 1896, the annual examination was conducted. Nalwadi had scored the highest marks in English, Kannada, Sanskrit, Sentence structures, Urdu, History and only in Maths he occupied third place in the class. Although Urdu was not his mother tongue, he had fared much better than the other Muslim students. Nalwadi loved drawing pictures in his notebooks. The Yuvaraja was not fond of drawing. The palace museum has preserved his drawings and sketches drawn at the age of ten. He drew such things as flower vases, cups, hammer, milk jug, knife, spoon, tongs, garden spade, trumpet, cricket bat, ball and wickets, football, garden scissors and vines. In his rough notebooks, he drew the royal mascot "*Gandabherunda*" (double-headed eagle), cows, sea, ships, boats, flowering plants, trees, arbour, Chamundi Hill, elephants, figures of divinities, etc. He always signed his name at the bottom of the page in fine handwriting. Even in his Maths notebook, there are illustrations of horses, which outnumber elephants and dogs. Nalwadi had a special fondness for horses.

The Maharani organised the "*upanayanam*" (initiation ceremony) in the palace for Nalwadi on 29th April (Wednesday) in 1896. At 11:00 AM, this religious ceremony was conducted by priests for the opening of the inner third eye. On the same day, his second elder sister, Sri Krishnajammani's marriage took place with Col. Desiraja Urs. These two functions were attended by members of various royal families and other important guests.

After the coronation ceremony, Nalwadi Sri Krishnaraja Wodeyar conducted himself with great dignity and reserve. He was not given to snobbery, but he was a man of few words. He expressed his opinion always in a few words and instructed servants through signs and gestures. But he never behaved as a superior individual and had an immense reserve of humility. He demonstrated his respect for elders and reverence towards holy men. He behaved in an informal manner with his friends in the school. The following incident proves how down-to-earth a person he was in real life.

Excellence in Studies

One day in the school, a teacher posed a question to the whole class. None of the students could answer it satisfactorily. So, the teacher decided to reward each student with two blows with the rod on the palm of the hand. This school protocol was observed with regard to general students. When the teacher came to the end of the line, he saw Nalwadi standing there with an outstretched hand to receive his quota of two blows, as he had not answered the question.

The teacher hesitated for two minutes because punishing a royal prince was an unthinkable act. Prince Nalwadi insisted on punishment as he had failed to give an appropriate answer. The teacher felt disgusted at his own conduct and announced that he would not punish any student in the future. He broke the lengthy bamboo stick into two pieces. This strange incident was reported to the Queen.

She was moved to tears by the noble act of her son and remembered her beloved husband, who would have been proud of his son's conduct. Nalwadi would not embark on a journey or an enterprise without consulting his mother. He always took her permission, and in the evenings, he reported his day's activities to the Queen mother. He valued her opinion and criticism highly. He sought her approval for his actions and words. If she reprimanded him for any wrongdoing, he would apologise and correct himself and desist from doing it again.

Bangalore to Nandidroog   Provincial Tour 1900   Oct 26th

We left the palace at 7-30 A M, party being H. H., Hy Naser, Captain Car White, Hy Raghavender Rao Alikhan, Basavaraja Urs and Shanker Rao. The Cyclone having blown over, the morning was fine though cloudy. The first place on the road Yalahanka; met here by assistant Com: K R Srinivas Iyangar, stopped at the Hunsmarana halli mutt. The Lingayat Guru is of some importance under the Baley Hormoor mutt. Has Seven Jodi villages worth about 4000 Rs per annum, partly given by Krishna Raja Wadiyar. Halted next at Jalar where we were met by Venkata Rama Chetty, whose grand father built a big Chakram at this place where travellors between Bangalore and Bellary used to halt at noon. Devandahalli met by Dep: Com: Venkata Varada Iyangar who had prepared refreshments. This is the place at it Seige of which Hyderali first distinguished himself and here Tippu was born. Three miles from here we entered the gravel road which was in very heavy condition after the rain and our pair, Bother and

ಆಳಿದ ಮಹಾಸ್ವಾಮಿಯವರ ಕೈ ಬರಹ
(ದಿನಚರಿ ಪುಸ್ತಕದ ಒಂದು ಹಾಳೆಯ ಭಾವ ಚಿತ್ರ)

Facsimile copy of a page from
Prince Sri Nalwadi Krishnaraja Wodeyar's diary

One day in a playful mood, he wore a tiger mask used in a Moharram procession and began to scare his younger sisters and brother. This prank gave Nalwadi immense enjoyment. But his mother did not approve of this sadistic behaviour. She told him not to indulge in this kind of prank again. He felt sorry and profusely apologised for his errant behaviour. He promised his mother that he would not repeat his act again.

Once, Nalwadi stopped talking to two of his classmates, because they had uttered lies. He had a great allergy to liars. Around the same time, two other boys quarrelled among themselves and stopped talking to each other. Prince Nalwadi approached the two boys and advised them to bury their hatchet.

One of them retorted by saying, "We two have stopped talking over some misunderstanding. Whereas the prince has stopped talking with two other classmates without any valid reason."

Then, the Prince told them that he was put off by their habit of lying. Anyway, the two boys who had quarrelled decided to bury their hatchet on the promptings of the Prince. The magnanimous prince agreed to build bridges with the two other boys with whom he had broken off his friendship.

Prince Sri Nalwadi Krishnaraja Wodeyar with his pet dog..

Prince Sri Nalwadi Krishnaraja Wodeyar with his riding horse

Prince Nalwadi always shared palace goodies like exotic fruits and dry fruits (dry grapes, dates, almonds and cashew nuts) with his classmates. He never showed any selfishness by way of hoarding sweets and fruits. In the mornings, he took his bath and performed devi puja and only then he would have his morning cup of coffee. Prince Nalwadi loved wearing simple and unostentatious dresses. He was not fond of expensive silk and woollen dresses. He wore expensive jewellery only on festive occasions like Dasara. He possessed a great sense of humour. Once in the evening, he dressed up as a servant and pretended to usher his sisters into the drawing room. They did not see through his game when Nalwadi disrobed his turban and removed his servants' uniform. They realised that they were being ushered in by their own elder brother. On another occasion, a classmate who had physical stature similar to the prince was made to dress up in the Prince's clothes. He was made to stand at a window gazing at the distant Chamundi Hill. The Queen mother entered the drawing room and mistook the look-alike boy for her son. She rushed towards the boy shouting, "*Ayya, ayya.*" But when she touched him, she realised to her horror that he was a total stranger. Soon, she came to know it was a practical joke played upon her by Nalwadi. Everybody had a hearty laugh over this subterfuge.

Prince Sri Nalwadi Krishnaraja Wodeyar with his bicycle

The British Raj was monitoring the education of Nalwadi Krishna Raja Wodeyar. They felt that he must master public administration, diplomacy and financial management. So, the Viceroy of India appointed Sir Stuart M. Fraser of the Indian Civil Service as the head of the royal school. At that time, the British government had not knighted him.

Arrival of S.M. Fraser

S. M. Fraser assumed duties as head of the royal school in the month of June 1896. He converted the day scholars' school into a boarding school. Now, students had to stay in Lokaranjan Mahal round the clock. Their sleeping dormitories and study rooms were prepared. They had a good dining room with a kitchen on the premises.

Misgivings of the Maharani

This new arrangement was not endorsed by the Maharani. The widowed Maharani had not spent even a single day away from her children. She was very much distraught that Nalwadi would be staying in the boarding school as a resident student. At night time, he was allowed to go to the Amba Vilas palace for dinner with his family members. But after dinner, he had to return to the royal school for the night. It fell on the shoulders of Darbar Bakshi Ambil Narasimha Iyengar to convince the Maharani to agree to this new arrangement. The Darbar Bakshi was an elderly courtier, who had taught the previous Maharaja Chamarajendra Wodeyar. He was also a close confidant of the royal family. The Maharani always observed purdah customs, while conducting official business. She would sit on a chair, behind a cloth curtain while talking with the officials. But Darbar Bakshi was an exception to this rule. The Darbar Bakshi pleaded with the Maharani that this arrangement was in the best interest of the royal Prince. All over the European continent, royal princes were educated in exclusive boarding schools. Finally, the Queen mother agreed to the educational reforms of S. M. Fraser.

The Royal School administration under S.M. Fraser

One day, S. M. Fraser took all the students on horseback for a cross-country ride. Until then, Prince Nalwadi had not been allowed to ride a horse independently by the servants. This was a sore point with the Prince. Here was S. M. Fraser, the head of the school, allowing the boy to trot, canter and gallop on the horse independently. When this news reached the Queen Mother, she was inconsolable and worried over the safety of the Prince. But the Prince relished this newfound freedom. He always possessed an adventurous spirit. The new head punished the students by asking a student to write imposition or stand on the bench or they were not allowed to play games in the evenings. The physical education given to boys consisted of "Round Athletic Races," "Cricket," "Football," "Tennis," "Rackets," "Polo," "Gymnastics," "Horse riding" and "Bicycling." This boarding school functioned between June 1896 to July 1902.

The Daily Schedule of Nalwadi

Prince Nalwadi woke up in the morning at 5:00 AM, and by playing on the bugle, he would wake up his other classmates. After taking a bath, he would go to the puja room for *Sandhyavandhana* (religious ritual) and he would worship the family deity Goddess Chamundeshwari. Afterwards, he played musical instruments like piano, violin, flute and *mridangam* (percussion instrument). Western classical music was taught by one bandmaster called Mr. Defries. Carnatic classical music was taught by court musician Veena Sheshanna. After these activities, one hour was spent on studies. Before attending classes, he would finish his lunch. Nalwadi's classes were conducted on the ground floor and his younger brother Sri Kanteerava Narasimharaja Wodeyar's classes were conducted on the first floor. The school session began with a religious prayer. Kavitilaka Sosale Ayya Sastri would request Nalwadi to recite *Shiva Tandava Stotra, Mukundamala Stotra* and *Shyamala Dandaka*. Occasionally, he would write a leave letter to Sir S. M. Fraser requesting him to permit the royal school children to visit the religious pilgrimage centre of Nanjanagud. There, he would offer prayers to Lord Shiva. This was done during school holidays.

The gymnastic lessons were given by Sri Viraswamy. The students practised "horizontal bars," "parallel bars" and "Roman rings." The instructor Vira Swamy was amazed by the virtuoso performance of Nalwadi. The gymnastic exercises were pursued for two days a week and on other days, the boys played "Tennis" and "Cricket." The boys rested in the evening for half an hour between 6:30 PM to 7:00 PM. They all assembled in the study hall to do assignments from 7:00 PM to 8:30 PM. Nalwadi would have a shower in the evening followed by Sandhyavandhana and brief puja. The students had their dinner at 9:00 PM and spent some time after dinner in informal chatting.

Nalwadi also received basic military training in this school under Colonel Cambell. Twice a week, military drill and parade were taught. Once, a boy had suffered a knee injury. So, he missed a few military drill exercises. He thought the knee pain was a good ruse for missing a few more military exercise classes. Nalwadi understood that the boy was feigning injury when there was none. So, he began to tease him by calling him, "Lame duck, lame duck, a liar." The boy felt ashamed and quit his act promptly. Colonel Cambell taught the Prince the art of driving a chaise. They also received shooting lessons at the firing range. Some hundred soldiers were invited to the royal school. Nalwadi learnt from military officers how to give orders to these soldiers during a parade. They were also taught battlefield manoeuvres by these officers. Later, Nalwadi confessed that this military training stood in good stead later in life.

S. M. Fraser also encouraged him to play polo to develop riding skills and dexterity with polo stick and ball. Nalwadi, S. M. Fraser and Sri Gopalaraja Urs went out on hunting expeditions. On the outskirts of Mysore, at a place called Ilavala, the residents of the village were troubled by leopards. This team went to the Ilavala neighbourhood to kill wild leopards. They got rid of a few of them during a hunting expedition.

Every year, for a few months, the royal school functioned from the Bangalore Palace. S. M. Fraser taught the students a hide-and-seek game called "Paper Chase." This game sharpened their skills of deductive logic and reasoning because they had to seek the boys hiding in unexpected places. The school head often invited the boys for a high tea in his Bangalore Bungalow accompanied by sandwiches and pastries.

The boys also learnt a playing card game called "Joker." They also imitated bird songs and animal sounds in a game of mimicry. They were taught a mime game called "Acting Game," wherein they had to enact different characters from history silently.

Nalwadi Krishnaraja Wodeyar had another interesting hobby of chopping the wood used in the hearth and in the bathroom. In this context, one is reminded of Prime Minister Gladstone of Great Britain who pursued a similar pastime of chopping wood. Nalwadi also relished driving a decorated ox cart with his brothers and sisters. Occasionally, either in Ooty or in Bangalore, the Queen mother was invited to join the ride on the palace estate. After the ride, the Prince would unleash the oxen and free them from the wooden yoke. He would give them a bath lovingly with his own hands. Later, he would feed the oxen with hay, ground chester beans and sweet balls of shredded coconuts.

During the hot summer months, the royal family left Mysore for the Imperial Fern Hill Palace to escape the heat and dust. In Ooty, family picnics were organised at such places as Doddabetta, Paikara waterfalls and to the nearby lake called "Lawrence Asylum." Whenever the Queen mother accompanied the children on these picnics, the young prince personally pitched a tent for his mother with the help of his friends. He wanted to protect his mother from rain and shine.

It is historically relevant to give the list of classmates of Prince Nalwadi Krishna Raja Wodeyar and Prince Kanteerava Narasimharaja Wodeyar. Some would leave the royal school to pursue formal education in the middle of their tenure. A few students joined the school a little later and remained with the royal princes till 1902.

Prince Nalwadi Sri Krishnaraja Wodeyar's classmates:
1. *Tirumala Swamy – left in the middle of the course*
2. *Gundappa – left*
3. *T. S. Alikhan*
4. *A. C. Basavaraja Urs*
5. *Badami Shankara Rao*

The following four students were sent to pursue formal high school education on scholarship by S. M. Fraser:
1. *Badami Lingopant*
2. *S. Shamanna*
3. *Gajanan Karvi*
4. *B. Venkata Subba Rao*

The following three students, after passing the matriculation exam in 1900, joined various colleges to acquire university degrees:
1. *Sir Mirza M. Ismail*
2. *M. S. Ramachandra Rao*
3. *Narasingha Rao*

The two students were also Nalwadi's classmates:
1. *C. V. Subramanyaraje Urs*
2. *M. C. Subbaraj Urs*

Prince Kanteerava Narasimharaja Wodeyar's classmates:
1. *M. G. Mekhri*
2. *M. Channaraja Urs*

3. K. Subba Rao
4. H. Mallaraja Urs
5. H. Muddaraja Urs
6. B. Dasappa
7. Kashinath Karvi
8. F. C. Devaraja Urs
9. B. P. Krishne Urs

Compassion Towards Animals

When Nalwadi was twelve years old, one morning, he witnessed a man trying to milk a cow. As the cow was a bit unruly in its behaviour, he had tied the two hind legs with a rope to restrict its movement. The cow had a young calf and it had been tied to a pole to prevent it from bothering the mother cow. As the owner of the cow squatted on the ground with an empty pail to milk the cow, the young prince noticed the wailing of the calf for milk. He also noticed tears flowing from the eyes of the cow. Nalwadi was extremely moved by the painful scene. He lamented sadly, "Why should we drink the cow's milk which is stolen from its young one?" The cow was poorly fed and it was emaciated. The attendants tried to console the prince by saying that the cow was unruly, and hence it deserved this treatment. Still, Nalwadi was not convinced by these lame excuses. So, they informed him that the poverty of the owner of the cow drove him to this state. Nalwadi said he did not want to partake in such milk. The attendant informed him that the calf will suffer from indigestion if it drank all the mother's milk. Nalwadi picked the pail of milk and offered all of it to the calf, much to the surprise of the bystanders.

He told the palace officials that they should procure a mild-mannered cow from tomorrow. He instructed that it must be milked without causing any hardship to the cow and calf. Moreover, at least half the mother's cow milk must be given to the calf. After this incident, whenever he came across a stray calf, he would hug and pat it with affection. He would take out one rupee silver coin and it would be rolled in a handkerchief and later it would be tied around the neck of the calf. He would order a trustworthy servant to escort it to its owner for custody.

Once Nalwadi saw a very pretty calf in a field and he wanted to own it. So, he sent for the owner, who was a washerman (Dhobi) by profession. The Prince Nalwadi made a generous offer to the washerman. But the washerman wanted a job in the palace for himself and for his successors. Nalwadi replied that such powers did not vest with him, but he was prepared to give either double or triple the price for the calf, that was normally paid for an ordinary calf. But the owner would have none of it, hence no deal.

On Krishna Janmashtami day (Lord Krishna's birthday) the children of the royal family took great pride in decorating their pet cows. Lord Krishna was a cowherd and he loved his cows very much. Moreover, the Wodeyars of Mysore belonged to the "*Yadu Vamsa*" (dynasty). Before Dasara festivities began, they participated in decorating palace elephants. Nalwadi supervised the painting of colour motifs and designs on the elephant. He personally used to feed animals such as cows, horses, elephants and dogs. He had a great rapport with the horses. When horses stood in a line on the parade ground, he would shout their names one by one. The horses came to him in an orderly fashion one after another. While riding the horses in the countryside, he did not ride one horse for a long time. He would change horses in the middle of the ride, so as to give respite to the exhausted horse. Nalwadi did not relish keeping birds in the cages. Hence, he did not keep parrots, mynas and lovebirds in his palace.

Nalwadi was fond of plants, trees and flowers. He firmly believed that the flora and fauna had a life of their own. He did not like people plucking flowers from the garden. He wanted visitors to admire them from a distance. Once a man plucked a beautiful rose flower. This was witnessed by Nalwadi. He admonished that man for plucking a beautiful flower. The man said that he had plucked the flower to offer it to God during the puja ceremony. Nalwadi asked the man to buy flowers from a florist, rather than ruin the beauty of the garden. He loved the well-laid-out garden on the premises (In fact, he has erected a statue of his favourite gardener Dorega (*name*) on Bangalore Palace grounds – *Ed. Note.*).

The two royal princes treated their classmates and friends as equals. They were not given to snobbery. They always shared all the goodies with their friends. The friends were always welcome at Bangalore, Mysore and Ooty palaces.

In the royal school, during a Maths class, S. M. Fraser had given a tough maths problem to work out. Nalwadi did very well in solving mathematical problems. But on that day, he could not solve the problem. Another student solved the difficult problem quickly. Nalwadi requested the boy to show his workbook. The boy haughtily refused to show his workout. S. M. Fraser asked Nalwadi why he had not solved it, that he was usually the first one to solve the problem. He advised Nalwadi not to seek any assistance from his classmates and to solve the problem on his own. Nalwadi remained silent and continued his efforts at solving the problem. The other boy gave a victorious glance at the distraught Nalwadi and beamed a sarcastic smile. S. M. Fraser angrily reminded the boy that every day Nalwadi solved Maths problems earlier than others. But he never taunted his classmates and remained composed. He told the boy to develop some humility and conduct himself with decorum. This student may go to Oxford University tomorrow and successfully write the senior wrangler test in Maths and pass it. But what is the use of all these achievements, if one lacks humility?

Peacemaker

Nalwadi showed often in his day-to-day behaviour a remarkable degree of generosity. One evening, the boys were playing a game of football. Nalwadi, before entering the play area, removed his expensive watch and gave it to another student, who was in the spectators' tent to keep it. Nalwadi did not collect his watch immediately nor bothered about it for a few days. The classmate approached him with the watch and reminded him that he had forgotten to claim it. Nalwadi replied by requisitioning it was not all that important and that if the classmate wanted it, he could retain it as a gift. The boy was scared of receiving such an expensive gift. He told Nalwadi that his family elders might take umbrage against this gesture. Nalwadi told him not to worry about his elders who might object to this transaction between friends. He informed the boy that he owned it and that he could gift it to anyone he liked it. So, the classmate came to possess a memento given to him by Nalwadi – an expensive watch.

Once the royal school students were trekking in the Nilgiri mountains and a boy stumbled on a stone, injuring one of his toes. He began to bleed profusely. Nalwadi immediately took out his handkerchief and used it as a bandage and tied it over the wound. He was ever-ready to help people in distress.

One day, the boys were playing a ball game called "Round Race." Nalwadi's team was led by a captain belonging to the Ursu community. One Muslim boy, who was not a student of the royal school, often came to Chittaranjan Mahal sports ground in the evenings to play various games. This Muslim boy was keeping the goalpost. When an opponent kicked the ball towards the goalkeeper, he allowed the ball to pass through his legs. The Ursu boy leading the team lost his temper. He scolded the Muslim boy of lassitude.

He also hit him with the ball on his head. The poor boy began to cry loudly. The teacher, Sri Bhima Rao, who was supervising the sports activity, became angry at this insolent behaviour of the captain. Sri Bhima Rao reprimanded the captain for his misbehaviour and questioned him, "Who gave you the authority to hit a fellow player?" The Ursu boy arrogantly replied that it was a captain's prerogative. Sri Bhima Rao did not appreciate this reply and told him to tender an apology to the hurt boy. The captain was advised by another Ursu boy not to offer apologies to a meat-eating Muslim boy, as they belonged to the ruling elite caste. The teacher would have none of this nonsense. He told the captain that if he did not apologise to the Muslim boy, he was not welcome to games from tomorrow. Nalwadi took the captain aside and advised him to offer apologies to the Muslim boy. It was not a demeaning conduct when one has committed a mistake. The captain told Nalwadi that they were Ursu community members and need not apologise to a meat-eating Muslim boy. Nalwadi stressed the fact that living in harmony in society was more important. Moreover, did they not respect their headmaster, S. M. Fraser, who was also a meat eater? Finally, the captain tendered an apology to the Muslim boy and made up with him.

Forgiveness as a Trait

Often, Nalwadi's heart melted at the sight of someone suffering. Once, S. M. Fraser punished a student with two strokes of a rod on the palm for some misconduct. Nalwadi, witnessing this incident, had tears in his eyes. On another occasion, the gold statues of Hindu deities were stolen from the Chittaranjan Mahal palace private puja room of the prince. The school head S. M. Fraser managed to catch the culprits. He was handing them over to the police, so that they could be packed off to the jail. Nalwadi pleaded on behalf of the criminals to show mercy and begged for a pardon. Whenever a palace staff fell ill, he would personally visit the sick person. He consoled the sick person with encouraging words. He ensured that the doctor attended to the sick person and administered him medicines. This genuine good conduct impressed the school head, S. M. Fraser.

Sense of Humour

Nalwadi had a great sense of humour. He gave nicknames to his classmates. A tall, lean student was named "General Stick," a round fat boy was called "Major Drum" and an adamant boy was called in Kannada "Kontu" (obdurate fellow).

Nalwadi loved jogging to the top of Chamundi Hill during the monsoon season. One morning, Nalwadi was jogging down the hill in ordinary cotton pants, sneakers and a white shirt on top. He was jogging through the fields with standing crops. Nalwadi was wearing an ordinary cap.

The owner of the fields saw a young boy wearing a cap running across the field. He shouted at the boy not to trample upon the crops. Nalwadi kept silent and continued running. Again, the angry farmer asked the boy rudely not to ruin his crops. Nalwadi returned to the Chittaranjan Mahal palace. He sent for the farmer. When the farmer turned up, Nalwadi asked him whether a young boy wearing a cap ran through his field trampling the corn. The farmer did not realise that the jogging boy and the Prince were one and the same person. The formally dressed prince went inside and came back wearing the jogging dress. The excited farmer blamed squarely this jogger for ruining his crops. Nalwadi enjoyed the confusion of the farmer immensely. He went inside and came back wearing the formal dress of the royalty. He told the farmer that it was himself who was out jogging in the fields. He compensated the farmer by gifting him with twenty-five rupees for inadvertently trampling on the standing crop.

The above-mentioned incident is comparable to another similar incident that took place in the life of Sir Ashutosh Mukherjee, the Vice-Chancellor of Calcutta University. Sir Ashutosh was working in the back garden of his bungalow. A gentleman entered the house from the back gate. He saw a gardener working on vegetable patches. He mistook him for a coolie and enquired with him about the Vice-Chancellor. The coolie told him to go to the front of the house and wait for Sir Ashutosh in the drawing room. After fifteen minutes, the soiled coolie turned up as formally dressed up Vice-Chancellor Sir Ashutosh Mukherjee to the surprise of the visitor.

Once, on a visit to Jog falls near Shimoga, Nalwadi came across an old octogenarian called Vrishabhayya. The old man narrated an incident connected with flooding in river Netravathi. This incident occurred before the Linganamakki dam was built across the river. The old man narrated the flooding that took place one year when he was a young man in a sing-song musical style much to the amusement of the young Prince.

He spoke in this manner, "Oh! What shall I tell you? I was wading through the river. Suddenly, there was a torrent of huge volumes of water flowing down in wave after wave. The river Sharavathi was ferocious and frothing at the mouth. This was really the jaws of death opening upon me. I realised the strong current of the river was going to drag me to my death. I loudly prayed to the Almighty to save my life." The old man said his life was saved by the ever-merciful God in a miraculous manner. This narration in the local rural dialect amused the Prince to no end and he would ask Vrishabhayya to re-tell the story again and again for the amusement of all.

There was another old retainer in the palace by the name Puttananjappa. He had a humorous anecdote to narrate to these students. He proudly claimed that when he took up employment in the palace during the late Maharaja Chamarajendra Wodeyar period, he was appointed as a "Kumandari." He pronounced the word "commander" as "Kumandari" in the local dialect. He was given the uniform of a guard of honour and asked to carry a sword tied to his ceremonial belt. Perhaps, the previous king thought that this villager did not fit into the uniform properly. The next morning, he was fired from his guard of honour post. This temporary glory lasted only twenty-four hours. But the old man was never tired of narrating his brief flirtation with glory and grandeur. Prince Nalwadi loved listening to the narration of the old man with his friends again and again. After dismissing the old retainer from their presence with a generous tip, all of them would have a hearty laugh.

Nalwadi had two gym instructors who gave him all the help required in the bodybuilding regimen. One was an infantry officer and another was a cavalry officer from the Mysore palace army. They often argued before the prince as to which was more important on the battlefield, infantry or cavalry regiments. We have to remember that this argument was taking place before WWI. We all know from history after WWI, that the cavalry regiments became outdated and faded from public memory. In the modern battlefield filled with tanks, cannons, machine guns and aircraft, the poor horse with its rider wielding a sword had no place in modern warfare. Nevertheless, Nalwadi enjoyed the endless debate between an infantryman and a cavalryman.

In the royal school, every morning, Nalwadi woke up his classmates with a bugle call. The punctual early risers were given a silver trophy as a memento. The snoring lethargic deep sleeping classmates were ridiculed and made fun of as lazy bones. While swimming in the pool, he often pushed his unsuspecting friends into the pool and enjoyed their discomfiture. During horse riding classes, he often arranged with lackeys to provide an unruly horse to a classmate. Then, he enjoyed their struggle on a wild horse. But he was always there beside these truant horses on another horse to control it, if necessary. But he would ensure these hapless riders were not hurt or injured in a fall.

Academic Performance of Nalwadi:

Nalwadi stood first for his class by his overall performance. When we look at the marks register, Nalwadi stood first on the basis of the monthly average marks obtained in each subject. The teachers evaluated the students' performance in an unbiased and impartial manner. When we study the marks scored by other students, we realise there was stiff competition among students. Nalwadi had mastered these languages English, Kannada, Sanskrit, Urdu, Parsi and Tamil. He studied books published in these languages. He was curious about science and technology. He updated his knowledge with the help of Sri P. Raghavendra Rao. He was a staunch supporter of the industrialisation of Mysore State. He was passionate about carpentry and indulged in "Fretwork." During his fourteenth year, he prepared a working model of a steam engine with cardboard, tin sheets and inside the engine, the piston and other moving parts worked. He showed his dexterity in preparing wooden models and sketching objects like a professional artist.

Nalwadi had proved himself as an able horse rider. He could tame even a wild and unruly horse. Occasionally, he would tie the reins to the peak of the saddle and ride the horse with his hands free. Sometimes, he used a short stick to guide the horse. If he touched the right portion of the neck with the stick, it would turn in the right direction. He loved cross-country riding. He easily made the horse to jump hedges, fences and water-filled ditches. Once, an unruly horse did not jump over a high fence. The rider, Nalwadi, fell down to the ground. He suffered bruises and injuries. A few days later, a determined Nalwadi jumped the fence successfully with the same unruly horse. His side grip of the horse with his thighs was pincer tight. He would often hold eight anna coins on either side of his knees tightly. He would return after a long ride with coins still held by his knees. When he loosened his legs, the coins would fall to the ground.

One of the teachers organised a trekking expedition to a hill in Nilgiris called "Cairn Hill." The boys carried rucksacks filled with food, drinking water containers and various other paraphernalia on their backs. Nalwadi had gone out for a long ride on his horse before the trek began at 4:00 PM. He was already exhausted by the riding exercise. They lost their way and they had to climb one rock after another rock to come back to the trail. All the boys were completely tired and they were complaining to their teacher. But Nalwadi kept quiet despite his double trouble. Meanwhile, the Queen mother had come from Mysore in a car. She was very much distraught as she could not find the heir apparent. She sent servants in different directions with lighted lanterns to look for the trekking troupe. But after an hour, they returned to the palace without achieving their objective. A little later, Nalwadi and his friends led by the teacher returned to the palace. All of them were hungry, tired and exhausted by this foolhardy expedition. The Queen mother was angry at the teacher, who led this expedition.

On another occasion, a trekking expedition to Mukurthi Hill was organised. This hill was some twenty miles away from Ooty. They could cover ten miles on their horses and they had to climb the remaining ten miles of the hill on foot. The peak of the hill resembled the nose of a sleeping giant. It was a steep climb to the top of the hill. Most of the students complained about their heavy rucksacks and water containers. Nalwadi willingly extended his help and carried their belongings on his back without a murmur. He was the first one to climb to the top of the hill.

This unique incident happened in 1885 when Nalwadi was eleven years old. There is a Sri Chandramouleshwara (Shiva) temple on the outskirts of Mysore on Mysore-Bangalore Road. Some one hundred and thirty years ago, this was a wild, desolate and uninhabited area (at present the busy vehicular traffic passes on the highway by passing a nearby village called Kalasthawadi – *Ed. Note*).

One official of the palace, perhaps on the instructions of the higher-ups took eleven-year-old Nalwadi late in the evening to this Shiva temple in a horse-drawn coach. They went inside the temple on the pretext of offering prayers to Lord Shiva. An accompanying servant lit a candle to assist the visitors. The young boy of eleven Nalwadi closed his eyes and began to recite *Shiva stotra*. When he was unaware of the outside world, the servant on the prior instructions of the official put off the candle. The palace official and the servant vanished from the sanctum sanctorum in pitch darkness. They got into the chaise and left for the palace leaving behind Nalwadi alone.

When Nalwadi opened his eyes, he was alone in darkness without any attendants. This old temple also harboured snakes, scorpions and bats. He groped his way out with difficulty. The horse-drawn coach and the other attendants were not to be seen on the highway. This eleven-year-old boy mustered the courage to walk back alone. It was a dark new moon night with only stars twinkling in the sky. Nalwadi was unafraid and remained courageous on the deserted highway. He was reciting the *Mruthyunjaya mantra* again and again to ward off the fear of death.

The Queen mother was informed by the palace official about this ingenious test conducted with the sole intention of making the Prince overcome his fears. But the Queen mother was furious and scolded the official for putting her son at risk. He could have been bitten by a Cobra or attacked by a wild leopard. She sent a coach for the prince with cavalry riders with flaming torches. Today, the distance between the palace and the temple is 5 Km. The palace officials, after 2 or 3 Km, saw an eleven-year-old boy walking alone in darkness reciting vedic mantras towards Mysore city. When Nalwadi was reunited with his mother, she was in tears and wanted to fire the errant palace officials who had put her son's life at risk from their jobs. The weeping Queen mother asked him, whether he was afraid of wild animals and the surrounding darkness. Nalwadi told his mother not to fire these officials from their jobs. They had done a favour to him by instilling courage in him. Moreover, the palace priest had told him that Mruthyunjaya mantra dedicated to Lord Shiva would always protect him from snakes, leopards, scorpions and tigers. The Queen mother admired his ardent devotion and faith in Lord Shiva. She blessed him to remain as an eternal believer in God's protection. Prince Nalwadi during his tender boyhood years was known to keep equanimity of mind and composure at all times. The three incidents that occurred during his childhood years demonstrate his grit and strength of will. They occurred during the 10th and 13th years of his boyhood.

The Maharaja Sri Chamarajendra Wodeyar had gone to Bombay with his family members in 1893. Some classmates of Nalwadi and Yuvaraja Sri Kanteerava Narasimharaja Wodeyar had also accompanied the royal troupe. Sri Ambil Narasimha Iyengar had organised a boat trip to Elephanta Caves situated on an island near Bombay City for students. On that morning, the sea was choppy and rough. While returning from the caves, the boatmen confronted huge waves in the Arabian Sea. One scared boy thought that his end was near. He shouted loudly "I am finished, I am finished." Prince Nalwadi and Yuvaraja at once shouted, "Do not be afraid, we are here to protect you." This was the first boat trip for the princes at sea. Nevertheless, they showed more courage in the face of imminent danger than the other boys. This incident left a great impression on Sri Ambil Narasimha Iyengar.

The Great Fire of Mysore City

Many great cities of the world have been destroyed by raging fire at different periods of history. The history of mankind has witnessed fires destroying Sri Lanka, Troy, Alexandria, Nalanda, London, Moscow and Tokyo.

The old Mysore palace was built out of wood. The roof was made up of planks and beams, and the tall pillars, doors, flooring and furniture were made up of Teak and Rosewood. On February 28th 1897, the Queen mother arranged the marriage of her eldest daughter, Princess Jayalakshammani, with Sri Kantharaje Urs. The old city of Mysore thrived inside the walls of the fortress. Like all ancient Indian cities Delhi, Jaipur and Lucknow, the city of Mysore was also a city within the fortress.

The marriage function was conducted in the morning. In the evening, there was a reception for the bride and bridegroom. They were supposed to indulge in a game called "*Uratane.*" They would be seated on a swing decorated with flowers. They would roll a ball covered with flowers at each other to the accompaniment of songs and music. Mysore City and Bangalore City had not been electrified. The lady servants of the palace are called "*Avvayara.*" They were using mainly oil lamps and torches at night time for illumination. It is due to the negligence of one of the lady servants, that a lamp got knocked down and perhaps hanging curtains or some other inflammable object must have got ignited by the fire. Soon, the raging flames spread from one quarter to the other. The wedding guests began to run out of the palace into the open ground to save their lives.

The palace guards and soldiers began to organise a team of firefighters. Their misfortune was compounded by the dry taps. The water pumps were out of order and hence, no water was flowing through the taps. The British Superintendent Engineer Macchain or Mackcheyn (?), Attachi Venkata Rao, Chenggiah Shetty and Amaldar of Mysore district organised a rescue operation. They also had the responsibility of saving gold and silver jewellery from inevitable theft. The people of Mysore City formed a human chain to pass buckets full of water from the lake in front of the palace to the burning portion of the palace.

At that time, there was a huge lake called "Doddakere." (Ed. Note: The Translator as a programme officer of the National Service Scheme attended a camp in a village near Heggadevana Kote in 1995. I happened to meet the oldest living person in that village. He claimed to be at least 110 or 112 years old. He was lying on a cot and his memory was still good. I asked him, "What is the earliest memory of an incident, you can recall"? He said, "Sir, I remember the burning down of the Mysore palace." He was ten or twelve years old at that time(1897). He had gone with his parents in an oxen cart to Mysore. In the evening, the wooden structure of the old palace began to burn. There was total mayhem and confusion. This centenarian villager recounted how dignified and respectable guests pinched gold and silver jewellery and scooted in different directions to avoid the palace cavalrymen. He expressed his great horror and shock at this pilferage by honourable citizens of the society. This young boy also began to run in the direction of the Vani Vilas market (Padma Circle, Mysore City). He was chased by a police guard on a horse. The boy was cornered and the guard demanded to see what he was carrying in a cloth bundle. The village boy opened the bundle and showed the two ragi rotis he was carrying for his supper. He was let off by the guard to go back to his village.)

The private secretary to the Regent Major Campbell, Sir S. M. Fraser and Sri Kantharaje Urs decided to send the royal family members to Sri Jagan Mohan Vilas palace for their night stay. They safeguarded the jewel-crested gold throne, *Vairamudi* (the bejewelled crown of Melkote Cheluvanarayana), the gold sword, *Chamarajamudi* (the diamond and gold crown of Sri Chamarajeshwara deity) and other valuable jewels were sent to a store room in Jaganmohan Palace for safekeeping. Many valuable gold ornaments, diamond necklaces, silver statues and priceless antiques were brought out by good Samaritans into the open ground. They were guarded by soldiers to prevent any more thefts.

The raging fire spread to Amba Vilas, which was in the South and it spread to Ragamala Mahal in the North. It was galloping towards Saraswathi Bhandar (Library of rare books and records) and the armoury section of the old palace. It also spread to other parts of the palace such as Sita Vilas Thotti (open-air quadrangle surrounded by halls or corridors) and Rama Vilasa Thotti.

Many valuables were lying in a heap in front of the palace including, Sri Kanteerava Narasimharaja's swords, a gold rifle sent by Queen Victoria as a gift to Mummadi Krishnaraja Wodeyar, gold daggers encrusted with precious gems, gold chains, etc. On the third day at midnight, the five gold cupolas of the palace came crashing to the ground. At that time, 2000 Mysore citizens, who were standing there wept profusely. The different parts of the palace like the stables, Hall of mirrors, Madana Vilas Thotti, Rama Vilas and Sajje were completely reduced to ashes. The British soldiers from Bangalore cantonment had brought water pumps to put off the raging fire. The local volunteers joined the soldiers to quench the flames by pumping water. Later, a committee of experts was appointed to investigate the cause of the fire. Their conclusion was on the wedding night a female servant had thrown ash with fire cinders near some inflammable liquid causing the fire to erupt and spread. The fire ravaged the palace for three days. When this disaster struck the Mysore royal family,

Prince Nalwadi was only thirteen years old. Nalwadi came to the palace on the second day morning, riding a horse. He was calm and showed a strong will to face this kind of adversity in life. In fact, he began to console the grieving Mysore citizens, officials and relatives. He saw an old Muslim retainer crying loudly and saying, "I joined palace service during Maharaja Chamarajendra Wodeyar's time. I have not witnessed this kind of destruction during my lifetime. Why should I live to see such misfortunes befall upon the Mysore royal family?"

Nalwadi said to the old man, "Life is an admixture of happiness and sorrow. God gives us sweet dishes as well as bitter medicines to consume. We must face bravely the bouquets and brickbats of fortune with equanimity of mind. Please stop weeping." As a young boy, Nalwadi showed grit and determination during a crisis.

Soon after the fire, the Queen regent, the British Resident to the princely state of Mysore and the then Dewan made a decision to re-build the Mysore palace. The British architect suggested shifting the inner residents from within the fortress to the newly planned suburbs outside the fortress (present-day Lashmipuram).

Diamond Jubilee of Queen Victoria

In the month of June 1897, the Mysore state celebrated the Diamond Jubilee of Queen Empress Victoria's long reign. The priests offered special prayers in temples, masjids and churches for the Queen Empress. Some prisoners languishing in jails were given back their freedom and released on this special occasion. The poor citizens were given free clothes and sumptuous food on that day. In schools and colleges, the diamond jubilee event was celebrated by organising sports events and various competitions like debating, essay writing and composing poems were conducted and prizes and trophies were given to the winners. The boys and girls were given sweet laddus in their institutions. The regent, Sri Vani Vilas Sannidhana, built a big hospital in Bangalore and it was called Queen Empress Victoria Hospital (Ed. Note: It still exists with the same name and it has been modernised.)

Passion for Theatre:

Prince Nalwadi showed immense interest in theatre. Maharaja Sri Chamarajendra Wodeyar was a great patron of theatre. In fact, he had founded a drama troupe called "Sri Chamarajendra Wodeyar Krupa Poshita Karnataka Nataka Sabha" in the Mysore palace. (It is reminiscent of Queen Elizabeth's

men in 16th century England – William Shakespeare's "Globe Theatre troupe."
– Ed. Note).

Once, a Marathi drama troupe visited Mysore and staged a modern play. In Mysore State, the folk theatre *"Yakshagana"* and *"Bayalata"* (open-air theatre), which specialised in plays based on Ramayana and Mahabharata *puranic* stories were popular. The Maharaja requested his court poets like Sri Basappa Sastri and others to write Kannada plays based on Sanskrit and English plays. These playwrights translated from Sanskrit: "Shakuntala," "Ratnavali," "Mricchakatika" and from Shakespeare: *"Hamlet," "Othello"* and *"Romeo and Juliet."*

During Nalwadi's time, the plays were staged in "Karikalla Thotti." Nalwadi loved the play *"Tulasi Farce"* and many short stories from various sources were adopted as one-act plays. Sometimes, Nalwadi played various roles on the stage by donning make-up and costumes. Otherwise, he would join the music ensemble to play either harmonium or tabla during the performance.

A few years after the death of Sri Chamarajendra Wodeyar, an opportunity afforded itself for the revision of the salary of actors and musicians. The palace accountants recommended a pay hike of ₹1, ₹2 and ₹3 to the artists over their present salary. Nalwadi summoned the list before it was sent to Queen Mother for her approval. Nalwadi took a blue pencil from the pen stand and struck off these meagre and paltry raises given to the artists. Nalwadi generously increased the salaries of these artists, much to the chagrin of accountants. They looked upon this instinctive gesture of a fourteen-year-old boy as a mere whim and fancy. Nalwadi told the officials that if artists were not properly looked after, how could they act on the stage with any enthusiasm? They needed food in their belly and hot milk down their throat to keep the act together. When the amended list reached the Queen mother, the officials criticised the generous hikes. The Queen replied my son has shown his magnanimous nature by generous raises, whereas your sole interest is to save the money for the exchequer. She appreciated the generosity of her son and further increased the hike by ₹5 for each artist.

One morning, while Nalwadi was climbing the Chamundi Hill to visit the temple, he lost one of his diamond ear studs on the way. Later, a villager, who found it on the road brought it to the palace. Nalwadi very much appreciated his sincerity and honesty. He not only rewarded him handsomely by paying him cash but also gave him employment in the palace.

The palace drama troupe received ample encouragement from Sri Chamarajendra Wodeyar. He spent a lot of money on lighting equipment, scenic backdrop curtains, costumes and various theatre equipment. He wanted to construct a state-of-the-art theatre in Mysore city. He instructed an architect to draw a blueprint for such a theatre. He wanted to take up this project after his trip to Calcutta. The palace troupe had many experienced and talented actors, who played both male and female roles. Sri Lakshmipathi Sastri was known for his role of Shakuntala, the heroine of Kalidasa's plays of the same name. The famous painter Raja Ravi Varma after seeing Sri Lakshmipathi Sastri's performance as Shakuntala exclaimed, "He is the best actor in the whole of India." Sir Dewan Seshadri Iyer offered the actor a permanent job in the government service with an attractive salary. But the actor declined this job offer because he loved the stage more than the lucre. Another famous actor, A. V. Varadachar, respected Lakshmipathi Sastri so much that he addressed him as "Guruji." Sri Subbanna another actor donned the role of Dushyanta, the hero of Shakuntala drama and he was admired very much by the audience. (Author's Note: Readers are not to confuse with the present-day actor Subbanna (1944), who is known for his female roles and the role of Lord Krishna. The Subbanna referred to here was active during the 1890s.) Another talented actor by the name Sri Viraraghava enacted the role of Mandaravalli before the Maharaja in an excellent fashion. The Maharaja was immensely pleased with the performance and he rewarded the actor on the spot with an expensive gold wristwatch.

Shakespeare's tragic play "*Othello*" had been adapted into Kannada language under the title of "*Shura Sena Charite.*" The role of Othello had been played by one "certain" Rama Rao. He had essayed the role to everyone's satisfaction. Once, the troupe travelled to the town of Bellary. The drama troupe performed in the British cantonment area before the Lieutenant Colonel who was the commanding officer of the regiment. After the play, in his thanksgiving speech, Lieutenant Colonel praised the troupe and the lead actor, a "certain" Rama Rao. He said this actor in his role of Othello was far superior to many of the actors of England, who had interpreted the same role. The citizens of Bellary took this actor in a grand procession through the streets of the city filled with cheering crowds. Many respectable citizens stopped this procession before their houses and performed "Aarati," the lighted lamps were brought near his face and it was rotated in a clockwise direction three times while singing auspicious songs. He was also profusely garlanded with flowers around his neck.

The story of "King Harishchandra" has remained a perennial source of inspiration for the Hindu soul. The protagonist of the story is a great stickler for truth. He is tested by God through hell-fire to find out whether he will give up his obsession with truth. Although he loses his empire and his son and wife get estranged from him, he still does not give up his adherence to the truth. Finally, he is reduced to become a keeper of a cemetery. Finally, truth triumphs and Harishchandra is rewarded with various boons by the Gods. This story was adopted to the stage by the palace drama troupe. The versatile actor "certain" Rama Rao was playing the role of the fierce reigning deity of the cemetery Kapalishwara. It is another avatar of Shiva. This tall gigantic black fearsome character with bloodshot eyes appeared on stage with long matted hair. "Certain" Rama Rao had managed to borrow a few poisonous Cobras from the snake charmers of Mysore. When he appeared on the stage, he had one snake coiled around his neck and one on his head. He held two snakes in his two hands. When he began to dance on the stage like Shiva to the music of nadhaswara, the snakes opened their hoods. The royalty and the lay audience were mightily thrilled by this exotic scene. Nalwadi was very much moved by the scene. After the play, he went to the green room to congratulate "certain" Rama Rao. He also wanted to touch these Cobras. Although he was a young boy, he had no fear of snakes. He was allowed to touch them. He rewarded this actor with a gold ring embedded with a diamond. The Queen mother watched the conduct of Nalwadi and she was extremely impressed by his generosity. She called Darbar Bakshi aside and asked him to give "certain" Rama Rao an adult-sized diamond ring and take back Nalwadi's small ring. The next morning, Darbar Bakshi gave him back his diamond ring. Prince Nalwadi thought that the actor was displeased with a small gift and hence must have returned it. But Queen mother asked him how his small ring could slip on the finger of a grown-up person. Nalwadi wanted to present the actor with an adult-sized diamond ring set in gold. But the Queen mother informed him that he had already been rewarded with a bigger-sized diamond ring. Sri Vanivilas Sannidhana the Queen Regent of the Mysore State during her reign proved herself as an able administrator. She continued the good work started by her husband, Maharaja Chamarajendra Wodeyar. Even the British resident was surprised by the progress of Mysore State. While performing her official duties, she sat behind a curtain observing purdah. She addressed Indian and British officials from behind the curtain. She kept Prince Nalwadi beside her during these official meetings. He gradually learnt the ropes of the administration in this manner. He lost his father at an early age. The heavy responsibility of administering Mysore state fell upon the shoulders of Nalwadi at a young age. The Queen mother often asked for his suggestion and opinion while dealing with complex problems. Gradually, he was entrusted with more and more responsibility. Earlier, his younger brother and three sisters approached their mother if they wanted anything. Later, they began to plead before their elder brother, Prince Nalwadi. He often complied with their requests.

Once, his elder sister, princess Sri Jayalakshammani wanted to go in her coach for a ride in the evening. She fancied a pair of white horses for the coach. She sent a message to her younger brother, Nalwadi. He tried to get this pair of white horses from the stables. But he was informed that one of the horses had gone lame due to an injury in one leg. So, he sent a message to his elder sister that he was not in a position to acquiesce to her request.

He offered her his profuse apologies for not being able to loan those two white horses. She did not take umbrage at him. Instead, she exclaimed, "I know how kind-hearted and soft my younger brother is and so, there's no room for misunderstanding."

Nalwadi always showed great sensitivity towards others. One afternoon, he visited his younger brother's bedroom. He found him fast asleep. He tiptoed out of the room without disturbing his brother. He also communicated to servants through signs not to wake up the Yuvaraja with heavy footfalls. The two brothers had great affection for each other. Their harmonious relationship was compared to the loving relationship between Sri Rama and Sri Lakshmana of the Ramayana epic. They had a good understanding between them.

Royal Students Go on a Tour

"Travel in the younger sort is a part of education; in the elder a part of experience" – Of Travel by Francis Bacon.

One has to whole heartedly concur with Francis Bacon that travel is a form of education. The young boys would be visiting new places and they would relish new sights. The school head organised a trip within Mysore State for the two princes and their classmates. The students of the royal school visited Shimoga,

Kadur and Hassan districts in Mysore State. They visited Jog waterfalls in Shimoga district and enjoyed its grandeur. The Sharavati river falls into the gorge from a height of 833 feet in four different streams called Raja, Rani, Roarer and Rocket. They visited ancient temples in Sagar taluk and visited the scenic village of Thirthahalli. They climbed Kodachadri Hill through a trekking route in the forest. They also climbed Bababudan mountain in Chikamagalur district. Finally, they made their way to the holy temple of Sringeri. The chief pontiff of Sringeri mutt was Sri Narasimha Bharati Swamy. They visited the Sri Vidyashankara temple built in the Hoysala style of architecture. Inside the quadrangle of the temple, we find twelve carved ornate pillars. It is strategically located by the architect and during each *Sankramana*, the early morning sunrays fall upon a designated pillar. The 12 signs of the Zodiac are important in Indian astrology. The sun transits from one Zodiac sign (*Rashi*) to another depending on the season. The travel of the Sun from south (*Dakshinayana*) to North (*Uttarayana*) through the 12 Zodiac signs is called Sankramana. Nalwadi and his friends watched the rays of the Sun bathing a particular pillar during their visit. In the evening, Nalwadi and friends visited Narasimhavana by crossing the bridge on the river Tungabhadra. The swamiji lived in the ashram on the other bank of the river. The swamiji received the princes with great love and affection. He gave them his benediction and blessings through his short lecture.

Nalwadi informed the Guruji that he liked the peaceful environment of the temple and the ashram. He expressed a desire to stay there for one more day. Swamiji told Nalwadi that as a ruler of the state, he could order S. M. Fraser and others to postpone their departure. But Nalwadi told Swamiji that as a student, he must obey his mentor. Swamiji was pleased with the reply given by Prince Nalwadi. Swamiji summoned S. M. Fraser and told him that it was the desire of Nalwadi to extend his stay in the ashram by a day. S. M. Fraser acquiesced to the request of the swamiji. During their return trip, the students of the royal school visited the famous temples of Halebidu and Belur built in Hoysala style.

The North India Trip of Nalwadi:

In the month of January 1900, Nalwadi, his classmates and teachers set on a tour of North India. They left by the royal train from Mysore to Madras. There, they got on to a ship called "*Dupleix*" at Madras port. They travelled to the capital city of British India, Calcutta. There they had an audience with the Viceroy of India Lord Curzon and also met the Chief of the Indian Army, General Lord Kitchener. During their stay in Calcutta, they were guests of Maharaja of Cooch Behar. They also visited the hill station of Darjeeling near Calcutta. Prince Nalwadi and his friends saw the snowcapped Himalayan Mountain range from Darjeeling for the first time in their lives. They travelled from Calcutta to Benaras by train. Here, they were guests of Maharaja of Benaras Sri Prabhu Narayan Singh. In the holy city of Kashi, they bathed in river Ganges and paid their respects to Lord Vishwanath. The royal troupe journeyed to the city of Agra. They visited the 7th wonder of the world "The Taj Mahal." Here, ordinary tourists were expected to remove their footwear to enter the Taj Mahal. But the V. V. I. P. visitors could enter the mosque and mausoleum with their footwear covered with a cloth sack. Prince Nalwadi was informed that he could enter the Taj Mahal with his footwear. But he said, "It is my bounden duty to show our respect and appreciation to this great object of beauty. Hence, I wish to remove my footwear and enter the premises barefoot."

They went to the nearby holy towns of Mathura and Brindavan connected with the life of Lord Krishna – a Yadava King and saint. They also visited the golden Sikh temple at Amritsar. They travelled to Lahore, Lucknow, Kanpur and Delhi. They travelled from Delhi to Baroda. Here, they were guests of Maharaja Sayyaji Rao Gaekwad of Baroda State. Then, they proceeded to the city of Bombay, the commercial capital of India. Here, they were guests of Jamshetji Nusserwanji Tata (1839 – 1904), who was a prominent industrialist and business tycoon of India.

They travelled from Bombay to Bijapur to see the famous Gol Gumbaz building. In this building, sound gets echoed seven times. The Nalwadi's party travelled from Bijapur (Vijayapura) to Hampi, the former capital of the Vijayanagar Empire (1336 – 1646 A. D.). Now, this vast capital lies in ruins. They visited many temples and buildings in this city. After a long trip all over North India, they returned to their hometown.

Somewhere in North India, Prince Nalwadi addressed a group of people in chaste Hindustani (Urdu). This surprised the North Indians because a Maharaja from South India could speak fluent Urdu. So, a gentleman exclaimed, "Your Maharaja speaks much more eloquently than most of us in Urdu language."

Marriage of a Monarch

The Queen mother wanted to conduct her son Nalwadi's marriage when he turned sixteen years of age. In those days, the boys and girls were cajoled to get married in their early teens. The Indian marriages were arranged by consenting parents taking into consideration caste and social status, and it had to be approved by astrologers after a comparative study of horoscopes. The Queen wanted a marriage alliance with a North Indian royal family.

The regent saw her brother Sardar M. Kantharaje Urs and Sri P. N. Krishnamurti call upon various North Indian royal families to select a suitable bride for Nalwadi. They finally selected a young bride aged 12 years belonging to the royal family of Kathiawad. She hailed from the Vana royal family and she was the daughter of Maharaja of Jhoola Rana Saheb Sri Vinaya Simha. The name of the bride was princess Sri Prathap Kumari Devi.

This marriage of Maharaja Sri Nalwadi Krishnaraja Wodeyar with Princess Sri Prathap Kumari Devi took place in Jagan Mohan palace on 6th June 1900 A. D. (As per the Hindu calendar, it was conducted on Wednesday on Jyeshta Shuddha Navami day in *Sarvarinama Samvathsara* (year) during *Simha lagna, Mithunamsha muhurta*). It was attended by the various royal house princes and princesses. The British governor was a special guest of honour. He conveyed the special greetings of Queen Empress of India Victoria and also the greetings of the Viceroy of India. Many expensive gifts were presented by the British governor on behalf of the Viceroy of India. The religious heads of Hindus, Moslems and Christians also presented their gifts and blessed the newly married couple.

On the same day, Nalwadi's younger sister Princess Chaluvajammani was given in marriage to Sri Sardar Lakshmi Kantharaje Urs. There was a special wedding reception in Mysore palace on 13th June 1900. It was attended by emissaries of John Taylor Gold mine company at Kolar Gold fields, the rich Indian and British coffee planters of Coorg and office bearers of various organisations and trade guilds of Mysore State presented letters of solicitation to the newly married couple and gave expensive gifts. At the end of the formal reception, Nalwadi delivered an impromptu acceptance speech in English. In this first public address, Nalwadi showcased his oratorial skills. It impressed immensely the British regent of the state and Dewan Sir Seshadri Iyer.

Maharaja Sri Nalwadi Krishnaraja Wodeyar's marriage reception with European and Indian Dignitaries in Durbar Hall

The palace authorities organised a royal wedding procession through the main roads of Mysore city on 14th June 1900. The newly-wed couple dressed in expensive silks and jewellery rode upon a richly caparisoned elephant. It was followed by a cavalcade of near relatives in horse-drawn coaches. It was escorted by palace cavalry, soldiers, officials and musicians. The procession left Mysore palace at 7:00 PM. The streets were filled with the citizens of Mysore State, who had travelled from far-off places, and when the royal procession returned to Sri Jagan Mohan Palace, it was 5:00 AM. in the morning. The subjects of Mysore State simply adored the newly married royal couple.

Nalwadi and Religious Vows

The pious Hindus observe various religious vows on auspicious days. They resolve to observe fasting on such occasions without consuming food and water. Sometimes, they go on a pilgrimage to temple towns on auspicious days.

Even after marriage, Nalwadi continued his studies in the royal school. Here, he excelled in academic pursuits and he also conducted himself in a very righteous manner. He was a stickler for truth, respected honest people and always kept his word of promise. Like many others, he was not fond of bakery products and pastries. He did not even drink soda water (bubble water).

On special festival days, he would not eat or drink until he completed the pooja rituals. On certain days, he fasted completely without drinking water. Once, the school head Sir S. M. Fraser organised a cross-country horse riding excursion to Kotagiri hill, which was 25 miles away from Fern Hill Imperial Palace. They started their ride early in the morning. Nalwadi could not take his bath and perform pooja before they started on their journey. Nalwadi never had his breakfast before a bath and pooja. It was a tiresome and exhaustive cross-country horse ride. He refused to have food, fruits and even drinking water during this trip. The other boys ate well and consumed fruits. But they were very much exhausted by this expedition. Even S. M. Fraser asked him to eat some fruits, but Nalwadi declined. He remained fresh and energetic throughout the trip. He kept smiling and joking with his friends. When they returned to Ooty palace, it was 4:00 PM. Nalwadi did not mind the inconvenience.

Royal School Students in Gymnasium
Background Sitting: (L – R) Maj. M. C. on Parallel Bar, Subbaraje Urs,
Janab T. S. Alikhan, Sardar M. Lakshhmikantharaje Urs
Front Row (L – R):? , Prince Sri Narasimha Raja Wodeyar
(sitting in the middle on the parallel bar),
Sir Mirza Ismail (standing)
Sitting: Left?

Rifle Shooting Training
L to R: Kneeling – Janab T. S. Alikhan,
Prince Sri Nalwadi Krishnaraja Wodeyar,?

Gymnastics and Antics

"When there is a circus in town, every boy wants to be a clown."
– *Mark Twain*. (Ed: Note)

Nalwadi definitely had an adventurous streak in him. His daredevil gymnastics and reckless horse riding shows before his mother and siblings caused quite a lot of anxiety and trepidation in their hearts. Even his friends and well-wishers who watched his antics became tense and worried about his safety. Once during a circus performance, he saw a gymnast doing a back somersault from a height. He wanted to try this before his younger brother and sisters. His elder sisters got worried about his penchant for risk-taking unnecessarily. They began to pray to Goddess Chamundeshwari to protect him from any injury. Nalwadi had kept himself fit through swimming, wrestling, horse riding, bicycling and gymnastics. He jumped from a great height and performed a somersault in the air, before landing on his feet safely.

Nalwadi loved animals and he had several pets. He had monkeys, goats, dogs and horses in his private menagerie. He had established a good rapport with these animals. He had trained them to perform various tricks before an audience. After the Dasara festival and during the Christmas holidays, he would make his animals perform before a select audience. He played the role of a ringmaster. All these animals obeyed him implicitly. He would come to the foreground of the palace, where a row of his favourite horses stood by. When he shouted the name of a horse, that particular horse would come running to him. He had proved himself as an able polo player. His fame had spread to all the corners of the Indian subcontinent. He also played squash, shuttlecock, badminton and tennis like a professional player.

The British aristocracy in India had brought along with them their tradition of fox hunting in the countryside. Maharaja Nalwadi Krishnaraja Wodeyar was invited to join the fox hunt in Ooty. He enjoyed riding his horse in a group led by a pack of barking hounds. They loved hunting hares and foxes in the Nilgiris.

Hydro-Electric Project

After the invention of electricity in England and America, it made inroads into India. The British rulers first electrified Calcutta in 1879. The regent of Mysore Sri Vanivilasa Sannidhana was keen on introducing electricity in Mysore State. Nalwadi also played an important role in the electrification programme of Mysore State. When Dewan Sir Seshadri Iyer proposed the generation of electricity from a hydro-electric project at Shivanasamudra water falls by utilising Shimsha river water, he was considered an imbalanced person. At that time, only at Niagara waterfalls in U. S. A., they were generating hydro-electric power and transmitting it to cities over a long distance with the help of cables and pylons. This high-profile project of the Dewan was ridiculed by his opponents. But Queen mother and Nalwadi trusted their Dewan and wanted to usher in industrialisation in Mysore State. The critics of the project described it as a grand illusion of the Dewan. The major presidency states and other princely states had not taken up any hydroelectric project. Because of the backing of the royal family members, the Dewan could execute this project. Hence, Bangalore city became the first South Indian city to be electrified on 5th August 1905.

The important high-ranking positions were held by the Britishers. They were expressing their diffidence about this expensive project. But some of the British experts like Mr. Edmund Carrington, Mr. Holmes, Col. Penny Quick and Capt. Lobinear assured the ruling class that it was a feasible project. In fact, one vehement critic of the project declared that Dewan Sir Seshadri Iyer was free to spend his personal fortune of several lakhs of rupees, but not the money belonging to the state treasury. Although Queen Regent reposed immense faith in the genius of the Dewan, she still had some apprehensions about spending several lakhs of rupees on this hydro-electric project.

At this critical juncture, Nalwadi played the role of a catalyst to trigger the required reaction. An American visitor visited Mysore state at this time. He toured extensively in the princely state. He met Nalwadi in the Mysore palace before his departure. Nalwadi asked a pertinent question to the foreigner, "Whether there were any similarities between U. S. A. and Mysore state?" The American citizen said there was one common factor between the two countries. Both nations had many scenic waterfalls. But Americans had taken a bold step to harness this power to produce electricity, whereas Indians had not taken advantage of this nature's boon. The electric power would ultimately transform the industrial scene of Mysore State. These words had a great impact on the mind of Nalwadi. If Americans could succeed in this endeavour, why not we Indians do the same?

So, Nalwadi requested Sir S. M. Fraser to explain the technological aspects of hydro-electric power generation to him. But S. M. Fraser told Nalwadi that Sir Dewan Seshadri Iyer was the right person to give him all the information.

Nalwadi requested the Dewan Sir Seshadri Iyer to enlighten him. The Dewan came with a big hard-bound technical book on hydro-electric generation and gave it to Sri Poorna Raghavendra Rao to go through this volume and explain it to Nalwadi. Sri Poorna Raghavendra Rao had studied Science subjects at Madras University. He explained all these things to Nalwadi after a thorough study of the volume. Whatever doubts that lingered in his mind were clarified by the Dewan later. Now, Nalwadi was convinced about the feasibility of the project. The Dewan had sent Mr. A. J. Lobin to U. S. A. to make trade enquiries about the electric machinery that the state government wanted for its Shivanasamudra hydro-electric station. He returned from his American trip and submitted a technical report. He informed the Queen Regent and Nalwadi that this project was feasible and profitable. Finally, electricity generation in Mysore State would transform the lives of the citizens forever. The state of Mysore would be holding a record in the whole of India for giving impetus to economic growth through industrialisation. Because of the efforts of the Queen Regent, Prince Nalwadi and Dewan Sir Seshadri Iyer, the hydro-electric project was completed by the Mysore State Government, thereby disproving the misgivings of the diehard critics of the British Raj. As Nalwadi matured into a young man, he was not satisfied with mere lectures on "Bhagavadgita." He began to study more serious texts like Upanishads and often discussed subtle nuances of Indian philosophy with scholarly pandits. One day, a great scholar was giving a sermon on "Brahma Sutra Bhashya" of Sri Adiguru Shankaracharya. Dewan Sir Seshadri Iyer, during a private study of the text, had stumbled upon a knotty problem. After an in-depth study of the philosophical problem, he had come to the conclusion that Sri Shankaracharya was in the wrong. Hence, he told young Nalwadi that a study of Shankara Bhashya was a mere waste of time. He said the Acharya Shankara's logical reasoning was wrong. The scholarly pandit laughed sarcastically and told the Dewan, "The Vedantins can enter upon a debate with other scholars, but one cannot argue with a high-ranking Dewan, who does not concur with scholars in a formal debate based on reason and logic."

Nalwadi told the Dewan to study the text once again for enlightenment because Acharya Shankara cannot be dismissed so lightly. Nalwadi said he was a young man with little knowledge and not competent to argue with an elderly Dewan. He gave an analogy to prove his argument. He said this scholar is like an oil lamp. The light from the lamp cannot shed light on distant objects. Whereas in the morning, the effulgent sunlight can brighten the whole world.

We cannot estimate the brightness of the Sun by comparing it with a lamp. He offered profuse apologies to the Dewan for his indiscreet observations. But the Dewan did not treat it as insolence on the part of a young man. He went home, and after dinner, began to study the contentious portion of the "*Shankara Bhashya.*" Around 11:00 PM, after pouring over the text for two hours, suddenly the truth dawned upon him and the clouds cleared. He loudly muttered in his mother tongue, if Nalwadi was not a Maharaja, he would have hugged him to his bosom and thanked him for his sagacious words. Indeed, Adiguru Shankaracharya was a bright Sun in the sky and we are all little lamps. The Yuvaraja Sri Kanteerava Narasimharaja Wodeyar emulated his elder brother Nalwadi in all aspects. He was a diligent student, played polo like a professional player and loved horse riding. He had a fondness for music, theatre and painting. Once a classmate misunderstood his statement and their friendship took a nose dive. The Yuvaraja apologised to his friend and cleared the misunderstanding by telling him that his words were not meant to hurt his feelings. He loved reading books on horses and on diet and nutrition. Once, when Yuvaraja was on a cross-country march with his classmates, he saw a cobra with its hood open under the shade of a huge tree. One of Yuvaraja's classmates was about to step on the snake. The Yuvaraja jumped to the rescue of this boy and pulled him aside, thereby saving the classmate's life. In this rescue operation, he took considerable personal risk to save another soul. The Yuvaraja often felicitated and honoured drama actors after their performance without fail.

In 1900 A.D. a Parsi Drama Troupe called "Appo Company" from Bombay visited Mysore. They staged 12 plays before the royal audience. On the final day, the Queen Regent showered encomiums on the actors and presented them with a fat purse. The Yuvaraja presented the exceptional actors with diamond rings and cashmere shawls. Sometime later, another Parsi Theatre group called "Patel's company" visited Mysore city. They also staged several plays before the royal audience. They also received sumptuous cash payments. One young actor by the name Krishna performed extraordinarily. Hence, the Yuvaraja honoured him with expensive gifts. In his thanksgiving speech, he lauded the performance of the actor with generous compliments. Somehow, this gesture of the Yuvaraja did not go well with his friends. Some of the pranksters made a cardboard coffin. They painted it in black. They kept a chess pawn in the coffin box and conducted a mock funeral for child actor Krishna. They carried the coffin in a procession chanting, "*Ram Nam*

Sathya Hai, Krishna Krishna Chatta (bier) hai." This angered Sri Kanteerava Narasimharaja Wodeyar greatly. He took another chess pawn and threw it at the boys' gang leader. It hit his cheek forcefully and he received a bruise. Soon, the Yuvaraja regretted his intemperate behaviour. He dipped his handkerchief in cold water and applied it to the wound. He sincerely apologised for his short-tempered behaviour.

During the month of November 1900 A.D., under the leadership of Sir S. M. Fraser, the royal school students went on a school trip to Nandi Durga, Maddagiri (present name Madhugiri), Devarayana Durga, Tumkur, Shivagange, Kunigal horse stud farm and Melkote. The Maddagiri town is close to a steep, rocky hill. It is difficult to climb to the peak by ordinary folks. But Nalwadi climbed it with ease. He reached the peak earlier than other boys. Even today, senior citizens of Maddagiri remember fondly how Nalwadi circumambulated the Nandi (Bull) statue three times. It was a very risky venture as the Nandi statue was situated on the edge of a precipice. During this trip, he visited temples, mosques and Jaina basadis. He paid his respects to these religious places.

Nalwadi made a close study of rural life and urban life during this tour. In most of these places, he addressed large gatherings of crowds. He distributed sweet laddus to boys and girls. He gave trophies to talented young students. Nalwadi spoke to people in a positive and optimistic way. They appreciated his words of encouragement.

Lord Curzon visited Mysore State in the month of December 1900 A. D. He was an honoured guest of the Queen Regent and Prince Nalwadi. Lord Curzon unveiled the marble statue of Sri Chamarajendra Wodeyar in front of Mysore town hall. He also inaugurated the Science and Art exhibition held at Jubilee Institute.

The Maharaja Sri Nalwadi Krishnaraja Wodeyar with his pet dog and the rescued goat from Burma.

Maharaja Visits Burma (Myanmar)

Maharaja Sri Nalwadi Krishnaraja Wodeyar decided to visit Burma with his entourage. He was accompanied by the Yuvaraja, his classmates and the teachers. After obtaining the blessings of the Queen mother, they left for Madras. During the month of January 1901, they boarded a ship called "*Jabingla*." When the ship was approaching Burma, they were surprised to see the welcoming party approaching them in mid-sea. The emissaries and officials of the Burmese government had travelled by boats and steamers to a distance of 18 miles to welcome the Maharaja of Mysore. They joyfully escorted the ship to the accompaniment of music and guided it to the harbour. They had erected a huge shamiana (tent) on the harbour to welcome the royal entourage. The harbour was crowded with at least 10,000 cheering citizens of Burma. The British lieutenant governor, elected representatives, and the leaders of Burmese, Chinese, Hindu and Muslim communities from India had assembled on the pier. The Burmese dignitaries presented a silver casket containing a lengthy salutation to His Highness the Maharaja of Mysore. This formal salutation was read by Rao Bahadur P. M. Madurai Pillai welcoming the Maharaja to the Burmese nation. Nalwadi made a grand eloquent acceptance speech in an impromptu manner.

This letter of salutation will make every citizen of Mysore proud. The letter states how the benevolent rule of Queen Regent Sri Vanivilasa Sannidhana and Sri Nalwadi Krishnaraja Wodeyar has made the state of Mysore a model state in India. It is more advanced than other states in India. The all-round development of the state has ushered in an era of peace and prosperity. The citizens belonging to different religions and castes are living in harmony. The rich culture and history of the state may be compared to any other civilised nation in the world. The state of Mysore can be described as a well-tended landscaped garden in India.

They also expressed their heartfelt desire that when Nalwadi takes the reigns of the state rule into his hands, the state will witness greater fast-paced progress. They also foretold the rule of Nalwadi would be far more illustrious than all his predecessors. The lieutenant governor escorted Nalwadi and his entourage to their guest house. Later, the Maharaja and other dignitaries were invited for a formal dinner at the Governor's house.

Nalwadi and his troupe travelled extensively throughout Burma. They visited Buddhist pagodas, the oil wells and thick tropical forests full of huge trees such as Burmese teak, Rosewood, etc. They visited big Burmese towns like Mandalay, Mechina, Bhamo and Prom. While they were returning from Mechina town on the Irrawaddy River in a steam launch, they saw the fury of the river. The strong current of the river took them head-on to the escarpment of a mountain. But at the last minute, it swerved away from the hill, on a different course. They travelled to Pakokku city on their way to a place called Mogok, which was famous for gems. But at Pakokku, they received the message of Queen Empress Victoria's death.

They cancelled the rest of the tour as per protocol. But Nalwadi and his friends also witnessed on the island of Cyria a petroleum refinery. It was processing petroleum into diesel, Vaseline, Kerosene, etc. They took a ship from Rangoon to Madras and reached Mysore by train. But the most memorable part of the tour was their train journey on the "Goteik viaduct" also spelled as Gokteik or Gonteik. This train journey is described as the scariest train ride in the world. The train runs on a trestle bridge situated in Nawngh Kio in Western Shan state. It is situated between the town of Pyin oo Lwin and Lashio town, which are approximately 100 km northeast of Mandalay in Western Shan state. Its length is 2,260 feet and the height of the bridge is 820 feet. It moves very slowly through tunnels and on the bridge taking passengers to the summer capital Pyin oo lwin of the British Raj. The passengers feel giddy when they look down into the gorge, where the river Gontwin flows.

Showering mercy on a goat

During their return voyage from Burma to Madras, an interesting incident occurred. When Nalwadi and his friends were on the deck of the ship, a beautiful white goat came running to him. It began to follow him everywhere. Nalwadi met the captain of the ship and enquired about this white goat, which had befriended him. The captain informed the Maharaja that it was destined for the table of the soldiers travelling on the ship. It had escaped from the hold of the ship, where it was kept with the other goats. The captain knew that the Maharaja was a vegetarian. Nalwadi wanted to buy this white goat for himself. So, he asked the captain whether he could buy it. The captain jokingly quoted an exorbitant price, thinking that Maharaja may not be serious about buying as he was a vegetarian. But the Maharaja insisted on buying the goat at the inflated price. The captain was willing to gift it to the Maharaja. But Nalwadi firmly refused a free gift and bought the goat at an exorbitant price. Finally, the lucky goat travelled with the Maharaja to Mysore and joined his menagerie. The Maharaja would personally feed the white goat often.

Sri Nalwadi Krishnaraja Wodeyar on a state tour prior to ascension to the throne with Royal entourage

Educational Tour

Nalwadi embarked on an educational tour on 18th November 1901 to Hassan, Belur, Gangamula and Sringeri. The earlier trips were meant for pleasure. This was a two months trip covering a distance of 1,700 miles. The purpose of this trip was to understand the problems of the common people. He studied the theories of public administration in practise. He also learnt how the age-old problems could be resolved by modern technology. During the year 1901, Mr. S. M. Fraser took Nalwadi to various government offices and courts. He was often made to work in different capacities to learn the ropes of administration.

Once, an important Civil Court case was in progress. S. M. Fraser took the Maharaja into the court hall. He followed the court proceedings over several days. Like a judge, he heard the arguments of the lawyers and depositions of the witnesses. After the conclusion of the case, S. M. Fraser asked Nalwadi to write his judgement. When he received a copy of the judgement, he was surprised to read it as it resembled the judgement delivered in a court by an experienced judge in every aspect.

During the visit to a village, Nalwadi called upon a farmer at his farmhouse. The farmer was asked to fetch his documents pertaining to the ownership of the farm. Nalwadi demanded to see annual tax receipts paid on the land to the Government of Mysore. The poor farmer told Nalwadi that the village accountant (*shanbhog*) had not mentioned the actual amount paid as tax. He had been given a tax receipt for a lesser amount. Nalwadi summoned the village accountant, who mistook the visiting dignitary as the new Amaldar of Taluq. The shanbhog was asked to bring the *Khata* and *Khirdi* account books. He poured over the accounts of the said farmer. The village accountant had not even entered the amount mentioned in the receipt. He had cheated the farmer by writing a figure, which was lower than what was actually paid to the official. He had misappropriated the money belonging to the state treasury. He had undercut what was due to the state government as well. Nalwadi was extremely furious with the erring official. He told the shanbhog to mend his ways or to end up in jail. In another village, the shanbhog was asked to bring the map of the village, so they could locate some lands belonging to a farmer. The local village and taluq officials began to search for the lands of the farmer on the map. Nalwadi took the map, and within no time, located the lands on the map. He laughed at the ineptitude of the officials who could not read a map.

During a visit to a dispensary (Primary Health Centre) in Hassan district during the year 1900, he noted a rusted injection needle in the clinic. He enquired with the local physicians, how this injection needle was used on a patient. The physician replied that it was used with a syringe to draw medicine from a bottle. Later, it was injected into the body of the patient. The medicine would spread all over the body and it would kill the infected cells. But Nalwadi laughed and held the rusted injection needle before the doctor and told him that the patient would be transported very quickly to the next world. He threw the rusted needle outside the window. Then, Nalwadi wanted the key to the almirah, where poisonous medicines had been stored. The key to the almirah is usually found in the custody of the resident doctor. But in this dispensary, it was found on the person of the compounder (Lab Assistant). Again, Nalwadi joked about the strange practise of this physician. In the same year, Nalwadi visited a village high school. The geography teacher in the classroom could not locate certain rivers and towns on a map. Nalwadi immediately showed those towns and rivers quite easily. He admonished the teacher to enter the classroom, after a few hours of study and preparation at home. Then, he asked the students to identify North, South, East and West on the map. One or two students showed the directions correctly. They were asked to identify the directions in real space. One boy pointed at the sky and identified it as North and the ground as south. The second boy confessed he was capable of identifying the East because the Sun rose every morning in the East and it would set in the West. But he was confused about North and South. This demonstrated the poor teaching skills of the geography teacher.

Once, Nalwadi visited the hydro-electric station at Shivanasamudra. At that time, the Chief Electrical Engineer was an American by the name Mr. Ex Throme, who had worked at the hydro-electric station at Niagara waterfalls. He knew how the electric turbines worked and produced high-voltage electricity. He was surprised that the young prince was so well-versed in electrical technology. In 1901, Dewan Seshadri Iyer retired from state service and died a few months later. Nalwadi was disappointed, because the noble soul, who envisioned the hydro-electric project did not live to see its completion. Sir S. M. Fraser, from time to time, submitted reports to the British resident about the progress of the two princes, who were under his tutelage. The seventh and final report was submitted to the resident on 14th July 1902. The two royal Princes had studied these subjects in great depth – languages, Science, History, Mathematics, Drawing, Philosophy, Geography, Trade and Business, International Law, Indian Civil and Criminal procedure codes and various political theories.

Sri Nalwadi Krishnaraja Wodeyar with his mentor Sir S. M. Fraser

They also studied various rules and regulations pertaining to the revenue and survey departments, income tax, commercial tax and customs and excise departments. Dispensation of awards and titles, Forestry, Famine eradication programmes, Hindu and Muslim Law, and their knowledge of Law and public administration were far beyond their seeming youthful appearance. They were competent to rule the state with diligence, responsibility and efficiency. They were competent to resolve any complex and difficult issue. They were experienced, honest, hardworking and could make sound judgements during a crisis. They were storehouses of patience. They were humble, well-mannered, dignified and commanded love and respect from all quarters. Even the European population considered them to be suave and sophisticated. They were superior to the European nobility in every aspect. In recognition of the yeoman service rendered to the royal family of Mysore and to the British Raj, the then King-Emperor Edward the seventh honoured Sir S. M. Fraser with the title of 'Companion Order of the Indian Empire' (C. I. E.) in recognition of his services. The British Government accepted the recommendations and submissions made in the report of Sir S. M. Fraser. The King Emperor Edward the seventh proclaimed Sri Nalwadi Krishnaraja Wodeyar as the full-fledged ruler of the princely state. It was decided that on 8th August 1902, Maharaja Sri Nalwadi Krishnaraja Wodeyar would receive the baton of state rule from his mother Queen regent Sri Vani Vilas Sannidhana.

Chapter 6

Background

******

*"Casyaathyanantham Sukamupanatham Dhukkamekanthatovaa|
Nechairgachhattuya paricha dashaa chakra nemi kramena||
Chakrar panktriva gatchathi bagyaa panktuah||*

******

"Who is utmost happy in life? Who is utmost unhappy in life? The cartwheel rotates clockwise. One half of the wheel remains at the ground level and the other half remains above, similarly the wheel of fortune turns up and down. So, everyman goes through a happy phase and an unhappy phase in life."

A Brief History of the Wodeyar Dynasty

It is relevant and meaningful to understand the background history of the Mysore Royal Family before Nalwadi Sri Krishnaraja Wodeyar's direct rule began in 1902 A.D. The Wodeyar dynasty was founded by Yaduraya and his brother Krishna Raya. A holy man ordered him to kill the troublemaker Maranayaka of Karugahalli near Mysore, who had 16 villages under his control. Afterwards, he could begin his independent rule of the Mysore region. He managed to defeat and kill Maranayaka. Yaduraya married Sri Devajammani daughter of Chamaraja. The successors of Sri Yaduraya expanded the Empire and Srirangapatna became the capital of part of Mysore state. Sri Kanteerava Narasaraja Wodeyar I (reign 1638 – 1659) proved himself as a powerful ruler and he defeated the ruler of Tirichinapally in a wrestling bout and the Empire stretched till Tirichinapally. The Muslim general Ramadullaha Khan came with his army and laid siege to Mysore fort. He was defeated conclusively and he turned his tail and went back to Bijapur. The King Dodda Deva Raja (1659 – 1673 A. D.) was a nightmare to his enemies. He defeated the Nayak ruler of Madurai and took possession of Dharapura. The shrewd and clever ruler Sri Chikka Devaraja Wodeyar (1673 – 1704) managed to win favours from the Mughal ruler Aurangzeb. He received the title of "Jagadevaraya" from Aurangzeb. He reformed the state administration by creating 18 departments (*Attara Kacheri*) to give a just administration. During his reign, Mysore state became a prosperous state and he was a generous patron to poets, playwrights and musicians. He was also the author of several books. He introduced an efficient postal communication system in the state.

The successors of Sri Chikka Devaraja Wodeyar were not competent rulers. The state administration deteriorated to a very low level. The Dalvoys began to exercise more and more political power in the state administration.

Hyder Ali (1722 – 1782), who was a commander in the Mysore army, usurped power by displacing Prime Minister Nanjaraja and Bettada Chamaraja Wodeyar VIII (1772 – 1776) and Khasa Chamaraja Wodeyar IX (1776 – 1796) were imprisoned. These rulers were puppet rulers of Hyder Ali and Tipu Sultan and they were kept under house arrest. Tipu Sultan (1782 – 1799) declared himself as an independent ruler and did not show any allegiance to the Mughal Emperor. He became a nightmare to East India Company's rulers. The British fought four Mysore wars against Tipu Sultan. He was defeated at Srirangapattanam and died on the battlefield in 1799.

The Role of Dewan Purnaiah in Mysore Political Affairs

Dewan Krishnacharya Purnaiah (born 1746 – 27 March 1812) had the rare distinction of working under three rulers – Hyder Ali, Tipu Sultan and Krishnaraja Wodeyar III. He worked as an administrator of the Mysore Kingdom from 1782 to 1811. He was known for his skill with accounts, prodigious memory and proficiency in several languages. He was also a wartime commander while serving under Tipu Sultan. Mummadi Krishnaraja Wodeyar was educated and trained by Purnaiah from 1799 till 1810 (when the Prince came of age). He took care of the administration of the state along with the British resident appointed by the East India Company. According to legend, Purnaiah, who hailed from Coimbatore was a Madhwa Kannada speaking brahmin. His first job was that of a book keeper and accountant with a big merchant, who was supplying goods to Hyder Ali. Gradually, he won the favours of the usurper Hyder Ali. He became a close confidant of

Hyder Ali. The following three incidents connected with Dewan Purnaiah's life demonstrate his wit and wisdom.

Once Hyder Ali saw a log of wood being carried by the river Kaveri in flood. He asked his courtiers, how come a log of wood, which is heavier than water does not sink. Even an iron ball sinks in water. None of the courtiers could give him a satisfactory answer. But Purnaiah replied that a tree grows big with water sucked from the earth. The current of water feels a responsibility towards the tree helps it to survive and carries it downstream. The modern-day scientists endowed with the Archimedes principle may laugh at this explanation. What we can appreciate here is the meaningful and emotional explanation offered to explain a natural phenomenon.

The second incident demonstrates Purnaiah's courage and intelligence. Once, one of the courtiers came under a cloud of suspicion. Some gossip mongers had poisoned the mind of Hyder Ali. The ruler had made up his mind to punish the individual. Dewan Purnaiah realised that an innocent man was going to be punished. Hence, he decided to plead this man's case before Hyder Ali. He told Hyder Ali to distinguish between truth and untruth. Only after ascertaining the truth of the matter, he should punish this person. Hyder Ali mockingly asked Purnaiah, what is the distance between truth and untruth?

Purnaiah replied that he knew the exact length between truth and untruth, that is 4½ fingers width. Hyder Ali asked in surprise, what does it really mean? Purnaiah replied it is the distance between the ear and the eye. What rumour the ear hears may not be true. But what the eye sees and confirms will be the ultimate truth.

These words of wisdom drove home a point and Hyder Ali pardoned the individual charged with various offences. Hyder Ali had gone to South Arcot with his army to quell a rebellion there. While returning from South Arcot, he developed Herpes. This illness aggravated and he succumbed to it. Dewan Purnaiah sent Hyder Ali's body secretly to Srirangapattanam. He sent a letter through messengers to Tipu Sultan, who was 500 miles away in the Malabar region. Purnaiah did not make any announcement of death. He did not want any rebellion to take place in Mysore State by disgruntled *Palegars*. Tipu Sultan managed to return to Srirangapattanam in time to take over the reins of the Kingdom. This subterfuge of Dewan Purnaiah has received accolades from British historians like J. D. B. Gribley, etc.

After the death of Tipu Sultan, the East India Company reinstated Mummadi Krishna Raja Wodeyar as ruler of Mysore State. The Queen mother

Lakshmiammani was appointed as a regent because Mummadi was five years old. Dewan Purnaiah was a caretaker of the prince until he came of age. The Queen mother wanted Sri Tirumala Rao to be the Dewan of State because he had helped the Wodeyar royal family in reclaiming the throne. But East India Company insisted that Purnaiah ought to continue as Dewan.

In 1799, the State treasury was empty after the IV Anglo-Mysore War. But the shrewd administrator, Dewan Purnaiah, managed to mop up more funds (1½ times) in the form of tax than before without hiking taxes. He managed to spend a huge sum of ₹77,29,310 on the repair of canals, tanks, highway roads, pilgrim inns, bridges and government buildings. Even in British-administered provinces, the Governors were not spending this kind of huge sums on public works. One Governor rejected a highway construction, by writing in his report that the state did not have enough numbers of oxen carts to ply on it. Maharani generously supported Dewan Purnaiah in his developmental activities. A political scientist wrote, "…This eminent statesman of whom India may well be proud of." In fact, even in the 19th century, Mysore State was considered a progressive state in India. In 1911, Mummadi Krishnaraja Wodeyar became a full-fledged ruler after coming of age.

The Dewan Purnaiah opted to retire from public service due to old age and ill health. He had served the Mysore royals for eleven years. The Maharaja had given him Yelandur taluq, in Chamarajanagar as a gift to him. His big mansion still stands today and it is maintained by the state government. Mummadi also granted a monthly pension of ₹1000 to Dewan Purnaiah. After three months, on March 27th night in 1817, he passed away. The Governor General of India, the Governor of Madras, the British Resident and the ruler Mummadi condoled the death of Dewan Purnaiah. The Maharaja continued the ₹1000 pension and it was granted to his children.

Mummadi Sri Krishnaraja Wodeyar's Rule (1799 – 1831 A.D.)

Sri Mummadi came of age and took the reigns of administration in 1811 A. D. After the retirement of Dewan Purnaiah the Maharaja appointed these Dewans in succession Balaji Rao, Sawar Bakshi Rama Rao, Babu Rao, Siddaraja Urs, etc. The initial few years of Mummadi's rule ushered in peace and prosperity in Mysore State. In 1817, the British fought a war against the Maratha army. In this battle, the Mysore army fought with exemplary bravery and finally, the Maratha army suffered a defeat. The Governor General of India wrote a letter to the Maharaja of Mysore praising the valour of the Mysore army sent to the aid of the British army. Mummadi was a great patron of fine arts. He encouraged scholars, physicians, sculptors, poets, painters and musicians and rewarded them generously. He spent more money on the up keep of temples, *agraharas* (Brahmin free housing quarters) and way side *choultries* (free inns) than the previous administration of Dewan Purnaiah. From 1810 A.D. onwards, Mummadi spent annually ₹ 42,500 per annum on public works.

Storm Clouds

After 1820, the monsoon rains failed and agricultural output decreased. The annual income of the Mysore State decreased to ₹ 76 lakhs from the previous average income of ₹ 87 lakhs. In 1823, the state was afflicted with a severe drought. During this period, Mummadi spent lakhs of rupees from state reserve funds to alleviate hunger and avoid inevitable deaths. The palace officials like Bakshi Narasappa and others rendered yeoman service to the state, which was wholeheartedly appreciated by the citizens of Mysore State. The annual tax revenue to the state treasury had declined by ₹ 11 lakhs, but famine relief work had shot the state budget expenditure to ₹ 90 lakhs. During this period, the East India Company wanted Mysore State to send army contingents for its war. This was an additional financial burden on the state treasury. Added to the existing woes, a cholera epidemic struck the population. The state incurred more expenditure fighting this epidemic.

In Mysore State, the land tax was collected by Subedhars through a procedure called "*Sharath*" (Eng: agreed conditions of payment). The Subedhars sent their henchmen to collect the annual land taxes from peasants. The Maharaja had imposed a condition that Subedhars had to remit a certain sum of money annually irrespective of the annual yield. Neither floods nor drought ever mattered to these Subedhars. This "Sharath" system of collection of annual taxes prevailed even during Dewan Purnaiah's time and it was in vogue in the neighbouring Canara district administered by the Britishers. The Subedhars should have collected taxes from farmers without harming them. But often, they resorted to torture and violence to extract money from poor farmers. The defaulting poor farmers were made to stand in the hot sun with a stone on their heads. They were beaten with sticks and whipped mercilessly. In extreme cases, these defaulting farmers were imprisoned and their properties were confiscated in lieu of taxes. These Subedhars fattened themselves on the surplus taxes collected by them. Only a small portion of taxes were remitted to the king. This led to a revolt in the Nagara (Hosanagara) area of Shimoga district. People began to find fault with the administration of Mummadi Sri Krishnaraja Wodeyar. We must take note of several revolts, which took place in British-ruled provinces of India also at this time.

The numerous revolts were first triggered by Tarikere Paleghar Rangappa Nayaka. This traitor with the help of one Haigamalla, a pretender caused much disturbance and trouble to Mummadi. Haigamalla claimed to be an adopted son called Boodi Basappa belonging to the ruling family of Nagara. This Paleghar of Nagara had been defeated by Haider Ali. Some mischief makers appointed Boodi Basappa as the new ruler of the Nagara principality. The Subedhars and Patels conducted a coronation ceremony to give this pretender legitimacy. These rebellions occurred in towns like Chennarayapatna, Doddaballapur, Chennagiri and Nagar region of Mysore state. These rebel armies looted citizens and committed various atrocities.

These developments forced Mummadi Sri Krishnaraja Wodeyar to take his army to these troubled areas to quell the rebellion. Mummadi requested assistance from the East India Company army in this endeavour. The British resident and the Governor of Madras came to the conclusion that the Mysore State army was adequate for this purpose. They declined to send the British army.

Maharaja's Journey Through the State

Sri Mummadi Krishnaraja Wodeyar left Mysore city with his army and arrived at Dasaraguppe on 14th December 1830. The Maharaja made enquiries about the welfare of farmers. He reduced the excess taxes collected by the Subedhars. On 17th December 1830, he visited Bookinakere and dismissed the corrupt Shirestedhar and Subedhar of that region. The royal entourage reached Chennarayapatna on 18th December 1830. At the same time, the British resident also arrived in the town. The Maharaja heard the grievances of ordinary citizens and came to know about the excesses of the Subedhar. He was dismissed from the service. He had kept in prison hundreds of farmers. They had not paid the exorbitant taxes demanded by the Subedhar and these farmers were starving. The Maharaja ordered his cooks to prepare a dish made up of flattened rice and yoghurt (curds) to be sent to these hungry prisoners. They were released from jail on the orders of the monarch. If Mummadi had been given a free hand, he would have brought the situation under control. But the British resident opined that a kid-glove treatment of rebels and corrupt officials would not produce the desired effect.

Dewan Venkate Urs and his cabinet members decided to implement the iron fist policy. On the advice of the British resident, they hanged two persons in Holenarsipura and two persons in Chennarayapatna. These actions provoked the rebels to put up stiff resistance. When the Maharaja was still at Chennarayapatna, he received a message that the rebellion had spread to Kumsi and Anandapura in the Shimoga district.

The Mysore army was sent to these troubled areas under a brave commander called Annappa. The British resident realised belatedly that the British army should have been called at the early stages of rebellion. He wrote to the Madras Governor requesting additional forces and warned that this rebellion may spread to British-ruled territories also. The East India Company army under Col. Evans was sent to Shimoga district to quell the rebellion. The Maharaja, after touring other troubled areas, returned to Mysore city on 10th January 1831. Though in large areas of Mysore law and order were re-established by the King, the troubles created by Rangappa Nayak and Haigamalla still persisted. Some of the Government officials like Subedhar of Honnale aided rebels secretly. Their treacherous activities against the Maharaja created chaotic conditions in the state.

Maharaja Loses Reins of Power

The Governor of Madras wrote a letter to Lord William Bentinck (Governor General of India) on 12th April 1831 complaining about the non-payment of annual tribute by the Maharaja of Mysore. He informed the Governor General that because of this, he was unable to disburse the salaries of soldiers. This would eventually lead to a mutiny by soldiers. This was a baseless allegation made by the Governor of Madras. When the accounts of the East India Company were audited later, it was found that Mummadi had not defaulted on payment of tributes to the British, even by a month. Lord Bentinck wrote a letter to Mummadi on 7th September 1831 stating that he had defaulted on the payment of tributes and he had awarded harsh capital punishments to rebels. The East India Company had to send its army to quell the rebellion in the state. Mummadi Sri Krishna Raja Wodeyar was ordered to relinquish his rule within ten days of receipt of this official letter and hand over the reins of power back to the British regent. This transfer of power must be published in the state gazette. The first complaint of the Governor General was a baseless allegation. It was true that commander Annappa had hanged many a mutineer. Because these rebels had killed many Government officials. At Chennarayapatna and Holenarsipura, two persons were hanged at the insistence of a British resident. Even then, the British army took one year to quell the rebellion in different parts of the state. Mummadi transferred power to British resident on 19th October 1831 A. D. The army officers like Col. Briggs suppressed the rebellion of Haigamalla and others by January 1833 A. D. The Governor General of India Lord William Bentinck appointed an experts committee to enquire into these rebellions. The report vindicated Mummadi of all allegations and Governor General realised that he had taken a hasty decision with regard to Mysore affairs on the goading of Maharaja's detractors.

Lord Bentinck met Mummadi in April 1834 A.D. and enquired about the political affairs of Mysore state. Later, he recommended the reinstatement of Mummadi on the throne and to return to him the Mysore districts of Manjirabad and Astagramas (eight villages) to form a truncated Mysore State. This recommendation was not favoured by the Directors of East India Company. We learn from the outspoken words of Col. Briggs, "The Governor General, as I did not understand till lately, was excessively anxious from the first and all through the business to screen the Resident casamaijor an old protégé and favourite of his own, so that while his dispatches demonstrated that gentleman's incapacity to the perception of the court of directors, he still supported him both publicly and privately and was glad to get me out of the way, because I frankly avowed my aversion to the residency party and my conviction that they were answerable for the misrule of Mysore," – "From the book – Modern Mysore, pg. 469."

Col. Briggs made several attempts to expose the nefarious role of the British resident in Mysore state affairs. He was punished by Lord Bentinck for his sincere attempt to redeem Mummadi from Calumny. Even after losing political power, Mummadi did not exhibit any rancour and bitterness towards the British. He kept up his good work through the highs and lows of political turmoil after assuming his office in 1811, he initiated many good developmental projects. In 1812, he laid the foundation for the first-ever modern hospital in Mysore State. After relinquishing his office, in the year 1840 on 1st October, he laid the foundation for an English Medium School in Mysore City. The State Commissioner taking note of this encouraged

Rev. J. Garett head of the Wesleyan Mission to develop the English school in Bangalore into a Collegiate School.

Good Deeds of a Disenfranchised Ruler

After losing political power, Mummadi Sri Krishnaraja Wodeyar received a privy purse of ₹ 13 lakhs. He cut down on his personal expenditure and lived a frugal life. Despite the crunch in funds, he carried on his charitable activities and still continued to function as a patron of fine arts. Mummadi and his well-wishers made repeated concerted attempts to impress upon the Governor General to re-instate the former ruler back on the throne.

In 1834, Col. J. S. Fraser was appointed as the resident and commissioner of the Mysore State. After ruling the state for two years, he wrote in his report, "We failed to give proper guidance to the young Maharaja Mummadi and when a positive action would have helped in quelling the rebellion in early stages, we instead remained quiescent. When the Maharaja was facing a severe political crisis, we withdrew his powers to rule the state. The Maharaja enjoys traditional hereditary powers over such things as adoption, marriage and Hindu religious practises. One day, after making sure that the East India Company receives tributes from the Maharaja regularly, we can transfer power back to him. This recommendation fell on deaf ears of the General and Mummadi's detractors and hostile critics were in greater number than the sympathizers.

The Maharaja wholeheartedly and without any prejudice admired the efficient administration of the commissioners, who worked for the welfare of the state. In 1857, all over India, the Sepoy mutiny took place as a reaction against the East India Company rule. It even reached some northern districts of Karnataka. At that time, Mummadi extended all help to the Britishers.

The Governor General of India, Lord Dalhousie (1848 – 1856) paid a state visit to Mysore. At that time, Sir Mark Cubbon was commissioner of Mysore State. In a selfless and self-effacing manner, Mummadi recommended, much to the surprise of the Governor General and Commissioner that the British should amalgamate Mysore State with the British presidency. After Lord Dalhousie relinquished office, because of Sepoy Mutiny and abolition of East India Company rule Queen Empress Victoria introduced the direct rule of the British monarchy. The post of Governor General of India was abolished and the first Viceroy of India Lord Canning (1858 – 1862) was appointed by

Queen Victoria. He declined to transfer back political power to Sri Mummadi Krishnaraja Wodeyar.

Lord Bentinck had introduced the doctrine of *theory of lapse* to deny an Indian ruler from adopting an heir to the throne if he or she was childless. Lord Bentinck opposed the princely states and he wanted the British to rule the whole of India directly to create a market for British manufactured goods. Mummadi did not have any children. Lord Canning the Viceroy of India interpreted the doctrine of lapse to mean that those Indian rulers, who had adopted heirs before 1858 A.D. would be allowed to continue their rule.

Attempts at Restoration of Monarchy

Meanwhile, Queen Empress Victoria honoured Mummadi with the title "G. C. S. I." (Knight Grand Commander – the most exalted Order of the Star of India) and sent him a gift of diamond studded watch. These developments enthused Mummadi and his followers to renew their efforts at claiming the political power to rule Mysore State. A leading businessman of Bangalore of Iranian extraction by the name Ali Asker vigorously championed the cause of Mummadi. This gentleman was Sir Mirza Ismail's father. He sent secret letters to the Governor of Madras and to the Viceroy of India pleading on behalf of Mummadi. He tried to woo high-ranking British civil and army officials. Many petitions and letters were secretly posted from Hosur (Madras Presidency) to Buckingham Palace, London. In 1864, the respectable citizens of Mysore state numbering 7,000 signed a petition requesting the reinstatement of Mummadi on the throne and it was submitted to the Viceroy of India. The well-known Doctor Campbell of Madras and Sri Lakshminarasa Shetty a member of the legislative assembly of Madras and a few others began to canvas for Mummadi. The ex-ruler remained calm and composed during this political storm. When a committee of British officials decided to erect a bronze statue of Sir Mark Cubbon, he generously donated ₹10,000 towards this project.

In 1865 A. D., the ex-Maharaja adopted a son by name Sri Chamarajendra Wodeyar. However, the British Government declared that the heir of Mummadi had only claims on personal movable and immovable properties of the palace. The heir had no succession right to the throne. This news disheartened Mummadi greatly. He again wrote a letter to the Viceroy demanding justice and equity before law. Many Indian, British and foreign newspapers criticised the move of the British Government's move to gobble up a princely state. Such eminent persons as Lord Morley, Lord president of the council and a member of the house of Lords and Rao Saheb Sri Vishwanath Mandalik and others began to argue in the British parliament on behalf of Mummadi Krishna Raja Wodeyar. A new ministry was formed in Britain after the elections and this cabinet of ministers was favourably disposed towards the Mysore ruler.

At last, the British Government decided to revert political power back to the Wodeyar dynasty. But Mummadi would not be reinstated as a ruler; his adopted son Sri Chamarajendra Wodeyar would become the next ruler of Mysore when he came of age. The British Government also raised the tribute amount to be paid by the Mysore state from ₹ 24.5 Lakhs to ₹ 35 Lakhs per annum. All these developments partially disheartened Mummadi, because he could not become a ruler of Mysore state in his own right. The consolation was that at least his adopted son would rule in the future. In a short while, on 27th March 1868, at 23:00 P.M. Mummadi Sri Krishna Raja Wodeyar breathed his last aged 74 years. The people of the Mysore state mourned the death of their beloved King, who was charitable, righteous, generous, erudite and caring for the welfare of one and all. During his rule, Mummadi had introduced street lamps in all the cities and towns. The illumination of cities and towns had made ordinary people to compose a ditty in this manner.

"*Krishnaraja Bhoopa Beedilella Deepa*" (Kannada)

"*Krishnaraja the sovereign gifted us with street lamps*" (Eng. Transl.)

At his death, they lamented that they would not see again such a just and fair ruler.

The Rule of Sri Chamarajendra Wodeyar

The British Resident made proper arrangements for imparting western education for the Maharaja Sri Chamarajendra Wodeyar. He got married to Smt. Kempananjammani. He was sixteen years old at the time of his marriage. This was a joyous occasion for the citizens of Mysore and a period of peace and prosperity was ushered in. The farmers were happy with a bumper harvest. Sri Chamarajendra Wodeyar came to the throne in 1881 A. D. The ruler of Mysore State with the help of the Dewans transformed Mysore State into a progressive state in just 14 years. This state became a model state for other princely states. The British Commissioners had ruled Mysore State from 1831 to 1881 A.D. During their 50 years of rule, they had laid a firm foundation for efficient administration. There was all round discipline and the law and order situation had improved greatly.

But during the three years in 1876, 1877 and 1878 a severe famine struck the state. It had a devastating effect on the population and economy. This great famine killed ten lakhs and fifty thousand people in Mysore state. If one took into account the total population of the state, a quarter of the population had been decimated by the severe drought that afflicted the state. Mysore State suffered a severe revenue loss to the extent of ₹10 Crores. The Maharaja was forced to spend from the state treasury ₹1 Crore and he had to borrow from the British Government ₹80 Lakhs for the drought relief work. There was all round deficiency in the collection of taxes. Mysore State also had to pay the British Government the recently hiked tribute money.

Although fair-minded Britishers did not grudge Sri Chamarajendra Wodeyar regaining political power, a large number of Britishers did not relish the fact of regional princes ruling their states. In a magnanimous gesture, the British Government deferred the payment of the hiked amount of tributes from Mysore state until 1896. One evening, in a "Victoria" chaise, the Maharaja, the Darbar Bakshi and a British nobleman were taking a ride in the beautiful countryside. The sun was setting in the west and a cool breeze was blowing in their direction. The English nobleman forgot for a few moments that he was in the presence of the Maharaja. He could not help but exclaim seeing the beautiful landscape, "What fools, these British statesmen are to hand over to native rulers, such a prosperous rattling country like Mysore!" from the book "Revised Memories" by Rao Bahadur Sri Ambigal Narasimha Iyengar. The Darbar Bakshi stifled a laughter with great difficulty and the Maharaja turned aside and pretended to be lost in thought. The Darbar Bakshi pinched the thigh of the Englishman and reminded him that he was in the presence of the Maharaja.

Many Europeans doubted the ability to rule by the native princes. They thought Indian royalty was not well educated and enlightened to give a good administration to the people. It is true that India at that time had some black sheep. But there were also exceptions like rulers of Mysore State, Baroda State and Travancore State, where the respective rulers ushered in a new era of development. In these princely states, important administrative posts were held by Indians. They had to prove that they were as competent and efficient as the British I.C.S. officers. Most of these states paid huge amounts of tributes to the British Government. They were also expected to keep up their former glory, pomp and dignity on reduced budgets. Often, their developmental projects could not take off without adequate funds in the treasury.

Sri Chamarajendra Wodeyar came to the throne in this kind of environment. He was handicapped by several factors. It has already been mentioned that Sri Chamarajendra Wodeyar had started a girls' high school in Mysore. The Maharaja created new departments in the state to improve administration and passed a legislation prohibiting child marriages. Sri Chamarajendra Wodeyar brought about a sea change in Mysore State within four years of taking the reins of power. The British Government and the other princely states took note of the progress made by Mysore State.

One British journalist wrote an article praising the good work of Sri Chamarajendra Wodeyar. This is what he wrote in an English newspaper, "In his personal life, the Maharaja does credit to the careful training which he received... ....He has a fine province to rule over, and should it be his good fortune to bring it again to a state of prosperity, he will do much to establish the fact that in good hands, native government can compare well with English administration."

Once, a good friend of Dewan Sir Seshadri Iyer visited him. During the conversation, the visitor made enquiries about the Maharaja. He asked the Dewan if he had the same job in another state, how he would have fared there. Sir Seshadri Iyer, replied that he would have lasted under some other Maharaja only for three months. He said that under Sri Chamarajendra Wodeyar, he could accomplish many things because the ruler was just, fair and encouraging.

The Maharaja appointed a high-level committee to give him advice and suggestions. It consisted of Dewan Sir Rangacharlu, Chief Justice Sri T. R. A. Thumboo Chetty, Sri Poorna Krishna Rao and Sri Ratna Sabhapathi Mudaliar as members. Dewan Sri Rangacharlu was appointed as the Chairman of this expert committee. This committee offered suggestions and recommendations to the Maharaja for approval.

All these years, the state government had followed a certain tradition in fiscal matters. The state government remitted $1/5^{th}$ of the state's revenue to the personal account of the Maharaja for palace expenditure. Maharaja received ₹13 lakhs for his personal expenditure. During 1881, Mysore State was afflicted by a severe drought. The people were dying of starvation.

Maharaja Sri Chamarajendra Wodeyar presented himself before the committee. He told Sri Dewan Rangacharlu that during 1881, he was prepared to receive only ₹10 lakhs. He contributed the surplus amount of ₹3 Lakhs for the drought relief work from his personal funds. The Maharaja showed great sagacity in the appointment of the Dewans. First, it was Sri Rangacharlu and the next Dewan was Sir Seshadri Iyer (*Dr. D. V. Gundappa has written extensively on their contributions to the Mysore State in his book – Ed. Note.*)

Dewan Sri C. V. Rangacharlu (1881 – 1883)
From: "An Art Gallery of Reminiscences" by D. V. Gundappa

Sri C. V. Rangacharlu served Mysore State in a selfless and dedicated manner. During the last phase of his life, his health deteriorated. Even on his death bed, he did not worry about his wife and children. Instead, he was lamenting that he could not serve his majesty in a much better capacity. He had joined palace service as a controller. He managed to run palace affairs on efficient lines. He brought in more discipline in managing the palace staff. He was able to save a lot of money by avoiding wasteful expenditures. Sri C. V. Rangacharlu was the Dewan of Mysore for one year and ten months.

The first major project taken up by the Dewan was the laying of the railway line from Bangalore to Mysore. He realised that during the drought period, thousands of people had died due to starvation because food grain could not be supplied to them quickly enough. He also requested the Maharaja to grant ₹20 lakhs to lay a railway line from Mysore to Tiptur. The railway train would transport food to the drought-hit region quickly. There was a severe famine during *Dhatu Eshwar* year resulting in the death of thousands of people. In his speech on 7th October 1881 in the legislative assembly, he declared that our farmers must grow more food to feed the hungry mouths. During the next year's speech, he wanted Mysore State to be industrialised quickly.

In Britain, the steam locomotives had come into existence. The spinning mills of Manchester were manufacturing cloth. There was stiff competition in trade between America and Britain. He condemned the age-old fatalistic attitude of illiterate Indians numbering 20 Crores people at that time. He wanted Indians to become more inventive and enterprising in the development of the economy.

Dewan Sir Seshadri Iyer

The Maharaja wanted a road constructed on Chamundi Hill for pilgrims to reach the temple of Sri Chamundeshwari on top of the hill. Many civil engineers thought it was not possible to construct a road, given its terrain.

Meanwhile, pilgrims had to climb 1000 steps to reach the top of the hill. The devotees and residents of Chamundi Hill regularly made these trips up and down. Dewan Seshadri Iyer took the help of a single surveyor to prepare a road project report. Often, he gave him suggestions on how to go about it. Ultimately, a smooth two-lane highway was built to facilitate vehicular traffic. It was inaugurated by the Maharaja, who made the first trip in his "Victoria" coach.

Once, Major Hancock introduced an Italian mining expert and geologist to Dewan Seshadri Iyer. After a discussion with the Dewan, he came out of the room and exclaimed, "This gentleman has previous experience in the mining field." The Dewan's knowledge of geology and mining was on par with experts. The two great accomplishments of Dewan Seshadri Iyer were the Shivana Samudra Hydro-Electric Project and Sri Vani Vilasa Sagar Project.

Dewan Seshadri Iyer was capable of finding flaws in the estimates submitted by the Royal Engineers of British India. When it came to the Indian School of Medicine (Ayurveda) or Western School of Medicine (Allopathy), Dewan Seshadri Iyer had a thorough knowledge of both systems. One day, the Director of Health Department – an Englishman – went to Sri Seshadri Iyer's office with certain recommendations to improve healthcare. He was confident that the Dewan would be unfamiliar with medical terminology and hence, approve his recommendations per se. He was flummoxed by the medical knowledge of the Dewan. The report had many inaccuracies and flaws, which were highlighted by the Dewan. This English doctor came out of the room in an exasperated manner saying, "How should I know this indomitable person possessed an encyclopaedic knowledge about the medical field?"

The long train of professionals, who went to meet him over some business or the other, the likes of doctors, pandits (scholars), lawyers, judges, engineers, legal experts, top bureaucrats or agriculturists came out of the office with a feeling that they were dealing with an expert in their field. He was a "Renaissance man" in his true element. His official reports and letters addressed to high-level dignitaries were written in the best English style. His letters were appreciated by even Viceroy Lord Curzon. One British resident, who knew him intimately remarked that you will not come across a genius like him either among Whites or among the Blacks ["*Black or White there is no equal to Seshadri*" - quote.]

Dewan Seshadri Iyer functioned as an administrator without exhibiting any fear or favour. This real-life incident is described in the book "*Revived

Memories" written by Rao Bahadur Sri Ambigal Narasimha Iyengar (pages 349 – 50). A top official of British India was invited by the State Government to complete a project on time. This Englishman assured the Dewan that he would be completing his project within the deadline. However, this work was not progressing at the expected pace. Dewan Seshadri Iyer kept a tab on the progress of the project. He soon realised that it would not be completed on time. So, he visited the work site in his horse-drawn coach. He met the Englishman and told him without mincing words that if he was unable to complete the project on time, he would have to face the consequences. The Englishman did not like the harsh language of the Dewan. He retorted by saying he was doing his best to complete the project on time, but several factors were hindering its progress. He also arrogantly remarked that if the Dewan was not satisfied with his performance, he could be sent back to his parent department in British India. The Dewan flared up and said, "I am warning you! If you do not conduct yourself like a professional, you will lose your job. I will see to it that you will not be retaining your previous job nor will you be getting a new assignment in Princely India. I will write letters to the Viceroy and to the heads of princely states barring you from any employment. If you do not mend your ways, you will have to pack up your suitcases and go back to Britain." These words had the desired effect on the Englishman. He worked day and night to complete this project on time. The Dewan honoured him with costly gifts and gave him a certificate of merit acknowledging his services afterwards.

A high-ranking British Engineer gave a statement to the newspaper "Madras Standard" (27th September 1902) in an interview, "As long as Sir Seshadri Iyer was Dewan of the Princely State of Mysore, it did not require the services of a Chief Engineer." Sir William Hunter expressed his high praise of Dewan Seshadri Iyer in these words, "Sir Seshadri Iyer was a statesman, who gave his head to Herbert Spencer and his heart to Parabrahman."

Development of Mysore State under Sri Chamarajendra Wodeyar

The Dewan administered Mysore State very efficiently and successfully with the help of his advisors, Sri Poorna Krishna Rao, Sri Ambigal Narasimha Iyengar, Sri Chancelraya and Sri T. R. A. Thumboo Chetty. More than all these people, he enjoyed the generous patronage of the Maharaja Sri Chamarajendra Wodeyar. The enlightened Maharaja stood by him and endorsed all the projects and enterprises embarked upon by the Dewan for the welfare of Mysore State. The Queen Empress of India Victoria bestowed upon him the title of "C. S. I" (Most Exalted Order of Star of India – Companion Commander) in 1887. He was honoured by the Queen with "K. C. S. I." (Knight Commander – Most Exalted Order of the Star of India) in 1893 A. D. He officiated as the Dewan of Mysore State during Sri Chamarajendra Wodeyar's reign for 11 years. The Maharaja passed away in Calcutta in 1894 A.D. The Queen Regent was appointed in 1895 A.D. by the British government to rule the state on behalf of the minor son Sri Nalwadi Krishnaraja Wodeyar. Dewan Sir Seshadri Iyer continued as Dewan for another 7 years until 1901 A. D. He enjoyed a very long tenure of 18 years as the Dewan of Mysore State.

Here is a brief report of his exemplary performance and a short list of achievements, which brought him immense credit and appreciation from citizens and observers. The total tenure of rule of the Maharaja Sri Chamarajendra Wodeyar was for 13 years. When the Maharaja came to the throne, the state fiscal record was poor. The state was in financial debt of ₹ 80 lakhs. At that time, the assets of the state were valued at ₹45,25,000. Hence, the state debt exceeded the total value of state assets by ₹33,75,000. When Maharaja Sri Chamarajendra Wodeyar passed away in 1894 A.D., the state finances stood on a positive note. Dewan Rangacharlu and Dewan Seshadri Iyer had managed to clear the state debts during their tenure. The state treasury had surplus cash of ₹2,75,50,000 in its chests. The Dewans had achieved this target without raising taxes.

Mysore State government extended the length of railway lines to a considerable extent between 1881 A.D. to 1894 A.D. The state government took the assistance of Southern Maratha Railway Company to lay new railway lines to the extent of 315 miles. The state government borrowed ₹20 lakhs to complete this project. During this period, new state highways were constructed covering a distance of 1,100 miles. The irrigation projects were taken up on a massive scale by the government. The water tanks were repaired, new canals were dug up and check dams were built. In the earlier budgets of the government, it was spending ₹ 3 lakhs. Now, the cost of irrigation works went up to ₹13 lakhs. The new dams built across rivers cost the exchequer ₹1 crore. Because of these developments, 350 square miles of acreage under cultivation received the benefit of perennial water supply to the crops. In a decade, 60% more acreage was added to the existing area of cultivation. The land revenue of the Mysore State increased from ₹1 crore and 3 lakhs to ₹1 crore and 63 lakhs. The number of government-run educational institutions and government-aided private educational institutions increased from 1,047 to 3,097 in a decade. The local cottage industries received a fillip from the government financial assistance. In 1884 A.D., three judges were appointed to the chief court of Mysore, which later came to be known as Mysore High Court. In 1885, the government created the posts of Inspector General of Police and Chief Conservator of Forests. In 1886, an independent department was created to deal with agriculture-related issues. The Kolar Gold mine began its operation in 1886. A textile factory was set up to manufacture cotton and woollen materials. The state administration brought about reforms in the field of healthcare and education. Some new government departments like the excise department, Muzrai department (temple endowment department), Military establishment, mines and geology department and several others were created. The Land Revenue Collection procedure was codified, leading to a better collection of revenue. The State Insurance department was created to give coverage to people of Mysore State.

The Maharaja introduced the Mysore Civil Service entrance examination in 1891. The government wanted to attract the best talent into Mysore's administrative service. The top rankers would be appointed as probationary Assistant Commissioners. The regional postal service was abolished. The state opted to be the part of All-India Postal Service operated by the British Government throughout the country. In 1894, the government allowed agricultural co-operative banks to help farmers. The Princely state started its own meteorological department to monitor weather in the state.

The post of Revenue commissioner of the state was created in 1894. The budgetary allocation for education was ₹3,15,000 in 1881 and it was increased to ₹ 8,20,010 by 1894. The number of boys studying in schools and colleges increased from 39,413 to 71,167. The number of girls in schools and colleges increased from 3,000 to 12,000. Mysore State had a railway line covering a distance of 58 miles in 1881. It increased to 173 miles by 1894. The extension of the railway line cost the exchequer ₹ 1 crore and 64 lakhs. The local self-government policy saw an increase in town municipalities from 83 to 107. In Mysore and Bangalore, several drinking water supply schemes were implemented. It came to the notice of the Maharaja that all over the state, the obnoxious practise of child marriages was taking place. The girls as young as 5 or 7 were married off to older grooms. Often, old widowers got married to pre-puberty girls. Hence, in the state legislature, an act was passed in 1894 prohibiting child marriages. We must take note of the shocking statistic of four-year-old girls, who were married off to aged grooms numbered 11,157 in 1891. The state had a population of young widows aged nine years to the extent of 3,560. The new legislative act laid the rule that girls below the age of eight could not marry. If the male widower was older than 50 years, he could not marry a girl aged less than sixteen. Although this looks today as an antiquated act, at that time, it helped many girls to escape early marriages. During the reign of Sri Chamarajendra Wodeyar, Mysore State witnessed an all-round development, which was not visible in any other princely state or in the British presidency.

This is what "Pioneer" newspaper wrote about the developmental activities of Mysore State, "Under a Maharaja with liberal views the abilities of the minister had a full scope and the record of the state was one of unparalleled progress and prosperity."

The rule of Maharaja Sri Chamarajendra Wodeyar came to symbolize the creative activity of the highest order. This appealed greatly to the sensibilities of Indians. That is why when the Maharaja died suddenly, people all over India mourned his death.

Regent's Rule

The Queen mother Sri Vani Vilas Sannidhana ruled the Mysore State as regent in charge of Nalwadi Krishnaraja Wodeyar for eight years. She ruled the Mysore State in an astute and enlightened manner. It called for tact, diplomacy, courage and moral strength. The ordinary citizens of Mysore State loved and respected the Queen Mother. In fact, the newspaper "Englishman" wrote in its columns, that in an under-developed country like India, where women stayed at home and observed purdah, it was a rare sight to see this royal personage, a widow with very little formal education conducting the affairs of the state in such a competent manner. This English-language newspaper compared the Queen Mother to Queen Empress Victoria. The two important projects executed during her reign – the Shivana Samudra Hydro-Electric project and Sri Vani Vilas Sagar reservoir project – were described by a newspaper, as two of the most remarkable projects of their kind in the world."

Another newspaper described the public works taken up in Mysore state viewed from any corner in India as, "…a splendid system of public works that might be envied from any part of British India." In another newspaper, it was reported, "Further, it must be placed to the credit of Mysore that, more than any other state, it is rendering to the Indian Empire the service of trying new experiments, which till recently the Imperial government have hesitated to attempt." One more newspaper wrote that Queen Mother's reign as regent of the state resulted in welfare schemes for people and there was all-round progress in education, health and business spheres. She treated her subjects as her own children.

When Sri Vani Vilasa Sannidhana came to power in 1894 A. D., it came to her notice that Areca nut farms in the Malanad region were taxed heavily. She reduced the taxes by 22 per cent, to make the growers happy.

The Plague Epidemic of 1898

The Plague Epidemic struck Mysore, Bangalore and many other towns of Mysore State in 1898. Sri Nalwadi was only 14 years of age at that time. He was moved by the plight of the people and he showered compassion on the suffering population. All kinds of help were extended to prevent further spread of the disease. When the plague first appeared in North India in 1897, even Viceroy Lord Curzon became distraught and disheartened. The disease appeared to be spreading rapidly in every direction taking a toll on millions of people.

When it first appeared in Mysore State, the government took the preventive and precautionary measures taken elsewhere in the country. The medical personnel were bewildered by the enormity of the problem. The doctors began to administer "Inoculation" to patients. The infected patients were sent to isolation hospitals. Many towns and villages were evacuated of their residents and often forcefully sent to camps. The Queen Mother and Nalwadi did their best to alleviate the suffering of the masses. The government of Mysore spent ₹20 lakhs to fight this deadly epidemic. These efforts of the royal family helped millions of people to overcome this deadly epidemic.

The Mysore state government act against cruelty to animals was introduced during this time by the Queen Mother with the active support of Nalwadi. Another Act was passed to regulate the hunting of wild animals indiscriminately. The Queen Mother had a kind disposition towards animals and birds. She was full of love and compassion for the speechless animals and birds. This genuine concern was expressed on many occasions.

Once, an employee had been recruited for palace service. But he was not taken on the job immediately by an official. When the prospective employee went to the official complaining about the delay in his appointment, the official snubbed him arrogantly. This was reported to the Queen Mother by the messengers. She shouted in exasperation, "If this official who receives his salary on the first day of every month, how can he understand the plight of a poor, hungry person? We must stop his salary for a month. Then, he will understand the privations of an individual." She ordered the concerned official to recruit this poor man immediately into palace service.

We can gauge the success and efficiency of Queen Mother's administration by the fact that state revenue increased by ₹36 lakhs in eight years. The Land revenue and royalty increased from the Kolar Gold mine increased by many fold and contributed surplus funds to the state treasury. The Queen Mother managed to clear the outstanding loans with Maratha Railway company and to repay the debts incurred by the Shivana Samudra Hydro-Electric Project. The arable land under cultivation in Mysore state in the year 1895 was 63 lakh acres. It increased to 66 lakh acres by 1902. The Queen Regent got three artificial lakes created at an expense of ₹5 lakhs at Mavatthur, Parasuramapura and Mir Sabhihalli. During the year 1897, the state was on the verge of a famine. The state government commissioned drinking water wells to be dug up in several villages. The needy farmers were given soft (means at a low rate of interest) agricultural loans. Some 500 new government schools were started during this period. The state budgetary allocation for the Education department rose from ₹ 8,50,000 to ₹ 11,50,000. The state education department started two new courses in Maharani Higher Secondary School for young widows so that they could get an education and become economically independent.

Mysore State had deputed four electrical engineers for higher studies in U. S. A. in high voltage engineering and in hydro-electric generation at government cost. Many new highway projects were executed to increase the length of motorable roads. The state public works department constructed bridges at Tadasa over the Bhadra River, at Yedatore (presently named Krishnaraja Nagara) over the Cauvery River and at Holenarsipura over the Hemavathi River. The Railway Train service between Birur and Shimoga began on 1st December 1899. "The Local Boards Regulatory Act" came into effect during this time. The number of town municipalities increased from 107 to 124, thereby increasing the burden of state expenditure greatly. The

Victoria hospital at Bangalore was inaugurated by the Viceroy of India Lord Curzon in 1900. The primary health centres and dispensaries (pharmaceutical outlets) increased from 116 to 135. In Bangalore city, an ophthalmic speciality institute called "Minto Eye Hospital" was built to help the visually impaired. The electricity generation in the state garnered an additional revenue to the state ₹1,50,000.

A foreign visitor by the name Sydney Low wrote in his travelogue about Shivanasamudra Gaganachukki waterfall and the hydro-electric station as,"…is worth coming a long way to see, by those who are interested in the future, as well as the present and the past of India. The mines and geology department and the Mysore army regiments received a fillip under Sri Vani Vilasa Sannidhana's rule. The Queen regent was not only a mother to her children, she became a matriarchal figure for the whole population of state numbering 5.5 million people."

Dewan Sir Seshadri Iyer's Superannuation and Death

Dewan Sir Seshadri Iyer went on sick leave on 11th August 1900. He retired from State Government service on 18th March 1901. He passed away on 13th September 1901. The Queen Mother made a laudatory speech praising him for his immense contribution to the modernisation of Mysore State at the farewell function. His vision for the future of Mysore and his long-term planning yielded very good results. The Dewan relied on his intuition and inspiration while taking major decisions. He had left his personal stamp on every department in the state.

His Majesty George the V and Lord Curzon Viceroy of India in their condolence messages acknowledged his brilliant and everlasting contributions to the state of Mysore. The citizens of Bangalore city collected funds to erect a bronze statue in front of the public library at Cubbon Park. The then Viceroy of India, Lord Hardinge unveiled the statue of the Dewan in 1913. In his inaugural speech, he said, "Dewan Sir K. Seshadri Iyer's imprint has been left on the pages of Mysore history forever. He became a Dewan of Mysore State at a time when a severe drought was staring in the face of the state administration. The Dewan received guidance and generous patronage from the ruler of the state, Sri Chamarajendra Wodeyar. The Dewan represented the best of the Indian Dharmic laws of Polity. When he took charge of state administration, the state revenue was ₹1 Crore. When he relinquished his office, the state revenue had increased to ₹1 Crore

80 Lakhs. There was phenomenal growth in the agriculture and business sectors. He rejuvenated every department of Mysore State to a very high degree of efficiency.

During his tenure, many famine relief projects were executed. The railway and road connectivity increased by many folds. The ordinary people received the benefits of universal education and health care. The drinking water supply schemes implemented by the Dewan greatly helped the inhabitants of Mysore and Bangalore cities. His achievements are remarkable and unforgettable. The generation of hydro-electricity with the technical help of J. D. Lobani is an extraordinary feat. I unveil the statue of Dewan Sir Seshadri Iyer with great pleasure" (Not a verbatim reproduction of the original speech). After the retirement of Dewan Sir Seshadri Iyer, the then-ruler Sri Nalwadi Krishnaraja Wodeyar appointed Sri P. N. Krishnamurti as the next Dewan of the state in 1901. He was a direct descendant of Dewan Sri Poorniah. This historical fact gladdened many a heart.

Chapter 7

The Investiture Ceremony of Maharaja Sri Krishnaraja Wodeyar IV

******

*"Rajadhi Rajaya prasahya sahine
Namo vayam vyshravanaya Kurmahe|
Same Kamanakamaya mahyam
Kameshwaro vyshravano dadatu|
Kuberaya vyshravanaya Maharajaya namah||*

******

"Let us pray to the King of Kings Vyshravana, who is strong and full of intrinsic worth. I desire to please every whim of Vyshravana. Similarly, I expect him to fulfil all my desires. King Vyshravana belongs to "Vishravas dynasty" of Prajapath lineage. I offer my humble prostrations to him."

Quality Education Imparted to a Scion of the Royal Family

Sri Nalwadi Krishnaraja Wodeyar had garnered through education and experience the requisite qualities to rule the modern state of Mysore as an able ruler. The youthful and energetic Maharaja had the ability to foster remarkable all-round development of the state. He had received the best of oriental and western education. He was well-versed in revenue laws, business management and public administration. When anyone who has travelled throughout India visited Mysore State, they noticed a refreshing change in the political climate. The newspaper "Madras Mail" wrote in its columns that no other Maharaja or Nawab in any other princely state of India had received this kind of education to rule the state in such a splendid manner.

Apart from all these qualities, Nalwadi had won the hearts and minds of his subjects, who hailed from different castes and religions.

Often, Nalwadi would visit villages and towns in plain clothes to interact with the common people. These first-hand encounters made him familiar with the day-to-day problems of ordinary people. Once, Nalwadi had gone to a village on a horse in informal clothes during the rainy season. He found on a village dirt road, where an oxen cart wheel had sunk in slush and mud. The cart was laden with heavy goods and the Oxen was unable to pull the cart. The poor farmer had resorted to whipping the animals and twisting their tails to make them draw the cart. Nalwadi saw many village bystanders not doing anything and standing as mute spectators. Hence, he told one farmer, "Why don't you assist the farmer in his attempts to extricate his cart wheel from the mud?" That man arrogantly replied, "It is not my cart and not my oxen. In what way am I concerned?" Nalwadi replied, "At least you must take note of the plight of the animals." He retorted, "Oh! It is easy for a well-dressed gentleman like you to offer free advice." Nalwadi quietly got down from his horse and approached the cart to assist the driver. He took hold of the spokes of one wheel and shouted at the villagers, "At least now help me by pushing the other wheel out of slush and mud." Now that vocal farmer came to the help of Nalwadi to extricate the wheel and soon the cart was on firm ground. In this melee, Nalwadi's fine black shoes, snow-white sherwani and kurta were muddied. He came to his horse and got on to his saddle. The awestruck villagers were taken aback by a well-dressed stranger stooping to help a poor farmer and his oxen in distress. One farmer exclaimed, "Oh! My Lord your shoes and clothes became soiled because of this incident. We feel sorry that your clean white dress has been ruined. May we know your true identity?" Nalwadi Sri Krishna Raja Wodeyar gave an enigmatic smile at the crowd and left the scene without revealing his true identity. In those days, millions living in villages had not seen the Maharaja and even photography was in its nascent stage in India.

The Investiture Ceremony of Sri Nalwadi Krishnaraja Wodeyar as the Maharaja of Mysore took place on 8th August 1902 in the august presence of Lord Curzon, the Viceroy of India as the Prince had come of age. It was a sheer coincidence that the Viceroy of India Lord Curzon was on a state visit to Mysore. A red carpet welcome was given to the Viceroy. The assistant residents C. L. S. Russell, V. P. Madhava Rao and Raja Sena Bhushana Sri Basappaji Urs travelled all the way to Hindupur to welcome the Viceroy on 3rd August

1902. He arrived at Bangalore by a special train from Madras on 4th August 1902 at 08:30 AM. The Viceroy was received at the railway station by British Resident Col. Robertson and by Dewan P. N. Krishnamurti. The Viceroy stayed in the residency bungalow as a V. I. P. guest of the British resident. Lord Curzon's entourage travelled by a special train to Mysore on 7th August 1902 and arrived at 08:30 AM. They also visited Shivana Samudra Hydro-Electric Project on their way to Mysore.

Lord Curzon, the Viceroy of India Arrives in Mysore

The Royal Investiture Ceremony took place in Jaganmohan Palace auditorium on 8th August 1902 (Friday, Shravana Shuddha Panchami in the Hindu Calendar year Shubha Krunnamma). The Viceroy of India Lord Curzon was received by Sri Nalwadi Krishnaraja Wodeyar and the British resident of Mysore State Col. Robertson exactly at 09:45 A. M. A grand stage had been erected to accommodate the two thrones. One was occupied by the Viceroy and the other throne was occupied by the young Maharaja. On the right side of the stage, in a row of chairs sat the British resident, European officials and army officers. On the left of the stage in a row of chairs sat the Dewan of Mysore state, council members, civil servants and very important Indian dignitaries. The Queen Mother, Maharani, the three Princesses and aristocratic ladies of the Urs community occupied chairs behind a thin cloth screen observing the purdah system. The royalty of various Indian Princely states with their Maharanis and Begums had come in expensive colourful dresses and jewellery. A British military band was playing music in the garden outside. In the auditorium, they had displayed expensive gifts and clothes given to the Maharaja of Mysore by these Indian Princes, the Europeans and the business community of Mysore State. The Maharaja had received special gifts from King Edward VII, the Viceroy and the British Resident. The Viceroy and the Maharaja entered the hall and walked on the red carpet in measured steps towards the stage. All the invitees stood up to welcome the guest of honour showing their respect and adoration. After the Viceroy and Maharaja took their seats, the others sat down. The Foreign Secretary of the Government of India had been delegated as master of ceremonies, but he was unable to attend the function. The Under Secretary of Foreign Office performed this duty and announced that the assembly was in session. He also welcomed the guests of honour. The formal inaugural speech was delivered by the Viceroy.

It was a grand eloquent speech delivered by Lord Curzon and the listeners felt they were fortunate enough to hear such a wonderful inaugural speech. Lord Curzon had proved himself as a great orator since his childhood. Now, he was delivering an investiture speech which would legitimise the rule of Sri Nalwadi Krishnaraja Wodeyar. Here is a summary of his speech. This Investiture Ceremony was the first one he was attending in India. If not for his love for Mysore State and the extraordinary affection he had for the young Maharaja, he would not have travelled all the way from the summer capital of India, Shimla.

Sri Nalwadi Krishnaraja Wodeyar with his favourite horse

Sri Nalwadi Krishnaraja Wodeyar with his pet dog

The Baton is Passed On

The Viceroy Lord Curzon thanked and congratulated Prime Minister and Foreign Minister of Great Britain Lord Salisbury, who moved the resolution to transfer power back to the Maharaja Sri Chamarajendra Wodeyar. "It was done to test the theory, of whether native Indian Princes were competent enough to administer their states or not. At that time, there was strong criticism against this move of the government. In fact, the British public was watching the whole experiment intently to know its final outcome. I will not claim on behalf of Mysore State that the experiment was flawless and perfect. There were occasional lapses and drawbacks, which were unavoidable. In public life, we spend more time discussing the failures rather than things accomplished by a ruler. But with regard to Mysore State, I can state frankly the rulers and administrators conducted the affairs of the state with complete dedication and patriotism.

Mysore State had the good fortune of having two able Dewans – Sri Rangacharlu for a brief period and Dewan Sir Seshadri Iyer, who had a longer tenure being at the helm of the development and progress of the state. The late Highness Sri Chamarajendra Wodeyar had a mild demeanour and pleasant manners, which endeared him to the public. His premature death is a regrettable fact.

I can state with authority as Viceroy of India that Queen Mother Sri Vani Vilasa Sannidhana as regent in charge of the minor Prince conducted the state affairs efficiently and momentous decisions were taken judiciously by the ruler. She conducted the affairs of the state and of the royal family in an able manner to the satisfaction of citizens and relatives of the royal family. She has won all-round admiration and appreciation from every quarter. Earlier, her Majesty's government had sanctioned a 19-gun salute to the Maharaja of Mysore. I am glad to make this announcement that His Majesty King George the V has given his royal permission for the continuation of 19 guns salute to the present Maharaja Sri Nalwadi Krishnaraja Wodeyar. The Queen regent has relinquished her rule and I am sure the enlightened rule of her son will gladden her heart."

A Brief Summary of Lord Curzon's Speech About Princes' Education

The Viceroy Lord Curzon made a significant reference to the education of two princes conducted by their mentor Sir S. M. Fraser. "Their eight years of formal education were not years of leisure and comfort. This education was meant to equip them with acumen and qualities, enabling them to shoulder greater responsibilities of state administration. The onus of giving a just rule to 50 lakh citizens of the state cannot be treated in a frivolous manner. An improper half-baked education will impair the rule. It will be a lack lustre performance of the ruler.

It was our good luck that we found Sir S. M. Fraser an able educationist, who could bring out the hidden talents of Sri Nalwadi Krishnaraja Wodeyar. The British Resident of the state Col. Robertson was compassionate and wise in his guidance of the Maharaja. Added to all this, the most beneficial boon came from an experienced ruler Queen Mother as Regent of the state. I am convinced that an inbuilt sense of fairness in judgement and possession of dispassionate qualities came to be nurtured by the heart of the Maharaja. This miraculous political evolution has enabled the Maharaja to take the reins of power and make a success of it. He has studied the problems of his subjects by travelling extensively in his kingdom. He has first-hand knowledge of their trials and tribulations. This acquired knowledge and his personal discernment of problems will help him resolve any crises. He is blessed with immense confidence and a perfect vision to guide Mysore State to a brighter future.

May Almighty bless his rule to be smooth and benevolent in the coming years." (*Translation from Kannada source – not the original speech*).

Later, Lord Curzon gave some suggestions about statecraft. He did not want it to be construed as high-sounding advice. Some guidelines were conveyed to Nalwadi:

a. The well-being and happiness of several lakhs of people depend on his political decisions.
b. They have reposed immense faith in Nalwadi's rule. If the rule is not benevolent, they will be disappointed.
c. The throne of Mysore is not meant as a couch for relaxation.
d. The people of the state will conduct themselves as law-abiding citizens if the royal rule is just and fair.

e. If you serve the people of the state with sincere dedication, your image will be etched permanently in their hearts. If not, your name will be written on water. A lacklustre rule will make people forget the ruler.

The Three Salient Points

The administration of the new Maharaja should not disappear into thin air like smoke. I reiterate once again please remember these words of good will at this crucial juncture. The ruler must strive to improve the lives of people with hard work. Let your rule be inspired by good will. You must be just, bold and compassionate towards the unfortunate and behave with everyone with modesty and humility.

Do rule the state with the belief that you are going to be alive for 5 years and not 50 years. In other words, you must be in a hurry to accomplish your goals. There is no place for lethargy and idleness. Every moment is precious and ought not to be wasted. Lord Curzon did not mince words while communicating with others. He believed in calling a spade a spade. This quotation from a biography of Lord Curzon written by Lord Ronaldshay sums up the man.

> *"Lord Curzon visited the native states in which no Viceroy had ever set foot before. Wherever he went, his utterances were followed with unusual interest, for in place of conventional compliments he spoke frankly what was in his mind."*

- pp. 144 – 45, Vol. II, **"The Life of Lord Curzon"** by Lord Ronaldshay.

This is what Lord Curzon said about the Indian Government,

> *"The Indian Government is like an elephant, very stately, very powerful, with high standard of intelligence, but with a regal slowness in its gait."*

(Vide page 64, Vol II, **"The Life of Lord Curzon,"** by Lord Ronaldshay).

These words prove that Lord Curzon was unsparing in his comments about the British Raj as well. He had reserved vitriolic criticism for Indian princely states, where the rulers were inept, corrupt and decadent

Lord Curzon was known for his frank and fearless comments. Such an individual blessed with fine critical sensibility expressed high praise for the rule of Sri Chamarajendra Wodeyar, Queen Mother Sri Vani Vilasa Sannidhana and Sri Nalwadi Krishnaraja Wodeyar as a future ruler of the state, because of his education and training. Lord Curzon gave Nalwadi sound advice and pointed out the essential qualities of a good administrator. Nevertheless, Nalwadi already possessed most of these qualities in abundant measure.

During his investiture ceremony, Nalwadi received very expensive mementoes, artworks and gifts. The Maharaja of Bhavanagar, in a rare gesture, had given Sri Nalwadi Krishnaraja Wodeyar a rare breed of white-bellied blackbucks with white spiralling horns as a special gift. The commander of the Warwickshire regiment having its headquarters in Belgaum requested the Maharaja to give one blackbuck as a gift to the regiment so that they could make blackbuck as their regimental symbol on the flag. But the Maharaja was unwilling to spare even one blackbuck. But had given several blackbucks to Sri Nalwadi as a gift on the occasion of the investiture ceremony.

The British Government had appointed Sir Evan Maconochie, K. C. I. E., C. S. I. as Private Secretary to the Maharaja of Mysore. These are the words of Sir Evan Maconochie, "A word of tribute is due to her highness the Maharani, late regent. A certain clinging to power would have been more than excusable on the part of a lady of character and education, who for the six (eight?) years of minority had ruled the state. But I can say that never during the seven years I spent in Mysore was I aware of the faintest indication on her part of a desire to intrude, even in minor personal matters upon her son's domain. Dignity and good sense could no further go" (p 140, "Life in the Indian Civil Service," by Sir Evan Maconochie, K. C. I. E., C. S. I.) The Private Secretary Sir Evan Maconochie writes in his memories, there could not have been a more valuable and rare gift than a few blackbucks sent by Maharaja of Bhavanagar. It is symbolic of his intense love and respect for the royal family of Mysore. The Queen regent came to rule the state under tragic circumstances. But even though she ruled the state efficiently for eight long years, she did not develop any special attachment to the post of regent. She gave up her post selflessly and encouraged her young son Nalwadi to take over the reins of power. Afterwards, not even once did she interfere with Nalwadi's decisions. She was not power-hungry in the least.

Lord Curzon led Sri Nalwadi Krishnaraja Wodeyar to his throne and assisted him in climbing the steps of the golden throne and occupying it. He occupied another equally regal ornate chair meant for the Viceroy. The master of the ceremonies the Under Secretary of the Foreign Department read out loud the honourable titles attributed to the Maharaja and announced that the baton of power had been passed over to the Maharaja from Queen Regent Sri Vani Vilas Sannidhana. Soon after this, the British Military Band played the British National Anthem "God save the King." The 21-gun salute was offered to the visiting dignitary the Viceroy of India and also to the new Maharaja of Mysore. The Viceroy of India presented the Maharaja with valuable gifts along with a certificate of appreciation.

Thanksgiving Speech of Nalwadi

Sri Nalwadi Krishnaraja Wodeyar stood up to deliver a thanksgiving speech as a reply to Lord Curzon's speech. The Viceroy was an elder statesman known for his oratorical skills, but still, he occasionally looked at notes he had brought with him to bolster his speech. But eighteen-year-old Nalwadi made an impromptu English speech which was marked by good diction and perfect pronunciation, which surprised the dignitaries and journalists alike.

At the outset, Sri Nalwadi Krishna Raja Wodeyar expressed his immense faith and respect for his majesty King Edward the seventh and informed the audience, how glad he was that the King-Emperor had recovered from his recent illness. Nalwadi also informed the Viceroy that the royal family and the citizens of Mysore State were happy to welcome him during his second visit to the state.

Nalwadi informed the Viceroy that he was fully aware of the enormous burden that had fallen upon his young shoulder. He said that he wanted to prove his sincere intentions through charitable acts and not by way of words. He was fully conscious of his rich legacy and inheritance from his ancestors. He was aware that the able rule of his predecessors like Sri Chamarajendra Wodeyar, Queen Regent and who were assisted by able civil servants and administrators was wholly responsible for the all-round development of the state. Nalwadi clarified that he would not rest on the laurels of his predecessors.

It was his responsibility to maintain the present amenities and comforts provided to the populace. In fact, he had the additional responsibility of improving their standard of living. "I hope my sincere endeavour to improve the quality of life will be blessed by the almighty God. I also look forward to an extended stay of British resident of Mysore State Col. Donald Robertson, who is a well-wisher of the state. This factor will be crucial in the modernisation of the state." - Sri Nalwadi.

The formal thanks rendered by Nalwadi, "I have also benefitted largely by the six years of higher education imparted by my mentor Sir S. M. Fraser. He has driven home to me, what a heavy responsibility lies on the shoulder of a ruler. On my part, I will make every sincere attempt to better the lives of the people and this desire will not be lacking in me.

The state of Mysore is blessed with bountiful nature, rich mineral deposits, forest wealth, dutiful law-abiding subjects and dedicated officials responsive to the needs of the population. I intend to provide a lasting safe heaven for the people. I pray to Almighty to give me strength and wisdom to rule the state without fear or favour in the coming years."

The British resident formally introduced the Viceroy of India Lord Curzon to the various dignitaries of Mysore State. Later, some of these eminent men including, Diwan P. N. Krishna Murti, Sardar M. Kantharaja Urs, Col. Desharaja Urs, Sardar Lakshmikantharaja Urs and Sri T. R. A. Thumboo Chetty and 46 others presented Nazar to Lord Curzon. The Viceroy symbolically touched the gold and silver coins proffered to him on a handkerchief and returned it.

The Viceroy of India Lord Curzon offered a silver tray of betel leaves, Areca nut and Attar (perfume) to the Maharaja. The Under Secretary of foreign affairs offered the "Tamboola" (the above-mentioned ingredients) to the Dewan of Mysore State. On behalf of the Under Secretary, the Mysore State Assistant Resident offered "Tamboola" to other Indian dignitaries. The Under Secretary of the foreign office declared that the investiture ceremony had come to a close.

When the Viceroy and the Maharaja left the hall, everyone stood up and showed their respect. At that time, 31 Cannon Gun salute was offered to the departing Viceroy. The Maharaja Nalwadi Sri Krishnaraja Wodeyar retired to his palace.

The august gathering consisting of Europeans and Indians expressed fulsome praise to the impromptu acceptance speech of the Maharaja rendered in King's English. The various English language newspapers expressed their opinion on Nalwadi's speech:

1. "The Speech of the Viceroy was full of advice to the young Maharaja and was delivered in such measured tone as to make a deep impression upon all present. With just a few notes in his hand, the Viceroy delivered his speech while the youthful ruler of Mysore excelled His Excellency by not having even a scrap of paper in his hand to refer to. The delivery of the

speech by His Highness was considered to be eminently good and his articulation exceptionally accurate."

2. "Though His Highness Sri Krishnaraja Wodeyar Bahadur, the newly installed Maharaja of Mysore is only eighteen years of age, still he seems to possess some of the qualities of more mature years. His reply to the address of the Viceroy was praised by everybody both in regard to diction and sentiment... ...the young Maharaja standing in a perfectly straight posture before the Viceroy and in front of a large and distinguished audience of Europeans and Indians burdened with vague notions of the gravity of the occasion and still with vaguer notions of the responsibilities that he was that day called upon to undertake, did not betray the least nervousness while delivering the speech. He did not have a printed speech in his hand nor any notes of catch-words to help him. Like that of a practised platform speaker in a loud and distinct voice, with manly intonation and without hesitation or omission of a single word, his delivery came on his hearers as a surprise. Everybody received the impression that the young Maharaja had a good deal of pluck and confidence in him."

In the afternoon after the investiture ceremony, the 26 leading citizens of the Mysore State presented the new Maharaja with various memorandums in English, Kannada and Urdu languages heralding his rule. The young Maharaja read these representations one by one. He gave suitable replies to these dignitaries in English, Kannada and Urdu languages depending on the respective language employed by that particular gentleman. The various newspapers of the state also praised the young Maharaja's excellent speech.

The Age of Reform

After taking over the reins of power, Nalwadi introduced several reforms in state administration. This entailed additional work for the ruler, who was already burdened with the daily chore of work. An English correspondent wrote from India about the new Maharaja in a British newspaper named "Western Daily Mercury" - "The Maharaja is to be no figurehead. His training has been conducted with a view to obtaining complete knowledge and mastery of the details of the administration of his country. He has been instructed in finance and law and has sat for practice in the Judicial capacity on the Bench with local Magistrates. Added to these qualifications, he has had an education of the best kind from a civilized point of view."

Nalwadi, with the help of his private secretary belonging to I.C.S, managed to effect many sweeping reforms. In the past, Dewans of Mysore State had appropriated many of the powers of the rulers. Sri. Nalwadi on the day of his investiture enacted a new legislative act, which revolutionised the state administration. These following rules were immediately introduced to awaken a moribund administration.

i. The Executive council chairman was Dewan of the Mysore state. Two members were appointed as councillors to this committee to assist the Dewan. This consultative committee has the power to make the required recommendations to the Maharaja. In the past, three elderly retired legislative assembly members were usually appointed as ministers to this committee to help the Dewan. These elderly gentlemen rarely expressed any dissent against the decisions of the Dewan. Those gubernatorial posts entailed additional income for these retirees. These members were handicapped by advanced age and poor health. Nalwadi stipulated that the two members of the committee should be around 55 years of age.

ii. Nalwadi introduced new rules to regulate the functioning of this executive council.

iii. The Dewan and two other ministers were allocated the responsibility of various state departments. They had to monitor the allotted departments for their successful functioning.

iv. The Executive council had to discuss the burning problems of each department and make suitable recommendations to the Maharaja for their rectification.

v. The routine business of these departments was to be conducted by the concerned officials of the department in consultation with the Private secretary and Dewan before making important decisions. The Government circulars had to be issued by the secretary.

The Executive council was authorized to impose new taxes, reduce or cancel already existing taxes, enact new laws appointing low-ranking and high-ranking posts and also empowered to create new posts, which often contravened the existing hierarchy of posts in the concerned departments. The Executive council had the power to dismiss a Government official from his post if found corrupt or inefficient. They also made provision for the modernisation of the state army. They prepared the annual budget taking into account state expenditure and income. They also deliberated on problems and issues referred to by the Maharaja. However, the final approval for any policy rested with the ruler of the state.

Even in matters that concerned a particular minister, where he had the liberty to make a decision if the decision was not to the liking of the Dewan, he could refer this matter to the Executive Council for a thorough discussion. After debating the matter, the Dewan whose prerogative it was to make an independent recommendation to the Maharaja, who either endorsed it or rejected it.

The two councils of Ministers had the power to pass a Government order related to their respective departments, if they failed to pass a relevant order, then Dewan could pass an order on their behalf. He was required to send a copy of the order with a written explanation to the concerned minister and also to the Maharaja. A new post of Revenue Commissioner was created and Sri. V. P. Madhava Rao, one of the council ministers was appointed as head of this newly created department. The functioning of the Secretariat at Bangalore was made more efficient and effective through various reforms. Even the palace administration was spruced up to function efficiently.

A highly respected elder statesman reacted to a press report that if the new reforms were implemented, in that case, Maharaja Nalwadi and his private Secretary had to slog like a lowly clerk in the Government department from morning to dusk. This comment was published in the newspaper "The Mysore Herald" dated 18th August 1902 and the editor wrote, "We wish that his Highness the Maharaja and the private secretary will practically show that they are prepared to work so." The news report irked the Maharaja greatly. Some four days later, the Maharaja ordered a special session of the people's representative council. While addressing the people's representative council, he remarked that the new administrative reforms are being implemented with diligence. Their success or failure depends on the efficient working of bureaucratic machinery headed by the Dewan.

It is wrong to assume that the ruler will agree with all the recommendations made by members. It is not realistic to expect that members of the council will always endorse a uniform opinion. We must remember even the dissenters have the welfare of the state in their heart of hearts. Soon, it became obvious to one and all that the new ruler meant well and worked very hard for the welfare of the state. There was no room for lethargy or procrastination.

Every day, the Maharaja devoted a few hours to going through the files sent to him for his scrutiny. He meticulously went through the files writing his comments, instructions and orders often running to several pages. Every morning at 11 AM, he entered his personal office located at Jagan Mohan Vilas palace and worked till lunch hour attending to the day's businesses. The files and papers would have been kept ready for his perusal by the private secretary. He did not keep any file in limbo and disposed of it with great alacrity.

The private secretary to the Maharaja, Sir Evan Maconochie K.C.I.E, C.S.I writes in his autobiography *"Life in the Indian civil service"* - "During the first year or two, the internal relations of the council were not always harmonious and the Maharaja was frequently placed in a position of having to decide between the view of the Dewan and of a dissentient councillor, who was as often as not in the right. It was essential for every reason, to support the minister as far as practicable and it was not always to reconcile that policy with the interests of efficiency and progress."

The onus was on the Maharaja to make an appropriate decision neither favouring the Dewan nor the concerned minister. Whenever the Maharaja appointed a qualified and experienced Indian official to a high-ranking post previously held by a Britisher, it often led to a lot of heartburn. The retired British official and his admirers frowned upon the new appointment as a policy of Indianisation or an instrument of compromise to promote mediocrity.

Some of the administrative reforms did not go well with even Mysore citizens, who had vested interests close to their hearts. If their privileges or financial interests were affected by the new reforms, they often complained to the British resident or Governor General against the Maharaja. They often blamed the Maharaja for taking bad advice from the British Private Secretary. The young Maharaja was often compelled to do a lot of tightrope walking. He openly expressed his love and admiration for upright, hard-working British civil servants. But he regularly faced flak from natives and also from the British community.

In his inaugural speech, he had assured the Viceroy Lord Curzon that he would administer the state without fear nor by seeking any favour from any quarter. The Maharaj proved himself as a good judge of men and matters. In the midst of a troublesome crisis, he often exhibited exemplary patience. He was not given to any severe agitation or unwarranted impatience in making vital decisions. The Maharaja faced innumerable problems and obstacles in the early years of his rule. His private secretary expressed immense praise for the Maharaja's administration. He ignored the unfounded criticism levelled by ignoramuses and uninformed critics. Some of them did not understand the complex nature of the problem. Some selfish people were grieved because their vested interests were affected. But Nalwadi never wavered from his decision and never went against his conscience during his rule.

He remained calm and composed during a crisis. He carried himself with a lot of dignity. The private secretary, Sir Evan Maconochie writes in his autobiography that although the Maharaja was junior to him in years, as far as wisdom and sagacity were concerned, he was senior to him in years. The private secretary writes 16 years after relinquishing his office with a finality that the Maharaja will remain so forever ("in some respects, he was and always will be an older man than myself"). He gives the instance of a hypocrite, who had impressed the private secretary with his false humility and modesty. This gentleman wanted some favour from the Maharaja. He pursued the private secretary with great diligence. Finally, Sir Evan Maconochie recommended the case of this favour seeker. But the Maharaja rejected the petition promptly. In a private conversation, the Maharaja briefed the private secretary about the man's antecedents. He was a worthless liar, hypocrite and lowly scum, who did not deserve any special favours from the Government. This came as a revelation to the private secretary.

Administrator Par Excellence

Sir Nalwadi Krishnaraja Wodeyar conceived many new and big projects which would modernize Mysore State. During the execution of these projects, the Maharaja remained calm and composed. He pursued these projects with single-minded zeal and enthusiasm. The princely state of Mysore achieved a rare distinction according to Sir Evan Maconochie – "It was in all essentials far ahead of any other Indian state of that day." Nalwadi, even in the midst of several onerous responsibilities and mental stress, never lost his cool or sense of humour.

One day, a few years into his reign, he visited a school in Mysore city. He found out that the school lacked basic infrastructure like sports equipment. Most of the sports items were old and broken, hence unusable. He questioned a student about this state of affairs. The student informed the Maharaja that they played no games in the playground as their sports equipment was useless. Maharaja went back to the palace and ordered the officials to deliver sports equipment lying unused in the royal school to the students of this particular Government school. Once upon a time, they were used by Nalwadi and his classmates in the royal school.

Since the time of Sri. Chamarajendra Wodeyar, the Mysore palace maintained a dairy. The royal family claimed to be the descendants of Lord Krishna of Hindu mythology. Bhagavan Sri Krishna is a well-known cowherd. The cows and calves were housed in a building called "*Karohatti.*" The cows and buffaloes were looked after by a manager called Daroga Chaluvaiah. He was an old man, who had taken employment here during the reign of Sri Chamarajendra Wodeyar. He was on familiar terms with Maharaja Nalwadi Krishnaraja Wodeyar.

The Maharaja had cultivated the habit of visiting the palace dairy on Friday mornings. He worshipped cows, which are sacred to pious Hindus. Daroga Chaluvaiah and his staff would bathe the cows and calves. They would clean the cowsheds with water. They also decorated the entrance arch and gate with banana plant stalks and Mango leaves. Due to a busy schedule, the Maharaja could not keep up with his Friday visits to "Karohatti" for a few weeks. Nalwadi visited "Karohatti" after a few days. Daroga Chaluvaiah, as an elderly caretaker, took the liberty to address the Maharaja on familiar terms. He prayed to the Maharaja to visit the cows on Friday mornings to perform Puja. The Maharaja would earn "*Punya*" (The benefits accrued by an individual, because of good (Dharmic) deeds and that could be shared by the attendants as well.) On Fridays, workers would keep the cattle sheds neat and clean. Once, the Maharaja noticed that buffalos were not receiving proper attention. He told the workers to give regular baths to the buffalos and treat them with equal love and affection. Nalwadi paid surprise visits to "Karohatti." On one or two occasions, instead of visiting "Karohatti" on Fridays, he visited the dairy on Thursdays. He found the sheds of the diary dirty and cattle being neglected. The workers were lazying around. He found even a sheep lying about and which did not belong to the palace. He reprimanded Daroga Chaluvaiah for neglecting his duties. But his immense affection for Daroga Chaluvaiah came to the fore and it was expressed through a work of art. He commissioned a painter to paint a portrait of the cattle caretaker. It hung in a hall in "Karohatti" for a very long time.

Once, the famous Indian painter Raja Ravi Verma visited "Karohatti" in the company of the Maharaja. He remarked that he has visited a number of princely states in India, but nowhere cows and calves have been looked after so well by a ruler. Nalwadi gave full credit to Daroga Chaluvaiah for its upkeep and maintenance. This high praise from the Maharaja elicited a tender reaction from Daroga Chaluvaiah, who could only utter "*Mahaswamy, Mahaswamy*" with tears flowing down his cheeks.

The Maharaja was soft-spoken, mild-mannered and gentle in his ways. But when the occasion demanded, he could rise above his soft nature and express his honest and frank opinion about an individual. Nalwadi's mentor, Mr. Fraser, has written in his assessment report that the ruler of Mysore State was capable of saying "no" on many occasions. Once, the Maharaja was on his way to Sri Chamundi temple on the hill. His car was blocked by a grieving lady, who wanted to plead with him. Her husband was in jail facing the gallows on the charge of killing a person. She requested the Maharaja to save her "*Mangala Sutra*" (A black beaded neck chain symbolizing her married status). The Maharaja Nalwadi very curtly told her, that her husband had snatched away the "Mangala Sutra" of another unfortunate lady, who was now a widow for no fault of hers. He refused to intervene. As a ruler, he never condoned the conduct of a criminal, who had violated the law of the land.

The Maharaja discovered that Rs. 3,000 (a very huge amount in the early decades of the century) had been stolen from his bedroom. The Police officials zeroed in on a domestic help, who had run away with the money. They managed to track him down and arrest him. The culprit was a trusted aide, who had served the Maharaja loyally for a very long period. On enquiry, it was found out that he had incurred a huge debt and to save himself from ignominy, he had resorted to theft. The Maharaja was not only magnanimous enough in pardoning the servant but also took him back to service. He was capable of chiding an arrogant and pompous fellow and bringing him down to the sober levels of behaviour.

Nalwadi decided to pay a visit to a government school in a nearby village. He went there incognito, wearing a simple dress. The school teacher received this visitor and assumed him to be a young clerk from the education department, who had come for school inspection. The teacher indulged in self-praise and boasted about his teaching skills. He informed Nalwadi that he was a nightmare to his young students. They obeyed his orders implicitly. Nalwadi told this uncouth teacher that his two disobedient students were standing behind the school building. He should exercise his authority to get them inside the classroom. So saying, he walked out of the school premises. The poor teacher who was preparing his snuff powder for inhalation was taken aback by these words. On that morning, three or four of his students were absent. He rushed to the backyard of the school to fetch his errant students. But he found to his dismay two donkeys lazying around.

The Hindu Maharajas, like the kings of ancient Puranas (epics), kept in their stables a sacred horse, an elephant and a holy cow, which were worshipped during nine days of the Dasara festival. The royal sacred horse of Mysore State had become very old. The Maharaja wanted to replace it with a healthy young horse. So, he sent a palace official to visit Gujarat, Kathiawada and Rajasthan to buy a good horse for the palace stables. After a prolonged tour of five or six months, he returned to Mysore state with a few horses. The Maharaja came to the stables to view these horses. But this vainglorious official began a long-winded speech about the travails of his tour, the difficulties and obstacles he confronted in these states. He would not conclude his tedious tale despite Nalwadi's disapproval. Nalwadi laughingly remarked to this tiresome individual, "I hope you will discuss the purchase of horses today itself. Will you be kind enough to show them today, so that I can select one of them as the royal sacred horse?" He was capable of throwing cold water on the face of any individual, who crossed the line of rubicon. During the early years of his reign, he worked hard day and night for the welfare of the state. His youthful years were not devoted to fun and frolic. Even during a severe illness, he carried on with his stately duties without showing any sign of discomfort or exhaustion.

The Royal school head Mr. Fraser writes in his autobiography, "In 1898, His Highness the Maharaja was down with Quinsy tonsils and suffered very badly. But it was most extraordinary that he never complained of pain and stoically bore it. It was remarkable for a boy of fourteen years."

Maharaja's Daily Chores

Nalwadi kept some of his residential school day habits even after assuming his office. He woke up very early everyday morning at 5 AM. After taking a bath, he would perform Puja. After drinking a cup of coffee, he went out to exercise his horses until 8.30 AM. He would have requested his Private Secretary and sometimes a few other high-ranking officials for a tete-a-tete. While riding their favourite horses, they would discuss state affairs.

Later, he visited the stables and kennels for an encounter with his pets. He would give horses sugar cubes, greens, carrots, turnips, etc. He loved to feed his dogs with biscuits. He would return to the palace at 9.30 AM. He again took a bath and got dressed up for breakfast with his family members. He promptly left for his office at 11.00 AM to attend to state affairs. He attended to files and wrote brief comments or instructions on them. They became state Government orders through the Private Secretary. In the afternoon, he met visitors and delegates who wanted to confer with him.

In the evening, he sometimes played polo or squash (racket) at Chittranjan Mahal palace. He often went with his friends in a horse-drawn coach on long drives to see the sunset from the foot hill of Chamundi or to drive through "Thandisadak." A street behind the zoo lined with long arbour with creepers grown over semi-circular steel structures throughout the length of the street. In the evening, he played his favourite musical instruments piano, violin, flute and Indian percussion instruments. He also read several English and vernacular newspapers. He loved listening to Carnatic classical music and read a number of books in English and Kannada. Again, he would take a bath in the evening. Afterwards, he performed "Sandhyavandan" (Evening offering of oblation to Gods) and performed Shiva Puja every day before dinner. It was his practice to spend an hour with his mother discussing state business and family matters. He always went to bed at 9:30 PM or 10:30 PM every day.

Chapter 8

The First 25 Years of Nalwadi's Reign (1902-1927)

******

Sam Gachhadvam Sam Vadadvam
Sam vo manamsi jaanathaam|
Devaa baagam yathaa purve
Sanjaanana upaasate||

******

Meaning 1: Let us march together; let us confer together. Let us understand our minds. In the hoary past, we worshipped our Gods after understanding their nature. (incomplete sentence)
Meaning 2: Like in the past, when Gods were worshipped after understanding them, let us march, let us develop one mind and let us speak in one voice being part of this heavenly assemblage.

Nalwadi began to rule the princely state of Mysore at the age of eighteen. Even though he was young, he exhibited a greater maturity in behaviour and thinking. He was considered a "*Karmayogi*" by many elderly courtiers. During his years of schooling, his mentor Mr. Fraser had given him training in public administration. He was also instructed by the British resident Col. Donald Robertson. He spent the hot summer months in Ooty, a hill station in Nilgiris. Many high-ranking British officials regularly visited Ootacamund to escape the hot and sultry Indian summer. These officials were often invited by the Maharaja to Fern Hill Imperial Palace for consultation. From these interactions with British civil servants, the Maharaja garnered quite a lot of information and useful ideas for the modernization of Mysore State. Many concluded that the hardworking nature of the Maharaja was an inherited characteristic. Again, we can generously quote Sir Fraser, "Most important for a ruler, the Maharaja is gifted in a marked degree with common sense and the strong qualities of readiness to form his own judgement, self-reliance, a reticent self-control and the power to say 'No.'" Because of the Maharaja's enlightened outlook and pragmatic vision for the future, the state of Mysore came to occupy a prominent place in the comity of nations.

The Maharaja and the Yuvaraja with two other Polo players after winning a trophy.

Yuvaraja and his friends during his trip to England in 1913.
Standing: L to R:? ,?,?
Seated on chair: Yuvaraja
Sitting: L to R:?, Rajmantra Praveena Dewan Bhadur Poorna Raghavendra Rao.

Delhi Durbar (1902)

Edward the Seventh became the King-Emperor of the British Empire in 1901. He did not come to India in 1901 and the Delhi Durbar was held on 1st January 1902. He had sent his brother the Duke of Connaught with a large retinue of dignitaries to India. Lord Curzon, Viceroy of India invited Indian Maharajas, Nawabs and rich Indian businessmen to Delhi Durbar. Nalwadi Krishnaraja Wodeyar, his mother, former regent, and his younger brother Yuvaraja Sri. Kanteerava Narasimharaja Wodeyar and Maharani Lakshmi Vilas Sannidhana, Dewan Sir. P. N. Krishnamurti and the British resident Sir Donald Robertson accompanied the Royal entourage. They travelled by a special train to Poona and Bombay. They travelled from Bombay to Delhi by the same train. Around this time, Mysore State also received automobiles from England.

The Indian Government had created a tent city for VVIPs some 7 miles away from Delhi city. The Delhi Durbar was going to be held in a large field. There was enough space for 12,000 people to witness the Delhi Durbar. Everything was on a grand scale and Government had decorated tents and Shamianas for the occasion. Many of the Indian princes had vied with each other to make their tents very impressive. They had not bothered about the cost of the decoration and furnishings. But the tent occupied by the Maharaja of Mysore was spartan in its simplicity. He had avoided ostentation and pomp.

An arts and crafts exhibition was going on at the same time. Mysore State had showcased its products in the showroom. The exhibition was inaugurated by the Viceroy of India Lord Curzon. In his inaugural speech, he made a special reference to teak wood, rosewood and sandalwood products displayed by Mysore State. He said they were incomparable and exquisite in their craftsmanship.

Again in 1911, there was another Delhi Durbar for the visiting King George V and Queen Mary, who were proclaimed on 12th December 1911 as Emperor and Empress of India. Even during this commemorative event, the Maharaja of Mysore stayed in his simple and unostentatious tent. Whereas the other Nawabs and Maharajas lived in grand style displaying their wealth. The press reporters asked the Maharaja why he lived in such a simple style. He replied that the state money could be better spent on improving the quality of life of his subjects. He did not believe in wasting money on mere display of pomp and power for a brief period while staying in a transitory camp.

After the Delhi Durbar of 1902, the royal family went to the holy pilgrim centre of Haridwar. Here, they bathed in the holy Ganga River and visited temples and ashrams. Afterwards, they visited Agra city to see the world-renowned Taj Mahal built in white marble. They continued their journey to Jhansi, Bhopal, Bombay and finally, reached Bangalore city.

Yuvaraja's Education and Illness

At the end of the year 1903, Nalwadi sent his younger brother Yuvaraja Sri Kanteerava Narasimharaja Wodeyar to Mayo college, Ajmer, Rajasthan for higher studies. The Mayo college had been started by the Britishers as an exclusive residential school for the scions of the various royal families of India. After a few months, the Yuvaraja contracted typhoid. This news reached Mysore palace on Ugadi day (Hindu new year) in the year 1904 via a telegram. On the very same day, by a special train, the Maharaja, Queen regent and others left for Ajmer. They travelled 1,400 miles over a period of four days and reached Mayo college. They attended to the sick Yuvaraja and he recovered his health after a few days. At the invitation of the Maharaja of Bikaner, they visited his state and enjoyed his hospitality over a period of three days. The Maharaja of Mysore went on a hunting expedition in the forests of Bikaner. He shot some wild boars during the hunt. They all returned to Mysore along with the Yuvaraja. Nalwadi had withdrawn his younger brother from Mayo college. His education continued in Mysore and the royal school head was Capt. R.J.W. Hill. He taught the Yuvaraja for 3 years and his other teachers were Sri. M. A. Narayana Iyengar (At present known as Sri Sri Vasaananda Swamy) and Sri. M. A. Singharacharya.

L to R: Lt. Col B. P. Krishnarajae Urs
Sitting Prince Sri Kanteerava Narasimharaja Wodeyar, Janab M.G. Mekhri
Standing (L to R) Sri F.C. Devaraja Urs, Sri K. Subba Rao

Death of a Sister

The Maharaja suffered another bereavement in the family when he lost his sister Sri. Krishnajammani in November 1904. She was suffering from tuberculosis for the last three years. All kinds of medical treatments were tried but to no avail. This prompted the Maharaj to start a Tuberculosis sanatorium on the outskirts of Mysore city with his own funds. The hospital was named after his sister and the most modern types of medical treatment were introduced here for the benefit of tuberculosis patients. At the inaugural function, the Maharaja broke down and wept for his sister. He was emotionally attached to his family members.

Once, while riding his horse in the countryside, the Yuvaraja suffered a fall. As the Maharaja was on another horse in the near vicinity, he came to the rescue of his younger brother. The Yuvaraja had fractured his collarbone due to the fall. He took it upon himself to bandage the neck and chest with splints to protect the collarbone. Later, Orthopaedic surgeons attended to him.

On another occasion, the Yuvaraja was bedridden with an illness. The Maharaja personally attended to him. He would often sit beside his bed and pep up his spirits with encouraging talk. On many afternoons, he was found beside the sick patient's bed past lunch hour. The servants would come and plead with him to come for lunch. He would tell the bystanders his brother's health was closer to his heart rather than perfunctory lunch.

Tour to Madras

Nalwadi went on a tour to Madras and other places in 1905. He had visited Madras City on an earlier occasion in 1903 when there was an industrial and craft exhibition. His simple unassuming ways and informal attire appealed to the citizens. According to Sir Evan Maconochie, people gathered on the pavements of streets to see him pass by in his car. This young Maharaja had won the hearts of ordinary people with his dignified behaviour. The Maharaja attracted greater crowds than the Governor of Madras Presidency. In the evenings, he took a walk on the Marina beach. If he came across some old acquaintance from Mysore State, he would talk to them informally. Nalwadi became very popular during his ten-day stay in Madras. Later, he also visited several other religious places in Madras State.

Electrification of Bangalore

The princely state of Mysore shot into fame on 3rd August 1905 through the electrification of Bangalore city. Electric power had been generated for the first time in Shivana Samudram electricity generating station. The British were keen on getting electricity to Kolar Gold field town. They wanted to mine Gold with modern machinery which worked on electricity. But Bangalore city became the first Indian city to be electrified. In the year 1906, Mysore city came to be electrified. In 1905, the co-operative societies regulatory act was enacted. Initially, co-operative societies were established during 1906-1907, the public health department and veterinary science department were established. In 1908, the Mysore State Government under the orders of the Maharaja donated 5 lakhs rupees towards the construction of Tata Institute Buildings (present Indian Institute of Science).

State visit of Prince of Wales

In 1906, the Prince of Wales (Future King George the V) and his wife Princess Mary visited the Mysore State. They had heard a lot about the visionary Maharaja Sri Nalwadi Krishnaraja Wodeyar and his modern state. In many respects, it was more advanced than the other presidency states, which were directly ruled by the British. In 1906, the Maharaja organized a banquet in honour of the visiting prince of Wales and Princess Mary. While raising a toast to Maharaja, the Prince of Wales said, "...Under the lead which we may expect from such a capable and enlightened ruler as our kind host, with the assistance of statesmen of the type of the late Sri. K. Seshadri Iyer, your province may look forward with confidence to making still greater strides." At that time, Nalwadi was in the 4th year of his reign and he was aged only 22 years.

In the English newspaper "Graphic" dated 10th March 1906, a correspondent from India wrote this, "There is a peculiar interest attached to the visit of the Prince and Princess of Wales to Mysore for this is a native state, which is governed so wisely, that it had earned the proud name of the model state – a title which could hardly be claimed by any other native state. Indeed, so truly is the title deserved that in the discharge of the administrative and judicial duties, the Government of Mysore compares very favourably with that of British India... ...Under the wise rule of the present Maharaja, H. H. Krishnaraja Wodeyar Bahadur, Mysore has flourished exceedingly. Justice is administered with impartiality, taxation distributed with equity, education for women as well as men are encouraged and industry fostered."

The cavalry regiment of the palace army had been trained by Nalwadi and by the late Col. Deshraja Urs. The lancers of the Mysore imperial service corps gave a display of their skill on horses before the Prince and Princess of Wales. This is how an English journalist wrote in a daily newspaper, "Among the entertainments offered to the Prince during his visit was an equestrian display by the Lancers of the Imperial service corps. These men showed that in horsemanship, they were second to none. They rode bareback, stood up on their horses when going at full gallop, and picked things up from the ground without slackening speed. There seemed to be nothing which they could not do with their handsome chargers. It is no wonder that the Prince was loud in his praise of these fine troops." The Maharaja had organised an exhibition to showcase Mysore State's industrial products.

The Prince and Princess of Wales were going to Srirangapattanam on 30th Jan 1906 to see historical places connected with Tippu Sultan. A police constable travelling on a bicycle was pedalling towards Srirangapattanam on the same highway. He happened to fall from the bicycle resulting in the fracture of a leg bone. He was lying on the road in a terrible condition. The Prince of Wales noticed this poor police constable lying on the road in a helpless condition. He stopped the car, got down from the car and rushed to the aid of the injured person. Soon, the other cars with dignitaries arrived at the accident spot. The Prince of Wales asked the medical staff to give the policeman first aid. Then, he was rushed to the hospital in another car. The Prince of Wales, future King George the V left the place after attending to this injured individual personally. The next morning, on 31st January 1906, the royal couple left for Kharapura. They stayed in the jungle lodge to witness the elephant khedda operation. It was scheduled for 2nd February 1906. The princely state of Mysore was famous for this khedda operation.

Once in 3 or 4 years, they would try to trap wild Elephants in a khedda operation with the help of tamed elephants. The soliga tribes would drive wild elephants from different directions towards the khedda pit. These tribal people would dig a circular deep pit. It would be surrounded by tall tree trunks erected like a barricade around the pit. One end of the tree trunk with a sharpened end would be placed in a hold in the ground and later it was all plastered up. The tree trunks placed next to each other were tied with coir ropes. There was one narrow entrance to the pit with wooden gates erected for the occasion. The path to the pit was a long narrow passage lined with tree trunk barricades. The circular pit had VVIP viewing machans (platforms) with sofas. The guests had to climb a step ladder to reach the viewing stands. The Soliga tribesmen knew how the wild elephants behaved and where they could be found in the forest. They usually made a lot of din to scare the wild elephants by beating drums, blowing trumpets and lighting firecrackers, which made very loud noise. They also carried with them burning torches. The elephants are afraid of fire in the forest. Then, scared elephants would begin to run and they were herded by tamed elephants to move towards the khedda pit. The angry and injured elephants with their young ones were trapped in the pit and its gates were closed. These wild elephants often turned violent. They would charge at the wooden barricade in great rage. The whole spectacle of trapping wild elephants in this manner greatly amused the Prince and Princess of Wales.

Women's Education

The women's education in Mysore State received a fillip from Maharani Regent Smt. Vanivilasa Sannidhana and later from Nalwadi Sri. Krishnaraja Wodeyar. A girls' school named after the regent was founded in 1881. Because of the Maharani's initiative, it soon became a high school. In the year 1889, during November Prince of Wales (Albert Victor) visited Mysore State. He paid a visit to the girls' high school and commented that it was a model school. In 1891, the Maharani Regent upgraded the girls' high school to the status of a second-grade college. In 1901, it became a full-fledged college called Maharani College with the introduction of the first-year degree course. A visiting British dignitary wrote in the visitors book, "It stands absolutely in the van (Vanguard?) of female education in India and may be regarded as one of the brightest jewels in the crown of H.H. The Maharaja of Mysore." – Sir Roper Lathebridge.

In 1902, the Maharani college for women announced that Muslims, Christians, Jews and others could join the college along with Hindu women. Each lady student was given a scholarship amount of Rs. 30 by the Maharaja. In 1905, two Anglo-Indian girls passed the Matriculation exams. In the lower secondary examination (present-day 7th standard) 50 girl students managed to pass the examination. One girl student had scored not only a high first class, she had scored the highest aggregate marks surpassing all the boys of the state. The Prince and Princess of Wales visited the Maharani college and appreciated the efforts of the ruler of Mysore State in making giant strides in women's education. Even in this respect, Mysore State was ahead of other Indian states.

dewan Retires and a New Dewan Takes Over the State Administration

Sir. P. N. Krishnamurti Dewan of Mysore State retired on 30th March 1906. As a judicial officer, he had passed many landmark judgements in several legal cases. When he was deputy commissioner of Tumkur district, he had to go to Mysore during the Dasara festival to attend the Indian Darbar. He was informed by the Police that there could be a Hindu-Muslim communal riot in Tumkur in his absence. During that period, the Moharrum festival coincided with Dasara festivities. So, he travelled throughout the night by car to reach Tumkur. The next morning, he summoned the Hindu and Muslim leaders to his residence. He requested them to maintain communal harmony and not to get involved in rioting. Thereby, he avoided trouble in Tumkur. Sir P. N. Krishnamurti relied on the advice of some well-wishers, who were not known for administrative experience or wisdom. According to Sir Evan Machonochie, the Dewan was not given to a disciplined regimen. He was not hard-working. He was a patriot and a loyalist. But he did not become popular with his subjects. Sri. V. P. Madhava Rao succeeded as Dewan for the next three years. Before becoming the Dewan of Mysore State, he was a member of the Executive Council and for a brief while, Dewan of Travancore State. In 1907, the king-emperor Albert Edward VII conferred upon Sri. Nalwadi Krishnaraja Wodiyar the title of G.C.S.I in recognition of his services to the state (Knight Grand Commander- Order of the Star of India). In Bangalore city, under the chairmanship of Dewan Sir. P. N. Krishnamurti a felicitation function for Nalwadi was organized at Lalbagh. The Maharaja was honoured and feted by the Bangalore public and he was presented with a grand eloquent memorandum and memento. In Mysore city, the members of the "Arasu Gymkhana club" under the auspices of Sardar M. Kantharaje Urs organised a felicitation function on 11th March 1907 and presented the Maharaja with a memorandum. The citizens of Mysore City organized a felicitation function for the Maharaja at Sri Rangacharlu Town Hall on 16th March 1907. They presented the Maharaja with a memorandum recording his extraordinary services to the state.

In his reply, the Maharaja stated modestly that he had completed only 4 years of his reign. In his opinion, what he had accomplished so far was very little and what had to be accomplished remained huge and stared at him in his face. He was aware of his immense responsibilities towards his subjects. I fully repose my faith in the Almighty to accomplish my goals. He said his goal in life was to make this beautiful state a heaven on Earth and he wanted to keep his subjects happy. He only prayed to God to give him good health and plenty of energy to work day and night for the welfare of the people. He did not want to hinder the fast-paced growth of the state even in the slightest manner. Throughout his reign, he never wavered from his straight path in achieving his goals.

We are aware of the fire mishap in the year 1897, wherein the old palace caught fire during a marriage ceremony and the centuries-old wooden building was reduced to ashes. Soon after that tragic incident, the new palace building construction began in earnest. It took 12 years to complete the construction of the present palace building. But a formal *"Gruhapravesha"* (house occupation ritual) was performed on 5th June 1907 on a grand scale.

Karnataka Legislative Council

The Legislative Council was established on 22nd June 1907 in the former Mysore State to associate certain non-official persons having experience and knowledge of local conditions to assist the government in enacting new Laws and Regulations. Besides the Dewan, the President and the Members of the Council, who were ex-officio members at that time the Council consisted of not less than 10 and not more than 15 additional members to be nominated by the Government, out of which not less than two-fifths were required to be non-officials. The strength of the Council was increased gradually and in 1923 it was fixed at 50. In 1914, the Council was empowered to discuss the Budget and in 1923, it was given power to vote on the demands for grants. From 1919 onwards, resolutions were discussed in the Council. The term of the Council was three years in 1917 and four years in 1940.

Nalwadi's father, Sri. Chamarajendra Wodeyar, had established for the first time in India People's Representative Assembly in 1886. After establishing the Legislative Council, the Government requested the Representative assembly to nominate two members to the new body.

Tour to Japan Cancelled

The Maharaja wanted to visit Japan in the year 1908. All the travel arrangements had been made on his behalf. Japan had made remarkable progress in Industrialization within a period of 50 years. The GDP of Japan had increased by six times within 12 years (1896-1908) [Ed. Note: It is relevant to note that Sir. M. Visveshwaraya, the former Dewan of Mysore state also visited Japan to study its economic miracle in 1898 at his own cost and he stayed in Japan for 3 months). But during this year, a severe drought afflicted Mysore State. Nalwadi did not want to forsake his subjects to the whimsical vagaries of fate. He decided to stay back and attend to massive relief work. Instead, he sent his younger brother Yuvaraja Sri Kanteerava Narasimharaja Wodeyar to Japan to study the changes taking place in that country.

The Maharaja asked the Dewan not to spare any resources or efforts in mitigating the suffering of the people in drought-hit districts. He told the Dewan to exhaust all the funds of the treasury, if necessary to feed the hungry people. He did not want any citizen to die of hunger.

He suppressed his irresistible desire to visit these drought-hit areas. Because his visit would only mean more expenditure to the villagers. In those days, the Maharaja was welcomed in villages with welcome arches, plantain stalks, Mango leaf decorations, Garlands, Fruits and other paraphernalia which cost them money. He did not want to tax them during a distressing period. He even told a confidant that he would cancel his summer vacation trip to Ooty if the drought did not subside by then.

Fortunately, all the efforts of the state Government to combat drought produced beneficial results. The efforts of the Government avoided deaths and immense hardship for millions. The state soon received abundant rainfall during the monsoon season by God's grace. In a palace banquet on 28th October 1909, Sir M. Fraser in his speech paid sumptuous tributes to the remarkable drought relief work done by his protege.

"I am not competent to evaluate the relief work executed by the Government officials. When the signs of a terrible drought appeared on the horizon of the Mysore state, a remarkable noble gentleman exhibited exemplary qualities of social work, not during normal times, but during a crisis. I am referring to the dedicated service to the people by His Highness Nalwadi Krishnaraja Wodeyar.

During last December the Maharaja was about to leave for Japan and his passage had been booked in advance. But he cancelled his trip in the interest of his suffering people. This noble gesture of the Maharaja had a great impact on his civil servants. They were enthused by this decision of the Maharaja to work with greater enthusiasm. These noble actions of the Maharaja have not only brought him accolades, but it has also earned him the immense love and affection of his people. God has blessed Mysore State with abundant rainfall during this year." The Maharaja in his reply remarked that, if he had gone ahead with his Japan tour, he would have betrayed the interests of his people, which was dearer to his heart. He was now very happy that those trying times were over. The Yuvaraja of Mysore had left for Japan on 26th January 1908 and he returned to his state on 21st March 1909. When he arrived with his retinue by a special train, he was given a warm welcome by the loving public consisting of the Dewan of the state, Sardars, officials, vedic pandits and relatives. They offered him garlands and bouquets as a sign of their love and respect. The soldiers of the Mysore army gave him a guard of honour and he was welcomed by the palace band. He was taken through the streets of Mysore in an open car. The streets were lined with thousands of cheering crowds. At the palace, Nalwadi received him with great affection and made enquiries about his trip. The Dewan V. P. Madhava Rao retired on 1st April 1909. The Maharaja nominated Sri. T. Ananda Rao, a member of the executive council as the in-charge Dewan of the state. When he was serving in the police department, he had reorganized the department on more efficient lines. He had introduced many reforms in the revenue department to improve tax collection. When he was a deputy commissioner, he initiated the digging of drinking water wells in his district. One Amaldar remarked that during hot summer months, only these wells replenished the needs of the villagers. These rural people remembered Sri Ananda Rao with gratitude.

End of the Devadasi Practise

Even in the princely state of Mysore, the Devadasi system prevailed; the girls belonging to this caste had been dedicated to temple deities. They were dancers and musicians by profession. However, the wealthy people had transformed them to the status of concubines. Nalwadi banned these inhuman and exploitative practices through a legislative act in May 1909. This was lauded by the English-language newspapers of Madras and other states. One Britisher appreciated the tough decision of the Maharaja to end this obnoxious practice. The Maharaja of Mysore appointed Sri K. P. Puttanna Chetty belonging to the Veerashaiva community as a council member of the executive council. The leaders of the Verashaiva community organised a felicitation function to thank His Highness Sri Nalwadi in Bangalore on 8th June 1909. They presented the Maharaja with a memorandum and thanked him profusely for his kind gesture. The Maharaja in his reply stated that educational facilities and job opportunities in Mysore State were open to one and all. Anyone who is talented and meritorious and deserves this kind of encouragement and due recognition were welcome. This is a good example of the state Government's preference for meritocracy in public service. Later, this person was elevated to the post of Dewan of Mysore state (The Bangalore town hall built in 1936 bears his name).

Animal Fair

In the city of Mysore, an animal fair was organised on the 26th and 27th of October 1909. These animals were on show-harness horses, polo game horses, dogs, cows, calves, buffaloes and sheep. Sri. Nalwadi was the chairman of the panel of judges. They identified the best breed of cows, horses and dogs, and their individual owners were rewarded with trophies and silver cups. He was very much particular that calves should not be denied their due share of mother cow's milk. When he was asked by a visitor why he had not visited a particular town in his state in recent times, he replied that good-quality milk was not available in that town. This news surprised the visitor and he said that his highness was in the wrong. Nalwadi replied that the people of the town sold all the cow's milk, thereby denying any milk to the calves. He did not frequent such a town and he was reluctant to consume that kind of milk.

In Mysore city, in November 1909, an exhibition of healthcare products was displayed in stalls. The ladies of the royal family led by Maharani Regent Sri Vani Vilas Sannidhana, Maharani Sri. Lakshmivilasa Sannidhana and the eldest princess Sri. Jayalaksmammani visited this health fair on 5th November 1909. Sri Sardar Kantheraje Urs escorted the ladies around the exhibition ground. On 6th November 1909, Yuvaraja Sri Kanteerava Narasimha Raja Wodeyar attended the valedictory function and distributed prizes to various participants.

The Equestrian Sports in Mysore

The Maharaja, Yuvaraja and other royal family's male members were interested in sports activities such as "polo," "rackets," "tennis," "Billiards," etc. The Mysore royal polo team enjoyed a great reputation all over India.

The Mysore royal polo team often gave exhibition matches and played in tournaments. The Secunderabad polo team had remained unbeaten in India. They visited Bangalore city to play a match against the Mysore royal polo team. This match was watched by thousands of spectators that evening. The Mysore polo team won the match against the Secunderabad team with ease. This was a surprise victory for the Mysore team.

The Mysore polo ground was considered the best playground in India. The Maharaja of Mysore played with such dexterity and skill, it took spectators by surprise and his reputation had spread to other countries. Once while playing a match, he fell off his horse. He was unconscious for several hours and required bed rest for several days. This accident occurred because he was galloping on the horse to hit the ball with his stick and the saddle strap came loose. He lost his balance and fell to the ground. During the year 1908, the Mysore royal team, led by the Maharaja, participated in several tournaments all over India. This team won many silver cups and shields in these tournaments. The silver was melted to make artistic mementos and they were displayed in the palace. In 1912, the Mysore royal polo team played a match against a formidable polo team called Golconda polo team. They were experts in "short hit," "long hit" and "dribble." This team was defeated by the Mysore team consisting of these players Nalwadi, Yuvaraja, Sardar Gopalaraja Urs and Sri Banni Singh. The Maharaja was an expert in dribbling the ball.

The Maharaja had several racehorses in his stud farm. They were thoroughbred horses of the best breed. They had many names, but it ended with the title "Chamundi." They won many prestigious races all over India. In 1903, the Maharaja rode many of these horses to victory in Gymkhana races (informal races) according to a British official. The Maharaja's Gold Cup race in Mysore and Bangalore racing seasons were major Derby events. Nalwadi was an expert "Racquets" (Squash) player with an international reputation. He could play three or four rubbers at the same time. There was hardly anybody in South India who could beat him at Squash. A reputed skilled player called Col. Jones often suffered defeat at the hands of the Maharaja. Some of the best players of the game like Col. P. H. Benson (former Surgeon General of Madras State), the Maharaja of Pudukkottai and Yedia king (Burma) could not defeat Nalwadi at the game of "Racquets."

In 1922, the Prince of Wales (Future King Edward VIII, who abdicated the British throne for an American divorcee called Mrs. Simpson) visited Mysore state. He played a game of squash with the Maharaja Nalwadi Krishnaraja Wadiyar and lost the game much to his chagrin. But he laughed it off by saying he would visit Mysore State once again only to win a game of squash. (In 1920, he lost another match against Rotund Governor General Lord Liverpool at Wellington, New Zealand during a state tour). After the tenure of Lord Curzon, Viceroy of India the Fourth Earl of Minto Gilbert Elliot (1905-1910 reign) took charge and he visited Mysore State in the month of

November 1909 with his wife Countess Mary Minto. The Maharaja had built an eye hospital in Bangalore named after Viceroy Minto. This hospital was inaugurated by Earl Minto and Countess Mary during their state visit.

The Sacred Thread Ceremony and the Marriage of Yuvaraja

The *"upanayanam"* the opening of the third inner eye (the sacred thread ceremony) of the Yuvaraja was conducted in the newly built hall on 16th June 1910 (Thursday). On the 15th June 1910 evening at 10 PM, women folk brought the *"Kalasha"* (the large silver vessel containing water (Ganga Jal), coconut, pan, mango leaves and a mirror from Doddakere (a big lake before the palace accompanied by the "Nadhaswaram" musicians.

The upanayanam was conducted by the Maharaja and Maharani Sri Lakshmivilasa Sannidhana in a Silver Mantap (Ornate platform structure with pillars and cupolas). The Ursu community courtiers and V.V.I.P guests from Bombay and Madras sat on the right side of the Mantap. On the left side sat the Maharaja of Baroda and Kashmir. The emissaries of Puddukotai, the Dewan of Mysore State and other high-ranking dignitaries also occupied the chairs. The chief priest performed the religious rituals before a fire pit by chanting mantras. The palace band and the nagaswara musicians provided music for the occasion. The Yuvaraja received the "Khilats" (gifts and honours) along with prasadam from various religious heads of Hindu Mutts. All the guests were garlanded and they were given "pala-Tambula" (fruit and pan leaves with areca nut).

The marriage of Yuvaraja Sri Kanteerava Narasimharaja Wodeyar took place on the 16th evening and on the 17th of June 1910 in the new palace. He married Sri Kempu Cheluvajammani, daughter of an aristocrat Sri Dalavayi Devaraja Urs, on the evening of 16th June 1910. The *"Kashi Yatra"* (ritual washing of the feet of the groom) of Yuvaraja was conducted by the father of the bride. This is a part of the Hindu marriage ritual. Every young bridegroom pretends to embark on a journey to Kashi. In the olden days, Kashi was the epicentre of higher education in India. The groom wants to join a "Gurukula" in Kashi. But his prospective/future father-in-law dissuades him from going to Kashi, instead, he offers him in marriage his nubile young daughter. On that evening, the Yuvaraja led by Maharaja and Maharani along with other courtiers and women went through the important roads of Mysore in a procession. Thousands of residents of Mysore City had lined up to cheer the

Yuvaraja and the Maharaja. The procession was led by six gold caparisoned elephants, cavalry, soldiers of the palace army in uniform carrying rifles and swords, servants carrying royal standards, musicians and royal courtiers in formal dress. They all walked on a red carpet. The event manager was hurrying up the progress of the procession, because of the impending rains. But the Maharaja ordered that the procession should go slowly so that the Mysore Citizens could relish it at leisure. The Royal procession returned to the palace before summer showers began to pour. The Yuvaraja was welcomed with a "Mangala Arti" (the auspicious lamp and red vermillion water in a silver plate was waved in a circular motion three times in front of the groom) to the accompaniment of melodious songs. This was done by elderly women folk to ward off the evil eye.

The grand marriage function of the Yuvaraja with Sri Kempu Chaluvajammani took place around 12 pm on 17th June 1910. Many memorandums in silver caskets were presented to the Yuvaraja by the representatives of all the districts of Mysore State. The representative of Shimoga district presented the memorandum in a sandalwood casket decorated with intricate carvings. The front piece had a scene of *Girija Kalyana* (Shiva – Parvathi Marriage scene). The back piece depicted the world-famous waterfall – Jog Falls. The Yuvaraja in his official address, expressed that the love, loyalty and devotion of the subjects was very much cherished and valued by the Mysore Royal family. He said his sole aim was to serve the Mysore State and its citizens in full measure. He wanted to emulate the shining example of exemplary conduct of his late revered father Sri Chamarajedra Wodeyar. His sincere desire was to follow in the footsteps of his elder brother Sri Nalwadi Krishnaraja Wodeyar as far as his public duties go.

On 25th June evening the marriage procession of Yuvaraja and his bride Smt. Kempu Cheluvajammani took place in Mysore City. A large crowd had gathered on either side of the main thoroughfares to view the grand spectacle and to cheer the royal couple. The procession was led by uniformed soldiers carrying swords, followed by camels, elephants and horses. The elephants carried floral garlands in their trunks and later, they garlanded the royal couple. The royal procession was led by a band of musicians playing marching tunes. There was also a nadhaswaram ensemble playing traditional Karnatak classical music. The centre of attraction was two elephants carrying "Golden Ambari" (Seating Howdas). On one elephant, the royal couple bejewelled and wearing expensive silk dresses sat and cheered by the public and on the other elephant sat the Maharaja. The Ambari elephants were followed by four auspicious women [Courtesans] carrying Kalasha [vessel with Ganga water, coconut and mango leaves], mirror and perfume in sprinklers surrounded by the ruler's bodyguards. The royal procession returned to the palace after two hours. They were welcomed by ladies after performing "Aarti," the lighted lamp set in a silver plate containing red-coloured (Vermilion powder) water.

The King Emperor George the Fifth succeeded to the British throne after the demise of King Edward the Seventh on 7th May 1910. King George honoured Nalwadi with the title of Colonel of the British army in the month of June 1910.

Congratulatory Messages

A grand royal banquet was organized by the palace authorities in honour of the Maharaja whose ascension day coincided with the marriage festivities of the Yuvaraja. Sir S. M. Fraser the British Resident of the Mysore State in his inaugural speech summed up his opinion about the Yuvaraja.

"Sri Yuva Raja Kanteerava Narasimharaja Wodeyar is loved by the citizens of Mysore for his endearing qualities like generosity of heart and kindness towards one and all. He is respected because he is the younger brother of the Maharaja and he received the best schooling at the behest of his mother Sri. Vanivilasa Sannidhana, the Regent of Mysore. I had the onerous responsibility of supervising his schooling.

There are not many people who can boast of as many friends and admirers as Yuvaraja can claim. I am not given to overpraise and unwarranted adulation of people. But I have known Yuvaraja since he was eight years old. I feel a bit embarrassed in his presence today even to grant him his well-deserved praise and appreciation of his noble virtues out of modesty.

The Yuvaraja is blessed with such inborn qualities as good manners, a genial personality and the spirit of a good sports person. Wherever he goes, he attracts admirers like a magnet attracting iron filings. If he had been born in any other household, he still would have been as popular with friends as he is now. Because of his informal behaviour, he is loved and respected by Indians and Europeans alike. The harmonious qualities found in him are by-products of his noble virtues, good education and extensive travel in India and abroad. That is why he may be described as the right hand of the Maharaja. The two royal brothers remind us of two ancient brothers

Rama and Lakshmana from the Hindu epic "Ramayana." The princely state of Mysore is fortunate to have such two giant pillars supporting the edifice.

One person plants a fruit tree, but another person belonging to the next generation enjoys its fruits. But I am fortunate enough to do both, that is plant a fruit tree and also enjoy its fruits.

In the past, I had dreamt of a ruler fulfilling a number of promises, because he had the vision and the energy to implement it. But now, as a British resident of the Mysore State, I can say with certainty that my nascent dreams have become a reality. I had noticed in him during his youth these qualities like a genuine love for his subjects, his sense of duty and admirable virtues like honesty and truthfulness. I was confident that my protégé one day would be among the galaxy of eminent men. I am glad to state that all the virtuous qualities have blossomed forth at present." (Translation from Kannada)

The Maharaja Nalwadi Krishnaraja Wodeyar, in his reply to the address of Sir. S.M. Fraser, said, "The British resident has highlighted the enormous love and affection that exists between me and my brother. These words well up from his kind heart. It gladdens my heart to know that my younger brother has earned so much love, affection and respect of thousands of people." (Translation from Kannada)

Soon, the fame of the Mysore Maharaja spread to other parts of India and the world. In a public reception at Bellary, the British governor of Madras presidency Sir Arthur Laly stated his opinion of Nalwadi, "I have come to Bellary Town from the neighbouring State of Mysore. The wise Ruler of Mysore followed the example of Queen Empress Victoria and King Edward of Britain in administrating the state in an efficient manner. His primary concern is to ensure that his subjects lived well. He believed that his comfort and well-being could be ignored in the interest of his subjects. He is very wise and prudent for his years. He has borrowed the best of western science and technology to improve the traditional lifestyle of the Mysoreans. He has achieved a unique harmony between western values and oriental values.

In the educational institutions run by the state, the students belonging to Hindu, Muslim, Christian and Jain religions could practice their religion without any outside interference and pursue their studies. They enjoy absolute religious freedom.

The Maharaja of Mysore is passionate about the all-round development and welfare of his subjects. He wants to imbibe in them high moral values through an ongoing dispersal of ethics based on Dharmic principles. He strongly believes that through sound education, the awareness and knowledge of people could be increased. He is ever willing to implement new economic policies to promote the prosperity of his subjects. He is marked by a high degree of culture and generosity of mind. I have complete trust and faith in him because he follows the dictates of his conscience. You have to excuse me for digressing from other important issues. I have given vent to my heartfelt emotions." (Translation from Kannada)

The European Darbar

Maharaja Nalwadi attended the Royal Darbar in the grand hall of the palace on nine evenings during Dasara festivities. On the Mahanavami evening (ninth day) the European guests were invited to the Royal Darbar. It was a long-standing practice that European guests of different ranks sat on chairs. But the Indian dignitaries were always made to sit on carpets in a cross-legged fashion. This was demeaning to the Indian officials because often their British juniors sat on chairs. The Maharaja did not relish this discriminatory practice. So, in 1910 Dasara European Darbar, he decided to do away with this humiliating practice. He took only two officials into his confidence and ordered that additional chairs were to be placed in rows for Indian Courtiers. When Indian officials came for the Darbar, they were pleasantly surprised to be ushered into the chairs. This decision of the Maharaja won all-round praise from the citizens.

A Trip to North India

In 1911, the Maharaja of Mysore embarked on a trip to North India, not once, but twice during this year. A grand Industrial and Arts exhibition on an all-India scale was organized at Prayagraj. The Maharaja decided to organize an all-India Industrial Fair at Mysore on a grand scale in 1906. The tradition of the All India Industrial and Arts Exhibition during Dasara began in 1906 and it still continues. The Industrial and Agricultural Fair attracted visitors from all parts of India. It began to generate substantial additional income for the state.

The Second Delhi Darbar took place in December 1911. The British Emperor King George the Fifth and Queen Mary's coronation took place on 22nd June 1911 at West Minister Abbey, London. As they were King Emperor and Queen Empress of India, a visit to the British Colony was inevitable.

Hence, the Delhi Darbar was organised at the behest of the Viceroy Lord Hardinge. All the important Maharajas and Sultans of India were invited to attend the Delhi Darbar. The British government decided to Confer (Knight Grand Commander of Indian Empire) order of the title of "K.C.I.E" upon the Yuvaraja of Mysore during Delhi Darbar.

The annual death anniversary of (Shraddha) of Sri Chamarajendra Wodeyar fell on *Shuddha padyami* day in *pushya masa* and it coincided with Delhi Darbar week. The Maharaja had requested the vedic pandits, Ritwicks and priests to travel with him on the train. He performed the "Shraddha" for his late father and offered oblations. He sent these religious men on a pilgrimage tour to Prayagraj, Kashi (Varanasi) and Gaya. He also arranged a trip to Kurukshetra for seventeen of his contingents.

Another incident in Delhi Darbar proved the generosity of the Maharaja. A group of tourists from Mysore had arrived in Delhi to witness the Darbar. But they had not booked rooms in Hotels or *Dharma Chatras* (Free travellers' inns). They could not find any place to stay. They came to Nalwadi's camp as a last resort. They met some officials and requested them to accommodate them in one of the tents. They promised to dine out every day. But the officers did not want to displease and inconvenience the Maharaja. Hence, they declined the request of the visitors. The Maharaja was watching this scene from afar. He guessed there was something amiss. He approached the group of visitors and enquired about their problem. They explained their plight to the Maharaja. This group of tourists was told by his Excellency that not only could they stay in one of the tents, but they could also enjoy the Royal meals.

Afterwards, Nalwadi travelled to Lahore, Amritsar, and Haridwar and performed "Shraddha" for his dead ancestors at Gaya. Then, the royal entourage reached Calcutta city. His late father's memorial stood at Kali Ghat. The royal family had made permanent arrangements for its upkeep. There was a well-maintained garden around the Brindavan (memorial). The permanent staff performed the puja to his portrait every day. Every day, some poor people were given food, ration and some money at the memorial. On new moon day, on the day of the eclipse and during the Dasara festival poor people received a lot of charity here.

The Maharaja inaugurated the "Economic Conference" on 10th June 1911 with the sole purpose of bringing about a co-ordination between government officials and citizens of the state. The State Government had taken up the railway line project from Mysore to Arisikere. Another expensive public works project had been taken up by the state. That is the Krishnaraja Sagar dam to be built across the Cauvery River at Kannambadi village to promote agricultural activity on additional acreage.

New Roles for the Yuvaraja

Nalwadi wanted to bring his younger brother, the Yuvaraja, into public life to utilize his services for the state. At this time, Colonel Jones the chief of Mysore army retired. Yuvaraj was appointed as the chief of the Mysore army and also as the Military secretary of the Maharaja. This move was very much appreciated by the "The Hindu" and "Amrita Bazar Patrika" daily newspapers.

The Maharaja made two significant breakthroughs during this period. He convinced the British Government to refund the surplus amount collected in the Bangalore Cantonment area to the Mysore State Revenue Dept. The taxes collected in the Cantonment area were spent on maintenance work. This area was directly administered by the Madras Presidency. The second project was building a dam across the Cauvery River near Kannambadi village. There was stiff opposition to this project from the riparian state of Madras. But it was overcome through diplomacy and negotiation.

Dewan Sri T. Ananda Rao retired from Mysore Government Service on 10th Nov 1912. He had been conferred with the title of "C.I.E" (The most eminent order of the Indian Empire – "Companion of the Indian Empire") by the King Emperor and the Maharaja had conferred upon him the title of "*Pradhana Shiromani.*" His father Raja T. Madhava Rao was the Dewan of Baroda and his father-in-law Sri Ramarao was the Dewan of Travancore State.

Sri T. Ananda Rao was a dedicated royalist, a disciplinarian and an enthusiastic administrator. He was a kind and compassionate patriarch. He was also an eccentric gentleman. A subordinate official came to his residence on a Sunday morning. He came seeking permission from the Dewan to visit Kharapura so that he could make a surprise inspection about the "Khedda" operation arrangements. The Dewan remained silent. The subordinate official assumed that the Dewan's regal and dignified silence as permission to go. The next morning, the Dewan noticed that this official was making preparations for a journey to Kaharapura. The Dewan called him to his office and told him curtly that on Sundays, he did not make official decisions unless they were very important. The Dewan told the official that he was announcing his decision, now, that his current dispensation to the official was not to go on this trip.

Contributions of Dewan Sir M. Visvesvaraya

Sir M. Visvesvaraya became the Dewan of the State on 10th Nov 1912. He had been appointed as a Chief Engineer of the state in 1909. He had worked in several British presidencies as a chief architect on irrigation projects. He had executed drinking water projects in Sukkur and Aden. He had also toured Egypt, Canada, the U.S.A. and Japan. He was the junior most member of the Executive council. The Maharaja selected him for the Dewan post by passing the two other Senior Executive council members (Perhaps, he was the first technocrat to occupy this post. -Ed. Note). Sir M.V. wanted Mysore State to achieve all-around progress in rural development, agriculture, education, commerce, Malnad area development, building big hydroelectric dams and giant industries was on the anvil.

During his tenure as the Dewan of the state, he accomplished these projects, the establishment of Mysore University, Krishnaraja Sagar Dam, the Sandalwood oil factory, Bhadravathi Iron and Steel factory and the setting up of the Economic Development Council. He encouraged non-government officials to participate in public administration. His tenure lasted more than six years and the British government conferred upon him knighthood. Sir M. Vishweshwariah hosted a dinner for the Maharaja and other high-ranking officials on 28th January 1913 in Balabroohie Bungalow in Bangalore. Nalwadi along with his brother attended this banquet.

The Maharaja inaugurated "Minto Eye Hospital" in Bangalore on 3rd Feb 1913. This Eye hospital was named after Lord Minto, who was the Viceroy of India. Lord Minto had visited Mysore State in 1909. His tenure had come to a close in 1910, and after his retirement, he was living in Britain. The Maharaja sent him a telegram conveying the good news that a new eye hospital in Bangalore was named after him. The Maharaja, on Feb 7th 1913, travelled to Chikkamagaluru to lay the foundation for the Veerashaiva Students' Hostel. Some time ago, the Maharaja had remarked in one of his speeches that Community-oriented student hostels must be built for the benefit of poor students. The pontiff of Yelahanka Mutt (near Belur) Sri Shiva Nanjuendendra Deshika Swamiji had donated funds for the construction of the hostel. Sri. C. Srinivasa Rao, a member of the Economic Development Council, took personal initiative to complete this project.

During the month of March 1913, the Maharaja inaugurated the Bank of Mysore to finance industries and commerce. This private bank collected deposits from the clientele. It began lending money on interest to businessmen so that they could start new industries. This banking activity, in turn, generated greater industrial development.

Yuvaraja's European Tour

Sri Kanteerava Narasimharaja Wodeyar embarked upon a European tour in the month of March 1913. His intention was to study civic planning and provide various amenities to city dwellers.

The Mayor of Glasgow gave a grand civic reception to the visiting Yuvaraja. The president of the committee, Mr. Bailey Plaxton, said in his welcome speech, "The visiting member of the Mysore royal family, who has crossed several seas to reach our shores from a faraway land called India, it is our pleasure to give him a warm welcome to our beautiful city. Many rulers and intellectuals from India have paid a visit to our city. But none comparable to Yuvaraja, who hails from the most modern state of Mysore ruled by his elder brother Sri Nalwadi Krishnaraja Wodeyar. The Mysore Dynasty stretches back to the time of Ptolemy of Greece. The Yuvaraja is assisting his elder brother in the administration of this princely state. Mysore State has become the most developed and most modern state in the whole of the orient.

This morning, the Yuvaraja visited electricity generation and distribution stations. He exhibited a fairly good amount of technical knowledge. He also studied the garbage and sewerage system of Glasgow. He was impressed with the disposal system. He already possesses sound knowledge, because Mysore State has hydroelectric dams and electricity generation system. The state is supplying electricity to the company John Taylor and sons which is mining gold at Kolar Gold Fields. The state administration is run by experienced Dewans. Mysore State boasts of advanced research laboratories, hospitals and reservoirs. Mysore State is spread across 29,000 square miles of land area. The population of the state is little more than fifty lakhs. The annual income of the state is Rs. 3 Crores. Hence, I heartily welcome the enlightened Yuvaraja of the Mysore Wodeyar Family." (Not a verbatim report only a translation from Kannada) ed: (John Taylor and Sons)

The Yuvaraja, after an extensive European tour, returned to his state in the month of October 1913. A grand gala civic reception was organized in Bangalore on 4th October 1913. The Mayor, civic officials and prominent citizens presented memorandums to the Yuvaraja in silver caskets.

The news of progress and development achieved by Mysore State under Nalwadi had spread to the East and West. All this came to a culmination when Lord Hardinge the Viceroy of India visited Mysore State in November 1913.

The British gave back the reins of power to Sri Chamarajendra Wodeyar in 1881 through an "Instrument of transfer of power" proclamation letter. In the past, they had withdrawn political power from Sri Mummadi Krishnaraja Wodeyar in 1831. The British ruled the state for 50 years until 1881. The draconian laws imposed on the rulers of Mysore were rescinded in 1913. In a banquet on 6th November 1913, Lord Hardinge read the official communiqué, which stated that all the curtailed political powers and privileges had been restored to the present ruler. Now, the ruler of Mysore was on par with other Maharajas and Nawabs of princely states.

All these years, Nalwadi argued persuasively with the Viceroy and the Royalty in Britain in a logical and dignified way for the restoration of his powers. He also wrote long letters with extreme politeness and courtesy to the higher officials requesting them to oblige his justifiable demands. The methodology and stratagem adopted by Sri Nalwadi received very high praise from the Viceroy. Even in the recent past, he had drawn the attention of the British Raj to the drawbacks and lacunae in the conditions imposed on the Mysore rulers.

Lord Hardinge's Visit to Mysore

The Maharaja was known for his hospitality and generosity in treating his guests. Nalwadi staged a 'Khedda' operation at 'Kharapur' to trap wild elephants for the benefit of the visiting Viceroy. He also took Lord Hardinge on a "Shikar" (hunt). The Viceroy shot and killed a fully grown tiger, which measured 9 feet and 4 inches in length from nose to tail. The Viceroy also unveiled the Statue of former Dewan Sir Sheshadri Iyer, which stands before the public Library in Cubbon Park.

In 1914, the Maharaja appointed his younger brother, the Yuvaraja, as an extraordinary member of the executive council. During his tenure, he demonstrated his thinking prowess, knowledge garnered from foreign travels and experience gained through interactions with Indian and European civil servants. His exemplary conduct during official meetings became an example to other members. He was always punctual and efficient in his official conduct. He was generous to a fault and frequently pardoned an erring official. After the incident, he would behave with the official, as if there was nothing amiss in their relationship.

The Yuvaraja did not make unilateral decisions in any meeting. He listened patiently to the lower-ranking official's dissenting presentation of arguments. If he thought the other person's opinion was more prudent, he would accept it. Once, while discussing certain matters related to the state army, a lower-ranking official argued at length against the proposals of the Yuvaraja. At the end of the presentation, he jocularly said, "Now, we will abide by your decision." But the Yuvaraja was nonplussed and he said, "We are all here to exchange ideas. You have been appointed to this post to think and act. You are not expected to toe my line of thinking blindly. Now, let us discuss this grave matter once again." After much deliberation, the Yuvaraja conceded to the argument of that official. He told the concerned official, a government order to that effect may be passed and implemented.

The King Emperor of Great Britain and India was very much impressed by the efficient functioning of the Yuvaraja, as an extraordinary member of the executive council. Hence, in 1915, he was conferred with the title of "G.C.I.E" [Grand Knight Commander of the Order of the Indian Empire.]

In 1919, the Maharaja started the Scout Movement in the state. He was impressed by the high ideals of the scout movement in the state. He was impressed by the movement started by Baden Powell. The Yuvaraja Sri Kanteerava Narasimharaja Wodeyar was made honorary "Chief Scout" to give the movement an energetic fillip. He extended all financial and infrastructural help to the scout movement.

More Powers to the People's Council and Assembly

The Maharaja of Mysore decided to make the legislative council more effective. Hence, he increased its strength from 18 to 25 in 1913. The legislative council was empowered to table questions during meetings and obtain replies from the government. They were entitled to debate and discuss the state budget. The legislative council consisted of 12 government officials and 13 non-government citizens. Out of the 13 non-government members, four were from the People's Representative Assembly. The remaining four were elected from 8 districts of the state. The two districts elected one council member. The remaining five members from the group of 13 were nominated members of the state government. In the year 1915, another additional power was granted to these 25 members. When they received replies to their tabled questions, they could proceed further and ask supplementary questions and get detailed explanations.

In 1915, Nalwadi gave further powers to the People's Representative Assembly. During the Dasara session, they could discuss the draft budget and offer suggestions. But by this time, the budget would have taken a final shape and moreover, very few changes were effected at this stage. Noticing this anomaly, Nalwadi proposed to have a special Budget Session during his coronation anniversary function in April month every year. The first budget Session took place on 22nd April 1917 in Mysore. Then onwards, the suggestions proposed by the people's representative assembly members could be given due precedence in altering the draft budget. Sri Nalwadi often introduced administrative reforms without anyone even demanding them.

The Role of the Mysore Army in 1st World War

The First World War in Europe began on 28th July 1914. The British declared war on Germany along with other allies on 4th August 1914. King George the Fifth requested citizens of the British Dominion including those living in colonies to contribute to the war effort. The Mysore State Army became part of the allied army and participated in many battles. Their sacrifice and show of valour impressed the British Government. In a letter to the Viceroy, the Maharaja wrote, "During this horrible crisis, the state of Mysore and its subjects are willing to make any sacrifice that is called for. Our army is in a prepared state. We are also contributing Rs. 50 lakhs as our contribution to the war fund." The Viceroy sent a telegram to Nalwadi expressing his gratitude and happiness at the noble gesture. The State Government and its citizens purchased "War bonds" worth Rupees 1 crore 27 lakhs. After a period of time, again the state government contributed Rs. 23 lakhs to the war fund. Apart from financial contribution, the Mysore State contributed minerals, Honne and Teak timber, woollen blankets, dry hay and other commodities to the war effort.

The Mysore army was led by Col. Desharaja Urs, the brother-in-law of Nalwadi. The Mysore army showed great valour and courage in the battles fought in Egypt, Mesopotamia and Palestine. When Col. Desharaje Urs and Mysore soldiers were leaving for the Middle East, the Maharaja in his farewell speech remarked that he would pray to Goddess Chamundeshwari for their safe victorious return. Moreover, all of them would be in his mind always and he would look forward anxiously for their "safe return." The Maharaja made a declaration that on behalf of the Royal Family members and on behalf of millions of citizens, he would express their solidarity and support to "Imperial Service Lancers." These printed copies of the official declaration were distributed to all the officers and Lancers. The declaration read like this, "The British Empire and its allies are at peril today. During this time of crisis, the British allied army is fighting to protect its freedom and uphold justice. You are a small fraction of a big army. But you have proved your mettle in various battles. Please uphold our glorious tradition and fame in whatever duties are assigned to you. You must redeem the trust posed in you by the British monarchy. We are praying to God every moment and our thoughts are dedicated to you eternally. It is our responsibility to take good care of your family members during your absence. Please remember you uphold the glorious tradition and honour of Mysore State. You must remember for Indians, honour is above life and it is considered more precious than anything else. You must keep faith in the Almighty. Our cause is a righteous cause. May God bless you with victory and a safe return to your homeland."

The Maharaja's message enthused the Lancers to fight much more courageously. During enemy shelling a lot of casualties occurred. But surprisingly, the Mysore army was very fortunate. They suffered very few casualties compared to other regiments. It appeared as if they were protected by Goddess Chamundeshwari. The British army officers called the Mysore contingent the "Jadu (Magic) Regiment." The Mysore soldiers impressed everyone with their refined, cultured and enlightened behaviour. The British Generals were surprised that 75% of the soldiers were literate. After the I World War, the Indian army took a cue from the Mysore army to educate its own soldiers. The Mysore soldiers showed a remarkable degree of self-discipline and their character was pure. There were no incidents of misdemeanour and misconduct during the First World War. The adage "Caesar's wife must be above suspicion" held good in their case. The high ideals of the ruler had percolated into the ranks. Many officers of the Mysore army were promoted to the rank of Brigadier, because of their bravery and good conduct.

The Mysore army laid siege to Aarpoli Aerodrome (the Former Aratot airport) held by the German army. They managed to defeat the German army and take over the Aerodrome. While fleeing from the battle scene, a German army official artist dropped his collection of sketches before escaping from Aarpole. These sketches were recovered by Lt. Col. B. P. Krishne Urs. He brought them back to Mysore and presented them to the Maharaja. I shall describe the magnanimous behaviour of Sri Nalwadi with regard to those German sketches while narrating the events of his European tour later.

The King Emperor of Britain conferred titles and medals to the officers and soldiers of Mysore Lancers, who had fought gallantly at Haifa and in other battles in the Middle East. These officers received special mention and honours. Col. J. Desharaje Urs of the Mysore army was made Hon, Lt. Col of the British Imperial Army, The Maharaja Conferred on him the highest State honour of the "Gandhaberunda" medal. (A gold medal in the shape of twin-headed mythical Eagle studded with diamonds).

The Following Heroes Received Special Bravery Honours
1) Sardar Bahadur B. Chamaraj Urs
2) Risaldar-Lt. Col B.P. Krishne Urs
3) Risaldar – Subbaraje Urs
4) Janab Turab Ali, etc.

The Maharaja provided many reliefs to the soldiers, who returned to Mysore after the 1st World War in 1920. The bereaved families were compensated financially.

Compassion and Kindness Towards Untouchables

I have already narrated in the previous chapter, how Nalwadi invited and welcomed dalit gentlemen to attend the Dasara Darbar in the palace. This event took place even before the Maharaja of Travancore allowed untouchable Hindus to enter the temples of the State.

Nalwadi visited Bombay on 31st January 1916. The Maharaja visited a school for dalit students in Parel, Bombay. The chairman of the school Sir Narayan G Chandavarkar and Sir Balachandra Krishna welcomed the ruler of Mysore with great respect and warmth. They showed the workshop, where students learnt carpentry as part of the job-oriented course. The library, laboratory and dining hall used by students were shown to him. Nalwadi wanted to know how non-dalit students and their parents behaved with dalit students. The chairman informed that the relationship between those two groups was cordial. The parents of the non-dalit students had no objection to the inter-mixing of caste students with dalit students. Sir Narayan G. Chandavarkar said the integration of dalits. into mainstream Hindu Society was of National importance. Whatever reforms the Maharaja was introducing in the Mysore

State had a national impact. In fact, Mahatma Gandhi had coined a new name for the downtrodden people "Harijan" (children of Vishnu).

The author wishes to state that in retrospect from the present time (1941), some 25 years ago the plight of Harijans all over India was pitiable. A ruler like Nalwadi with foresight and vision initiated social reforms to improve the lot of the downtrodden. He gave importance to educational schemes for Harijan students. The state offered scholarships, waiver of school and college fees, free student hostels and financial assistance to poor parents who sent their sons and daughters to school. The students were given free uniforms and books. The farmlands of Harijans enjoyed a tax rebate, separate housing colonies, separate cooperative societies and finally job reservation in government service came into practice. Reservation of electoral wards was initiated so that they could get elected to Municipalities, District boards and the legislative council. The government passed an order stating that they could draw water from public wells and ponds for their use. The ruler of Mysore received universal recognition and honour because of these social reform programmes.

Hydro-electric Generation and Development of Mysore Railway Network

In Mysore State, the hydroelectric generation project at Shivanasamudra became the first electricity-generating project in the whole of Asia. The electricity generated was used in Kolar Gold Mines for extracting gold. Cities like Bangalore and Mysore came to be electrified for the first time in India. Till 1916, the hydroelectric station had only four turbines to produce electric power. A fifth one was built to generate 22,650 units of horsepower and it began generation in 1916.

The state railway network received a new fillip, because of the extension of the railway line from Mysore to Arisikere. A tramway was built from Tarikere to Narasimharajapura. A new Kolar District Railway network was started with links to Chintamani and Chikkaballapura.

Mysore State Municipalities Revised Act (1918)

As per this new act, the state municipalities were divided into three categories: City Municipality, Town Municipality and Minor Municipalities. The state also hiked the number of members who could conduct business in these institutions. The Municipalities elected a chairman to conduct business in the city or town. Bangalore City Municipality enjoyed the privilege of electing its own chairman. The Mysore municipality and other civil bodies had government officials functioning as chairmen. In Mysore and in other towns, Deputy Chairmen were respectful citizens of society. So, famous public men of stature and reputation occupied these positions.

The First Convocation of Mysore University

The first University in Princely India came to be established in 1916 in Mysore State. The Maharaja was the first Chancellor and the Yuvaraja was appointed as Pro-Chancellor. The first convocation of Mysore University took place on 22nd October 1918. The Maharaja in his capacity as Chancellor of the University distributed degree certificates to the successful candidates. This grand convocation was attended by 2000 dignitaries and invitees.

Later, Nalwadi also officiated as the first chancellor of Benares Hindu University. He participated as Chancellor in two convocations held in 1919 and 1921 at Kashi.

Dewan Sir M. Vishweshwariah resigned from his post in 1918. He went on six months' leave before retirement from 10th Dec 1918. [Ed. Note: He opposed Miller's committee recommendation of reservation of jobs for backward caste citizens. He endorsed reservations in educational institutions. He was a champion of meritocracy and he was from a very poor family himself.]

The Maharaja appointed Sardar Sri A. Kantharaja Urs as the next Dewan of Mysore State on 14th June 1919. Later, his yeoman services were recognized by the King-Emperor and he was honoured with Knighthood ("Sir" title). Nalwadi conferred on him *"Raja Seva Dhurina"* (one who excelled in Royal Service). He retired on 30th April 1922.

Sir A. Kantharaja Urs was the first Ursu gentleman to take a B.A degree from the Mysore University. He joined State Government service as a probationary Assistant Commissioner. In 1917, he had visited Japan to study the political Administration, progress of Industrialisation and cultural hallmarks of that society. He was a staunch Royalist. He treated the rich and the poor alike. He was kind-hearted and courteous. Once, a classmate of A. Kantharaja Urs, who was in the lower rung of state administration, went to see the Dewan in the "Lakeview" bungalow. The Dewan received him with a lot of love and affection. He took him into his drawing room on the first floor. He offered him a seat and talked with him for over an hour. He took leave of his friend by coming down the staircase and saying "goodbye" to him in the foyer. He also requested him to visit him more often. During the Dewanship of Sir M

Kanthraja Urs, Mysore State saw various economic and political programmes being implemented. The Steel Mill at Bhadravathi, free school education for boys and girls until 7th form (middle school), scholarships were offered to students belonging to backward castes and the government appointed the "Millers Committee" which introduced job reservation for depressed classes. For the first time, the Dewan established the Central recruitment board to recruit employees to various departments. In 1919, the "Economic Conference" organization was revived.

The legislative council had one member representing two districts (4 members from 8 districts). Sir M. Kantharaja Urs recommended to the Maharaja that election rules be changed to receive one member from each district. The Mysore University Senate was empowered to send one member as their representative to the legislative council. The State government could nominate 4 members to the legislative council. Because of all these changes, the total number of members of the council rose from 21 to 30.

After the First World War, food prices skyrocketed in the state. The government employees could not make both ends meet with their meagre salaries. Hence, the state government hiked their salaries and imposed curbs on the export and import of grains. Another factor added to the woes of the fiscal balance – the pound-rupee exchange rate increased. The State had to part with more rupees while buying imported goods. The state government took an important decision to introduce income tax to generate revenue.

Many public sector industries were forced to exhaust their capital. The State exchequer found it unprofitable to fund these industries to fill up the deficit gap. It consulted the well-known economist Sri Datta for advice. He suggested to the State Government on 1st July 1920 to raise money through loan-bonds from the public thereby extending loans to the sick industries with this fund. This fiscal arrangement started in 1920 and lasted till 1940.

During the month of December 1919, the Viceroy of India Lord Chelmsford and during the month of January 1921, the Prince of Wales visited Mysore State and enjoyed the hospitality of the Maharaja.

Another important milestone in the history of state healthcare was the establishment of a sanatorium for Tuberculosis patients. Nalwadi's elder sister Princess Sri Krishnajammani had contracted Tuberculosis. This proved fatal not only for her but also to be a harbinger of death to her three daughters. This was a tragic blow to the members of the royal family. Nalwadi took a decision to help other victims of Tuberculosis. Hence, it was decided to establish a state-of-the-art Sanatorium in the name of Princess Sri Krishnajammani on the outskirts of the Mysore city. He consulted his mother Vanivilas Sannidhana and Col. Desharaje Urs before establishing this sanatorium. The Mysore city did not have an exclusive Tuberculosis Hospital until then. Sri Vanivilasa Sannidhana laid the foundation stone for the hospital on 6th April 1918. The total cost of the project was Rs. 1,03,959. The royal family members contributed Rs. 75,000 and the balance amount was paid by the State Government. The Maharaja of Mysore inaugurated the hospital on 18th November 1921.

In his inaugural speech, he said, "The audience before me is aware of the tragic calamity suffered by the royal family members because of this deadly disease. This hospital is named after my sister Princess Krishnajammani and it is also a memorial for her three daughters, who also succumbed to this deadly disease. I do not want my subjects to suffer from a similar fate. My mother and I pray to Lord Almighty to grant good protection and health to our fellow sufferers of this disease. May God give them a long life."

Yuvaraja Sri Kanteerava Narasimharaja Wodeyar Bahadur, G. C. I. E, Seated on his lap – Sujaya Kanthammanni, To his left – Vijayalakshmi Ammani, Jayachamarajendra Wodeyar to his right.

Prince Sri Jayachamarajendra Wodeyar and his younger sister Princess Sri Vijayalakshammani on horses during birth anniversary celebration of the Maharaja Sri Nalwadi Krishnaraja Wodeyar.

The Birth of Sri Jayachamarajendra Wodeyar

The Yuvaraja Kanteerava Narasimharaja Wodeyar's consort delivered a male child on 18th July 1919 [*Bahula panchami* day, *Ashada* month, *Siddharthi Samvatsara* (Hindu Year)]. The present ruler was born on a Friday evening at 6 o'clock and 13 minutes. His birth star was *uttarabhadra* and Lagna was *Dhanur lagna* (Hour Marker). On that day, there was a gentle shower in the capital city. The palace was illuminated with electric bulbs.. The Maharaja ordered that cartloads of sugar must be distributed to the city's citizens so that they could all prepare sweet dishes and eat them. A large crowd gathered in front of the palace and cheered the newborn prince and future heir. The next morning, the townspeople were woken up to the booming sound of a 21-gun salute.

29th July 1919 (Tuesday) happened to be the 12th day after the child's birth. The naming ceremony of the child was performed at 10.30 AM in Sri Amba Vilas Darbar hall. The *"Namakarana"* (naming) ceremony was sanctified by the presence of the pontiff (Raja Guru) of the Brahma Tantra Parakala Mutt. The Maharaja and the Yuvaraja washed the feet of their family Guru with Ganga water. Then, the Raja Guru was given fruits, flowers and a Cashmere Shawl. The Raja Guru gave in return flowers, fruits and shawls to the Maharaja and the Yuvaraja. The swamiji blessed the newborn infant and the other royal family members by sprinkling holy rice grains upon their heads. They were also given holy water to drink. The male child was given the name Sri Jayachamaraja Wodeyar. Afterwards, the Dewan Sir M. Kantha Raja Urs presented the male heir with a diamond necklace and two silk shawls. The other courtiers presented expensive gifts to the child. The whole of Mysore State celebrated the arrival of a Royal heir. In all the towns and cities, thousands of people belonging to different castes and religions were served hearty meals in public charitable halls.

The incumbent Dewan Sir Kantharaja Urs decided to relinquish his office because of poor health. He retired on 1st May 1922 and the Maharaja appointed Sri A.R. Banerjee an Indian Civil Service officer as the new Dewan. He administered the state for four years and the King-Emperor conferred Knighthood upon him. The Bhadravathi Steel mill was commissioned eight months after A.R. Banerjee took over the office of the Dewan. The Steel Mill Furnace began to produce steel from 18th January 1923.

The state government of Mysore wanted to build a dam across the Cauvery River to harness it for agricultural purposes. The Madras Government opposed it because it felt that most of the Cauvery water would be appropriated by Mysore State. The Madras Presidency, as a riparian state, was insisting on its rights. Ultimately, on 18th February 1924, the two states signed an agreement to share the water without causing any hardship to the riparian state farmers. The sharing of Cauvery water depended on the annual rainfall and inflow of water to the Krishnaraja Sagar Dam. The Farmers of Mysore state could irrigate more acreage to grow rice and sugarcane.

The state had empowered some revenue officials in a few districts to act like Magistrates. They could hear criminal cases and pass judgments. These extraordinary powers were withdrawn from them and in all eight districts, Magistrate courts were established to try criminal cases. Many administrative reforms were initiated to cut costs as per the recommendations of the "Retrenchment Committee" set up in 1922. The fiscal deficit was narrowed to some extent by these economic measures.

Sri Nalwadi repeatedly gave several representations to the Viceroy of India and to the British monarch requesting them to rescind the annual tribute paid to the British Government as the state was a welfare state. The Maharaja of Mysore visited the summer capital of India, Shimla to negotiate this waiver with the Viceroy.

The Yuvaraja's wife delivered three daughters after the birth of their son Sri Jayachamarajendra Wodeyar. The first daughter Sri Vijaya Lakshammani was born on 28th August 1922. The second daughter, Sri Sujaya Kanthammani, was born on 6th February 1924. The third daughter Sri Jaya Chamundammani was born on 30th October 1927.

The council was empowered to discuss the budget in 1914. In 1923, it was given power to vote on the demands for grants. In 1923, it was enacted that the council would not have the power to amend the legislative assembly regulation and legislative council regulations.

The Loss of Close Relatives of the Royal Family

A series of deaths of the close relatives of the royal family impacted the Maharaja and the Yuvaraja.

The brother-in-law of the Maharaja Col. J. Desharaja Urs passed away on 8th October 1922. Another brother-in-law, Sir M. Kantharaja Urs, died on 2nd October 1923. His wife and elder sister of Nalwadi, Sri Jayalakshammani passed away on 8th December 1924. These untimely deaths caused immense grief to the Mysore royal family.

The Maharaja wanted the public to be involved in Civic administration; hence more devolution of political power was initiated. More and more elected members were inducted into the Legislative Council and the People's Representative Assembly. The village panchayats, local boards and municipalities enjoyed more political power because the "new Mysore State Municipalities Act" had been enacted in 1918. The municipalities were classified into three categories - Minor Municipalities, Town Municipalities and City Municipalities. These Municipal boards had more civilian members than official members. These civic bodies could plan and implement their own budgetary proposals. They were empowered to link villages and towns by constructing highways.

Nalwadi wanted to delegate more powers to these civic bodies. During October 1922, the Dewan proclaimed in the Dasara Darbar to the members of the Representative assembly that His Highness intended to vest more powers to them. The Maharaja appointed a committee under the chairmanship of Sir Brajendranath Seal the then Vice-Chancellor of Mysore University to suggest further reforms. The recommendations of this committee were accepted and the new regulations to guide the functioning of the Mysore Legislative Council and the Mysore Representative Assembly were made public through a state government Gazette notification in 1923.

Because of the reforms, the strength of the Legislative Council went up from 30 to 50. The Council could seat 30 civilian representatives and 20 nominated Government officials. The 30 civilian components in the council had 22 elected members and 8 government-nominated members. The legislative council already had powers to table questions on important issues and also to make decisions to promote the welfare of the subjects. Now, they could make proposals during budget motion and also make necessary allocation of funds for that purpose. The legislative council members would not debate upon certain matters like palace expenditure and defence outlay in the budget.

Because of the new regulations, the representative assembly came to be empowered. In the earlier times, the house had 250 members. It was felt that certain groups did not get adequate representation in the assembly. Hence, the house strength was increased to 275. The representative assembly had the power to discuss the budgetary proposals and also to suggest changes.

The assembly could send eight of its members to the state legislative council. They also elected members to officiate in various capacities in different "Standing Committees." It became mandatory to consult the Representative Assembly before the enactment of new laws and also before new taxes were imposed on people. The State Government had stipulated certain preconditions to eligible voters. These gentlemen had voting rights. Landlords with stipulated land holdings, income taxpayers and graduates with property. Later, women with property and education were empowered to vote during elections to council and assembly. Because of these reforms, the number of voters strength increased by four-fold.

Some minorities like Christians and Muslims did not find adequate representation in the assembly and council. So, a certain number of seats were reserved for them. The members from minority communities, representatives of the University of Mysore, representatives of John Taylor and Sons (Gold Mine and co.) at KGF and some prominent businessmen got nominated through their official and unofficial guilds to the assembly. It was also resolved to conduct official business in the Kannada Language in the assembly and in English in the council like in the past.

The re-constituted Assembly and council was inaugurated by His Highness Sri Nalwadi Krishnaraja Wodeyar on 17th March 1924. In the joint address to both the houses, he expressed his future vision and a deep concern for the welfare of his subjects. He stated in his speech, "It is my desire and hope that citizens of our state will develop the self-confidence and self-reliance to conduct the legislative business. They ought to develop the required strength, courage and energy to take up challenging schemes and projects to enrich Mysore State. They shall chart their own destiny to achieve all-round development. I wish to see this true democratic spirit prevail in our state. The whole purpose of political reform is to achieve economic and social progress. The whole purpose of democracy is to empower ordinary citizens to develop a capacity for shaping their own future. We want all sections of the society to strive with the ruler for the welfare of the state. You must assist the state government and you must also function as guardians of the state to make it an ideal place to live in." It was truly a historic day, which heralded a new revolution in the political administration of a princely state. At that time, even in British-ruled presidencies, this kind of empowerment of elected representatives had not taken place. The princely state of Mysore proved to be a pathbreaker.

The Two Royal Weddings

Nalwadi's third sister, Princess Chaluvajammani's daughter Sri Chennajammani got married to Sri Dalavayi Madangopalaraja Urs on 21st June 1924 in the palace Kalyana Mantapa. Nalwadi's elder sister Princess Jayalakshammani's daughter Sri Lilavathi Kumari got married to Sri K. Basvaraja Urs on June 13, 1926, in Mysore Palace.

Floods in State

Due to heavy downpour of monsoon rain, the rivers Cauvery, Kabini, Hemavathi and Tungabhadra were in spate. These rivers in flood destroyed crops and ruined agricultural fields with river sand. Some lakes and ponds breached the check dams. Many people lost their houses. In Manjrabad near Sakaleshpura, one house in a village collapsed and a young boy died. The flood-affected people were given aid by the State government. They were also helped by the Maharaja and also by some rich people.

The late Sri Lala Lajpath Rai was truly a great patriot. He never minced words and never spoke against his conscience. He wrote an article on Mysore's ruler in 1925 for the "*Swarajya*" newspaper published from Madras.

> "It adds considerably to one's feeling of pleasure and pride when one comes across a prince who continues in his person the ancient nobility of his family with the characteristics of a great and good personality. Such is the present Maharaja of Mysore, handsome in appearance, highly religious in character and simple in habits and he has none of the vices, which disfigure some of the royal houses today. His purity of life, his devotion to his own faith accompanied by high regard and tolerance for other faiths, his great personal charm, his regard for learning and his desire to introduce all the methods of good government in his state endear him to his people and place him high among the present ruling princes of India. In these days of bitter communalism in India, the first thing that attracts the notice of a visitor is the fact that the most religious of Hindu princes has a Mohamedan as his Private Secretary who enjoys the implicit confidence of his master… …what, however, pleased me most and made me proud of the administration of Mysore is its individuality. It distinguishes Mysore from all other Indian States and even from British India…"

– Late Mr. Lala Lajpath Rai

The newly enacted Gramapanchayat (Village Council) and District Board regulations came into force in 1927. The Gramapanchayats were freed from the control of District boards. They came under the purview of the Revenue officials of Taluq Boards. The Dewan of the State Rajamantradhurina Sir A.R. Banerjee, M.A, C.S.I, C.I.E, ICS retired on 1st May 1926. The Maharaja appointed Amin-ul-Mulk Mirza M. Ismail C.I.E. D.B.E as the next Dewan of Mysore State.

Lalitadripura – A Model Village

A model planned village was built behind Chamundi Hill in 1926 at the initiative of the Maharaja. This experimental project came for very high praise in "The Hindu" newspaper. Nalwadi wanted other States of India to emulate this project. The villages must provide a healthy environment to its inhabitants.

The Maharaja entrusted this novel project to Advocate H. Narasingha Rao and to Raja Sena Tilaka Major Gopala Rao of Mysore. There was a small insignificant village called Sakkahalli. Nalwadi generously donated 20 acres of reserve palace land for this project. He also gave local farmers additional acreage of palace lands. The villagers would be accommodated in the newly built houses. The villagers were given plots of land free of cost. They were given soft loans to construct well-planned houses. The Maharaja advanced a loan of Rs. 60,000 to the farmers to build houses on a nominal rate of interest. In the past, the farmers had borrowed agricultural loans from the Maharaja. They had repaid these loans with interest. Nalwadi ordered that this fund must be spent on the development of the village and it should not be credited to the palace account. The villagers were given 15 years' time to repay these loans. They were given permission to fell trees in the state government forests and make use of the timber in the construction of buildings. The state government spent Rs. 3,000 to rejuvenate the village lake by desilting it.

The Maharaja commissioned a school building for Lalithadripura. He wanted the boys and girls to receive quality education. These students received education in agricultural sciences. They were taught the technique of spinning thread from cotton. They also received religious education.

The Maharaja gave a financial grant for the construction of a cooperative society building, a hall for prayer and singing bhajans and a grama panchayat building. Everyone, including young and old people, was told to become members of the Co-operative Society. Nalwadi advised them to settle disputes in the grama panchayat, without resorting to expensive legal battles.

The whole of India admired this model village, which embodied inner spiritual aspirations with the external aesthetics of town planning. The newspapers and magazines praised the experiment as worthy of emulation by other states. The Maharaja not only gave generous donations but also supervised the construction of the houses. Nalwadi, by unveiling the nameplate of the village, inaugurated the occupation of the model village. After a while, the villagers requested the Maharaja to give their village electricity and piped water. This facility also was provided with the personal funds of the Maharaja.

The Royal family deity, Goddess Chamundeshwari temple was on top of the hill. There was a small township surrounding the temple. The inhabitants of this hamlet relied on a small pond called "Devi Kere" for their drinking water needs. This pond containing water often became polluted and caused health problems. The Maharaja commissioned a water pumping facility from the base of the hill. The people who lived on the hill could receive Cauvery drinking water from July 1927 onwards.

Yuvarani Sri Kempuchaluvajammani (sitting in the middle),
Prince Sri Jayachamarajendra Wodeyar (on arm rest),
Sitting: Princess Sri Vijayalakshammani (left) and
Princess Sujaya Kanthammani (right)

Chapter 9

The post-Silver Jubilee Reign of the Maharaja

******

Samano mantrasamitisamaani
Samaanam manasah Chitta meshaam|
Samaanam mantramabimantrayevah
Samaanena vo havishaa juhomi||
Samaniva akoti samaanaa hridayani vah|
Samanmastu vo mano yatha vassusahaasati||

******

"Those who possess an equanimity of mind blended with consciousness (perception) and remains calm during discussions or negotiations, to such a person I offer my mantras and invite you to this august gathering. During Homa, I offer oblation (Havis) generously. May your ideas and opinions give gentle happiness, feelings and finer emotions to everyone gathered here."

It was declared by the State Government that on 8th August 1927, all over the state the Silver Jubilee of Nalwadi's rule would be celebrated on a grand scale. Prior to this celebration, the then Viceroy of India Lord Irwin and Lady Irwin paid an official Visit to Mysore State. They spent one week as V.V.I. P guests of the Maharaja from 25th July 1927.

During the official Banquet, the Viceroy Lord Irwin in his after-dinner speech announced that the British Imperial Government had passed an order stating that the princely state of Mysore need not pay an annual tribute of Rs. 35 Lakhs to the British Government and instead it could pay Rs. 24,50,000 per annum. This gesture was made by the King-Emperor in recognition of the benevolent rule and the modernization of the State, achieved under Sri Nalwadi Krishnaraja Wodeyar.

Lord Irwin said, "Through appropriate means, state development had been accomplished during the last 25 years. Moreover, it was constantly revised time and again to make further improvements. Nalwadi has set an example to other states on how a princely state could make progress in the briefest period. All this has not escaped our notice." This financial concession to a princely state by a mighty colonial power gladdened the hearts of its subjects. The Silver Jubilee Celebration of Maharaja's rule was celebrated in all the towns and villages on 8th August 1927. The religious leaders of different faiths offered special thanksgiving prayers in temples, churches and masjids. In all the schools and colleges of the state, the boys and girls participated in the function with enthusiasm. They garlanded the portrait of the Maharaja and saluted the red state flag which sported *"Gandhabherunda"* symbol and also to the Union Jack. They also sang the state anthem *"Kaio Sri Gowri"* wishing long life to the ruler and victory to the state [Ed Note- An Indian version of "God Save the King" as state anthem.]

The Maharaja conveyed a special message on this occasion to his state's subjects, "We express our heartfelt emotion that all the citizens of Mysore State should live happily and their welfare is of utmost importance to me. On the completion of 25 years, I express my desire to ensure the well-being and happiness of our subjects through various further endeavours. I pray to lord Almighty to grant me strength and wisdom to accomplish these goals."

The Maharaja woke up early on 8th August 1927 (Silver Jubilee Day) and was given an auspicious shower (*"Mangala snana"*). He prayed and performed the pooja and Sandhyavandana. He visited the family deity, Goddess Chamundeshwari, who was enthroned in the big temple on the hill. He prayed and took prasad from the priests. Later, he went to see his mother former Regent Vanivilas Sannidhana. He took his mother's blessings and from there, he proceeded to attend a conclave of eminent Sanskrit pandits at Kalyana Mantap. They blessed the ruler of the State by reciting appropriate vedic mantras in his honour. He addressed them in the following manner in chaste Sanskrit: "….."

"Bo boha nigamaagam aparadhrshavanah, Shishya prashishya nivahai prakayapitha digantha vishranth keerthayah, yaadava bhumipaalaanam shreyase nirantara nidyaatha devatha paramparaaha, mahashayaah, panditavarayah, yathah tatrabhavathaam bhavathayam amoghashirvadaasya asmin smarneye sudivase paathrataam nithosmi, athohamaatanam, dhanyam maneye| Shubhasamayesminidanim astaan mandape bhadrapitamaardum anugnam praratheye|"

Translation

"Oh Ye! great reputed veda-vedanta scholars blessed with immense knowledge, your fame has spread in all four directions through your disciples. You have been praying to God for the well-being of the ruler of the Yadava Dynasty all these years. On this auspicious occasion, I am fortunate enough to receive your blessings and benedictions. You are entitled to my respectful homage and veneration. You are the chosen ones among the great scholars. I am grateful to you for your generous and kind-hearted divine sanction. I humbly seek your permission to occupy this sacred throne on this happy occasion of the silver jubilee of my ascension."

He sought their consent and approval to sit on the throne and continue his rule as per the injunctions of the Dharma Sastras.

The Maharaja made his entry into the Darbar Hall at 10 AM along with his younger brother Yuvaraja Sri Kanteerava Narasimharaja Wodeyar. He ascended the throne and sat on it. A renowned Sanskrit scholar recited a long Sanskrit verse praising his glorious rule and the benefits enjoyed by his citizens. He recited vedic mantras, praying to God for the long life and well-being of the ruler.

Afterwards, the Diwan Sir K.P. Puttanna Chetty on behalf of the subjects of the Mysore State presented the Maharaja with a memorandum in a silver rotund casket.

God Bless Our King
[SRI RASTU]
May God protect our king and bring auspicious tidings
[Svasti]

The princely state of Mysore was also known by the name of Mahishura Kingdom situated in the subcontinent of Bharathakanda, where the reputed Kannada-speaking population dwells. It is ruled by the Monarch Sri Nalwadi Krishnaraja Wodeyar G.C.S.I, G.B.E who is also known by the titles such as the bravest among the brave, sovereign supreme ruler, a symbol of utmost courage and valour and one who holds many more titles attributed to him. We submit this humble memorandum to His Highness.

On this auspicious day in the *Shalivahana Shaka* Era of 1849 *Prabhava* year on the 10th day (Monday) in the month of *Shravana* this representation is submitted by the people of Mysore State belonging to different castes and religions. This memorandum conveys the genuine devotion and love for our monarch. In good faith and humility, this thanksgiving letter of commendation is offered to the ruler in good faith.

Our Highness Sri Nalwadi Krishnaraja Wodeyar belongs to an ancient royal lineage of Yaduvamsa, who ascended the throne 25 years ago taking on his shoulders the responsibility of governing this hallowed state. During this long period, our monarch has given the state an efficient administration laced with goodwill and plenty of boons in the form of projects of development and progress. The needs of the general population have been quite well taken care of by our ruler,

The Mysore clock tower in front of the Town Hall. Silver Jubilee Memorial

The innumerable achievements of the Maharaja Sri Nalwadi Krishnaraja Wodeyar deserve to be written in golden letters in the annals of Indian History. According to discerning observers, our ruler is a role model for the other rulers of India and the world. This is the general consensus among the citizens that the state of Mysore is blessed by the Almighty to possess such a visionary ruler.

The political scientists are generous in their praise and admiration for the Maharaja's efficient rule on democratic lines. Our Maharaja has been pruning and reforming various organs of the state like the Executive, Legislature and Judiciary. All these revolutionary changes have quadrupled the state's income and correspondingly the government welfare schemes have ushered in a better quality of life. Because our Maharaja has paid a lot of attention to widespread access to quality education, it has resulted in a thirst for knowledge among the masses. More and more people are learning the language of the Gods, "Sanskrit" (Girvani). Our educational institutions are spreading Western science and technology. Our ruler has been a generous patron of music and fine arts. The numerous educational institutions, schools, colleges and Mysore University stand as remarkable monuments to the idealistic foresight of Nalwadi Krishnaraja Wodeyar.

The innumerable achievements of our beloved ruler may be listed here. Sri Krishnaraja Sagar dam, new wells, lakes and irrigation canals benefitting our farmers, new State highways and railway lines, Electricity generation stations, mining, chemical industries, modernisation of agriculture and fillip to mass communication and improvement of trade skills among artisans are some of them.

The Maharaja is also credited with building new hospitals, veterinary hospitals for animals, magnificent town halls, parks, reading rooms and libraries and money-lending co-operative societies, all of which have helped the common man to improve his lot.

Sri Krishnarajendra Silver Jubilee Technological Institute

Dewan of Mysore State – Dewan Amin – Ul – Mulk Sir Mirza. M. Ismail, K. C. I. E, O. B. E (1926 – 1941)

Standing L – R: The Maharaja and Sir Mirza. M. Ismail

The people's representative Assembly, the legislative council, the town municipalities and village panchayat boards have amply proved the democratic spirit of our ruler. These institutions will inspire people to take an interest in politics, get involved in public affairs and they will participate in nation-building activity. Due to these activities, ordinary citizens will develop a sense of duty, a craving for justice, self-reliance sagacity of mind and a feeling of oneness among the masses. This will promote the smooth functioning of the government. This will ensure prosperity, progress and peace to prevail in our kingdom.

A View of Brindavan Gardens

The Water Fountains in Brindavan Gardens

Gateway to Brindavan Gardens

Our highness is blessed by God with these noble virtues –faith in God, compassion towards animals and birds, good conduct, faith in tradition, respect towards gurus, an affection for erudite scholars, an adherent of dharma sastras, easy access to the grieving public, a willingness to consult experienced administrators and ministers, an instinct to please the world with right action and last but not the least, possess a pure soul.

All those pure virtues make our monarch a perfect ruler in the mould of the mythical King Janaka and King Yudhishtra of yore. These qualities of the ruler have resulted in peace and tranquillity prevailing in the Mysore State.

In recent times, the British government has taken note of the efficient and competent rule of our monarch. All the remarkable achievements of Mysore State have received due publicity in Europe and America. All this resulted in a friendly gesture from Lord Irwin the Viceroy of India announcing a reduction in the amount of tribute paid to the British Raj. The state was remitting annually Rs. 35 lakhs and now, it has been asked to pay a tribute of Rs. 24 lakhs and 50,000 only. A remission of Rs, 10,50,000 has been given to the state.

We pray to the Almighty to grant long life, good health, fame and wealth to our Monarch and to Yuvaraja and to the Queen Mother Sri Vanivilasa Sannidhana. May the great reputation of our Monarch spread to all continents. Let our ruler be victorious in all his endeavours. We pray to God to give us a similar opportunity to express our heartfelt appreciation for our king during the forthcoming Golden Jubilee celebration. We, the citizens, pray to almighty God to grant our Monarch bountiful gifts.

Place: Mysore City
8th August 1927
This is the humble appeal and submission made by the loyal subjects of Mahishura Kingdom.

On this occasion, a 21-gun salute was given to His Highness Sri Nalwadi Krishna Raja Wodeyar. The Maharaja in his thanksgiving speech said,

"My dear Citizens,
I receive your memorandum, which embodies your respect and love for your sovereign gratefully. It has gladdened my heart immensely. God has not only blessed Mysore State with natural wealth, but he has also granted a broad-minded, generous populace. The State of Mysore has earned the sobriquet of a modern state because of your sincere efforts. The British government has given

us a remission in payment of annual tribute, because of your contribution to the development of the state.

In a similar fashion, we must all strive in the future like brothers to develop agriculture, industry and commerce. We must create equal opportunities for all. We must make our state stand among developed nations on an equal footing.

The future generation of youth must endorse brotherly love and encourage the formation of a people's republic. The future of the state depends on the love they show for their motherland. I wish to state at this juncture that we all must show love and compassion towards speechless animals and birds.

I urge the people of Mysore belonging to different religions and castes to forget their differences and they must remember that all were born in this state to help and uplift their less fortunate brethren.

We personally believe that the well-being of people is our well-being. I pray to Almighty to grant me wisdom, determination to achieve my goals and financial bounty to enhance the wellbeing and happiness of my subjects."

The Maharaja inaugurated the Silver Jubilee Clock tower in front of the palace in the evening at 5.30 PM by pressing an electric button. This clock tower was a gift to His Royal Highness by the Palace officials and courtiers. Then, the Maharaja in an open chaise drawn by four horses went in a procession to the government house grounds to watch the evening pageant. The Mysore army battalions paraded before him. The boy scouts demonstrated their gymnastic skills by forming human pyramids, etc. Some blind students performed *"Harikatha"* (Recitation of Puranic stories), music concerts, acrobatics show and at the end a grand display of fireworks. The Maharaja returned to the palace in an open horse-drawn carriage and he was cheered by thousands of people who had lined up in the streets. He was welcomed by Prince Desharaja Urs and other senior dignitaries of the Ursu community. Prince Sri Desharaja Urs washed the feet of the Maharaja with water. He performed the puja. They offered a garland, shawl and fruits to the King expressing their loyalty and devotion to him. The next morning, the boy scouts gathered at Jagan Mohan Palace. The chief guest was Yuvaraja Sri Kanteerava Narasimharaja Wodeyar. The scouts expressed their respect, love and devotion to the monarch. The Maharaja's message was read. It had expressed his desire that the scouts should lead the lives of ideal citizens of the society. They must also harbour goodwill towards one and all. The presence of Yuvaraja and his son Prince Sri Jayachamarajendra Wodeyar added lustre and colour to the function. It gladdened the hearts of boys and girls.

Sri Krishnarajendra Hospital, Mysore

The Maharaja was invited to Bangalore City in September 1927. He was accorded a grand civic reception in his honour. A memorandum was presented to him in a gala reception at Cubbon Park.

In the evening on an elephant, the Maharaja and the Yuvaraja sitting in a golden Ambari went through the main streets of Bangalore. They were cheered by the Bangalore public.

During Silver Jubilee celebrations, a lot of citizens donated to the jubilee fund. It was decided that $1/3^{rd}$ of that amount would be spent on the construction of libraries, reading rooms, free highway inns (*Dharmashalas*), orphanages and maternity wards in small towns of Mysore State. It was decided to start a technical training institute with the remaining $2/3^{rd}$ of the amount.

"The Krishnarajendra Silver Jubilee Technological Institute" was started to give professional job-oriented education. It is relevant to quote the words of Mahatma Gandhi, who described the Princely State of Mysore as modern-day "*Ramrajya*".

According to M.K. Gandhi, "Mysoreans are doubly fortunate; firstly, nature is kind and beautiful to them and their climate fine and salubrious. Secondly, their Maharaja is a ruler of great nobility and character. He is dharmic. I have heard from everyone good accounts of the Maharaja. He is kind and always thinking of the good of his people." The other gentlemen who have heaped praise on the Maharaja are Sir Prafulla Chandra Ray, Sir P.S. Shivaswamy Iyer and the Right honourable V.S. Srinivasa Sastri. During the silver jubilee celebrations, the state had received another great patriot in the person of Sri Pandit Madan Mohan Malvia.

This is his opinion of our Maharaja, "You Mysoreans are a happy people. You are happy to have such a beautiful province, situated between two to three thousand feet above sea level, neither very warm nor very cold, with a salubrious climate and great natural resources. You are also happy to have the present Maharaja as your King. His Highness' purity of private life combined with his solicitude for the welfare of his people, his genuine conservatism and firmness of his own faith combined with a full appreciation of the requirements of modern progress and unaffected religious toleration have marked him out for honour among the rulers of men. His wise choice of selection of successive Dewans and his encouragement of numerous schemes for the best administration of the state and for the advancement of his people and the Highness' impartiality towards the sections of his subjects have rightly won for him the gratitude and affection of his people… His Highness the

Maharaja has been really happy in the choice of his successive Dewans and it is, therefore, not surprising that the administration of the state has attained its present excellence."

Sir Mirza M. Ismail was appointed as the next Dewan on 1st May 1926. He was very well known for his strong patriotism, loyalty and political acumen. He proved himself as an able administrator. The Maharaja, during Dasara festivities, was accorded the title of "Amin-ul-Mulk" in 1920. The British Government honoured him with these titles – D.B.E in 1923, C.I.E in 1924, Knighthood in 1930 and K.C.I.E in 1936. Sir Mirza M. Ismail's grandfather Janab Ai Askar had wholeheartedly worked in favour of Mummadi Krishna Raja Wodeyar regaining his kingdom. Sir Mirza's father had served Sri Chamarjendra Wodeyar and Sri Nalwadi Krishna Raja Wodeyar as a bodyguard. Sir Mirza M. Ismail was a trusted classmate in school and a good friend. He had held several administrative posts in the government and had proved himself as a skilled and able administrator. During his tenure, the British Raj gave a remission of 10.5 lakhs in the payment of tributes. Instead of 35 lakhs, the state was asked to pay a tribute of 24.5 lakhs to the British Government. His aim is to achieve zero tribute to the British government from Mysore State.

Sir Mirza M. Ismail has proved himself to be a courageous and adventurous administrator. In the case of the Bhadravathi Iron and Steel factory, which had proved to be a loss-making enterprise year after year was turned around to make profits. It came to such a pass that the members of the People's Representative Assembly and Legislative Council were urging the Mysore State Government to close this industry. But Sir Mirza M. Ismail was not dismayed by these huge losses. He was determined to make this steel mill a profit-making enterprise and save thousands of jobs. The iron mill had these subsidiaries added to it, a steel manufacturing unit, a cement unit and a paper manufacturing unit. On the whole, the Bhadravathi Iron and Steel enterprise became a profitable one. During the last fourteen years, Mysore State has witnessed many such miracles performed by Sir Mirza M. Ismail. Lord Samuel recently in London made this statement during his speech, "…Incidentally, one example of his wisdom and his foresight has been the appointment as Dewan Saheb of Sir Mirza M. Ismail, undoubtedly one of the ablest administrators to be found, not only in India but anywhere within the bounds of the British Commonwealth."

The president of Bombay State Congress Party Sri B.G. Kher has expressed his admiration and appreciation for Sir Mirza M. Ismail in this manner, "I am dumfounded by his remarkable character, integrity, loyalty, generosity and his commitment to public service." Sir Mirza M. Ismail possesses erudition and wisdom which is laced with compassion and humility in good measure. He is definitely a good role model for others. He is extremely sympathetic to the people, who have suffered misfortunes in life.

Once, Dewan Sir Mirza M. Ismail was proceeding to Doddaballapur to inaugurate a Primary Health Centre in his official car. Some *Adikarnataka* (untouchable caste) people approached him near Nelamangala town. They were in dire straits as their huts and belongings had been engulfed in flames, because of a fire accident. They had lost all their possessions in the fire mishap. They begged for help. He summoned the *"Amaldar"* (officer in charge of Taluq) and ordered him to provide those unfortunate victims with food and clothing. The funds were sanctioned immediately for the construction of houses. An elderly man hearing these words of Dewan came forward and thanked the Dewan profusely with tears in his eyes. When the official car resumed its journey, after a few minutes, Dewan Mirza M. Ismail remarked before the co-passengers that the government officials were meant to help the needy persons. They must place themselves in the shoes of the unfortunate victims to feel their pangs of suffering.

Another touching incident occurred on the same day. The Dewan Saheb enquired about a blind beggar who sat usually on the outskirts of the town. He used to sing devotional bajans so as to collect alms. But on this particular day, the blind beggar was absent. Some people informed him that he could be found in another street. While returning from the town after the inaugural function, he asked the chauffeur to drive to the street where the blind beggar could be found. The Dewan gave him fruits, money and also a garland as parting gifts. The blind beggar was overjoyed by this unforeseen bounty. Later, the Dewan remarked, if only the blind person could see his gifts, how much more pleasure he would have derived from it.

Whenever the Dewan Saheb left his residence, he made sure his pockets were full of sweets, chocolates and candies. If he found children at the place of visit, he would distribute sweets to them.

The Dewan Saheb believed in self-reliance. He loved Mysore State deeply and wanted all citizens to consume products produced within the state. Dewan Sir Mirza M. Ismail followed the secular philosophy practised by the Maharaja Sri Nalwadi Krishnaraja Wodeyar. Firstly, he was a devout Muslim but respected all other religions. He sincerely believed that by helping people of all religions, he was pleasing "Allah" greatly.

Once the Muslim Dewan in a Hindu temple accepted the "Mangala Arti" (a ritualistic offering of a lighted lamp to a God or Goddess) much to the amazement of the assembled Hindu devotees. When asked by someone about his unconventional behaviour, he replied, "I feel the presence of God here, because for centuries Hindu devotees have worshipped in this temple. How can the prayers of millions of people go to waste?"

The Dewan is a shrewd politician and given to deep thinking on matters of administration. His fame has spread to all the four corners of the world. In India, he is considered as the best Dewan (Chief Minister) taking care of a princely state.

The well-known politician, diplomat, newspaper editor and private secretary to British Prime Minister Sir Lloyd George and a Scottish aristocrat Philip Henry Kerr Marquis of Lothian (1882-1940) has expressed his admiration for the Dewan of Mysore State in these words, "Sir Mirza M Ismail is an old friend of mine. I have sat beside him during round table conferences that were conducted over a period of three or four years. He is a very good debater and presented his argument with lot of prudence. He has a thorough knowledge of Indian political scene and knew the due process of law. When I visited Mysore State in 1938, he escorted me to 3 or 4 places of historical interest. But I saw as firsthand witness only during this visit to Mysore State, his remarkable achievements as an able seasoned administrator. One is wonderstruck by his vision and planning."

A famous American scholar by the name Dr. S. Ralph Harlow a missionary and a college professor and his lawful wife visited Mysore State which was making progress as a modern state at that time. In a letter to a friend, this is what he wrote,

"We feel it our bounden duty to inform the American public about a wonderful progress made by this princely state in the field of Industry and Commerce, Social reform and Education. The state is not lagging behind in town planning and beautification of public parks. The hydro-electric generation station and the beautiful KRS dam with its aesthetically designed garden with fountains can rival the garden and fountains of Versailles in Paris."

Sir Mirza M Ismail was also a lover of Kannada language. When he was presented with a memorandum by the office bearers of Kannada Association of Channarayanapattana, he replied that his love for Kannada and Kannada newspapers was boundless. Mysore State Government allotted a plot of land for construction of building of Kannada Sahitya Parishat. But the Dewan found it inadequate and located in an insignificant area of Bangalore. He questioned the City Town Planning authorities, "Why have you allotted a small plot of land for the Kannada temple patronized by the Maharaja himself?" The present building came up on a plot opposite Sri Chamarajendra Sanskrit Patasala (Presently Karnataka Sanskrit University building) in Chamarajapet.

Dewan Sir Mirza M. Ismail was blessed with a good aesthetic sense. He began in 1910 his government service as an Assistant Secretary to the Maharaja in the Palace. Since then, he has been obsessed with the beautification and town planning of Mysore and Bangalore cities.

When Nalwadi assumed powers in 1902, he appointed Sir Evan Maconochie as chairman of the newly formed "City Improvement Trust Board." The Maharaja gave his advice from time to time. After Sir Mirza M. Ismail joined the working committee, wherein he initiated many beautification programmes. According to the guidelines of the ruler, the roads in the city were laid in straight lines, which criss-crossed each other. A new planned elite extension was planned in the Southern part of the city called Lakshmipuram. [The first planned extension in Bangalore South came up and it was called Chamarajpet- Ed note] Mysore and Bangalore cities came to possess beautiful parks and streets which were lined with electric lamp posts cast in iron and made in England. His love of gardens prompted him to develop "Brindavan Gardens" in the vicinity of the KRS Dam modelled on the Mughal Gardens (Designed by Krumbigal). Every year, 2 lakh visitors visit Brindavan Gardens, thereby bringing much-needed revenue to the State Treasury. [I have already quoted the letter of Marquis of Lothian and opinions of Sri B.G. Kher and Dr. S. Ralph Harlow on Brindavan Garden]

If we study annual budgetary allocation of funds to various sectors, we realize the progress made under Nalwadi's rule. When Nalwadi began his rule, the state revenue was Rs. 2 crores. Gradually, it increased to Rs. 4 crores and 39 lakhs. In the beginning, Rs. 6 lakhs was spent on education. At the end of his rule, (1940) it touched Rs. 60 lakhs which included expenditure on the University of Mysore. The expenditure on the state healthcare quadrupled. Earlier Rs. 27 lakhs was spent on public buildings, highways and bridges. Several more lakhs of rupees were allotted to public works department in annual budget.

Sri Nalwadi dispensed justice to people of all religions and castes without any discrimination. A delegation of non-Brahmins and Muslim community leaders met the Maharaja on 18th June 1918. During the parleys, they appealed to Maharaja to give representation to non-Brahmins and Muslims in Government service. As such, a majority of officials were from the Brahmin community. The Maharaja replied to these people in the following manner, "It is my desire to see proportional representation of civil servants of all religions and castes in the state Government Service. Hence, I do not want to make fresh promises. The Brahmins are in majority in the Government service, only because of their educational background and a high level of literacy. This is the natural outcome of their advantage enjoyed, since time immemorial. At present, people of all communities are receiving the benefits of universal education. Henceforth, they will compete for jobs along with Brahmins. In due course, people of other religions and castes will fill up government jobs. You must not expect me to either punish or create hurdles for Brahmins in the matter of jobs. Like all other community members, the Brahmins have served the state and the royal family loyally and their patriotism and dedication to the causes are a proven fact. Their yeoman service in the past and at present has been recognized by us. It is our aim to create an environment conducive for all castes so that they can thrive and prosper. I neither want to give any extra fillip to one community nor block the progress of another community."

The Maharaja also stated that the backward caste citizens will be provided more facilities and given more privileges. They should not disturb the harmony that prevails in the society. Nalwadi advised Brahmins not to harbor any ill will or hatred towards the depressed castes. Their natural desire to improve their station in life should be viewed sympathetically.

Because the ruler of Mysore state practised true secularism and tolerance, communal riots and disturbances between Hindus and Muslims were almost unknown.

Lord Walter Samuel 2nd Viscount Bearsted (1882-1948), owner of Shell Oil Company has got this to say, "With respect to the third great problem, the conflict between the Hindus and Muslims, I was grieved to learn when I was in India – and fact has been confirmed in many enquiries – that the condition in that respect is rather worse in these years than better. That has been an indirect effect of recent constitutional development, but here, Mysore is an example for the rest of India. Here, with a ruler of Hindu faith and a Dewan who is a Muslim, and all the offices of the state open to men of both communities, Mysore stands as an example of peace and harmony in this unhappy conflict." – Lord Samuel

Because of election reforms, women gained voting rights. They were encouraged to contest the elections. This is because both the Maharaja and the Dewan encouraged women's education. They effected an amendment to Hindu law, so women could lay claim to ancestral property and also lay claim to a share in their husband's property. The downtrodden Adi Karnataka caste people and tribals could enjoy equal rights before the law. It is because of Nalwadi's benign rule the State of Mysore moved from No. 2 position to No. 1 position among Indian princely states. This is how Madan Mohan Malviya summed up the progress of Mysore State,

*"Excepting one state which I have not yet had the privilege of visiting, you are ahead of every other Indian state in the progress you have achieved."
– Pandit Madan Mohan Malviya

The princely state of Baroda was the No.1 state until Mysore State overtook it around 1930.

"Mysore continued in 1938 to live up to the expectation as the most progressive of the Indian States" – a quote from Encyclopaedia Britannica, Book of the Year 1939 (page 446)

Heir-apparent for Sitamau State in Madhyapradesh Maharaja Kumar Raghubir Singh, D.litt. evaluates princely states in this manner –

"The systems of administration also differ widely. Some states like Mysore, Baroda and Travancore can claim systems of administration, which are more efficient, better organized and more solicitous for the welfare of the people than even British Rule in British India; at the same time, it must be admitted that there are states whose administration is medieval in structure and feudal in spirit." From the book *"Indian States and the New Regime,"* by Maharaja Kumar Rahubir Singh, D.litt., (Heir-apparent for Sitamau State). These are the words of praise coming from a scion of the royal family.

The princes of Thiruvananthapuram, Akkalakote and Mir Sahib of Khairpur received administrative education in Mysore. Even today, princes from different parts of India come to Mysore to receive training in political administration. I wish to make a survey of the progress made in Mysore during 13 years after the Silver Jubilee Celebration. Due to the paucity of space, I cannot give a detailed report. Here is a brief report of progress made in the last thirteen years:

> The Maharaja has given priority to rural development and health care. The present Dewan has dedicated himself to the increased generation of electric power and to the development of heavy industries. He also took up public building projects and improvement of small town infrastructure.

The state government is trying to increase the revenue by way of taxes, including income tax and tax received from K.G.F goldmine, chrome mines and from sale of sandalwood grown in state reserve forests. The state is collecting sales tax on goods produced within the state. From factories, government revenue is three times larger than the farm lands tax collected by the state.

Boost to Agriculture Sector

The Maharaja has shown utmost interest in the agriculture sector. He wants to provide farmers with the latest equipment, machinery and better quality seeds and fertilizer. Nalwadi has commissioned Agriculture Research stations at Baboor, Marthur, Nagenahalli, Balehonnuru, etc. An agriculture school has been started at Hebbal in 1913 to impart agriculture training to young students (Present Gandhi Krishi Vikas Kendra University of Agricultural Sciences at Hebbal). Many extension lectures were organized in towns like Ramakrishnapura. The state Agriculture Department scientists successfully fought areca nut palm tree disease called "Fruit-rot disease" and they also fought diseases which affected coffee shrubs and cotton plants. The efficient agricultural practices of Mysore State has become a role model for the rest of India. The farmers are supplied with hybrid seeds of cotton, ragi and sugarcane at a nominal price. They have encouraged farmers to produce white jaggery from the sugarcane harvest. The farmers are encouraged to grow fruit trees at Ganjam, Irwin canal area and in Hesaraghatta near Bangalore. The state government is offering soft loans on low interest rates to farmers during sowing season. They are also given long term soft loans, meaning loans on meagre interest rate, to clear the earlier loans borrowed from private individuals.

The state also sold electric pumps to farmers to irrigate their lands. They could buy these pumps by availing loans. They were asked to clear these loans through a payment of equal monthly instalments. In the areas where crops failed, they were offered tax waivers.

The construction of Sri Krishnaraja Sagar Dam across Cauvery River is the largest water body or water reservoir in the state. At the time of construction, it was the largest water reservoir in whole of India. The construction work began in 1911 and concluded in 1931. There is another water reservoir built in British presidency state, which is at present bigger than this dam. The height of the dam is 130 feet and the length of the dam is one and a half miles. The whole project cost is Rs. 2 crores and Rs. 42 lakhs. After Sir Mirza M. Ismail took charge of the Dewanship as per the orders of the Maharaja, the Irwin canal project was taken up at a cost of Rs. 2 crores. This canal will be irrigating 1,20,000 acres of arable land. Already more than 60,000 acres of land in Mandya and Maddur Taluqs are receiving water and fields are turned into a rich green expanse. The establishment of a sugar factory at Mandya has benefitted thousands of growers. The Dewan Sahib started an agricultural research station near Irwin Canal zone. Because of the canal, Mandya became a prosperous Taluq and later, it attained the status of a district.

After Mirza Sahib became the Dewan, the following reservoir projects at Anjanapura, Gopalapura, Bhimanahalli, Chandhanhalli, Nelligere and check dam for Bhrigu River were completed. The Markonahalli reservoir project in Kunigal Taluq was also completed.

One more dam at Lakkavalli in Shimoga District was built across the Bhadra River. The waters of Bhadra River is irrigating 2 lakh acres of farm land. In the last 13 years, the state government has spent Rs. 3 crores on irrigation projects. The state government is trying to rejuvenate barren dry lands by repairing old dams and water bodies. They have spent huge sums of money on new projects.

In the British Presidency states like Madras, Bombay, etc., the state governments are particular that the revenue yield on the investment must be at least 6% of the corpus fund. If the revenue is less than 6%, they will not take up expensive projects. But the Maharaja of Mysore is extremely compassionate towards the poor. So, he always ignored the profitability factor and has taken up new irrigation projects.

During the last 13 years, the Mysore government has spent Rs. 62 lakhs on restoring 7,400 lakes. Apart from this, 23,453 lakes are maintained in good shape to conserve rainwater. Some new water bodies have been created at a huge cost. The following 9 new lakes have been created by the government:

1. Ketohalli Lake (Bangalore District)
2. Maralavadi Lake (Bangalore district)
3. Hirige Lake (Mysore District)
4. Tumbadi Lake (Tumkur District)
5. Dalvaiy Lake (Tumkur District)
6. Nidasale Lake (Tumkur District)
7. Bavanhalli Lake (Tumkur District)
8. Kamasamudra Lake (Kolar District)
9. Savlanga Lake (Shimoga District)

The total cost of these projects is Rs. 22 lakhs.

The state government has created a new corpus fund called "Irrigation Development Fund" with an outlay of Rs. 28 lakhs. The scheme was started on 1st July 1939 to develop backward drought-prone areas of the state. At present (1940), the government not only wants to take up new projects in these areas, but revive old lakes to help farmers. The state government has passed an order to build 4 new lakes with this fund at those places.
1. Byramangala Lake (Bangalore District)
2. Alahalli Lake (Bangalore District)
3. Tippaganahalli Lake (Kolar District)
4. Ragimakalhalli Lake (Kolar District)

The total cost of the project is Rs. 9 lakhs and Rs. 50, 000 only.

The state government is contemplating of building new dams in Shimoga and Chitradurga districts across the Tungabhadra River. This mammoth project can irrigate an additional 32,000 acres of farmland. It is also planned to rejuvenate small lakes and ponds at a cost of Rs. 2 lakhs on a tri-annual basis. The following four dams were built at a cost of Rs. 22 lakhs and Rs. 50,000 to irrigate 7000 acres of farm land.
1. A dam across Kanva River at Kannamangala, Channapatna
2. A dam at Parasuramapura Lake, Challakere Taluq
3. A dam at Honnemachanahalli Lake, Kunigal Taluq
4. A dam across the Yennehole River at Kadakola

Revival of Villages

The Maharaja and the Dewan were keen on improving the quality of life in the villages. The creation of a model village behind Chamundi Hill called Lalitadripura is a good example. The state has decided to develop and construct at least one village in each district. The Maharaja has encouraged the villages to take up small-scale cottage industries and devote their spare time to generating additional income. For example, a Khadi Cottage Industry has come into existence at Badanal. Even in some British provinces, Khadi cottage industries have come up to generate substantial income for the poor.

In the last 13 years, the silk industry has received a fillip from the government. They have managed to overcome stiff competition from Japan. The state government has encouraged sericulture by leasing government lands to farmers to grow mulberry plantations. The state has opened sericulture

Research Stations with the latest equipment to produce hybrid silkworm eggs. They are sold to farmers at subsidized prices. They are also given soft loans at nominal interest rates. Today, 2,00,000 silk farmers are earning a good income from sericulture. Formerly, silk yarn was wound around a wheel (Charaka) in the silk factory. Now, silk yarn is drawn from the cocoon through the filature process. The silk fabric produced in Mysore is superior to French silk fabric. Now, Mysore State is exporting silk cloth to Australia also.

Another cottage industry which has produced a good income for poor people is the wood industry. The Dewan observed that the local sheep produced rough and short wool fibre. The government decided to improve the local breed of sheep. Hence, sheep-raring stations were established at Hebbal, Anjanapura, Yelechihalli and Kolar. The government has imported Merino Sheep and goats from foreign countries. Recently, 27 Merino sheep were imported at a cost of Rs. 6,000 from South Africa. The government has interbred the imported variety with Indian sheep to produce hybrid sheep with superior wool. So, many sheep farmers are rearing these hybrid sheep on their farms.

In rural India, cows and oxen occupy an important integral part of the village economy. An average farmer ploughs his farmland with a plough and oxen. The village women generate substantial income from selling cow's milk and butter. Mysore State has 81 veterinary hospitals for cattle and other animals. Because of Dewan Sir Mirza M. Ismail's efforts, 41 hospitals came into being after 1926. Because of the research work done by government veterinary college scientists, a cure has been discovered for the "Big mouth disease" among cattle. The vaccine developed by Mysore scientists is in use in other states of India as well. Government veterinary doctors visit the houses of villagers to treat this disease. The Government has started high-breed bull-producing animal husbandry centres at Hunsur and Anjanapura. They are producing hybrid bulls to inseminate local cow variety in different towns. These bulls are also sold to village panchayats at a nominal price. The state government is also encouraging poultry farming and aviary. In the state, there have been 11,918 grama panchayats since 1927. These grama panchayats are developing road networks, schools and temple maintenance, upkeep of ponds and lakes, selling modern agricultural machines and hybrid seeds, improving drainage systems, reading rooms and libraries, prayer hall construction and building of panchayat offices. They have also started co-operative societies in the villages. They are responsible for village sanitation.

Sitting: Mahamathusri Maharani Sri Lakshmi Vilasa Sannidhana
Standing: Prince Sri Jayachamarajendra Wodeyar

Electrification of Towns and Villages

In 1926, only three towns had electric power supply. They are Bangalore, Mysore and the gold mining town of K.G.F. In recent years, more villages and towns have been electrified. Until June 1940, in Mysore State, 204 cities and villages have been electrified.

Drinking Water Supply Scheme

Dewan Sahib made a decision to implement drinking water schemes in all the villages of the state within five years. The government has sanctioned Rs. 5 lakhs, to dig new wells in villages. There is an attempt to revive traditional crafts, which have gone into decline. They have extended healthcare and educational facilities to villages. In many poor areas of the state, land tax has been reduced, even though state revenue dwindled considerably in the last 5 years. The rural development programmes are utilising the benefits extended by the benevolent government. I wish to conclude this section with a quote from Sir Marcus Samuel, 1st Viscount Bearsted (1853-1927) Lord Mayor of London and founder of Shell Transport and Trading Company,

"I had an opportunity of motoring through a large part of Mysore and of visiting several of the villages and of hearing much of the village upliftment movement, which is so dear to the heart of both His Highness and of the Dewan, and there, very much has been achieved. The results in many places are remarkable. I visited seven of the provinces and seven of the states of India and from all I saw and heard and from all I learnt and read, among the provinces, one stands at the forefront of the work done for village improvement, and that is the Punjab, and among the states, one stands pre-eminent, and that is Mysore."

Industrial Development in Mysore State

Agriculture and Industry contribute immensely to the National Development of England, Germany, Russia and Japan and hence they have become wealthy nations, because of these two sectors. Sri Nalwadi realized in 1911 that when compared to developed countries, we realize that our country lags behind only because of a lack of education, ignorance is widespread and the longevity of our people is below the global average as a result of poverty. So, the Maharaja came to the conclusion that only by learning from the examples of developed nations could we become rich and powerful. In fact, the Department of Industry and Commerce was started in 1911.

The state government encouraged the setting up of industries by private capitalists. The Maharaja founded a private bank called "Mysore Bank" to lend money to entrepreneurs in 1913. In 1916, the "Mysore Chamber of Commerce" was established to bring together the Business Community. It was also decided to offer scholarships to students to go abroad and study. The small-scale cottage industries were encouraged by offering soft loans at low-interest rates to businessmen.

The Mysore government started these industries:
1. Bhadravathi Iron and Steel plant
2. The Mysore soap and detergent factory in Bangalore
3. Cast Iron Foundry to manufacture machines
4. Sri Krishna Rajendra Textile Mills at Mysore
5. Handicrafts Emporium at Mysore

The British Empire Exhibition organized at Wembley, London in 1924 was visited by Queen Mary. She visited the Mysore State showroom. She admired the handicraft works of Mysore artisans. She purchased a few decorative works. Many artworks were given gold medals and certificates.

During the last thirteen years, after the Silver Jubilee year, the state witnessed a remarkable degree of industrial progress. Sir Mirza Ismail had taken inspiration from Nalwadi's vision of the future. The development of the state is achieved through four ambitious objectives.

(a) Import substitution of consumer goods- Nalwadi wanted industrialists to manufacture goods indigenously and save precious foreign exchange.
(b) To manufacture electric transformers in the state and stop importing them from abroad. The state was collecting excise duty on opium, ganja, liquor and toddy. The state was collecting duty imposed on gold being mined at KGF. But one day, the excise on gold will dwindle and stop. The Maharaja wanted to increase excise income by increasing industrial and agricultural production.
(c) The third aim was to develop industries in cities and towns. A lot of migrants will migrate to towns in search of jobs. It will ease population pressure on agricultural lands in the villages.
(d) Nalwadi wanted to improve the quality of life by making use of Mysore State's natural resources.

Many new big industries have come up in towns like the silk factory at Mysore, the porcelain and electrical factory at Bangalore, the cast iron factory, the steel and cement factory at Bhadravati, etc. The manufacture of steel from scrap iron became a profitable venture. At Hassan, a steel implements factory is coming up to manufacture spades, crowbars, plough shares, knives, sickles, etc.

The state-owned public enterprises are doing well. But the state has also invested money in shares and stocks of joint stock companies. A few companies can be named here – the sugar factory at Mandya, the silk factory at Channapatna, the paper mill at Bhadravati, the tobacco company, the glass factory at Bangalore, the sulphuric acid plant in Belagola, hydrogenated vegetable oil, usually palm oil (Mono-saturated) manufacturing factory and an electric bulb manufacturing company. The state government has provided subsidies like inexpensive industrial plots, cheap electricity and water.

The state government wants to start industries based on new technology. Hence, the government has enhanced electricity generation. At Shivana Samudra Hydro-electric station, earlier, 34,000 horsepower of electricity was being generated and at present, 56,000 horsepower of electricity is being generated. In 1926, the state earned a revenue of Rs. 26 lakhs 68 thousand from selling electricity. Now, in 1940, the state revenue has increased to Rs. 50 lakhs. At Shimshapura, an additional 23,000 horsepower of electricity will be generated from June 1940. This hydro-electricity project has been completed at a cost of Rs. 56 lakhs. The state government has drawn a blueprint to generate electricity (70,000 horsepower) from the Sharavati River near Jog Falls. Sri Nalwadi laid the foundation stone for the project on 5th March 1939. The estimated cost of the project is Rs. 1.5 crores. When this hydroelectric project is completed, the state can supply electricity to the nook and corner of the state.

Mysore State is at the forefront of sandalwood oil extraction for the perfumery and soap manufacturing industry. But businessmen of Mysore could not export it easily to foreign countries. Hence, the Maharaja thoughtfully created the post of Track Commissioner in London to promote sandalwood oil sales. The Mysore state made great strides in Industrial development during these 13 years (1927-1940). The state government invested Rs. 5 crores in the industrial sector and created 20,000 jobs. The MySugar Company has declared annually a dividend of 15% to shareholders. The company share of

Rs. 10 face value is being quoted on the stock exchange at Rs. 40. The excise revenue to the state from sugar stands at Rs. 13 lakhs. Sir B.G Kher, President of Bombay Pradesh Congress Party has praised the benefits of Irwin Canal which brought prosperity to thousands of farmers. The farming community in Mysore State is quite prosperous.

The Bhadravati Iron and Steel factory and the soap factory are raking in good profits. The sulphuric acid manufactured at Belagola has a ready consumer in Mysugar factory at Mandya. In this factory, the fertilizer Ammonium Sulphate is being produced. The state can stop importing fertilizer from abroad. The Mysore Paper Mill is producing paper and cardboard. A lot of foreign exchange is saved by the state. It is beyond doubt that during the tenure of Dewan Sir Mirza M. Ismail, the industrialization of Mysore was accomplished in a planned manner.

Public Civil Works Projects

Industrial and Agricultural progress was enhanced by various civil works like building dams, bridges, highways, railways and irrigation canals. The following bridges were built at a cost of Rs. 19 lakhs during the last 12 years:
1. Bridge at Gorur across Hemavati River
2. Narasimharajendra Bridge at Akkihebbal across Hemavati River
3. Krishnarajendra Bridge at T.Narasipura across Cauvery River.
4. Bridge at Ramanathapura across the Cauvery River
5. Jayachamarajendra Bridge at Halaguru across Shimsa River,
6. Three more bridges are being built in different places.

The new railway lines were being laid in Shimoga and Chitradurga districts at a cost of Rs. 59 Lakhs covering a distance of 74 miles in 1926. The Mysore state government has acquired the ownership of two railway lines, one from Bangalore to Harihara and another from Bangalore to Hindupur from "Madras" and "Southern Maratta" Railway companies. Another proposal that is pending before the government is to lay a railway line from Chamarajanagar to Sathyamangalam. The railway journey from North India to South India to reach many big towns in the south and also holy places, without passing through Madras (Chennai) becomes a feasibility. It also brings in additional revenue to the state exchequer. The able negotiator Dewan Sir Mirza M. Ismail will bring this project to fruition in the near future. The citizens of Mysore State are eagerly awaiting clearance from the central government. The number of buses, lorries and cars in the state has increased to a large extent. But the conditions of the roads are terrible. The State has initiated a "Road Fund" for the maintenance of roads.

These majestic buildings designed by experienced architects were built for the use of the public:
1. Life Insurance Company building, Bangalore.
2. Sri Krishnarajendra Institute of Technology, Bangalore.
3. Sri VaniVilasa Maternity Hospital, Bangalore.
4. Mental Hospital, Bangalore.
5. The diagnostic laboratory to examine the origin of diseases at Mysore.
6. The Mysore Dasara Exhibition building.
7. The Mysore State Railway headquarters.
8. McGann District Hospital, Shimoga.
9. The Narasimharaja Hospital, Kolar.
10. Many schools and hospitals were built in small towns.
11. The Thippagondana Halli reservoir was built near Bangalore to supply drinking water to the city.

These construction projects provided employment to needy persons.

Medical assistance, Healthcare and Education in Mysore State

Dewan Sir Mirza M. Ismail paid a lot of attention to the development of the healthcare system. At present, Rs. 17 lakhs is spent on medical assistance. This scheme was started in 1926. In the last 13 years, the State Government has built 84 new healthcare institutions. The Dewan has managed to collect Rs. 25 lakhs from philanthropists. The State Government has contributed Rs. 15 Lakhs to the health care fund. Many District Hospitals are equipped with state-of-the-art medical equipment. Anti-malarial programmes are being implemented. In the Malnad region, doctors are going to remote villages to treat patients. The Public Health Department has implemented many new schemes to improve healthcare. Some of the deadly diseases like malaria, hookworm disease and gangrene are tackled on a war footing.

The State Government has started a medical college at Mysore to impart medical education. Near Closepet (present Ramanagaram) a central healthcare centre has been opened.

Sri B.G. Kher, President of the Bombay Pradesh Congress Committee has praised various developmental activities like model village programme at Bogadi, electricity generation, industrialization, and educational and health infrastructure development in the state.

In Mysore State, women's education, especially Muslim Women's education, received impetus, and incentives were given to schedule caste and tribal students to pursue higher education. The education offered to students combines professional skills with life-shaping ideology. At the high school level, History and Mathematics are taught in Kannada medium. But English as a medium of instruction continues in the State. The University graduates from the state have fared well in the Indian Civil Services Examination.

Various Other Reforms

In 1930, the Mysore State Chief Court was designated as the High Court. Earlier, the Chief Court had one Chief Justice and two other judges. Now, the present High Court has six judges. All necessary steps have been taken to speed up the dispensation of justice. Legislation was passed under labour laws to compensate an injured worker immediately. Hence, cash compensation is given to an injured worker. The state government brought about an amendment to Hindu Darmasastra Legal Canon to give equal rights to women in property matters in 1934. An Aerodrome has been constructed at Jakkur, Bangalore. Many Aeroplanes fly via Bangalore from Hyderabad to Madras and back.

The government wants to establish an Aeroplane manufacturing factory in Bangalore. The state has a good telephone network. The government wants to establish two radio broadcasting stations in Mysore and Bangalore. In this regard, a budgetary allocation has been made during the year 1940-41 to begin this project.

Nalwadi Sri Krishnarajendra Wodeyar has inspired and enthused the state Civil Service. They are guided by the Maharaja to achieve excellence in every field. The ruler has become a role model to the other Maharajas and to the rest of the civil service in presidency states. All the civic works in cities and towns owe their existence to the Maharaja's initiatives. The former resident of Mysore State Lt. Col. C.T.C Plowden while addressing Rotarians said,

"...whatever has been done for his people proceeded from His Highness the Maharaja who has set a high standard to all his officers and his people..." (30th November 1937)

The Maharaja is a charismatic person. He is an expert negotiator and a clever debater. He has managed to win over the Viceroy and the Governor. He is good at official correspondence. He has accomplished a lot through courteous behaviour and polite demeanour.

When the Mysore State government wanted to raise the K.R.S dam's height, there was stiff opposition from the Madras State Government. Many rounds of talk between officials and engineers took place but to no avail. But the Maharaja regularly kept up the official correspondence with Lord Willingdon (1931-1936), Viceroy and Governor General of India and many others from 1922 onwards. If one studies the Maharaja's official correspondence, one understands his adventurous spirit, patriotism, concern for his subjects, courage and negotiation skills. He is capable of voicing unpleasant truths and conducting business without rancour and hatred. Many British dignitaries have praised Nalwadi's strength, courtesy, humility, dignity and extraordinary personality in their letters to him. Because of his charismatic personality, he could score over his opponents. Mysore State benefitted greatly through his skills.

Dewan Sir Mirza M. Ismail attended the All Party round table conferences held in 1930, 1931 and 1932 in London. He represented the princely states of Mysore, Travancore, Cochin and Puddukottai. He gave bold suggestions with regard to centre-state relations under the constitution. He is still striving to bring down the financial burden of annual tributes paid to the British Government. He is also trying to bring the Bangalore Cantonment area under the Maharaja's rule. This area was administrated by the Madras Presidency.

The Viceroy and Governor-General of India Lord Willingdon and his wife visited Mysore State in December 1933. The Maharaja gave a Gala Banquet party in honour of visiting dignitaries on the night of 4th December 1933. In reply to the Maharaja's Welcome Speech, the Viceroy of India said, "The princely state of Mysore has made great strides in progress during the last eleven years. I last visited the state eleven years ago. These last eleven years have been difficult years globally. The great economic depression has dealt a harsh blow to people all over the world. Mysore State cannot be an exception to the rule. But still, Mysore State has achieved considerable success in the field of agriculture and industry. The present ruler has made the lives of his citizens attain a much better quality of life. They have been provided with better facilities." (Not the actual words; only a translation from Kannada)

The British Government has conceded to the Maharaja's request to legislate their own laws. As per Article 18 of the 1913 agreement, the Mysore State Government did not have the powers to make laws on their own. This prohibition was withdrawn to facilitate the princely state to frame its own laws. This was a major Constitutional Victory for the Maharaja.

The Maharaja, Prince Sri Jayachamarajendra Wodeyar and Yuvaraja on the occasion of the Upanayanam ceremony (initiation ceremony)

Prince Sri Jayachamarajendra Wodeyar with
Princess Sri Vijayalakashammani (left) and
Princess Sri Kempuchalvajammani (right) on the upanayanam day.

Chapter 10
Maharaja as a Game Hunter

******

Medashechedha krushodaram lagu bhavathuythaana yogyam vapuh
Sattvanamapi Lakshyethe Vikrutimacchittam baya krodhayoh|
Uttkarsha sacha dhanvinaam yadishavah Siddyanthi Laksheye chale
Mithaiva vysanam vadanthi mrigyaamdrugvinodah kutah||

******

There are wild animals (deer, leopards, etc.) which are sleek and slim. They have flat stomachs, which enables them to leap and fly in the air. Their awareness is filled with anger and fear. The true hunter is one, who can shoot an arrow at an animal, which is leaping and flying in the air and kill it. A hunter who kills a stationary animal is only pursuing a hobby. Why indulge in such fanciful pursuits? (English Translation)

The Maharaja has created many wildlife sanctuaries in Mysore State. The state is blessed with stretches of thick forest teeming with wildlife. He has built many forest lodges for game hunters. Nalwadi is known for courage and strength. He is a good Shikar. He even vibes with Kadu Kurubas (tribals), who dwell in the forest. He jokes with them time and again and shows great love and affection for them.

Today, game hunting is a frowned upon hobby of the rich. In many countries, it is banned. But when you see a game hunter exhibiting extraordinary bravery in the face of danger, unafraid of death and the adventurous spirit involved, it overwhelms you. A hunter often resorts to killing wild animals to protect villagers and cattle. The menace of man-eating tigers and leopards is well-known in the Indian subcontinent. Sometimes, a tusker goes on "Mast." Then, it causes a lot of havoc, destruction and death.

Once, a tiger strayed into the pastoral grassland, where cows were grazing. It caught hold of the leg of a cow. But the group of people armed with sticks chased the tiger back to the woods. This poor cow lost its leg and no one in the village took its responsibility. It found its way to the palace dairy, where the Maharaja made its stay as comfortable as possible. But it was a pitiable sight to watch the cow struggling with its three feet. The villagers and the forest dwellers look upon those game hunters as their saviours.

In his youth, the Maharaja was often seen in the hill station of Ooty, riding his horse followed by greyhound dogs. He would often gallop on narrow mountain paths with gay abandon. Even the European hunters admitted his mettle. The Maharaja was always prepared to kill dangerous animals like tigers, leopards and elephants in heat. He did not kill nilgai, deer and bison. He also believed in killing animals instantly by aiming at their brain or heart. When other hunters prolonged the pain of animals and delayed death, he did not like it in the least. He made sarcastic remarks about their poor hunting skills.

The evergreen thick forest cover in Mysore State was once called "*Dandakarayana*" and traceable to the Ramayana epic. In the depths of rain forest, hardly any sunrays penetrate the green foliage. The tall age-old trees and bamboo groves give shelter to a variety of wildlife.

A game hunter in an Indian forest finds all these exotic wild animals, birds and fishes:
1. Elephants
2. Tigers
3. Leopards
4. Bison
5. Wild Buffalos
6. Barking Deer
7. Antelope
8. Stags
9. Elks
10. Bears
11. Wolves
12. Wild dogs
13. Mongoose (Weasel)
14. Snakes and pythons

15. Porcupines
16. Crocodiles
17. Beavers and otters
18. Peacocks and other birds
19. Wild fowls
20. Hyena
21. Wild boars (which can tear the ribs of hunting dogs with its canine in a fight)
22. Mahseer fish found in Cauvery River

One of our beautiful forests can be seen in Kakankote. Nalwadi has regulated hunting in Mysore forests through a legislative act. Even overhunting can drive an animal to extinction. Hence, there are guidelines for hunters.

The visiting European dignitaries and many Indian aristocratic gentlemen love to catch "Mahaseer" fish in the Cauvery River. It weighs more than a hundred pounds. The fishing equipment required for this expedition costs Rs. 7,000 (1940s rate). The hunters go after man-eating tigers and leopards and often kill some tuskers who are on the rampage. They also kill wild bison which damage standing crop in farms.

Tiger Hunting

In Mysore State, the tiger population is quite high in these four districts - Mysore, Hassan, Kadur and Shimoga. Tigers have immense strength and agility. Once a hunter shot a tiger and the wounded tiger snapped at the root of a tree with its jaws. It soon died and the hunters could not free the jaws from the root. They had to cut the root to free the animal, before taking it away to a taxidermist. When a tiger pounces on an ox or buffalo and bites its back, the sharp canine makes holes even in the skeletal bones of these animals. Once, a hunter thrust his double-barrel gun into the mouth of a tiger. Later, the tiger's teeth marks were found on the steel barrel. A cheetah can outrun a gazelle at a speed of thirty miles per hour. But a tiger can be swift in its run and kill the animal with its strength. An average tiger weighs 500 to 600 pounds. But it can easily kill a bison, which weighs 2,800 pounds. The tiger consumes it over two or three days in the forest. A tiger can consume at one sitting 150 to 200 pounds of meat. If it is unable to hunt an animal, it can still fast for twenty-eight days easily. Once, a caged tiger dashed against iron rods, which measured ¾" in size. The forceful impact of the tiger had bent the rods outwards to the extent of four inches. Normally, a *matchan* (a hunter's platform) would be built on a tree at a height of 9 to 12 ft. A hunter will not be able to kill a tiger if the matchan is above twelve feet. But a wounded angry tiger can leap to a height of 20 feet. Many a time, the wounded tiger has leapt at the matchan and dragged the hunter down. Several hunters have been killed by wounded tigers. It is undoubtedly a dangerous sport.

The Maharaja on a hunt

Prince Sri Jayachamarajendra Wodeyar (Holding Solar pith hat) with other shikars. The tiger has been killed by the Prince.

The hunter who wants to kill a tiger must possess an adventurous spirit, physical stamina and immense courage. The hunter must sit patiently on a matchan waiting for a tiger to come in the vicinity. Normally, a bait in the form of a goat or a sheep is tied to the tree. The hunter must resist thirst, hunger and sleep to achieve his goal. The Maharaja had the patience and stamina to keep a vigil on a matchan for two or three consecutive nights. He often spent a whole night on a matchan sitting like a stone statue. Occasionally, an injured tiger escapes leaving a trail of blood. The brave Maharaja would come down from the matchan and follow the tiger's trail of blood to finish the job. The accompanying hunters would plead with the Maharaja not to take such risks. Moreover, the Maharaja often succeeded in killing the tiger with one bullet as he was a good marksman.

During a hunt, the Maharaja would trek a distance of twenty-five miles in the forest. He also rode his horse covering 30 or 40 miles in the jungle. The same hunting abilities are seen in the present ruler, Sri Jayachamarajendra Wodeyar.

Nalwadi improved the hunting infrastructure and various other facilities for hunters. He raised hunting sport to a level of fine art. In the past, the hunters went in search of a half-eaten carcass of an animal in the forest. If they found one, they would climb a tree and wait for the tiger to return for its kill. Then, they would take aim and kill it with a double-barrelled gun. Sometimes, the tribals would beat drums and blow trumpets to drive the tiger towards the carcass of an animal. Sometimes, an injured tiger would attack these tribal herders and kill them too. Often, a tiger would rush in at great speed towards the vicinity of the matchan. The hunter often fired a gun without taking proper aim. This injured tiger would wait in a crouched position in the grassland unseen. It would spring upon an unsuspecting passerby with ferocity and maul him to death.

Nalwadi avoided accidental deaths of tribals and hunters by adopting various measures. He studied the behaviour patterns of wild tigers. He realized that they preferred water holes surrounded by grass and bushes. It always came to the water source unseen by human beings. These wild animals not only came for drinking water but also to lick the earth for salt. The tigers after a hunt would drag an ox or bison into the deep forest. Otherwise, vultures and scavenger animals like hyenas would devour the dead animal.

The morning ritual – Nalwadi feeding the holy cow with Bananas.

The Maharaja and a European guest. The giant tiger shot by Nalwadi on the foreground.

Maharaja Sri Jayachamarajendra Wodeyar with his kill

The Altered Hunting Landscape

Nalwadi created tiger trails for hunters in different forests. Some distance away from Mysore city, deep in the forest, an Omkareshwara temple exists. There is a holy tomb of Saint Kendaganna Swamy. Here, in the middle of the forest, a clearing area was created. A path for the tiger was created with grass and bushes planted on either side. They had removed big trees standing in the vicinity of the spot, where a tiger normally brought its kill. In the clearing, a hunter would be sitting on a matchan with his rifle. When the tiger turned up to have its dinner, it would be shot. Sometimes, the tribals of the forest would drive a frightened tiger towards the matchan by beating drums and blowing trumpets. If the tiger got injured, it could run away, because of the noisome tribals. It runs on the path to another clearing, where another hunter would be waiting on a matchan to finish the job.

In the past, a tiger ran helter-skelter, because of the din created by the tribals. Often an injured tiger would attack these herders and kill a few of them. Now, Nalwadi has dispensed with these noisome tribals. Instead, one or two tribals sit on the branch of a tree. The tiger is a highly suspicious animal. The tribals would snap at a branch to alert the tiger. It runs away in the opposite direction. Sometimes, those tribals drop one or two stones from the branch to the ground. Once again, a scared tiger is made to run away towards the clearing through the trail.

Another stratagem adapted by hunters now is to signal other hunters and tribals by blowing a whistle. If the tiger got killed by one bullet, then one continuous whistle was blown. If the tiger got only injured, then the hunter would blow the whistle with several pips. Unnecessary deaths of other hunters and tribals would be avoided. If these people heard one strong whistle signalling the death of a tiger by one bullet, then they would come down by cheering "Jai Chamundeshwari. Jai Chamundeshwari."

Several Viceroys of India, including Lord Reading and Lord Hardinge, appreciated the Maharaja's efforts at modernizing tiger hunting expeditions. In fact, Lord Reading followed the instructions during a hunt. The Maharaja had explained from what direction the tiger would enter the clearing. Lord Reading was asked to aim his gun at a particular angle and wait for the tiger. A tiger appeared as predicted by the Maharaja and Lord Reading was able to kill it with one bullet. The Viceroy praised the Maharaja for making such meticulous arrangements for a tiger kill.

The elimination of tigers and elephants helped farmers. Their lives were protected and standing crops were saved from destruction. The hunters on the matchan were always exposed to the danger of a wounded tiger either mauling or killing them. On 4th March 1939, the Maharaja went after a dreaded man-eater, which was partially wounded in a previous encounter and succeeded in killing it. People living in several villages on the periphery of the forest heaved a sigh of relief. This brave act of the Maharaja was appreciated by all.

Nalwadi discovered a new method of trapping tigers alive. Maharaja and the tribals would study the regular trails of the tigers. In a suitable place, they would dig a pit with a circumference of eight feet and a depth of eighteen feet. This pit was carefully covered with branches and grass. They would sprinkle this terrace with dry leaves and some earth. A buffalo would be tied to a tree as a bait. It so happened often a tiger would avoid the covered pit and kill the buffalo and after a heavy meal would walk away alive.

Nalwadi thought of a plan to trap the tigers more efficiently. Some trees and stakes were planted in a semi-circular fashion around the pit. Inside the pit, a pathway or tunnel was created to lead the animal to a cage. The buffalo was tied at the clearing of the pit to a tree. The tiger always leapt upon the back of an animal to kill it. If it could not leap in one go, then it would make a double or triple jumps to reach the animal. It always bounded in the direction of the animal at great speed and pounced upon it ferociously. The covered pit came between the tiger and the bait. The rest of the area had tree branches and stakes, which made it look like a natural forest. When the tiger attempted a second leap, it often fell into the deep pit. After a day or two, this hungry tiger was driven to the cage by the tribals. They would pelt stones and sticks at the animal. When the tiger entered the cage, the door would come down, thereby imprisoning it in the cage. Later, this caged tiger was transported to a zoo or circus as the case may be.

Nalwadi's Sense of Humour

The Maharaja had a unique kind of sense of humour. It was of a refined and cultured variety. He often joked even with the European dignitaries in a sophisticated and subtle way. It was unhurtful and harmless, but often enjoyed by both the parties.

Once a visiting Viceroy of India and his wife were being taken to Kharapur forest to witness the Khedda (elephant trapping) operation. The

Vicereine picked up a pillow from the front seat of the car, so she could use the cushion to prop up her back. Nalwadi who stood outside told her curtly, it belonged to the chauffeur. She naturally felt hurt by this remark. How could a lowly chauffeur be superior to a visiting Vicereine? Meanwhile, Nalwadi had signalled servants to fetch extra pillows or cushions. A few minutes later, they saw the Maharaja sitting in the driver's seat. Both the Viceroy and the Vicereine had a merry laughter over this little prank.

Once, the Maharaja visited the Wildlife Sanctuary for a hunt. In those days, the new technique in tiger hunting had not been evolved. Nalwadi fired a bullet at the tiger, but the tiger managed to escape unhurt. He returned to his palace. Later, a list of names of tribals was placed before him. They had assisted in the hunt and had to be compensated for their efforts. The Maharaja joked, "I suppose this refers to our recent hunt. Have you sent anyone to locate the dead tiger's carcass? Who is going to skin it?" What he meant was it was a futile expedition. The tribals were collecting wages for a non-event. Nevertheless, they were paid their dues.

Nalwadi was waiting for a tiger during a hunt and he was sitting patiently upon the matchan. Even after a wait of several hours, the tiger did not turn up. He asked the accompanying forest official as to why no tiger was seen. The official replied innocuously that the tigers in that forest had become clever and wily. Some of them had been hit by bullets and they had recovered from their injuries. So, these tigers had become doubly cautious after their encounters with human beings. After a gap of two years, the Maharaja was hunting in another forest with the same official. Nalwadi asked him whether this forest was well stocked with tigers. The official gleefully replied that their population was good in that forest. The Maharaja jocularly asked whether they were clever and wily or too docile by nature, making the kill an easy affair. The Maharaja had not forgotten the official's previous flippant remark concerning the unavailability of tigers.

On another occasion, the Maharaja noticed the officials running here and there with their guns and they did not know that a tiger had escaped unhurt. None of the hunters had been able to fire at the target. Hence, he joked, "Do not kill all the tigers in the forest today. Spare a few of them for the future."

Once, the Governor of Madras Presidency visited Mysore State to hunt wildlife. After a successful hunt, he could not but help admire the new arrangements made for a tiger kill. He greatly admired the tribal people, who co-ordinated his hunt. He said, "Hats off to your Highness' men. They are wonderfully clever and courageous."

Nalwadi remarked that the forest officials had done a good job with tribals (Shikaras). The officials said after a tiresome hunt, "Shikaras are exhausted and hungry. Now, they have to go in search of ragi flour to make ragi balls for lunch." The Maharaja was magnanimous enough to invite these tribals for a grand lunch prepared by the palace cooks. After a sumptuous lunch, they prostrated before the Maharaja and thanked him. They represented a problem that they were facing in the forest. The state government gave them plots of land for growing grass for their cattle and sheep. But these tribals had to pay "*Hulubanni*" (grassland tax) annually. The state received a revenue of Rs. 2,400 from Hulubanni tax. The "KaduKurubas" requested the Maharaja to waive this tax. Nalwadi readily agreed to dispense with this tax.

This generous gesture made them plead for another favour. They told the Maharaja that they wanted to build new homes in their villages. They wanted good timber from the forest free of cost to make door frames and windows. The Maharaja saw plain human greed making its appearance. Each tribal member wanted to build 10 square foot of building. The Maharaja sarcastically said that if all the 2,000 inhabitants decide to build 2,000 houses and claim free timber from the government, it would only lead to the depletion of a good forest. These tribals wanted to sell free timber in the open market and earn profits. Nalwadi saw through the scheme and put an end to this enterprise.

Once, a newly recruited official made an innovative arrangement in the construction of a matchan. It was covered with foliage on all three sides. There was an opening only in one direction to fire the gun. The Maharaja asked the official, that if the tiger appeared in that direction, then only a hunter could kill it. The official said that this arrangement had been made after studying the tiger's behaviour and Shikar's performance. Nalwadi wanted to find out if this new innovative arrangement was a well-thought-out plan or an accidental development. He grilled the official thoroughly and was pleased to know it was a well-thought-out plan.

One early morning, in Kemmanagundi, the Maharaja came out in plain clothes walking a horse. Some villagers had come to see the Maharaja. Nalwadi enquired with them what they were seeking. They replied that they wanted an interview with the Maharaja. None of them had seen the Maharaja before. Nalwadi deliberately told them that the Maharaja would soon follow him. After a long wait, they asked when the Maharaja would be making his appearance. The people who appeared after him did not possess any regal bearing. They were informed that the first person in plain clothes they met was the Maharaja. After a while, Nalwadi returned from the ride and roared with laughter. The poor villagers prostrated before him and presented him with their complaints and appeals. These villagers were invited to a grand lunch by the Maharaja afterwards.

On another occasion, the Maharaja and his officials trekked in the Kemmangundi area for twenty miles. All of them were tired, and after lunch, they were sleeping in their bedrooms in the travellers' bungalow. The Maharaja came to see them and peeped through the windows. He collected some Kadupatre tree nuts and threw them into their bedrooms. Later, they complained to their Maharaja that somebody had thrown Kadupatre nuts into their bedrooms. The Maharaja told them that no trespasser could have passed through the security guards. This must be the handiwork of a mischievous malevolent spirit. He blamed it on the priests, who did not purge these spirits after a religious ritual. So, the next day, a grand lunch was prepared to ward off the evil spirits after a ritual. Some became convinced about the existence of ghosts and spirits. Some rationalists refused to believe them. No one suspected that it was a prank played by the Maharaja.

In another camp, when the officials were having their siestas post lunch, Nalwadi stealthily entered their rooms and walked away with their handkerchiefs, gold shirt buttons, gold cuff links, wallets and watches. After they woke up, there was a big commotion. Some blamed it on burglars, who must have sneaked in despite vigilant guards. The guards were blamed for these thefts as they had become negligent. So, they demanded that the police be called or the case must be handed over to the C.I.D (Central Investigation Department). How could these thefts occur in Maharaja's private camps? Nalwadi told them that the valuables must have been spirited over by malevolent spirits. Then, with a mischievous smile, he began to produce them one by one from his pocket. Watches, gold buttons, cuff links, wallets and handkerchiefs. This practical joke was done by Nalwadi merely for everyone's amusement.

Once, the Maharaja visited a temple deep in the forest of Kalanathgiri late in the morning. The temple doors were locked. He came across a Kadukuruba tribal person. This conversation took place on that occasion.

M: To which God is this temple dedicated?

K: My Lord, it is a Virabhadra temple.

M: Who is Virabhadra?

K: What, sir, you do not know Virabhadra? (One of the Ganas of Shiva) "Virbhadra means fire, fire, fire and fire."

M: Fire? What goes on inside the temple?

K: On certain nights, a burning fire is seen. Our ancestors have seen lighting strike here.

M: The doors of the temple are locked.

K: The priest will come and open the doors. You seem to be a stranger here.

M: Why can't you open the doors?

K: I have not had my purification bath. I must take a dip in the lake and come here in wet clothes to worship. Otherwise, Virabhadra will roast me over the fire.

M: I have taken a bath in the morning. Can I open the door?

K: No, no, no. You are sweating after a trek. You should take a dip in the cold water and come here in wet clothes to do puja.

M: At least can I offer prayers to the locked doors?

K: Sure, sir. I will fetch some flowers for you.

Nalwadi enjoyed the implicit faith and belief of the innocent tribal fellow.

Once, in the Kakanakote forest, a wild tusker had gone on a rampage. It also killed a few persons. The Maharaja visited this forest area on his elephant with the intent of killing this rogue elephant. He asked a forest official to hand over his double-barrelled gun. The gun was not loaded with bullets. The Maharaja joked, that at any moment, the rogue elephant may attack them. Here, he was with an empty gun. He curtly asked for bullets.

On another occasion, an officer known for his lethargy garlanded His Highness. Nalwadi sarcastically smiled and remarked, that the concerned official must prove his worth through diligence and hard work and then expect compliments from the ruler.

This incident happened near the Kakankote forest. Maharaja gave a basket of fruits as a gift to an Amaldar (a Taluq-level official). He requested another official to proceed in the official car along with the Amaldar. After some time, in his private vehicle, he drove towards Mysore. The official who had escorted the Amaldar stopped well before the place, where roads diverged, one towards Kasaba Hobli and another towards Mysore. He forced the Amaldar to get down from the car and trudge a long distance with a basket of fruits to his Kasaba Hobli. The Maharaja travelling in his private car noticed the poor Amaldar walking in the hot sun with a basket of fruits. He overtook the first car of the official and stopped him. The errant official came running to Nalwadi's car. The Maharaja told him to send his car back with the driver and drop the Amaldar at his residence in the village. Next, he started his car and began to drive. The distraught official began to run next to the car. After some distance, the Maharaja stopped his car. The panting and breathless official joined him. His Highness asked him why he was breathless and red-faced. The official complained that it was a hot day and how he could keep up with the moving car. The Maharaja asked, "Why did you make the Amaldar trek in the hot sun with a heavy load?" Whether the sun is any milder for the Amaldar? The errant official apologized profusely for his arrogant and insensitive behaviour. Then, he was asked to sit in the car and their journey ended in Mysore.

Once, a pompous hypocritical official pretended to be afraid of the Maharaja. He blurted, "Sir I am scared of your very presence. I am unable to decide what to say and what not to say. I am worried about my omissions and commissions in formal speech. I am shy and fearful in your company." The Maharaja laughed aloud and said, "In that case, you can keep your mouth shut."

Another forest official during the Khedda operation was pretending to be an overworked official. He approached the Maharaja like an exhausted official. Nalwadi remarked, "Oh! I see you appear to have roamed all over the forest." The official complacently replied, "The Khedda operation is not a cake walk." Nalwadi retorted, "Yes, yes. You have gone to all four corners of the forest to distribute invitations to wild elephants, asking them to come and get trapped in Khedda." Nevertheless, he was a very good judge of human character.

Often, Nalwadi played deliberate practical jokes upon others to test their intelligence. The Maharaja was in Kemmangundi and some hunters came to him with a tiger skin and gave it to him. The skin was sent to Mysore Palace with an official letter dictated to Darbar Bakshi and this Royal message was conveyed to the palace official in charge of game hunting. The Maharaja had conveyed to the official that on the second day of his visit, some people came to him and informed him about a dangerous tiger. So, the Maharaja went to that area of the forest and climbed a matchan. Soon, a big tiger appeared before him and it was killed with one bullet fired from an old gun. He wanted the tiger skin to be sent to a taxidermist. That official had a sense of humour and wrote in his letter – 'I have sent the skin to a taxidermist for treatment. But by my study of the skin, I could discover that the bullet after entering the mouth appears to have come out of the back of the animal ripping its tail. There is no gun in the world that can accomplish this feat. It also looks like a very compliant tiger, which offers itself before the hunter to be killed. Moreover, it has left behind its claws in the forest before it offered itself to the hunter. One must be very lucky to find such a pliant tiger.' The hunters of Kemmangundi wanted to cheat the Maharaja with this concocted story. Nalwadi noticed that these people had severed the claws and the tail from the body. They had fired a bullet through the mouth of a dead tiger. He admonished them for their white lies and still gave them some money with a warning not to try such dirty tricks.

Nalwadi had a firsthand knowledge of Mysore forest. He had trekked extensively inside the forest. The officials could not mislead him about the topography. Once, Nalwadi asked a forest official to show him Kalkere hill. The official spread a map of that area and pointed to a hill on that map. The Maharaja asked him at what distance this hill was situated. The official replied it is at a distance of one and a half or two miles. But the Maharaja insisted that if you trusted the map, the hill must be at a distance of fifteen miles. He stuck to his claim and pointed at a nearby hill and declared it was Kalkere Hill. There stood a tribal fellow called Belle. The Maharaja asked him whether the hill shown by the official was Kelekere Hill. Belle replied in the negative and told everybody that he had accompanied the Maharaja to Kalkere Hill on several occasions. He emphatically stated that the nearby hill was not Kelekere Hill. The official was crestfallen by this exposure.

The forest officials were good at enacting a drama before the Maharaja. They would bring a tribal before the Maharaja completely tutored and coached. The dialogue was conducted in this fashion.

(1) X official: Hey fellow in this area, do we find Bisons?

P tribal: No sir, they do not live here.

(2) Y official: Isn't it true that until yesterday Bisons were here, but now they have gone elsewhere?

K Tribal: Yes, your honour.

(3) Z official: Bisons do not live in this forest area.

C tribal: Yes, your honour. This is not their habitat.

But Nalwadi was familiar with this game of subterfuge. Nalwadi had named these official stock responses as "Departmental replies" (*Ilaake Uttara*). The Maharaja only respected the deserving officials.

Lord Hardinge the Viceroy of India paid a second official visit to Mysore State. He was very fond of Nalwadi. The Maharaja organised a tiger hunt and the Viceroy managed to kill a tiger. The next morning, they set out to hunt a bison. A tribal fellow was leading the hunting party in the forest. Soon, they encountered thick bamboo groves blocking their path. It took twenty minutes to clear the bamboo branches with a machete to make way for the elephants. At this moment, an experienced forest officer turned up on the scene. He informed the Maharaja that the path was not suitable for the hunting party. The Maharaja enquired again with the tribal fellow, who insisted it was the right path to find bison. Nalwadi told the official the native-born forester was more reliable. But the prudent official informed the Maharaja that it was good enough for a tribal trekker, but not suited for an elephant party as tall bamboos blocked their way. Nalwadi conceded to his argument and replied, "This is not officialise."

On another occasion, a hunting party was led by a tribal called "Bella." They wanted to hunt a bison. He was making the party trek for a long time. Whenever he was asked where they would find a bison he would reply, "It is near the bank of a lake." Their conception of distance could be 500 meters or 5,000 metres. Now, an experienced forest official said the bison herd must be nearby. The Maharaja asked for reasons. The official said that in this area, it rained heavily half an hour ago. The grass on the ground is wet. But in one particular patch, the grass was dry. He said a big bison must have stood in this spot. Beneath the bison's body, the grass was dry. Now, it must have moved away to a nearby pasture after the rain had stopped. Nalwadi called it an explanation based on experience and common sense. Indeed, the hunting party found a bison herd in a nearby grassland. Nalwadi killed a bison with one shot. Later, this official was honoured with flowers, fruits and a ceremonial robe.

The Role of Tribals in Hunting

In the forest of Mysore State, many tribes have lived for thousands of years. They have an intimate knowledge of the forest. Sometimes, either a tiger hunt or an elephant Khedda operation required 2 to 4 thousand "Shikaras" (tribals). These shikaras hailed from Karimuddanahalli, Aswala and a few nearby villages. They belonged to Kadu Kuruba, Besta, Parivar and Adi Karnataka castes. The Maharaja was affectionate and loving towards these tribals. In many villages, primary schools were run with financial grants coming from palace funds. A visiting aristocratic English lady, the wife of a resident, who saw Nalwadi's initiative in rural education, wrote a Letter to the Editor of a London daily newspaper praising these efforts in 1936. In some villages, Nalwadi ordered separate water wells to be dug for Adikarnataka people (untouchable caste). He knew many Shikars by name. He arranged grand feasts for 3 to 4 thousand shikars during hunting expeditions. He sometimes distributed 3 to 4 thousand *jubbas* (long shirts) to these Shikars. The tribal women received free sarees and children school uniforms. The tribals who lived in higher regions of the Nilgiri mountains received woollen quilts to bear the cold winter. The children received laddus (sweets), toys and trumpets.

Once, the Maharaja out of sheer love for the forest dwellers, organized a trip to Mysore city. They were brought to Mysore in palace vehicles. They were taken on a sightseeing trip. They went to cinema halls and watched movies. But they were not enamoured by the city lights. As someone remarked, that it is like bringing a wild tiger to the city. Nalwadi asked an elderly tribal leader whether he liked urban life. This man replied, "In the forest, we drink natural spring water and, in the city, we drink tap water."

The Maharaja often used to organize a fox hunt in Ootacamund hill station for Europeans. The tribals and horse attendants numbering three hundred were engaged in this exercise. They were treated to sumptuous lunches and dinners. The Maharaja never lost his temper with a tribal. He exhibited immense patience with them. When they made unreasonable demands upon him, he tried to convince them through reason that their demands could not be fulfilled.

Once, a group of tribals came to the Maharaja with an appeal. They wanted gun licenses to hunt tigers, bison and elephants. Nalwadi at once realized that it would lead to the depletion of wildlife. So, he asked their leader how they hunted a tiger or a wild boar in the past. He explained their traditional style of hunting. They dug pits in the forest and covered it with branches and leaves. They would also use strong nets to catch these animals. The animals were chased by a group of tribals with tom-toms, trumpets and burning torches. When a tiger or a boar was caught in the net, the animal would be attacked with spears and arrows. They showed remarkable bravery and courage. The Maharaja smiled and asked them to preserve their hunting traditions. Those hunters who lacked courage and strength may resort to guns.

Once, a forest dweller complained to the Maharaja that a particular Forest Ranger and a game officer troubled them a lot. They were not allowed to take out firewood from the forest in bullock carts. They demand 4 annas (25 paise) as tax on one cartload of firewood. Nalwadi wanted to know how much it fetched in the market. The tribal fellow said, if it was transported to Mysore City, they would get six rupees. The Maharaja told him forest trees belonged to the state government and these officials protected it. Shouldn't he pay at least four annas as tax to the state over a profit of Rs. six? He pleaded for sufficient time to pay back taxes. Nalwadi advised him to pay state taxes promptly. But on that day, the Maharaja ordered payment of Rs. One to each transporter of wood from palace funds so that a tribal can take out four cartloads of firewood to the nearby town and earn a living.

On another occasion, the Maharaja and Deputy Commissioner of Mysore district returned from a hunt on an elephant to Kharapur Forest bungalow by crossing the Kabini River. The other minor officials took time to cross the river on a raft. The tribals, noticing the absence of overseer, came to the Maharaja with a complaint. They informed the Maharaja that the lower rung officials were fleecing them for money. Nalwadi asked them why they were penalizing them with fines. They said in the vast grounds of Kharapur lodge they had grown grass (lawn and flower beds). The tribals illegally herded cattle into the compound for grazing. The officials confiscated these animals and sent them to a pound. The villagers got back their animals only after paying fines. The Maharaja told them not to graze their cattle inside the compound. The village elder informed him that it was their traditional grazing ground (*Gomala*). The Maharaja told them he will find an alternative grazing ground for them.

Nalwadi initiated improvements and innovations in Khedda operation (Elephants taming programme). Inside the large Khedda arena, a pool was dug out for freshwater. The Kapila River water was channelized to this elephant pond. These animals drank water and frolicked with their young ones in the pond. When the water became dirty, it was pumped out and fresh water was pumped into the pond. The wild elephants were not starved as in the past. They were supplied with grass, tree leaves and sugarcane.

In olden days, Shikars used to dig big pits of the size 10.5 feet in length, 7.5 feet width and a depth of 15 feet. This pit would be covered with branches and leaves. The Shikars would chase the wild elephants by beating tom-toms and by blowing trumpets. An elephant would fall into the pit during the wild chase. Sometimes, the fall resulted in broken legs or even death of the animal due to head injuries. These elephants in the pit were not given drinking water and made to starve. After a few days, these exhausted elephants were brought out of the pit with the help of tamed elephants. Then, they were roped in and chained to big trees. Sri Chamarajendra Wodeyar banned this cruel hunting or taming practice of elephants. In the 17th or 18th century, small cannons with a cannon ball weighing half a pound was fired at a standing elephant, thereby killing it. In the 19th century, the menace of wild elephants was kept in check by private individual hunters. After killing the elephant, they would slash ears or tail or toes and then it would be produced before the Maharaja. If they had killed a tusker, then they would produce its ivory tusks. The Maharaja would give them Rs. 25 for each elephant killed.

Sometimes, a lone elephant was chased by tamed elephants with hunters straddling on it. They would exhaust the wild elephant. It was not allowed to rest or sleep. The totally weakened animal was tied with chains and ropes to a tree. After a week or two, it would become a mild-mannered tame animal. During the run, the wild elephants exhibited more strength and stamina. The Mahouts (chief rider or driver) resorted to the cruel practice of stabbing the backsides of the tamed elephant with a sharp iron implement. This practice was resorted to enhance its pace of run during the hunt. It caused lot of pain and the wounds took a long time to heal. Nalwadi did not tolerate cruelty to animals and this obnoxious practice was stopped. If a rogue male elephant went on a rampage, then Nalwadi came to the rescue of villagers. These tuskers on "Masth" (Sometimes a bull elephant became aggressive, because of a large secretion of reproductive hormones) damaged standing crops and houses of villagers. Nalwadi would track it alone, carrying a double-barrelled gun on his shoulder and when found, he would kill it with one bullet. He was a sharp shooter of great repute. He usually aimed either at the brain or at the heart. In this manner, the villagers were protected from Elephants, Tigers, Bisons and Leopards.

Maharaja Sri Nalwadi Krishnaraja Wodeyar leaving Kharapur Forest Lodge to inspect Khedda arrangements.

Khedda Operation in Mysore State

The elephant catching Khedda operation had gained global popularity. This operation was conducted in Kharapura located in Kakanakote forest, Budhipadaga in Chamarajanagar Taluq and in few other places. This was a big operation involving thousands of Shikars and hundreds of officials. The wild elephants were chased towards a large pit by making them cross the river or sometimes, through forest trails. The evergreen thick Kakanakote forest was always pleasing to one's eyes. The tamed "Kumki" elephants herded the wild elephants towards the pit. The Shikars with great dexterity tied thick ropes to its legs. The four ropes extending from the legs were in turn tied to the trunks of huge trees.

Often a "Salaga" (Male or Female wild elephant) which is strongest of the herd and the group leader gave immense resistance.

This Khedda operation was conducted once in 5 or 6 years. If the elephant population had increased, then Khedda operation was conducted to capture the surplus ones. Sometimes, it was conducted to impress the visiting Royalty or Viceroy or Governor.

Khedda operation in progress

"Kumki" elephant taming the wild elephant

A wild baby elephant tied to the trees

Wild Elephants are herded by tame "Kumki Elephants"

A lone tusker "Salaga"

Kumki Elephants marching towards the Keddha pit.

Maharaja Sri Jayachamarajendra Wodeyar with a dead rogue elephant killed by him

The Maharani Sri. Sathyapremadevi and Maharaja Sri Jayachamarajendra Wodeyar proceeding on an elephant for tiger hunt soon after their marriage.

The Shikars (Tribals) exhibited great courage, ingenuity and tact in trapping these animals. They would form three groups. One group made a lot of noise and goaded the wild elephants from the left and another from the right. The third group worked at the back of the elephants. They used fire crackers, burning torches, tin drums and split bamboo hand-held noise making device called "*Kadaku*," which was extensively used. They also blew the wind horn instrument called "*Kombu*."

When the herd of elephants numbering 15 or 20, crossed the river by swimming, it was a beautiful sight to watch. The mother elephants helped baby elephants, while crossing the big flowing river. The young ones were rescued from possible drowning by big elephants. The Shikars created another ruse to trap these elephants. They make tamed elephants to drop dung on the trail leading from the river to the Khedda pit. The wild elephants traverse the path thinking it is a regular elephant migratory route. Finally, they are pushed into the deep pit.

The VIP visitors sit at a height on platforms built behind the log wall. The path leading to the pit gets narrowed and on either side, tall and strong trunks of the trees are bound with rope. They are erected to act as a wall. Of course, the large pit is surrounded by a big barricade created in a semi-circular fashion with tall tree trunks. They are inserted into earthen pits and tied to each other by thick ropes. This logwood barricade ought to be able to withstand the battering of the wild enraged elephants, who try to bring down this man-made trap.

The entrance to the pit was narrow and Shikars would have installed a sliding tree trunk gate. This they would have hoisted to a great height with the help of ropes. These ropes are tied to tall tree branches adjacent to the Khedda pit's entrance. After herding wild elephants into this large pit, the Shikars lower the large gate with the help of ropes. It blocks the exit path. Three rows of tree trunk barricade is erected near the gate to withstand the constant ramming of big elephants with their heads at the gate and nearby walls. Then, the Shikars surround the pit and they truly create mayhem by beating drums and by blowing trumpets. They keep big bonfires burning for several nights. The main objective is to exhaust the energy and anger of the wild elephants.

These wild elephants are provided with ample supply of fodder and drinking water. After one week or ten days, these elephants are herded out of the pen with the help of tamed elephants. They tie big ropes to the legs of wild elephants and also run a rope around its neck like a collar. They tie these rope ends to tree trunks. Then, elephants are fed with sugarcane and jaggery to entice them with delectable desserts.

When future George the Fifth and Queen Mary visited the Mysore State in 1906, an interesting incident took place. At that time, King George the Fifth was only a Prince of Wales. The Shikars were trying to capture a "Salaga" the group leader of wild elephants. It could be either a male or a female elephant, which becomes the pack leader. In this case, a female Salaga was surrounded by Kumki (tamed) elephants. One Shikar was tying a rope around the leg and it kicked him suddenly. He was thrown to a distance and he was unconscious. This man was carried out on a stretcher.

The other Shikars continued with their task of tying ropes around legs and neck. The loose ends were tied to Kumki elephants' legs and necks. When the Kumki elephants began to pull the wild Salaga out of the pen, it became enraged and attacked the escorting elephants. It angrily pulled a wooden stake from the ground and threw it aside. The mahouts jumped from their Kumki elephants and ran away in fear. At this moment, the Maharaja rushed into the pit and ordered to bring six more elephants to assist the five Kumki elephants which were struggling to subdue the Salaga. Sometime later, after a bitter struggle, the eleven elephants escorted the Salaga out of the pen. The Royal couple, the Viceroy of India and Governors were greatly impressed by the courageous behaviour of the Maharaja, who risked his precious life to help the Shikars. The other wild elephants belonging to the same herd saw their enraged leader and they began to go amuck. They began to pull at the tied rope and thereby the Kumki elephants were also dragged. They attacked bamboo groves and standing trees. The Royal couple saw Nalwadi walking behind wild elephants nonchalantly along with other Shikars. They also imitated the Maharaja and walked on foot for half a kilometre which became an international news.

On November 14th in the year 1913, Khedda operation took place in Kharapura. On that day, one wild elephant aged about sixty years began to throw tantrum. It remained quiet when ropes were tied around its legs. But when the ropes were put around its neck, it went wild. It put up stiff resistance to its enslavement. On 10th November 1913, the Shikars did not come across any stiff resistance from a Salaga after it was captured. Then, the Maharaja ordered the strongest elephant from the palace stables to be brought forth. It was called by the name of Motilal. The two elephants began to fight it out to everyone's surprise. The wild animal attacked Motilal with immense force.

The head on collision made Motilal totter around. But with renewed energy, it attacked the wild one again and again. But the wild one had more strength and energy. It almost knocked down Motilal. It managed to kick back two Kumki elephants, which were in front blocking its path. It then attacked the gates of Khedda with great force. Some logs of woods tied across the gates came off. In its second knock, it brought down with its trunk two or three stakes. One mahout jumped from his Kumki elephant in fear and sprained his leg. Another Mahout sitting on a Kumki elephant caught the wooden beam on the gate and was seen hanging from it, as the elephant ran out in fear.

At this moment, the Maharaja and a few other officials took charge of the situation. They ordered mahouts to bring in more Kumki elephants. These tame elephants surrounded the wild elephant. From the pit, the Maharaja gave directions to escort the wild one in a tight packed formation to the field outside. The wild elephant made loud angry noises on its way out. The Viceroy of India was immensely impressed by the bravery of the Maharaja.

When the elephants were taken out of Khedda pit into the open forest, they often got injured, sometimes in a fight with another elephant. Many elephants refused to eat and drink water. The tightly bound thick ropes around legs and neck resulted in heavy wounds. Sometimes, these wounds festered. Hence, the Maharaja asked Shikars to tie only two front legs first time. After a while, the other two hind legs were tied with ropes. The earlier ones were withdrawn and sometime, neck ropes were taken off. The Maharaja told the vets to apply medication to the wounds. Later, the Maharaja ordered soothing music to be played by palace band. (In ancient Indian texts, it is mentioned that king Udayana played Veena in the forest to tame wild elephants. Some singers used to sing melodious songs to pacify elephants.)

The Greek Ambassador Megasthenes visited the court of Chandragupta Maurya in 3rd Century B.C. He narrated how Indians cleverly trapped wild elephants and tamed them. In some respects, the ancient and modern trapping methods are identical. But Nalwadi has reformed greatly the Khedda operation in the 20th Century. He has undoubtedly improvised both tiger hunt and elephant trapping Khedda exercise.

Chapter 11

Patron of Arts and Music

******

"Raso vy sah|"
"Kalabyam chudalankrutha
Sashi kalabyam nija tapah
palabyaam bhakteshu prakatith
palabhyam bavathu mae|
Shivabyamstoka tribhuvana
Shivabyaam hridhi punarbavaabyamnanda spurdanubavabyam nathiriyam||"
"Nadopaasnaya deva Brahma
Vishnu Maheshwarah|
bavanthyu paasita noonam yatha yethe tadatamkaha||"

******

I. The divine one who wears a crescent moon on his head, one who manifests himself before our eyes, after our arduous penance you grant to us our boons, one who ushers in an auspicious environment in *swarga*, *amartya* and *patala* (Tribhuvana), one who invokes positive emotions in one's heart again and again, one who personifies the cumulative experiences gained by oneself, the divine couple Shiva-Shive, I offer you my humble prayers to you as you are personification of universal knowledge and 64 *kalas*."

II. The reverential worship of musical notes (sound or tone) helps us to realise triumvirates (Brahma, Vishnu and Maheshwara), because they personify melodic aspect of music. My sincere pursuit of music is one form of worship of the three triumvirates.

The present Mysore Amba Vilas Palace

The Mysore Wodeyar rulers, throughout history, were known for their generous patronage of fine arts like drama, poetry, music and painting. Sri Chamarajendra Wodeyar and Sri Vanivilasa Sannidhana decided to educate their daughters and sons in fine arts.

The eldest daughter, Princess Sri Jayalakshammani, received music lessons. She could play piano with one hand and press the foot pedal when required and keep the rhythm by playing on a *tabala* with the other hand. Sri Krishnajammani also played veena with great dexterity. [She was blessed with green fingers. She loved gardening and had her own personal vegetable patch.] Both the sisters, that is Sri Krishnajammani and Sri Chaluvajammani excelled in music and portrait painting. I can quote one instance to showcase their artistic talent. They both used to prepare exquisite ornaments for goddess Sri Chamundeshwari from pomegranate fruit seeds and make beautiful garlands of *Thumbe* flowers (Leucasaspera: genus *Lucas* and the family *Lamiaceae*). They would present it to Goddess Chamundeshwari during the Chariot Festival. Their brother, Yuvaraja Sri Kanteerava Narasimharaja Wodeyar acquired musical skills, but did not excel in painting. But in later life, he became a generous patron of painters.

The Rajendra Vilas Palace on top of Chamundi Hill

Nalwadi had several artistic talents like painting and music. He could play several Indian and Western musical instruments with great ease. The Maharaja was a connoisseur of all the three schools of music – Carnatic, Hindustani and Western Classical music. A large number of people develop in-depth knowledge of one musical school. Whereas, Nalwadi possessed expertise in all the three classical schools of music to everyone's surprise.

The Maharaja was trained by the conductor J.M D'Fries of Mysore Palace Band in the subtleties of western classical music. In 1900, an American musician visited Mysore city. He happened to listen to the saxophone performance of 16-year-old Nalwadi. He was greatly impressed by the virtuosity of the young prince. He exclaimed that Nalwadi's talent was a boon given by the almighty. Nalwadi devoted himself to the learning of violin. Nalwadi was able to impress able violinists of the palace band like Col. Fox and J.M.D'Fries. In western classical music, the instrumentalists follow the musical score sheets before them. They master compositions after long and arduous practice. But Nalwadi could play on violin a new composition at first sight and without any prior practice. This has amazed many a great visiting musician.

This incident took place in Mysore prior to 1914. Three European musicians of repute called on the Maharaja. They had performed in Europe before the Czar of Russia, Emperor of Austria and the King of Italy. They had received great accolades from connoisseurs of music. They had developed super-size egos due to this mass adulation. But before their visit to Mysore State, they had heard great praise from discerning European lovers of music that the Maharaja possessed immense talent as a musician and moreover, he was known for his critical evaluation of artistic performance. These three brothers on the day of the concert developed stage fright and anxiety. During their performance, one of the brothers played a false note much to the dismay of the audience. This faux pas became a subject of discussion in the elite circles.

Nalwadi encouraged the three princesses (daughters of the Yuvaraja) to learn piano. In those days, overseas examiners used to visit India from Trinity College of Music, London. One famous pianist Mestowski (?) came to conduct tests for the princesses. The examiner gave them very high grades and he was full of praise for them. Later, they often performed over All India Radio for the benefit of lay listeners. Nalwadi's grounding in all the three schools of Classical music made the performing artists nervous wrecks before him. Their concerts on many occasions fell short of expectations of the audience.

Nalwadi's first musical guru in Carnatic music was Sri Veena Shamanna. The second most important guru was Sri Veena Sheshanna. Here is a brief biographical sketch of Veena Sheshanna. The veena maestro Sheshanna hailed from the family of Veena Kuppaiah. This ancestor lived even before the time of Hyder Ali (1720 – 82). Kuppaiah had travelled through Tamil Nadu and he had defeated the other eminent veena artists of the time in virtuosity. He had won several veena instruments as trophies once owned by these eminent artists. The Maharaja Sarabhoji Bhonsle I (1675-1728) of Tanjavur had honoured Veena Kuppaiah with titles and cash rewards. Veena Sheshanna's father Chikkaramappa was a musician and Veena player in the court of Mummadi Krishnaraja Wodeyar (1794-1868). Veena Sheshanna was a child prodigy and unfortunately, at a young age, he lost his father. He was trained in veena playing by Dodda Sheshanna, father of Veena Subbanna. The elder sister of Veena Sheshanna Smt. Venkamma had a profound knowledge of Carnatic classical music. She would ask Sheshanna to play a "new *Sangathi*," otherwise lunch would not be served to him. A musical improvisation of each line in a song is called "Sangathi." This raw diamond was honed and polished by a great many contemporary musicians. This genius began his career in the court of Sri Chamarajendra Wodeyar and continued to garner fame and fortune in the court of Nalwadi Krishnaraja Wodeyar.

These two famous incidents took place during the lifetime of Veena Sheshanna. The renowned violinist of Tamil Nadu Sri Thirukoddikaval Krishna Iyer visited Mysore once. He called on three famous instrumentalists of Mysore city and requested them to play Carnatic classical music. All the three veena players played the Kalyani composition "*Taraka brahma Swaroopini*" in *pallavi* form. Then, he visited the house of Veena Subbanna. He also played the same raga and composition in pallavi form. In an aside with other musicians, he jocularly said the Mysore artists knew only this composition in Kalyani raga to render it in pallavi style. This light hearted remark did not go down well with Veena Sheshanna.

Later in the mansion of Darbar Bakshi Basappaji, during a religious festival, a veena concert of Sheshanna was organized. His highness Sri Chamarajendra Wodeyar was also present. Veena Sheshanna was accompanied by the violinist Sri Krishna Iyer and ghatam player Sri Ananthacharya. Sometime before the evening concert began, Sri Krishna Iyer the accompanying violinist condescendingly told Veena Sheshanna not to worry too much about matching his skills with other artists. Krishna Iyer treated the concert in a casual manner and with disdain. But Veena Sheshanna was known for his fiery temper and acidic tongue. He remained quiet for some time. Veena Sheshanna began his concert with Raga Todi. On that evening, he played as one possessed by the spirit of Goddess Sharadha. He played the musical notes of Raga Todi in a variety of permutations and combinations. In the beginning, Ari Ananthacharya could not even guess the rhythmic Tala adopted by Sheshanna. He humbly asked Veena Sheshanna to delineate the tala for him. The violinist Krishna Iyer could not follow the complex Raga Todi exposition. He kept his violin on the ground and prayed to the Maharaja that he was not competent to follow the Veena artist. He requested Sheshanna to proceed to pallavi stage of performance.

Normally for instrumentalists to render a pallavi for a long duration is a challenge because they had to follow the tala mentally. They could not keep tala by slapping the right palm on the thigh back and front and sometime keeping count of tala time lapse with fingers like vocalists. That evening, he played Raga Todi pallavi for half an hour. At the end of the concert, Sri Krishna Iyer said he had not heard Raga Todi played so exquisitely and in such detail during his lifetime. Most instrumentalists resort to simple talas like *Aditala* or *Trishrajati triputa tala* during pallavi rendition. But Veena Sheshanna could play pallavi of a raga in any tala of his choice with ease. He also had the talent to render Carnatic compositions in the Western Classical notation or in the style of Hindustani Raga. There are many common ragas shared by Carnatic and Hindustani schools of classical music.

A seasoned connoisseur of classical music expressed this opinion to the author about Veena Sheshanna. The veena maestro Sheshanna was known for his virtuosity and creativity. He could play a Carnatic Raga for four or five hours. He could elaborate on the ascending and descending notes of a Raga in one thousand varieties of permutations and combinations. The average musician may demonstrate five or ten variations of the Raga theme. After that, he becomes repetitive and monotonous.

During Navaratri (Dasara) festive days, Veena Sheshanna especially on Saraswati festival day, he worshipped Goddess with flowers and by offering incense. A vocalist relies on the words of poetic composition to bring out its hidden meaning in the concert. But an instrumentalist has to rely on his musical instrument to express varied emotions and feelings. Veena Sheshanna's dexterity made the instrument "talk" to the audience. He could make the audience laugh, weep and cry. He also instilled the *Bhakti* aspect of the music into the hearts of the listeners. Occasionally overcome with emotions, he would shed profuse tears. He took the music lovers into a trance-like mystical state. He was capable of casting a magical spell on the audience. On rare occasions, Veena Sheshanna would attain a state of "Samadhi" and the instrument would slip to the ground from his hands.

The well-known Sanskrit quotation on the effects of music goes like this – "*pasurvetthi shishirvetthi Vetthi Ganarasam phani*" (Animals, infants and even snakes exhibit a taste for music. They feel the amorous effects of music.)

Once during a veena concert of Sheshanna a huge cobra wound its way into the auditorium much to the horror of the audience. This snake stopped in front of Veena Sheshanna with its open hood. It was swaying this way and that way during the rendition of a Raga. When the musical number concluded, it quietly slithered away from the concert hall without causing any harm to anyone. This rare sight inspired the wealthy patrons so much one individual exclaimed "Shesha (snake) has come to listen to Sheshanna's music." These admirers got a silver open hooded snake made by a silversmith in the capital city and presented it to Veena Sheshanna. This appurtenance could be fixed to the curved neck [Yasi] of the peg box of veena instrument.

Veena Sheshanna has composed complex and intricate *Tillanas* and *Varnas*. His famous composition "The Vanquisher of Mahishasura" in seven different rhythmic (talas) scales is very popular with listeners. This is a difficult Raga composition for ordinary veena players. Once, he was invited to Dharwad by Sir Evan Maconochie the British civil servant to perform there. The local population loved his music so much that they forced him to spend an extra fortnight in Dharwad. These are the words of Sir Evan Maconochie,

*"One year, I got an old Mysore friend Mr. Seshanna, the head *Vina* player at the palace, to come and play to the guests. The *Vina* is an instrument of the lute type of great beauty and delicacy, and when properly played, appeals to the Western ear as much as to the Indian, Mr. Seshanna a handsome and charming old gentleman, was a great artist; and his instrument, which had been in his family for two hundred years or more was a Stradivarius among *Vinas*. Dharwar went into raptures over him, and for a week or two declined to let him go; so, his visit was a great success from every point of view."

Veena Sheshanna earned immense fame and fortune during his musical career.

Sri Nalwadi Krishnaraja Wodeyar honoured Veena Sheshanna with the honorific title "*Vainika Shikamani*"(Crest jewel among Veena artists). He was presented with a gold band worn as an armlet. He was also given a ceremonial silk robe. The Maharaja of Ramanad invited Veena Sheshanna to his royal court. He was an honoured guest of the Maharaja. Veena Sheshanna gave many concerts before the Maharaja. On the penultimate day, he was taken in a ceremonial procession on an elephant through the streets of the city. He was felicitated with a costly Cashmere shawl and gold ornaments. He was invited by the Maharaja of Baroda H.H. Sayaji Rao Gaekwad to perform before him. After listening to him for several days, he honoured him with an expensive shawl and a gold medal. He was taken in a procession through the streets of Baroda in an expensive palanquin. Later, this costly palanquin worth Rs. 1,500 was presented to Veena Sheshanna as a gift.

In 1911, Nalwadi honoured Veena Sheshanna with a ceremonial robe and costly gifts. He was garlanded with two rows of flowers and pan leaves. He was taken in a procession with a group of nadhaswara musicians from Karikallu Totti to the Brahmapuri gate of the Mysore palace. When Queen Mary visited the Indian pavilion during the Festival of Empire in 1911, her eyes took note of small statues of Veena Sheshanna with a veena. She had listened to his concert with rapt attention. She purchased a small statue of Veena Sheshanna at the exhibition in London.

His Highness received veena lessons from the two eminent artists Veena Shamanna and Veena Sheshanna. The classical Carnatic music benefitted from their efforts in making the Maharaja not merely a connoisseur, but also an accomplished artist. He had inherited musical genius from his previous birth and his rigorous practice honed his skills further.

While talking with a courtier, Veena Sheshanna said he had performed before the previous ruler Chamarajendra Wodeyar on several occasions with ease. But before the present ruler, Nalwadi Sri Krishnaraja Wodeyar, he had to play veena with double caution, as the Maharaja possessed in depth knowledge of Carnatic classical music. He would notice the slightest slip or deviation in a Raga.

Once, Veena Sheshanna was informed by the Maharaja Sri Chamarajendra Wodeyar that he had only two passions in life – one horse riding and the other was music. But Nalwadi was a greater patron of music and fine arts. He not merely honoured them, but many were made court musicians on a regular honorarium. They were permanent employees of the Mysore Palace. He not merely played the role of a generous patron, but also a discerning music critic.

Once, the famous sitarist Afta-be-Sitar Ustad Barkatullah Khan, remarked that many Maharajas and Nawabs listened to classical music without understanding its nuances and subtleties. They would order the musician to perform by shouting "Bajav." They would sit like a statue during the concert non-plussed. But Nalwadi judged a musical performance by its intrinsic merit. His mere nod or a smile of appreciation meant so much to the artists, because he had an in-depth knowledge of all the three classical schools of music. Even Ustad Barkatulla Khan played sitar before the Maharaja with trepidation and anxiety.

Another renowned Carnatic vocalist had this to narrate. He had already received accolades and honours in several royal courts of India. In 1927, this famous artist (author withholds the name) was invited to perform before the Maharaja in Mysore Palace. The concert was held in the private drawing of the Maharaja. The musician took a look at the seated Maharaja. He took him to be an ignoramus as far as classical Carnatic music was concerned. The performing artist underestimated the musical scholarship of the Maharaja. The singer presented a Carnatic varna on that day. His highness sat like a statue unmoved by the performance. The next morning, the palace officials visited the artist and gave him sumptuous money. But the Darbar Bakshi informed the artist not to leave the city. He was requested to perform again. The vocalist sang for half an hour. The Maharaja continued to sit like a statue, unmoved. He did not sway his head or swing his hands. The vocalist noticed that the Maharaja was keeping the count of tala with his big toe. The next day, a palace official visited with a request. He told the vocalist that the Maharaja was impressed with the *Goula* Raga composition performed before him.

The artist presented a new "Raga *Ratna Malikache*" and the Maharaja wanted a personal copy of that "*Chitte*" (The musical notations and sahitya). The official wrote down the Raga Ratna Malikache and delivered it to the Maharaja.

The vocalist was asked to perform for the third time before the Maharaja. This time, the vocalist sang Raga Bhairavi for one hour and fifteen minutes. This time, he sang with more seriousness and application of mind. The Maharaja expressed his appreciation by saying that he had listened to this kind of fine music some twenty years ago. He elaborated on the finer aspects of the Raga Bhairavi like a seasoned musician. Later, the vocalist told someone that the Maharaja made him feel like he was born again. It was a journey back to his mother's womb to be born again. The Raga Bhairavi's prime musical note is *"Shadja Madhyama"* ("Sa" as the fourth note). This Raga hovers around the Shadja Madhyam note during the rendition and the vocalist essays this musical note in permutations and combinations. ('Do' in western classical music). Nalwadi had a deep understanding of Raga, Tala and *Bhava* (mood) of a musical composition. Some compositions had an emotional appeal and he was completely immersed in *"Rasanubhava."* He was attentive to the *"Shruti"* (pitch) of Tamburi (Tanpura). Once he was staring at the Tamburi of a musician. After the rendition of the Raga, the artist checked the Tamburi. He discovered that "Mandara" (Ma) had a lower pitch. He adjusted the bead near the bridge of the Tambura to correct its Sruti (pitch).

Once, the Maharaja was driving in front of Nishad Bagh (Public Park) where the palace band house was situated. The Carnatic musicians were rehearsing for a concert. Nalwadi stopped his car for a minute. Later, he drove off slowly from the park area. The next day, he complained to the main vocalist that his accompanying *mridanga* player was playing on the out-of-tune percussion instrument. When forty musicians played different musical instruments before him in an orchestra, he could identify with precision the artist, who had played a false musical note.

On one occasion in his private Bungalow, one European pianist and another Indian jalataranga artist were playing a musical composition based on western musical notations. The Maharaja noticed that the jalataranga artist was striking with a stick the water bowl, which was producing an "off key" or "out of tune" "pa" (*pancham*) (G musical note in Western music). The Maharaja brought it to the notice of the erring musician and asked him to make the required correction. Nalwadi was capable of memorizing a musical composition sung by another artist within a few minutes and play it on a single string of his violin without any note missing.

Nalwadi did not make a distinction between a highly talented artist and an average artist. He always listened with equal seriousness to both the artists. He did not look upon with disdain the music produced by a street-side snake charmer. Sometimes, he showed infinite understanding and patience in the lacklustre performance of an artist. He knew the artist performed well or badly depending on his health, mood and temperament on that day. He often gave them another opportunity to do better. But once, one artist fared badly despite giving him three opportunities. He was promptly blacklisted as a poor performer.

In 1910, Yuvaraja Sri Kanteerava Narasimharaja Wodeyar got married. In the evening, Carnatic classical musicians performed a concert. Nalwadi had invited one Mridangam player (Percussion instrument) to perform on the occasion on the recommendation of a courtier. However, the artist did not live up to the expectations. But the courtier confessed that on the evening of the concert, the artist was running a high temperature because of a fever. Moreover, he had developed stage fright because of the Maharaja's presence. This mridangam player was given another opportunity to make good his earlier lacklustre performance. On the second time, he performed extremely well. Nalwadi praised the skills and artistry of the musician, before the courtier. But with a laugh, he asked the courtier, why the mridangam artist suffered from stage fright. The courtier replied that most of the artists became nervous because they knew that the Maharaja was an unsparing and discerning music critic.

Once, a vocalist came to the palace to perform after eating a heavy breakfast. The concert was marred by frequent belching and hiccups. He was given another opportunity to perform in the palace. He improved his performance and overcame his earlier handicap. When a palace artist erred and produced a false note, the Maharaja reprimanded him, either with a cold stare or a knowledgeable wink. Once, the reputed sitar artist Ustad Barakatullah Khan noticed that during a concert, the Maharaja sat unmoved like a statue. The sitar player deliberately produced a false note. The ruler smiled sarcastically and his eyes narrowed to show his displeasure. Later, the musician confessed to Nalwadi that it was a deliberate act on his part to test the musical reflexes of the Huzur.

Nalwadi's tender heart oozed with love and affection for musicians. But he did not tolerate arrogant artists. Such artists were taught unforgettable lessons in a humorous vein. Once, a vocalist came to Mysore Palace with a letter of introduction from his illustrious Guru (…Bhagavathar) in 1923. He praised his guru and sang encomium about himself sky-high. He was asked to perform before the Maharaja. He sang the famous composition *"Vathapi Ganapathim baje"* in Raga Hamsadhawni. The tambura's pitch and the pitch of the *harmonium* did not synchronize. Moreover, the vocalist presented the Raga in a different pitch. Nalwadi asked the artist why he had engaged a tambura artist and a harmonium artist. The vocalists concluded that the Maharaja was an ignoramus as far as classical Carnatic music. He proudly retorted that the two musical instruments were used to maintain "Sruthi" (pitch). Nalwadi asked whether "Sruthi" was essential to Carnatic classical music. The artist laughed jeeringly and told His Highness "*Sruthir Mata Laya Pitah*" and without them, music would be bereft of musical aspects like melody and rhythm. The Maharaja retorted that the concerned musician must go back to school and learn how to synchronise the singer's voice with the tambura and harmonium. Then, he can safeguard his illustrious Guru's reputation.

One South Indian mridangam player [who claimed to be a disciple of ... Muthu Swami Thevar] visited Mysore court to perform before Nalwadi. This arrogant and vainglorious musician demanded from Darbar Bakshi a gold arm band studded with precious stones even before the performance. The percussion artist also had the first name "Muthu" (pearl). So, in this instance, the court musician, Muthu Swami Thevar and the artist shared a common name. Nalwadi exclaimed, "Let us see who is a genuine pearl of Carnatic music between the guru and his protégé." He meant whether the guru was a true artist or the percussion artist from the South was a true musical genius. This Mridangam player presented his finale, wherein his percussion instrument did not blend harmoniously with the main vocalist and other instrumentalists in "Sruti." He also shouted in an abrasive manner "*Gana Lola*" (one who savours music) as a compliment to the ruler. Later, Nalwadi requested the Mysore court musician Sri Muthu Swamy Thevar to perform the same musical composition on the mridangam. The local artist played the percussion instrument without missing the Sruti. He concluded on the right musical note along with other musicians and pronounced "*Nada Lola*." Nalwadi clapped loudly at the end of the concert to show his appreciation. Of course, the visiting artist was adequately rewarded for his poor performance. But the court musician Sri Muthu Swami Thevar received not only a cash reward but also an expensive silk and velvet Mridangam cover and a gold statue of goddess Lakshmi valued at more than Rs. 1000.

A similar incident is narrated by the famous violinist T. Chowdaiah in his article published by "*Thainadu*" newspaper recently. T. Chowdaiah mentions that a famous mridangam player from South India arrived in Mysore to perform before Nalwadi. The artist suffered from excessive hubris. He believed that no vocalist or instrumentalist was talented enough to accompany him on the mridangam. He had come there along with the vocalist Sri Salem Doreswamy Iyengar. One concert was organized along with Mysore court mridangam player Sri Muthu Swamy Thevar, who was alive at that time. T. Chowdaiah accompanied these artists on the violin. Sri Doreswamy Iyengar sang a Bhairavi raga composition, "*Ma Madura Meenakshi*" in pallavi form (Pallavi is the equivalent of a refrain in Western music).

The visiting Mridangam player presented "*Tani Avartanna*" in cycles as presented by the singer. But it did not conclude on the proper note at the end of the interlude. The Maharaja asked Sri Muthu Swamy Thevar to repeat the cyclical pallavi as the singer repeated the concluding part of the raga. This time, the court musician demonstrated his tala gnana by concluding it on the right musical note. Nalwadi clapped his hands energetically to show his approval. He rewarded all the musicians adequately, but never missed an opportunity to teach an arrogant, errant musician a lesson which he would never forget.

Another outstation mridangam player who was given to bragging about his skills appeared before the Maharaja. All his self-praise proved to be a hollow claim. In fact, that evening concert was a big disappointment to the audience. The musicians left the concert hall for their overnight stay at the guest house. The Maharaja noticed that the mridangam player had left behind the rice flour paste with ferric oxide powder and starch used as a black disk on the sides of the percussion instrument. The next morning, the Maharaja got it gift-packed and sent it to the artist. The Mridangam player received it. He opened it with great glee thinking that His Highness had rewarded him in a grand manner, but he was disappointed to see that his Mridangam black paste had been returned to him as a gift. The arrogant musician had learnt a lesson in his life. Of course, he was given his monetary remuneration as per palace rules.

Nalwadi always listened to musicians during a concert with rapt attention. But even seasoned musicians occasionally erred during the concert. Nalwadi observed other musicians through the binoculars and noticed these artists exchanging glances, knowing smiles and sarcastic expressions to express their displeasure or approbation. Nalwadi often exclaimed before the confidants that these artists were intolerant and lacked patience. He believed in the dictum that to err is human. A child who has learned to walk sometimes stumbles. He criticized the artists who neglected the literary aspects of a composition. If an artist during *Alapana* showed his jugglery skills by singing *Kalpana swaras* did a lot of harm by neglecting Laya aspect of raga.[2]

---

[2] Pallavi: "pa" pada (words), "la" laya (rhythm) and "vi" vinyasam (variations). The pallavi is usually a one-line composition set to a single or more cycles of a tala.

He frowned upon artists resorting to exaggerated facial expressions or hand gestures. He compared it to a pounding of rice with a pestle or grinding of ragi into flour with a circular stone grinder.

Nalwadi admired and enjoyed the other fine arts like dance, recitation of puranas (*gamaka*) and various musical instruments. He never discriminated between local artists and visiting outstation artists. He was equally at home in Carnatic, Hindustani and Western classical music. He had a collector's instinct to record and store rare musical compositions with proper notations in a notebook. His personal library with rare compositions was a music scholar's delight. He had a thorough knowledge of the text *"Natya Shastra"* by Bharath Muni. He often invited great Bharatanatyam dancers to perform in the palace, especially on his coronation anniversary day. He also invited Kathakali, Manipuri, and Yakshagana artists and puppeteers to perform in the palace. The famous drama troupes performed well-known plays in the Jaganmohan Palace auditorium before an elite audience.

The Mysore Palace had its own drama troupe with the title "Sri Chamarajendra Karnataka Nataka Sabha." He had imposed certain restrictions on the drama troupe. He did not want them to sing songs in Hindusthani style in a mythological musical play. The puranic theme is best suited for Carnatic raga compositions. He was also particular about certain emotions (rasas) that could be best expressed only through selected ragas. He also instructed actors who played traditional characters like Valmiki, Lava and Kusha should wear only proper period costumes. He was a generous patron to various visiting drama troupes from faraway places.

In 1915, the Maharaja started a free music school in Mysore Palace. Anyone interested in classical music could go there and learn vocal or instrumental music. The western concept of Philharmonic orchestra did not prevail in Indian classical music. So, he formed Carnatic and Hindustani palace orchestra ensemble.

The important aspect of Western classical music, that is harmony and synchronization of various musical instruments to produce music was taught to Indian musicians. All of them were taught Western musical notations and sheet music was given to Indian ragas for the first time. The very idea of 15 or 20 musicians playing different instruments together in harmony was a new development in Indian music. Nalwadi instituted graded musical honours by instituting titles and awards like *"Vainika Shikamani," "Gayaka Shikamani." "Vainika Praveena," "Gana Visharadha," "Sangeetha Sastra Ratnam"* and

"*Sangita Ratna.*" The artists who played "nadhaswaram" (Clarinet) and dolu (huge drums) were rewarded by Nalwadi generously. The clarinet players were given gold mouth pieces and drum players were given gold pendant with Goddess Chamundi embossed on it with a gold chain. They were also presented with velvet and silk covers for the Mridangam. Many musicians were nominated as "*Asthana Vidwan*" (court musicians). They received a monthly remuneration. The outstation musicians were expected to remain in Mysore during special occasions like Dasara, Nalwadi's birthday and Ascension Day. They lived in far-away towns during the rest of the year in Hubli, Calcutta and Travancore. He respected the vocalists who pronounced the words of the lyrics correctly, and the artists who kept "Sruti" (pitch) and "Laya" (rhythm) in the rendition of a raga. He enjoyed the performance of artists who brought out the "Rasa" (emotional) aspect of a particular composition. Nalwadi had told the palace officials to fix the loudspeakers to the ground floor pillars also facing the parade ground in front of the palace. When the great musicians performed in the Darbar hall before the Maharaja, the commoners assembled before the palace could also relish classical music. He got a palace musician to master the Western wind instrument called "Caliphone" to play Indian ragas on it. It was played in public parks so that the common man could relish this music. The palace Carnatic band regularly performed in cities and rural towns. They were ordered to perform in Smt. Krishnajammani T.B. sanatorium once a week for the benefit of the patients.

Nalwadi honoured talented musicians like Sri Muthaiah Bhagavathar and Sri Mysore Vasudeva Charya who composed rare compositions. Sri Muthaiah Bhagavathar composed 108 kirtans on Goddess Chamundeshwari.

Once, Nalwadi saw a young man practising mridangam on top of Chamundi Hill. But he was playing awfully. Nalwadi questioned him, why he was playing talas wrongly. He replied that regular practice would hone his skills. Maharaja replied if you learn talas wrongly you will be a poor player. So, Nalwadi invited the young man to learn mridangam from a good guru free of cost. He also enrolled him in a good school to pursue higher education. He once noticed a young man in the palace garage singing a song. He possessed a good voice but lacked formal training in classical music. At that time, he was drawing a salary of Rs. 12. He withdrew him from the garage and enrolled him with a good Carnatic musician. After a few years, he blossomed into a good singer. He was employed on a salary of Rs. 40 and became part of the Carnatic music palace band.

The visiting Western classical musicians were astounded by the in-depth knowledge of the intricacies of the Western Classical music possessed by the Maharaja. He played the generous role of a patron of Western classical music as well. One major instance of Nalwadi's devotion to Western classical music came to the fore in 1920. It was the year of Ludwig Van Beethoven's (1770 to 1827) sesquicentennial celebration (150th birth anniversary) all over the world. The Maharaja commissioned a statue of the great composer Beethoven. Perhaps, he is comparable to the great Carnatic classical music composer Saint Tyagaraja (1767-1847). A grand function was organized in Bangalore palace in honour of Beethoven. The statue was draped in silk cloth and profusely garlanded. The Mysore palace Western classical music band performed in front of an elite audience peppered with a lot of Europeans. The concert began with the orchestra playing the famous Beethoven's "The Symphony No.5 in C minor" in a lucid and grand manner. The native Indian musicians playing a difficult composition so ably astounded the assembled audience. The evening concert performed by local artists in such an excellent manner won the hearts of the listeners. The Mysore palace bands had formed music bands such as "Reed Band," "Cavalry band" and "Carnatic Band." It is relevant to make note on a regular basis the music examiners from Trinity College of Music, London came to test the skills of musicians playing violin, piano and other musical instruments. The members of the royal family and palace band members passed these exams and received diploma certificates from this august institution. More often, teachers and students were native Indians. Nalwadi encouraged one native piano tuner, who could fine-tune the 200 strings of a piano to proper pitch. Although he belonged to the Urs royal family, he pursued this profession. Once, Nalwadi came across a 12-year-old Sri Vaishnav boy prodigy, who could play Western music compositions without looking at musical notation sheets. He gave him ample encouragement to pursue a musical career. Another gentleman evinced a great interest in playing the "Harp." He could not afford this musical string instrument. So, the Maharaja imported a good harp from abroad and presented it to this budding artist. The Maharaja had a vast collection of musical instruments of the East and the West. He also acquired from Europe an electric pipe organ which was installed in his green drawing room.

Love for Paintings

The Maharaja loved paintings and sculptures passionately. He has collected a number of paintings from artists and they were on display in his drawing rooms and bedrooms. One of the palace painter's sons, Sri. Venkatappa, as a young man, had copied a famous western painting. This was greatly appreciated by Nalwadi. He rewarded the young boy with Rs. 100. Later, this young man was taught English and Hindustani languages. The Maharaja offered him a scholarship and sent him to Shantiniketan in Bengal to learn painting from Sri Abanindranath Tagore. When he returned from Bengal after a few years, The Maharaja commissioned him to paint several paintings and also he created plaster of paris bas relief works for the palace. He encouraged the artists like Sri Keshavaiah and Sri Nagarajaiah to produce masterpieces. In Mysore state, many institutions requested His Highness to present portraits of Sri Chamarajendra Wodeyar, Sri Nalwadi Krishnaraja Wodeyar and later,Sri Jayachamarajendra Wodeyar to their organisations. The Jaganmohan Palace art museum has a very valuable collection of art works. Some of the famous paintings are "Bhagavad Gita Scene" by Sri Appaji, Nalwadi's portrait by Abdul Aziz, and Sri. Venkatappa's painting "Mahashivaratri" adorn the walls of the museum. There are some very good paintings of horses in the palace stables.

Nalwadi commissioned the artists to paint portraits of high-ranking palace officials and the Dasara procession on Vijayadasami day painted on the walls of the Kalyana mantapa are some of the examples. There is also a portrait of the nadhaswaram player Sri. Kandaswamy. His Highness encouraged the Mysore school of painting.

When the then Prince of Wales and at present the King-Emperor George the Vth visited the princely state of Mysore in 1906, the Maharaja organized a Fine Arts and Crafts Exhibition in honour of the visiting dignitaries.

(Ed. Note: Sri Raja Ravivarma and Nicholas Roerich paintings collection speaks volumes about the esoteric taste of the ruler)

The famous Indian self-taught painter belonging to one of the Royal families of Kerala Sri Raja Ravivarma displayed a mythological scene from Mahabharata. The painting depicted an enraged Satyaki glaring at Duryodhana. He is being pacified by Lord Krishna. Satyaki's arm is held back by Lord Krishna. Nalwadi, taking the proportions of the characters in that scene into account, noticed that one arm of Krishna was longer than the other. This critical comment was reported to Raja Ravi Varma. The artist came running to the art gallery and saw the anomaly in the painting from the exhibition and rectified it by making the required corrections. This corrected version is now on display inside the palace.

Passion for Architecture

Nalwadi had an ingrained ability for architectural planning. He could advise well-educated architects and engineers in planning a highway, a bridge or a fine building. He would study blueprints and find fault in it. If there was a disagreement, he would ask engineers to prepare a scale model. Then, he would pinpoint technical flaws in the model. Once, Nalwadi was driving his motor car on the newly built road on Chamundi Hill. He told the engineers the road was uneven. They argued that the Maharaja was wrong in his observation. So, Nalwadi asked them to bring levellers to test the road. It was observed that the road did not have a uniform depth. He was good at assessing the road curves. He would tell the engineers you can take a turn in your car at 30 M.P.H or 40 M.P.H at those curves. Once in Bandipur forest, the engineers had built a road with many hairpin bends causing inconvenience to motorists. The Maharaja told the Engineer that a motor car cannot make a 'u' turn at 30 M.P.H. The engineer quoted an English road planning textbook as a reliable authority to reinforce his argument. Nalwadi told him mere bookish knowledge is useless. He took the Engineer in his car and demonstrated that at 30 M.P.H, it was not feasible to make a 'u' turn.

In another instance, an Engineer was supervising the construction of a building. Nalwadi drew the attention of the engineer to the flaws in the building plan. The engineer, in an afterthought, made a remark, "Don't show your project to the ruler when it is half finished." This statement was reported to the Maharaja. The ruler kept quiet about the project during construction. When the building construction was over, Nalwadi and other engineers noticed numerous flaws in the building. The engineer in charge of the project became a laughing stock. He had to redo the whole thing again. This engineer, after this debacle in his professional career, had fulsome praise for the Maharaja's abilities as an architect.

Nalwadi commissioned the statues and busts of his father Sri Chamarajendra Wodeyar to be installed in Bangalore and Mysore. He also commissioned the full-scale statue of Goddess Cauvery, which can be seen in Brindavan Gardens (K.R.S). He has immortalised ordinary people, who served Mysore State in their individual capacity. One Sri Venkataka Swamy Raju was the chief administrator in the Bangalore Palace. He has been immortalised through a statue and it can be seen in Bangalore palace premises.

Several statues and art works like Sri Krishnarajendra Wodeyar's statue seated on a chair can be seen outside the Darbar Hall. Nalwadi also commissioned a marble statue of Sri Madabhinava Valukeshwara Bharati Swamy to be sculpted by Sri Basavaiah. This swamiji was known as Vidhyanidhi Vedhamurthy Brahma Rishi Sri Virupaksha Sastry before he embraced sanyasa. This great soul had passed away recently. The Maharaja commissioned many art works made from plaster of Paris in bas relief by the famous artist K. Venkatappa. Famous artworks are "Siddharth's Sacrifice," "Sakuntala," "Ganda Bherunda" (Mythical twin-headed eagle), "Shiva Tandava Dance," "The great archer Sri Dhronacharya teaching his disciples" and "Ekalavya," etc. The Maharaja got his mother "Mathusri Vanivilasa Sannidhana's" miniature statues commissioned to be manufactured at Bangalore porcelain factory. Later, they were gifted to high-ranking Ursu courtiers of the palace.

The Maharaja loved his capital Mysore city. A lot of dedicated town planning went into the planning of Mysore. The broad tree-lined avenues ran criss-cross to each other. Where the major arterial roads met the Maharaja got roundabouts constructed either with a flower garden or a decorative lamp post with five lights or a fountain, which beckoned the visitors. The major avenues in the city were lined with asymmetrical buildings well designed by architects using the streets on either side of the street. This overall harmony and aesthetically created balance in the landscape pleased one's eyes and gave Mysore city a European ambience. The beautiful city had numerous parks with band stands and public radio transmission rooms to cater to the citizens of Mysore. These public radio sets played music, radio plays and news readers gave global news to the listeners. The beautiful avenues like the road leading to Lalita Mahal, the Sayyaji Rao Gaekwad Road, The Jhansi Laxmibai Road that leads to the railway station, the Vanivilas Road and Sri Chamarajendra Wodeyar Road demonstrate to the world the Maharaja's passion for town planning.

The old Mysore palace caught fire during a wedding on 28th February (Sunday) 1897 in the evening during a marriage function. The old palace building was built out of wood and the fire spread fast and reduced it to ashes. The firefighting measures were inadequate. After this great fire of Mysore, it was decided to build a modern palace. (Ed. Note:Today, the Mysore palace architecture is described as an Indo-Sarcenic style of Architecture. The old city within the fortress with its residents was shifted to a new suburb called Laxmipuram.) The leading European and Indian architects were employed to design the new Mysore palace. The different kinds of artists from North India and South India converged in Mysore city. Many artists hailed from families which had pursued respective professions for thousands of years. These talented and experienced artists were architects, marble artisans, sandalwood craftsmen, gold and silversmiths and many painters and sculptors who worked on this lifetime project. The famous painter Raja Ravi Varma collaborated on this huge project. One well-known art critic exclaimed, "This was not a building project. It had become a cradle for the best artistic creative activity. He is raising an edifice which will attract universal admiration and at the same time, he is also reviving the art of carving in stone and wood in the style so much admired in the Chalukyan and Dravidian temples. The palace, when completed, will be a monument to Indian art which will serve to inspire and elevate the ideas of future generations."

These are the dimensions of the Mysore Palace. It faces the auspicious direction of the East and faces the Chamundi Hill. The length of the building is 245 ft; the width is 156 ft and the height from ground level to the top of the gold-covered cupola tower is 145 ft. Inside the palace, the stone platforms of the pillars, in the pillar creches and on the outer walls, one can see Hoysala-style temple decorations carved in soapstone. The Mysore palace has three floors. The exterior and the interior of the palace are decorated with electric bulbs. The walls are adorned with paintings and the floor is covered with expansive Persian carpets. The ground floor has an armoury, Kalyana Mantapa and Saraswathi Bhandar. The visitors are overawed by the rare pieces of armoury like Shiva Prabhu's (Emperor Shivaji) Vyagraha (Tiger Claws) made with fine steel and worn by a fighter on his hand. There is on display "Sri Ranadhira Kanteerava Narasaraja Wodeyar's special sword called "Pancha Katari." It can be worn like a belt and in one's hand, it becomes a long, flexible and sharp weapon. The other weapons on display are "Vazra Musti" worn on hand by wrestlers. Pistols, spears and one sword is etched with figures of Dasavataram on the blade. There is a big heavy double gun used in elephant hunting. Even a strong man had to heave it up with difficulty and he would be out of breath after lifting the gun. Many of these weapons were handled with ease by soldiers in the past centuries, but now, the modern man lacks the strength and stamina to use them.

In the adjacent hall, the gifts and souvenirs received by His Highness Sri Krishnaraja Wodeyar are displayed. This hall displays fine art works, silver caskets (boxes or chests) engraved in style, and portraits of Viceroys and Maharajas. In this hall, we see horses and bulls carved in Heggadadevanakote black stone. There are also gold and silver statues of dancing damsels from the Halebidu and Belur temples. The palace library has a fine collection of rare manuscripts and books in the Saraswathi Library.

The way to the first floor of the palace is by way of a grand marble staircase. On the second floor, one section is called "Ambavilas" (*Zanana*) restricted enclosure meant for the princesses and royal family ladies. There is a big hall to hold musical soirees. The second hall has a large Darbar hall also called by the name "Sajjae." The big two main doors are covered with sheets of silver. The doors depict the embossed silver figures of Dashavatara of Vishnu. The diametrically opposite doors are made of silver. The third floor is covered with ivory decorations. The ceiling of Ambavilas is decorated with finely carved teakwood lotuses and leaves. Many of the palace doors are adorned with wood panels depicting Goddess Chamundeshwari, Sri Venugopala and cows. This Amba Vilas also has a silver throne of Mummadi Krishnarajendra Wodeyar. It also has many ornate silver cushioned chairs for dignitaries. Among the chairs, there is a crystal glass chair with velvet cushions. The private drawing room of Sri Nalwadi Krishnaraja Wodeyar has a green colour theme. The expansive green carpet covers the floor. The sofa sets are of green shade. The drawing room has many paintings and marble statues. The pride of place is taken by the bust of Sri Krishnajammani. The walls are covered with portraits of royal family members. On one side of the drawing-room, next to the wall stands an expensive imported piano. In the drawing-room, we also see a cow carved in marble and a buffalo carved in emerald.

The music hall has a collection of Indian and Western musical instruments from all over the world. Nalwadi was a skilled player of veena, violin, sitar, mridanga, flute and nadhaswaram. All the musical instruments displayed here are of the best quality. The passage that leads from the private drawing room to Darbar hall is graced with portraits of near relatives of the royal family like uncles and brothers-in-law. Maharaja has also honoured the past Dewans with their life-size portraits. The back portion of the Darbar Hall dates back to earlier times. Nalwadi extended the Darbar Hall in the eastern direction. The Indian and European dignitaries during the Dasara festival sat on either side of the throne to the left and right. The evening musical concert was the high-water mark of the evening Darbar. The musicians were seated on a platform and they were raised from ground level with the help of a large mechanical elevator. The courtiers, guests and the Maharaja could see the cavalry marching, the gymnasts and the acrobats performing on the grounds before the palace. The assembled commoners on the green could view the Darbar and parades. They also could savour western classical music broadcast on the loudspeakers. In later years, "Akashvani" the local Radio Station began to transmit these musical performances to listeners all over the state. The new Darbar hall measures 80 ft in width, length 245 ft and 50 ft above the ground level. This new Darbar Hall gave a grand stand view of the parade ground in front of it.

The Durbar Hall walls are adorned with the paintings of Raja Ravi Varma such as "Samudra Garvabhanga" (Sri Rama subduing the God of the seas), "The abduction of Sita," "Bhisma's vow" and "Sri Krishna's diplomacy," etc, The three previous rulers of Mysore State, the late Yuvaraja Sri Kanteerava Narasimharaja Wodeyar and Sri Nalwadi's life-size portrait hang in the Darbar Hall. The ceiling is decorated with pictures of the triumvirate of Hindu mythology Brahma, Vishnu and Maheshwara. We see guardian deities of eight cardinal directions, the nine divinities, who represent nine planets, twelve zodiac signs and Goddess Chamundeshwari. All these beautiful pictures were painted by Mysorean painters. The interior and the exterior of the palace are decorated with electric lights. The quadrangle in front of the palace is used for wrestling bouts, acrobat performances and cavalry charges. The Mysore palace is surrounded by a strong fortress. It has five entry gates called Balarama, Jayarama, Jaya Martanda, Varaha and Brahmapuri. The tourists and local population enjoy grand spectacles staged on Mysore palace grounds.

Patron of Multilingual Literature

The Maharaja was a rare polyglot, who had mastered several languages like Sanskrit, Kannada, English, Urdu, Parsi and Marathi. He was well-read in Kannada, Sanskrit, English and Urdu literature. Once, Nalwadi visited the princely state of Cooch Bihar. He was taken to a Sanskrit *pathashala*. Here, the head of the pathashala welcomed him with a speech in Sanskrit and presented him with a memorandum. Nalwadi delivered his speech in Sanskrit. It was an impromptu speech delivered in grand style with perfect pronunciation of words. The speech dealt with lofty ideas and it was marked by its brilliance and fluency. He could compose Sanskrit verses instantaneously. When he wrote congratulatory letters to his Sanskrit mentors on the eve of the coronation day, he invariably wrote them in chaste Sanskrit. The letter always began with an independent new composition in a poetic style in Sanskrit..

Nalwadi, on a visit to Kashi, composed two Sanskrit shlokas on the presiding deity Sri Kashi Vishveshwara. Inside the temple, there is a portrait of Nalwadi hanging on the wall with these verses in Sanskrit written at the bottom of the painting. Every day, a few hours were reserved for his private study. He always welcomed new ideas with an open mind. He often consulted visiting European and Indian experts on the latest developments in administration and economic policies. Inside Jagan Mohan Palace Museum, Ludwig van Beethoven's statue and veena maestro Sheshanna's statue face each other. It shows the catholicity of musical thinking. He was a great lover of books and encouraged others to read books to garner knowledge. He would buy expensive books and donate them to the public library. He conducted a statewide poetry competition and rewarded the winners with prizes. He organized lectures in different towns by well-known writers and scholars. He often invited intellectuals to the palace to debate and argue about various socio-political issues. He loved Sanskrit and Kannada languages immensely. He granted generous donations to Sanskrit Mahapatashalas and Kannada Sahitya Parishat. Often, he donated prime vacant plots to build aesthetically beautiful buildings for these august institutions. (Kannada Sahithya Parishat, Sri Chamarajendra Sanskrit Pathashala and The Mythic Society.)

The Sanskrit pathashala threw open the doors to students from all castes to learn vedas and vedhantha. The students hailing from the Sudra community could now learn Sanskrit. The teachers in the Pathashala once received a pittance of a salary of Rs. 17. This was gradually raised to Rs. 100. A new magnificent building with a hostel and kitchen facility was provided to the students. Like in the olden days, a provision was made for weekly oil baths. The graduates and rank students of this venerable institution had their graduation ceremony once a year. The toppers were given gold medals and cash rewards along with their degree certificates on Ashwija Shuddha Dwadashi day every year in Darbar Hall of Mysore Palace.

The Mysore Sanskrit Pathashala celebrated in 1926 its Quincentenary (500 years) on a grand scale. In the inaugural speech, he mentioned how his father the late Maharaja Sri Chamarajendra Wodeyar was devoted to the cause of Sanskrit studies. He gave generous donations for the development of infrastructure, library, etc. Similarly, the present ruler has continued his patronage of this venerable institution.

The Maharaja said that the Sanskrit language and literature have espoused a high level of culture, education system, and humane philosophy and it is a repository of ancient wisdom. No other system of education can impart these values. The great temples and monuments occupy a pride of place in our history. The tall majestic towers (Vimanas) of our temples, the dancing *panchaloha* statues of Nataraja or the magnificent serene and calm statues of Lord Buddha, the most valuable paintings of Ajanta and Ellora and the Raga Ragini miniature paintings of Kangra Valley cannot be understood without a study of Sanskrit poetics. Only a thorough study of great Sanskrit works of poetics and Vastushastra can alone open the doors of the treasure house of knowledge. After the conclusion of the function, there was a group photograph session with the scholars and students. The Maharaja remarked that he considered the photo opportunity as an extraordinary privilege bestowed upon him. It was a great moment to be cherished and valued because of the company of eminent vedic pandits. He considered it as his good fortune to be seen in their company. The Mysore palace regularly gave emoluments on a monthly basis to poets, litterateurs, scholars and pandits, who had special repositories of knowledge of various sastras. In fact, their number increased during Nalwadi's reign. These scholars were classified as "vidhwan" and "*Mahavidhwan*." The "Asthan Mahavidhwans" were bestowed with honours and titles such as "*vidhyanidhi*," "*Pandit Ratnam*" and "*Pouranika Ratnam*." The Maharaja had appointed four elderly scholars on a permanent basis as "Dharma Adhikaris" of the palace. At present, one more Dharma Adhikari has been appointed to the post. They all receive Rs. 50 as honorarium. The other vedic scholars receive Rs. 15 as remuneration for lifetime. The palace had on its roles, 10 ritwiks who conducted vedic yagnas (sacrifices) during different seasons. The palace had four purohits (regular priests) and astrologers. The Maharaja honoured writers and authors. All three kalas – Sahitya (Literature), Sangeetha (music) and Chitrakala (painting) received their due share of munificence. The talented artists living in a distant town were not neglected. The body builders and comic actors also received cash rewards and expensive shawls from His Highness.

Chapter 12

The Torch Bearer of Dharma

******

"*poornamadaha poornamidam poornath poornamudachayathe|
Poornasya poornamaadaaya poornamevava Shishyathe||*"

"*Eshavasyamedam sarwa yathikincha Jagatyam Jagat
Tena takteyana bhunjita ma grudaha kasyaswiddanam||*"

"*Kurvenneveha Karmani jijivishechattam samaha|
Evam twaye nanyatetosti na karma lipyathe nare||*"

"*Sathyam vada| Dharmam chara|
Swadayaanma pramadah|*"
"*Dharmo Dhaaryathi prajah*"|

******

This is whole, that is whole; from whole entity the wholesomeness is garnered and what remains ultimately is also whole? Everything in this universe is the repository of the creator. What we gather and consume are blessed by him.

Do not covet the wealth and material possessions of others.

Do live on this earth for one hundred years performing your assigned duties. There is no alternative to this conundrum.

When one's assigned duties are performed selflessly one is not tainted by any sin."

"Abide by Truth, perform righteous action and never stop from studying, learning and contemplation."

"It is "Dharma" that envelops and protects us from ruination and damnation."

Nalwadi Sri Krishnaraja Wodeyar was a pious, religious and fair-minded Hindu king. He did not neglect his religious duties. He went on long pilgrimages with his family members, officials and priests. He followed the injunctions of the dharma sastras diligently. Many rationalists with a so-called scientific bent of mind may express a condescending attitude towards these religious practices.

I wish to quote here the former Prime Minister of Great Britain.

*"If one were to turn to any great philosophy or any great system of thought upon which could be built up a harmony between races, a harmony between conflicting thoughts where could one go to find it more readily than to the great philosophies of India itself, those philosophies where brotherhood is inculcated, where peace and harmony and co-operation are enjoyed, those philosophies which look at the world not in a mere abstract way but something that is essentially composed of differences than a mere uniformity of thought of action." – Right Honourable Ramsay Macdonald.

This statement reiterates the philosophical thoughts of India which preaches love, harmony and peace to the world. This antidote was required to a world, which had witnessed the I^{st} World War. The brotherhood of mankind was at peril. Soon, a more devastating war was going to engulf the world.

Maharaja alighting from the car in front of Sri Chamundeshwari Temple

Nalwadi leading Goddess Sri Chamundeshwari Palanquin Procession

The famous French novelist, dramatist and Nobel Laureate (1915) Romain Rolland says global peace could be achieved only by blending western and eastern philosophies. This is his opinion,

*"For a long time to come the most intense joy which man can know on earth will be derived from supplementing ideals of Europe by the ideals of Asia."

It is relevant to note here that he is the author of a fine biography of "Sri Ramakrishna." (During his lifetime, he also met Swami Vivekananda and Mahatma Gandhi.)

These words of famous philosopher Dr. S. Radhakrishnan sums up the essence of varieties of religious experience.

*"Simply because there are persons to whom religious experience is unknown, we cannot say that it is unreal or impossible. Our limited experiences are not the standard for all. There are many for whom beauty is a word and music only a noise, but that does not mean that there is no reality in the artist's experience... To suggest that men who have religious experiences are mental invalids is inconsistent with the well-known fact that some of the greatest mystics are men of remarkable intellectual power, shrewd discrimination and practical ability."

Sir James H. Jeans, a famous physicist, astronomer and mathematician feels that man may achieve powers to control and regulate nature. But he has not understood his own mind. Perhaps, psychology and philosophy may help him to "Know Thyself." Thus, he writes,

*"Science has given man control over nature before he has gained control over himself. Thus, with respect to knowledge, each generation stands on the shoulders of its predecessors; but in respect to himself, both stand on the same ground... ...Psychology holds out a hope that for the first time in his long history, man may be enable to obey the command, Know Thyself."

Sir James Jeans feels that Indian vedanta is ideally suited for realizing the nature of one's soul. It is a practical philosophy for day-to-day living. The great Indian thinkers are not handmaids to any theories of philosophy. They have a practical approach to life. The great Indian texts like Upanishads, Brahmasutra Bashya or Bhagavad Gita eternally open new vistas for truth seekers. One eminent scientist, who has bagged the Nobel prize for scientific discoveries has stated that a handful of "Riks" from Rig Veda describes various scientific theories dealing with the universe more clearly, ably and more succinctly than new modern day scientific theories. We are left wondering how those ancient rishis, who lived thousands of years ago could have developed a scientific and rationale approach to nature. Some of these seminal ideas from Hindu scriptures will remain relevant and meaningful even in the coming centuries.

In a speech delivered by Nalwadi Krishnaraja Wodeyar at a public function summed up the crisis in the modern world in these words.

"To enhance knowledge, the scientific knowledge of the physical world is alone not enough. The human soul is a witness to the day-to-day transaction of the physical world. Our ultimate goal must be to realise the nature of the soul. To achieve *"Atma Gnana,"* the language best suited for this purpose is Sanskrit. It is known as the language of the Gods. It is spoken by the Goddess of learning Saraswathi and hence, called *"Geervani."* No other language is best suited for pursuing this goal, except Sanskrit. At present, science and technology are not used for the welfare of the world. It is used for the destruction and decimation of nations. Peace and harmony in the world could be achieved only through a study of Sanskrit texts. Each citizen will be happy if all are treated with equal love, kindness and compassion. The *Sanatana* (ever new) Hindu dharma inherited from our ancestors is a great treasure house of wisdom."

The Hindus worship God with attributes and God without attributes. The devotees worship God in different shapes and forms. They conduct rituals according to different paths paved with "Bhakti" (devotion), but ultimately, they all lead to the same goal. Even Adi Shankaracharya, the propagator of Advaitha School of philosophy has advocated "Bhakti" as a feasible means to realize God. Many of his Sanskrit hymns laud the quality of "Bhakti" as being a very important step in the spiritual progress made by man. The offerings made by a "Bhakta" (devotee) reach the one supreme God.

Nalwadi happened to visit Srinagar on Sri Krishna Janmashtami day. He was given a civic reception by the ruler of Kashmir. He was presented with a memorandum. In his speech to the august gathering, he stressed about the holy and auspicious occasion of Sri Krishna's Birthday. "Lord Sri Krishna took birth on this earth to redeem mankind. He is an avatar of Vishnu. But all the incidents of his life demonstrate that his purpose on earth was to vanquish evil forces and to uphold "dharma." His glorious noble life becomes an eternal inspiration to purify our mind and heart. We cannot fathom the spiritual greatness of Lord Krishna. But he is worth emulating in our day-to-day life. His immortal message conveyed to us through "Bhagavad Gita" must be our guiding star. If we take him as our ideal figure in life, we can overcome our petty problems. Lord Krishna through "Gnana yoga" cleanses our hearts. We can achieve salvation and shake off the fetters of our karma by adopting the teachings of Lord Krishna." These words of Nalwadi are words of wisdom.

*Dharma: This Sanskrit word defies English translation. It is variously defined as "righteous living," "way of life" and "Religion." Here, it is broadly used in the sense of "Raja Dharma."

Sri Chamundeshwari Chariot festival
Top photo: High-ranking officials awaiting Maharaja and
Yuvaraja's arrival at the temple
L to R front row: Assistant Secretary Rajasevasaktha Sri. M. Rama Rao,
Deputy Commissioner Sri K. Subba Rao and
Mysore District Board President Sri P.S. Puttaswamy

Sri Chamundeshwari Chariot festival
Maharaja and Yuvaraja leaving Sri Amba Vilas Palace for the Chariot festival.

Dedicated to "Karma" – Dharmic rituals

Nalwadi knew that in the final reckoning, "Gnana yoga" helped in achieving our personal salvation. But he did not neglect the "*Karma Khanda*" of dharma sastra. At a young age, he had been initiated into "Srividya" by the then pontiff of Sri Shankaracharya mutt of Sringeri.

On auspicious days, he performed Sri Vidhya puja from 6 AM to 9 PM. He fasted during this passage of time called one mandala. In the evening, he would perform puja to a pre-puberty adolescent girl and then take his evening meal later. Once in Sringeri, he fasted and meditated from morning till night. But he told his family members and officials to consume food at regular intervals. At 9 P.M, the Maharaja ate some fruits only, skipped his dinner and went to sleep.

People have seen the Maharaja on top of Chamundi hill on hot sultry mornings sitting on a rock and meditating on Goddess Sri Raj Rajeshwari. He was unmindful of the hot rock on which he was sitting cross-legged. Even when he was suffering from high fever, he would not forgo the mandatory Sandhya Vandhana rituals normally performed in the morning, afternoon and evening. He took a bath before doing these religious rituals. Once, a palace official came to give him the prasad from Sringeri Mutt. Nalwadi was suffering from a high fever, but he was doing Sandhya Vandhana. He tried to stand up immediately to receive the prasad but overcome by exhaustion, he was about to collapse to the ground, but he was held up by an assistant at that instant thereby avoiding a fall.

The Hindus perform the annual "Shraddha" (death anniversary) of one's own father and mother on a fixed day in the Hindu calendar coinciding with the time and date of death of the deceased. The oblations are offered to one's father, grandfather and great-grandfather on that day. One priest officiates as the spirit of the dead father. He is worshipped with due honour and his feet are washed with the waters of Ganga. This sacred water is sprinkled over the head of the performer of this sacred ritual and also on the heads of the family members. In the past, the Maharaja would order a pandit to wash the feet of the ordained priest. But Nalwadi changed this practice. He began to wash the feet of the ordained priest with all the devotion and accorded him the status of his late father.

On the festive occasion of "*Upakarma*" (The upper caste Hindus wear a new sacred thread on this day after performing rituals) Nalwadi personally worshipped the "Sapta Rishis" (7 ancient sages) on this day. Every morning, he conducted puja of Gods and Goddesses by reciting appropriate mantras. During the chariot festival of Goddess Sri Chamundeshwari on the hill, he along with the commoners pulled the rope of the chariot and took the deity of the Goddess around the temple.

He has donated expensive gold and silver gifts to famous temples of India. The gold necklace with precious stones was presented to the deities, gold and silver masks, and Nagabharana (The head ornament shaped like a cobra) were given as gifts to Lord Shiva. These ornaments in their own right are artistic work.

The long years of religious austerities had effaced in him all traces of ego and attachment to material things and treated everyone on equal terms. The steadfast devotion, humility and one-pointed mind aimed at God realization remained with him till the end. During the Deepavali festival on "Balipadyami Day," the statue of King Balindra was brought in procession to the Darbar hall and installed with due reverence on the throne. On that day, the Maharaja and the Royal family members paid their due respect to the greatest king on earth, who gifted his whole kingdom to Lord Vishnu. He took the third and final step of Lord Vishnu on his head and went into the nether world only to return to earth on Balipadyama day. On this occasion, Nazar (a show of respect) was offered to King Bali. Nalwadi did not receive any royal honours on that day. [Trans. Note: After a one-to-one personal meeting of the Maharaja with Sri Bhagwan Maharishi conducted in total silence at Tiruvanamalai, the Bhagwan later gave his opinion of the Maharaja – "He is a ripe one in spiritual evolution" Maharishi. [The highest accolade from a realized soul.]

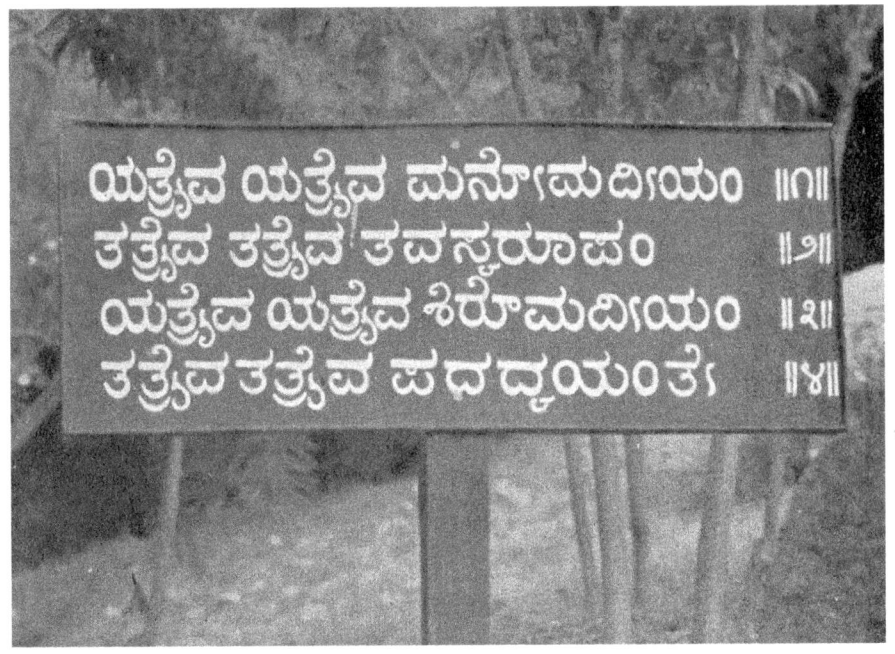

Sanskrit shloka from Lalita Sahasranama

Sanskrit Shloka from Lalita Sahasranama

When we travel on Chamundi Hill road in our vehicle, we see a big wooden hoarding displaying a Sanskrit shloka.

"*Yathraiva yathraiva manomadhiyam|*
Thatraiva thatraiva tava swaroopam||
Yathraiva yathraiva shiromadiyam|
Thatraiva thatraiva padadwayamte"

Wherever my mind dwells, I see your divine form,
Wherever and whenever my mind is subdued,
There the word of God multiplies by many folds in my heart.

On many rocks, shlokas from "*Lalitha Sahasranama*" are inscribed to instil devotion in pilgrims. The inside wall of the temple is adorned with a portrait of Nalwadi absorbed in bhakti. One can find many Sanskrit shlokas written on walls. One Sanskrit shloka declares his total surrender at the feet of Chamundi Devi and prays for her benign blessings.

"*vignaptiravadehime Sumahataa Yethenenathe te Sannidhim*
Praptam maamiha kandhishikamadhuna martana duri kuru|
Chittam tattpadbhavane whybecharedrugvakcha me jatuche
Tattasowmye swagunairbardhana na yatha bhuyo venirgattachati||"

I have surrendered at your feet, after making several repeated attempts to reach you with great difficulty.
    I am a coward and lack courage, but I have come to you seeking refuge, do not reject me.
    My mind, eyes and speech do not rest in you. They are fickle by nature and wander away.
    Therefore, this is my humble prayer.
    Mother, tie me with strong ropes to yourself. Your divine power bids me to you. Your noble qualities make me a slave of you eternally. Never ever separate me from your blessed company.

A Portrait of the Maharaja

Pilgrimages to Holy Towns

Nalwadi went on several pilgrimage tours across the length and breadth of the country. In each and every holy town, he performed poojas, made offerings, and conducted homas and rituals as per the dharma sastras. He would bathe in the cold water, observe fasting and perform special poojas. The local residents were astonished by the sincere devotion and fastidiousness shown by the Maharaja. He also performed the Kailash Mountain and Manasa Sarovar pilgrimage on foot. I shall describe some of these tours briefly. He was invited by the Maharajas and Nawabs of various princely states as a state guest on many occasions. In turn, he also played host to British royalty, many European aristocrats and Indian princes on several occasions.

In every holy city, on an auspicious day, special poojas for the welfare of the royal family members were performed. On the next day, at the same shrine, a special pooja was performed for the welfare of his subjects. He gave generous donations on the second day during the pooja ritual performed for the wellbeing of his subjects, because this was a more important duty to be performed as a king. These rituals began in early mornings and lasted till 8 PM in the evening. He would be inside the temple throughout the pooja and performing of homa on an empty stomach (fasting). During his stay in a holy city, he would fast, pray and meditate for the well-being of his subjects. The observers had fulsome praise for the Maharaja and called him "Raja Rishi." They also came to the conclusion that they would not see another monarch like him during their lifetime.

The Pilgrimage to Rameshwaram

Maharaja Nalwadi Krishnaraja Wodeyar visited Sri Rameshwaram in 1917 along with his mother Sri Vanivilasa Sannidhana, the Yuvaaja Kanteerava Narasimharaja Wodeyar and Maharani Sri Lakshmi Vilasa Sannidhana, etc. They reached the princely state of Ramanada on 16th February 1917. The ruler of Ramanada Raja Muthu Ramalinga Sethupathi received the Mysore Monarch and his entourage with due honours. Nalwadi visited Sri Raja Rajeshwari temple consecrated by the pontiff of the Sringeri Mutt. The next morning, he visited Navapashana to perform *"Hiranya Shraddha"* (to give gold coins to the priests) for his departed ancestors. On the same Saturday evening, they arrived at the holy city of Rameshwaram.

On Monday, the royal entourage visited Dhanushkodi to perform pooja to the Golden Bow of Sri Rama. "Maha Shivaratri" was observed on Tuesday at the Rameshwaram temple. The Maharaja requested the priests to perform *"Abhisheka"* (ritual bath) to Shivalinga with Ganga water. Nalwadi gifted to God Rameshwara two expensive shawls, silk cloth to wrap the Shivalinga, a pair of Dhotis and along with a length of silk cloth with gold brocade and *"Ashtothara pooja"* was performed. The Godess Parvath Vardhini the consort of Shiva was worshipped by the family members. Nalwadi presented the Goddess with an expensive silk saree with a gold border, silk blouse cloth, a pearl necklace and "Ashtothara pooja" was performed. He had a tete-a-tete with Raja of Ramanada who was waiting in the Mantapam. He walked back to the guest house with his family members like ordinary pilgrims through the streets of Rameshwaram.

On Thursday, he performed *Naga Pooja* by consecrating the statue of entwined cobra snakes at the holy enclosure of a peepal tree. After the pooja, the Brahmin priests were sumptuously rewarded with shawls and gold coins. The local Brahmins were served with a grand lunch on this occasion. On Friday, the royal party visited the famous Gandhamadana Mountain of mythological fame.

Nalwadi visited Darbashayana on 24th February 1917 and performed Hiranya Shraddha for his departed ancestors. Later in the day, he called on the Raja of Ramanad at his palace for formal leave-taking. He also sent an expensive saree and blouse to Sri Raja Rajeshwari temple. That evening, he travelled by a special train to Madurai and Tiruchirappalli. Everywhere, he donated money to religious endowments. He returned to Mysore with his family members after a fortnight.

During this trip, one particular incident stands out. He trekked 13 miles to Dharbashayana on a muddy and slushy road. After performing Shraddha (Obsequies) to his ancestors, he then had to return by the same road. He told the Dharmadikari, (chief priest) "You must be exhausted by now. Please travel back to town by a bullock cart." The chief priest replied, "Your highness is trekking through the same road and how can we travel in the comfort of the bullock cart?" So, the whole party walked back covering a distance of 13 miles.

Trip to Kashmir; Amarnath Pilgrimage

The royal entourage led by the Maharaja left Mysore on 3rd July 1918 and reached the capital, Srinagar, on 9th July 1918 in the evening at 8. They were received by the Maharaja of Kashmir and the royal family members were lodged in "Chasmashi" palace. They spent one week in Srinagar. The silk manufacturers of Kashmir were supplying Mysore silk farmers with disease-free silk cocoons to be used in silk cloth manufacturing.

The state of Kashmir is known for its natural beauty. The state boasts of snowcapped Himalayan mountains, green valleys and clear streams running through valleys. The Dal Lake at Srinagar is known for its picturesque scenery with boat houses. Emperor Jahangir described Kashmir as heaven on earth. Kashmir's flora and fauna are world-famous. Here the very best quality fruits like apples, almonds, guava, mulberries, figs and walnuts are grown. The figs grown here are as big as oranges and mulberry plants grow to the size of peepal trees. They grow lemon fruits in plenty.

Srinagar is full of boats that are used for transportation. A river flows through the city. The residents use boats for transporting goods and passengers. During severe winter, the Maharaja and his government move to warmer climes of Jammu. So, the state has two capitals, the summer capital of Srinagar and the winter capital of Jammu. During winter, the elite of Kashmir go to Lahore City for their comfortable vacation. Only the very poor are left behind in Srinagar to live during harsh months of winter.

The Maharaja of Kashmir took Nalwadi on a tour of Kashmir and showed him the Mughal gardens, etc. The Royal entourage left Srinagar on the day of *shuddha panchami* for Amarnath yatra. They trekked and travelled on mules to the Amarnath cave. They stayed in tents during their journey. They reached the Amarnath cave on 11th August 1918. It was a full moon day and they performed pooja to the Shivalinga formed by ice. The Amarnath cave is situated at a height of 15,000 ft.

The Maharaja of Kashmir warned Nalwadi about the rarified air with less oxygen. The Himalayan valley was prone to heavy rains, snowfall and avalanches. Hence, they were warned not to take this pilgrimage. But Nalwadi gave a cryptic reply, "If Almighty wills it, all dangers will vanish." So saying, he resumed his trek. During his eleven days' trek, Nalwadi took a bath in the early morning. He would do pooja and Sandhyavandhana before breakfast. Most of the members of the royal troupe travelled on mules. Nalwadi covered the distance on foot, and when he had to cross a stream, he would sit on a horse to cross it.

On their way to Amarnath cave, they saw fields of saffron flowers. The ruler had a monopoly over the production and sale of saffron. The saffron seeds resembled garlic seeds and each plant produced 10 or 12 flowers. The pollen collected from these flowers were dried, packed and sold abroad as an exotic spice.

One day, the royal family climbed Shankaracharya Hill close to Srinagar. The sage Shankaracharya is believed to have installed a Shankareshwara linga in the temple on top of this hill. Nalwadi presented a big electric lamp post to be erected in front of the temple. These five lamps were called "Pratap Singh Hira" after the ruler of the state. On another different hill, a temple dedicated to Goddess Sri Sharika Bhagavathi was being worshipped by the local population. When Nalwadi visited this temple, a grand pooja was performed for the welfare of the royal family members.

The ten-day trek to Amarnath cave from Srinagar is taken up by pilgrims, priests and petty traders. Nalwadi walked through the valley and climbed the Amarnath mountain. On the way, he saw the ruins of Avantipura, an ancient city which had 30 lakh population once upon a time. He saw the temple ruins of Avantipura, Martandapura, Chandravana, Sheshnag and Panchatarani. The Maharaja of Mysore distributed warm woollen blankets and sweaters to poor pilgrims. He gave old Sadhus Rs. 240 to make the to and fro journey by a palanquin (Dholi).

The cave of Amarnath is huge. The large ice lingam is formed by water droplets falling from its roof. It is a strange phenomenon on a full moon night the ice Shivalinga grows to a great height. During the summer months, one does not see ice or snow in the surrounding area. But throughout the year, the ice lingam keeps growing or shrinking. In the words of His Highness' private secretary R.H. Campbell, C.I.E, I.C.S. (Retired)

"Under the rock, in the interior of the cave, are two frozen springs of clear ice resembling lingam in shape and it is these that are worshipped by the pilgrims. It is certainly a curious phenomenon – the existence of solid ice in this open cave – as there is no real ice anywhere in the neighbourhood, nothing but thawing snow."

Near the Amarnath cave, the visitors see a massive waterfall. This waterfall is called "Amaraganga." The Hindus believe that if they bathe in Amaraganga and worship the Amaranath linga, then they can attain salvation. But the water is ice cold and the outside temperature is always on the minus side. Some pilgrims just take a little water and sprinkle it on their heads. Most of the pilgrims wear flannel and woolen caps, gloves, sweaters and socks. Because the cave is a sacred sanctum, they wear shoes made of dry grass called *"Ghas ka Jootha."* On that day, Nalwadi took a cold shower under Amaraganga waterfall. The only other person who took this risk of hypothermia on that day was the chief priest Vedamurthi Brahma Sri Panditratnam Kanakanahalli Narayana Sastri. The Maharaja had managed to procure cow's milk and Bilva leaves (*Aegle marmesos*) for the pooja of the Shivalinga. The chief priest performed *Ekadashavara Rudrabhisheka* with cow's milk and recited *Sahasranama Archane* to the Shivalinga with bilva leaves. After his bath, the Maharaja wore a dothi and upper cloth to cover his chest. He recited for one and a half hours the *Shivapanchakshari japa* and *Rajarjeshwari japa*. The visiting pilgrims were struck by wonder on seeing the Maharaja doing "Tapas" for such a long time in that extremely cold weather. They felt privileged to see such an ardent Shiva Bhakta. The Maharaja was repeating the japa mantra *"Hara Hara Om, Hara Hara Om, Amaranath ki Jai."* They looked upon him as a divine figure.

Later in the Srinagar camp, the chief officer of the entourage, Amin-ul-Mulk Sir Mirza M Ismail questioned pandit Sri Narayana Sastry about the wisdom of exposing His Highness to the high risk of hypothermia and probable death. This genuine concern of Mirza M. Ismail was conveyed to the Maharaja. Nalwadi laughed and replied, "I have come here to worship God Shiva. My humble life is in the hands of the Lord. If I do not worship Lord Amarnath as per religious injunctions, what is the use? Lord Krishna has said, '*Tena Vina Thruanamapi Chalathi*' (Even a blade of grass does not stir without my consent.) My fate is in the hands of the divine force. Why should I worry about my life?"

The people of Kashmir saw the Maharaja taking a bath in rivers at regular intervals during the Amarnath pilgrimage. They admired his resolve to observe all the religious injunctions like fasting and praying with total dedication. He took the cold water bath in extreme weather conditions twice. On the penultimate day, he ordered a grand lunch for all the pilgrims and *Bairagis* on Mount Amarnath. They were also given thin wool shawls and generous alms as gifts.

Pilgrimage to the Holy City of Kashi

The Maharaja of Mysore visited Kashi sixteen times during his lifetime. Before 1919, the Maharaja often took a holy bath in Kashi or Prayagraj in a special boat called *"Saraswathi Boat."* This was a large square boat with a bench running on all four sides. The centre of the boat had a wooden shallow pit, where pilgrims could stand and take a bath. This square shallow pit was replenished with fresh water as the boat moved in the middle of the river along with the current. The devotee would collect water from this pit in a vessel and pour it over the head. One day, the Maharaja asked one of the priests, whether he could take a proper holy bath in the Saraswathi boat. The Sastri replied with some hesitation that the wealthy could afford the luxury of a bath in the Saraswathi boat. But poor ordinary people like him took a bath in one of the ghats situated in the upper part of the river. There, the water was less contaminated or polluted. The Maharaja replied that the Almighty alone is fortunate in his dealings. All human beings are subject to the vagaries of fate. Who is really rich and who is really poor? Please tell me about your holy bath. The pandit said at Prayagraj, they walk along the shore for three miles. They arrive at the confluence of Ganga, Yamuna and the hidden stream Saraswathi. There, these priests take a dip in the river thirty-six times chanting mantras. The Maharaja replied he would accompany them the next day for a plebian bath. Early in the morning of the next day, the Maharaja walked three miles with them and took a bath like them. He made a resolve (*Sankalpa*) and took a dip in the river thirty-six times.[3] Later, he described it as a proper holy bath and then onwards avoided Saraswathi boats. The Maharaja Nalwadi Sri Krishnaraja Wodeyar was a patron and chancellor of Benaras Hindu University. He visited Kashi in 1919 to preside over the first convocation (Graduation Ceremony) of the University. It was conducted on 17th January 1919 in Benaras.

During this visit, he also took the plebian bath at Hanuman Ghat. He fasted from 6 am to 6 pm and performed Japa (repetition of Shiva's name internally). He took his dinner only after performing pooja in the Kashi Vishweshara temple.

On another visit, he took the plebian bath on fourteen mornings. He meditated from early morning till evening pradosha pooja. One day he was

---

[3.] Pradosha: It is a bi-monthly occasion dedicated to lord Shiva. It falls on the thirteenth day (Trayodashi) of first fortnight in the Hindu calendar. It is an auspicious three-hour period of twilight considered best time for Lord Shiva's worship. (Wikipedia.)

walking towards the Kashi Vishweshara temple, a stray cow was lying in the middle of the road. His attendants wanted to shoo it away as it blocked the Maharaja's path. But the Maharaja told the attendants not to disturb the holy cow. He was prepared to go around the cow without much difficulty and reach his destination.

One morning, after the bath in the Ganges, Nalwadi was sitting inside a stone mantap and meditating until evening. When he rose from the sitting position, his head got knocked down by the low ceiling of the mantap. As this Hanuman Ghat belonged to the Maharaja of Kashi, he wrote a letter to him expressing his willingness to get the mantap renovated. The Kashi Maharaj wrote back stating that the surrounding area of Hanuman Ghat has been gifted away as a public ghat. The various royal families of India had their private ghats named after them. Jaipur Ghat, Scindia Ghat, Kashmir Ghat, Kapurthala Ghat, etc. Nalwadi felt elated to receive the news. The Mysore guest house was some distance away from the banks of the Ganga River. Now, if he acquired the Hanuman Ghat, he could build Mysore guest house on the banks of the Ganga. He offered to buy this area from the Kashi Maharaja. But the Kashi ruler replied that he considered it as a privilege to gift it to Nalwadi. The Maharaja of Mysore replied that if that parcel of land belonged to his kingdom, he would have received it as a gift. But as a *Kshatriya*, he could not receive the gift of land belonging to another ruler. The official correspondence between the two rulers transpired over a period of six months. Finally, the Maharaja of Kashi agreed to sell it for Rs. 30,000 to the Maharaja of Mysore. Later, the Mysore choultry and bathing ghat came to be constructed here.

On one occasion, Nalwadi ordered that the priest of the Vishweshwara temple should conduct a *mahapuja* on an auspicious day for the welfare of the people of Mysore State. His Highness' servants waited outside the precincts of the temple with 2 silver salvers with fruits, coconuts, flowers, shawls and Pithambar (silk brocade cloth) to offer it to Lord Shiva. When Nalwadi arrived there, he noticed that 3 to 4 thousand devotees had been held back to facilitate the ruler's visit to the temple. This caused considerable anguish to the Maharaja. He expressed his pain and sorrow that 3 to 4 thousand ordinary devotees were kept waiting for hours. So, he declared that let these thousands of devotees perform pooja first and then he would follow suit. The officials, priests and commoners were taken aback by this unexpected kind gesture by the Maharaja.

The Maharaja's mother, the Queen Dowager Sri Vanivilasa Sannidhana, completed sixty years. Her birthday was celebrated on a grand scale in 1926 at Kashi with Shanthi Homa, pooja, etc.

Pilgrimage to Badarinath

The Maharaja of Mysore set out on a pilgrimage tour to Badarinath in 1925. Badarinath (Vishnu temple) and Kedarnath (Shiva temple) are two holy pilgrimage centres for devout Hindus. The Badarinath temple is in the middle of a Himalayan valley on the banks of the Alakananda River. It is at a height of 12,000 ft above sea level. It is surrounded by snowcapped Himalayan mountain ranges. A European visitor wrote in his book that during a stay in Badarinath as a non-believer, he felt blessed to be there.

"Whether temples are useless collections of mere stones, or whether gods are figments of primitive man's imagination, to live in the Himalayas for a while is itself a memorable blessing."

The believers found great bliss and felt a divine presence there. This is a holy place because the great sage Vasista did tapas here and wrote a philosophical text called "*Yoga Vasista*." In this place, the famous Maharshi Agastya did tapas (austerities). In a nearby cave, the famous Maharshi Vyasa dictated the epic "Mahabharata" to Lord Ganesh. The 8th century Saint Sri Shankaracharya re-installed the statue of Sri Badarinarayana and consecrated the temple. Even today many Buddhist monasteries in Tibet send gifts and donations to this temple annually.

The sacred Brahmakapala Kshetra is situated on the banks of the Alakananda River. According to Mythology, Lord Shiva cut off the fifth head of Lord Brahma as he had committed a sin by marrying his own daughter Saraswathi. This entailed Shiva with the sin of "Brahmahatya." The 5th head of Brahma was still stuck to his trident. He knocked it off at this place and by performing rituals, he got relieved from the curse of Brahmahatya. This sacred place is used by visiting Hindu pilgrims to perform Shraddha (Obsequies) for their departed ancestors. It is believed that an oblation offered to ancestors ensures them a place in the heavenly abode or a better *janma* (re-birth). This place is eight times more holy than Gaya for performing Shraddha. Anyone who offers oblations to the forefathers here need not do annual Shraddha henceforth.

Nalwadi trekked from Nainital passing through Almora, Ranikhet and Joshimath before reaching Badarinath. This narrow hazardous mountain path posed a lot of risk. On one side, the gigantic mountain rose to great heights and on the other side in the deep gorge a torrent of stream would be gushing forth. In some places, the low stone ledge made them crawl on all their fours. Even where he could have engaged a mule or a palanquin, he preferred to walk. Often, they trekked during the night time after 11 PM and walked till 7 AM to reduce day time fatigue. He completed this journey in thirteen stages. At Badarinath, the river Alakananda flows down at great speed and the water is extremely cold. At a height of 50 meters on the way to the temple, we come across a hot spring. This hot spring joins the Alakananda River and the pilgrims take a bath before performing Shraddha in this luke-warm water.

Sri Shankaracharya selected this spot amidst the Nara Narayana Mountains as a sacred place for establishing Badarinath Statue. The priests of this temple hail from Kerala and they belong to the Namboodari caste. They are addressed as "Raval." They are selected by the Maharaja of Travancore and appointed by the Maharaja of Tehri State.

The Maharaja stayed in Badarinath for five days. He had obtained Tulasi leaves (Basil leaves) from a town situated some forty miles away. He did "*Sahasranamaarchane*" (one thousand names of Vishnu are recited) Mantra with basil leaves. He performed Mahapuja and distributed gifts and cash to priests and sadhus. The pilgrims were awe-struck because he had trekked 170 miles distance like a commoner. They looked upon him as a Raja Rishi and fell at his feet seeking his blessings. Many old women were seen shedding tears. They praised him greatly and they were expressing their elation at seeing him in person. They sang his hosannas in different languages of India.

During his sojourn in Nandaprayag, he was given a grand civic reception by a rich Brahmin businessman. He honoured the Maharaja with garland and fruits. He prostrated before the Maharaja and held the feet with his hands. With tears in his eyes, the businessman invited him for an overnight stay. The Maharaja readily conceded to the request of this brahmin. The next morning, he compared the Maharaja of Mysore to the other Maharajas of India and said the Mysore ruler personified the sattavic qualities of a nobleman. He quoted a line from the ancient text. "*Na Vishnuha prithvi patiha*." It means God Vishnu and this ruler of earth are one and the same (*Raja Pratyaksha Devata*).

During the trek, Nalwadi was shown utmost reverence and respect by young and old alike. A servant accompanied the Maharaja on his horse. The ordinary people could not believe that a Maharaja with an income of 4 crore was traversing the distance on foot, whereas his servant was riding a horse.

They all shouted that the citizens of Mysore State were lucky to have such a great monarch.

While returning from Badarinath, Nalawadi was given a civic reception in a town. Here, they were running a Sanskrit pathashala. They had come to know that the Maharaja of Mysore was a lover of the Sanskrit language. Hence, they requested him to give a generous donation to this institution. Nalwadi delivered his speech in Sanskrit. He informed them that he had to look after the welfare of his 60 lakh subjects. They gave him a privy purse annually out of love for the royal family. This corpus fund was spent on the subjects in various ways for their welfare. So, he could give only Rs. 2,500 as his donation to the Sanskrit pathashala. He requested them to accept it. This generous gift was accepted heartily by the trustees of this institution.

Trip to Jwalamukhi Temple

The Maharaja visited the Jwalamukhi Kshetra in Punjab in 1927. There, a temple has been constructed around a rock. Through the crevices of the rock from the depths of the earth hot molten lava sends flames to the rock situated up the mountain. This is the holy pilgrimage centre of Jwalaji temple. When people of this area came to know that the pious and devoted Maharaja of Mysore was coming there, they thronged to that place from 15 or 20 villages. They had come to know that he had travelled on foot to Amarnath and Badarinath. They were overjoyed to see him and sought his blessings by touching his feet.

The Maharaja of Mysore (in turban) with the royal entourage before Kedarnath Temple.

Pilgrimage to Kedarnath

The Maharaja went on a pilgrimage to Kedarnath in 1930. It is surrounded by snowcapped Himalayan mountains rising to 23,000 ft from the sea level. Sri Shankaracharya, after completing his life's mission, disappeared into a cave and gave up his mortal coil. This is also the seat of pancha pita of the Veerashaiva community. The chief of this mutt is also called "Raval." Most of the pilgrims and sadhus visit Kedarnath to have a darshan and return to towns at lower heights on the same day. This is an extremely cold place and it snows often. Here, Nalwadi stayed for five days. It was the most difficult pilgrimage for Nalwadi. The travellers are exposed to landslides, avalanches, tropical diseases, heavy rainfall and snowfall.

The devote Hindus call this area "Devabhoomi." The great Sanskrit poet of India, Kalidasa has called this land "Devataatma." One Westerner has written here he was completely lost in this scenic beauty. He became one with the Deodar trees of the Himalayan Mountain ranges. He felt that his soul was merged with the universal soul. The well-known Botanist Dr. Kashyap has remarked that the snowcapped mountains of the Himalayas could transform an atheist into a believer. The beautiful evening sunset over the Himalayan snowcapped mountain is breathtaking and unforgettable. The people of Tibet describe Mount Kailasha as a rare gem among the Himalayan Mountain ranges.

Maharaja taking a ritual bath in ice-cold Manasa Sarovar Lake

Kailash and Manasa Sarovar – A rare photo of Maharaja on a Pony. For most of the distance during Parikrama, he had trekked.

The Trip to Mt. Kailash and Manasa Sarovar

The Maharaja started his journey from Mysore on 18th June 1931. The royal troupe had these officials and doctors – Janab Siddique-ul-Mulk Sadeg Sad Shaw, Raja Sena Bhushana Lt. Col. A. V. Subramanyaraje Urs, Rajasena Tilaka Lt. Col. S. Gopal Rao, Capt Nabhi Khan, Lt. Nanja Raja Bahadur, Dr. N. Rangacharya, Sir C.V. Subramanyaraje Urs, Sri A. Venkatasubbiah, Sri C. Krishnappa, etc. This royal entourage reached Bombay on 20th June 1931 from Mysore. They reached the mountain town of Almora on 24th June 1931. The state of the United Provinces had appointed the Almora Tashildar Sri Prathap Singh to be in charge of Mysore Maharaja's travel arrangements to Mt. Kailash.

They began their trek to Manasarovar on 27th June 1931 from Almora. They reached a village called Ganayi after two halts on their way. Thousands of villagers welcomed with the slogans "Mysore Maharaja Ki Jai, Kailash yatra ki Jai." They continued their journey from Ganayi and after ten halts on their way, they reached a town called Malpa on 10th July 1931. They had to cross the Kali River, which was gushing forth in torrents. From Malpa, they travelled to a border town called Taklakot through Budi, Garbayang, Kalapani, Siyangbam, etc., in seven stages of travel. In Taklakot, the local people gave a civic reception to the Maharaja. A very old man, who had come from his village 20 miles away presented his highness with fruits and flowers. In his welcome speech, he said, "Our people who live in this area are hesitant to take this arduous pilgrimage, whereas the Maharaja of Mysore has travelled from Rameshwaram in South India to the upper reaches of Tibet. The Commissioner and the District magistrate of Taklakot called by the name of "Jangpan" had come there with his two daughters, to receive His Highness. He welcomed the Royal entourage through an interpreter and presented him with carpets. In turn, Nalwadi presented them with a gramophone player and discs. They had not seen a winding gramophone player. He also gave silk shawls and sandalwood craft works as a gift to the Dalai Lama, the religious leader of Tibet. They left Taklakot on 20th July 1931 and trekked through Gurla valley, which is 16,000 ft above sea level to reach Manasa Sarovar camp on 22nd July 1931.

Manasa Sarovar Lake finds mention in Hindu and Buddhist mythologies. This lake is surrounded by very high snowcapped mountains of the Himalayas. The Manasa Sarovar is green in colour and resembles an emerald gem stone. The orange setting sun in the evening gives a special hue to the white snow of the mountains and emerald green waters of the holy lake. Here, even the dead fish does not stink, when taken out of water for sun drying.

It appears to be a green lake from the distance. But when we stand near the shore of the lake, the water is crystal clear. The Maharaja and the Hindu members of his troupe took a bath in this ice-cold water. They offered oblations to their dead, According to Dr. N. Rnagacharya after a bath in this freezing water, at least half an hour of massaging and warming up is required to regain normal blood circulation.

The Royal troupe had pitched tents on the Western side of Manasa Sarovar Lake. They began to travel in the northern direction on 23rd July 1931 to see Jio Gompa Buddhist monastery perched on top of a mountain (Chiu Gompa). This is the oldest monastery in Tibet (Red Hat Monastery). They admired the numerous beautiful birds, which visit the lake during summer. They walked eleven miles to see the birth place of Sindhadi-Brahmaputra River. They stayed overnight here in tents. The next morning, they began their trek and reached a plateau named Barkha situated at the base of Mt. Kailash. They also visited a hot water spring near Chiugompa and they saw adjacent fields rich in gold veins embedded in rocks. As they approached Mt. Kailash, they saw plenty of rabbits running helter-skelter.

(*Four important rivers take birth here, Sindhu, Brahmaputra, Karnali/Ghaghara and Sutlej)

They saw the flat grassland dotted with wild blue flowers resembling our native Chrysanthemums (*Seventhige*). The Mt. Kailash looks beautiful from this plateau. In this grassland, there are only two houses. One house belongs to a Tibetan government official, who is lower in rank than Jangpan. He invited His Highness to his simple cottage. He welcomed the Maharaja to his house and sang two welcome songs to the accompaniment of a Tibetan stringed musical instrument. Nalwadi also visited the second cottage owned by a shepherd. This house was situated in a dug-up square pit in the ground. It was ten feet deep from the ground level may be to keep off the cold wind of the steppes blowing from the North. It was a simple house with a hearth in a corner and a Buddha statue in another corner with lighted lamps, gongs and bells. Nalwadi and his troupe started their journey at 5 AM for Darchen. The parikrama starts from this place and every morning, they would start at 5:30 AM. During their parikrama, they saw the south face and west face of Mt. Kailash. They camped at a place called Dedepo. Here, they went to see Mt. Kailash during sunset time. They did not feel like returning to their camp as the sight of Mt. Kailash was so spectacular. The night was falling and they all forgot their tedious and exhaustive journey from South India while watching the sunset scene of Mt. Kailash. One great observer has opined that Mt. Kailash makes a visitor experience a sublime state of mind. He merges with the landscape. The realization dawns upon him that the universe is not a mechanical clock. He experiences the universal spirit of harmony. He realizes that he is a mere speck of dust in this vast universe. Even an atheist realizes the universal spirit that is the vital force (chaitanya) and runs like current through living and non-living things. He gets absorbed within himself and forgets the external world.

While travelling to Barkha plateau they noticed that two layers of snow had covered Mt. Kailash from base to the peak. They looked like a staircase to heaven. The scene is reminiscent of poet Kalidasa's description of Mt. Kailash in his play "*Meghaduta.*"*

Lord Shiva after discarding the snake on his shoulder must have taken the hand of his wife Gauri, while ascending these steps of ice to reach the peak, which is their amorous playground. Kalidasa instructs the clouds to hover above the peak and the rain-bearing cloud must shower snow and icicles to the summit of Mt. Kailash. This snow is doubly blessed as they are trodden by the feet of Shiva and Gauri.

*"*Hithva tasmin bhujaga valayam Shambunaa datta hastaa*
Kridashyle yadi cha vichretpadchaarena Gauri|
bangi bhaktya virachitavapuh stambitamtarjalougaha
Soapnattavam kuru Manitata rohanayaagrayaye||"

- Megaduta of Kalidasa

The Buddhists believe that the liberated souls of the monks after pari-nirvana reside on top of Mt. Kailash. It is a holy mountain for both Buddhists and Hindus.

Maharaja performing Sandhyavandhana in Manasa Sarovar

Mt. Kailash

Nalwadi described the landscape in these words, "It looks as if the scenery is beautified by various elements found in nature. The majestic tall snowcapped mountains kissed by the golden rays of sun in the morning and in the evening are a sight to behold. The lower reaches of the mountain covered with tall deodhar and pine trees are an impressive sight. In these valleys, the running streams rush at a great pace often carrying blocks of white ice. They join big rivers in a torrent. This place is of exceptional beauty and even a poet cannot describe this scenery adequately with his limited vocabulary. This is a fit place for a hermit to sit and meditate. He can forget the hurly-burly of the external world.

Moreover, a pilgrim who comes here overcomes his petty pre-occupation with worldly temptations. His mind can concentrate on the almighty without any disturbing vibrations. Here, one loses himself in the mystical beauty of nature. This is an ideal "Tapovana" for a seeker of truth." This beautiful description of Mt. Kailash – Manasa Sarovar region was expressed during a public speech.

The author wishes to quote from Paul Brunton's book the words of Swami Pranavananda, "I became a sanyasi thirteen years ago giving up my family. I have not known pangs of sorrow. But when I left Mt. Kailash area, I was overcome with grief. Here, I tolerated extreme cold weather, and food and fuel shortages. But in this beautiful environment, I forgot my privations. I felt sad to leave behind the sublime Manasa Sarovar lake and magnificent Kailasha Mountain. Our subtle mind simply crumbles while staring at this magnificent scenery. This snowcovered peak is called "*Rajathagiri*" (Silver Mountain). We Hindus believe Lord Shiva sits on top doing tapas. Buddhists believe that Lord Buddha sits on top of the peak in meditation. I do not endorse the view that Lord Shiva lives on top of the mountain in his physical form. I believe his spirit and vital energy pervades the peak. An unseen force fills the atmosphere. In this place, the visitor goes into a meditative mood. This kind of experience cannot be had anywhere else.

While returning to the camp, Nalwadi saw a number of flowers of "*Brahma Kamala*" (*Saussurea obvallata*) and they were greyish light red colour. Many members of the party collected them to take them back to Mysore. The petals of this flower remain soft even after drying.

The second stage of their parikrama began on 27th July 1931 at 5:30 A.M. from Dedepo to Jindipuvi. The twelve miles trek was most arduous and harsh. They began to climb the upper regions to reach a place called Gaurikund situated at a height of 18,000 ft above sea level. The Gaurikund lake was frozen and covered with ice. They began their trek the next morning (27-7-1931) from Jindipu to Darchen. They had walked a distance of 21 miles to complete the parikrama. They reached Barkha on the same day. The next day was *Vysapoornima* day. They all took a holy dip in the lake. In the evening, they saw the full moon rise over the lake. The silvery moon shed its cool light upon the mountain and lake. The next stage of the journey from Manasa Sarovar began on 31st July 1931 and reached Rakshas Sarovar (Rakshastal). On that morning, it was extremely cold and it reached even their bones after penetrating their woollen sweaters. After a few more stages of trekking, they reached Taklakot on 1st August 1931. The next day, they visited the Buddhist monastery of Khojarnath. Here, the huge walls had beautiful paintings depicting the life of Buddha, flowers, wild animals and dragons. At the entrance to the monastery on either side two huge 8 ft height mortar statues of two demons guard the shrine. Inside the temple, the main prayer hall measured 20' by 50'. At one end a huge Buddha statue surrounded by pooja articles was being worshipped. A little behind the Buddha statue stood the statues of Rama, Sita and Lakshmana measuring 7 or 8 feet in height. These three statues had an ornate bronze arch covering all the statues. In front of these Hindu deities in silver and gold lamps the wicks dipped in oil were burning round the clock. They asked the lamas how old were these statues. They replied that they were not made by human beings but by divine spirits. In the left side room, they saw some statues of Maharishis. In another room on the right side, they saw statues of Saptharishis (7 Maharishis). On the first floor of the monastery, there was a large library containing many old Buddhist texts. They also saw statues of Goddess Laxmidevi and Kalikadevi. The royal troupe member Dr. Rangacharya opined that this must have been a Hindu temple in ancient times and later Buddhists must have converted it into a monastery.

Nalwadi presented to the Chief Lama of the monastery two lengths of red and blue woollen embroidered cloth. He also made a cash donation to the monastery. That night, they stayed in Khojarnath. The next morning, they began their trek to Kalapani via Taklakot. From here, they trekked back via Garbayayng, Malpa, Galagar, Titla, Khela, Darchula, Askot, Saamdev, Thaal and Berinag to reach Bageshwar town situated at the confluence of

Sarayu and Gomati Rivers. While trekking near Malpa town, some pilgrims were hurt by rocks which came rolling down from the top of the hill. Near Titla, a huge boulder came rolling down and narrowly missed a high-ranking official of Mysore Palace and rolled down into the gorge. The Maharaja and his royal entourage were given grand civic reception in towns. They threw flowers upon him. They gave the royal pilgrims fruits. At Bageshwar town, the Maharaja was given a memorandum. They reached Almora town on 24th August 1931 after four stages of trekking. Here, they stayed for two days. Here, the Maharaja honoured the local officials with shawls and mementoes. Even the caretakers of mules received gifts. After trekking for a day, they reached Haridwar on 28th August 1931. They continued their journey from Haridwar to New Delhi by train. They reached Bombay city on 9th August 1931. They travelled by train to Poona and reached it on 4th September 1931. They travelled by a special train from Poona and reached Mysore on 7th September 1931 via Arisikere and Hassan. The royal family members, especially Queen-Dowager Sri Vanivilasa Sannidhana were overjoyed by their safe homecoming.

During the Navratri celebrations, thousands of citizens came from far away villages and cities to see the Maharaja. On Navratri Padyami day, in the evening, there was a mammoth crowd to see the Maharaja, who had returned from Mt. Kailash and Manasa Sarovar after an arduous pilgrimage. A senior courtier exclaimed, "See our Monarch and rejoice! We are fortunate to see such a monarch." He was shedding tears of joy. The documentary film was screened before the Queen mother and other family members. The Queen mother told Nalwadi, "Oh! My beloved Aiyya, what hardships did you undergo?"

The prasadam was sent to the pontiff of Sringeri Mutt with palace officials. They wanted to screen the documentary before him. The swamiji said watching the home movie was not a religious taboo. The pontiff saw the documentary film all the time exclaiming "This is Sattvik Kingship! These are the virtues of a true king."

Tolerance Towards Other Religions

The Maharaja had immense faith in the Hindu religion. But he exhibited equally great tolerance toward other religions. In Tibet, he visited many Buddhist monasteries. He paid his utmost respect to Lord Buddha and also to the Lamas. He gave generous gifts and donations to these institutions.

When he visited Badarinath and Kedaranath, he took with him Muslim and Christian officials also.

Nalwadi invited preachers from other religions to deliver lectures in the palace. He wanted to understand the essence of all religions. He did not relish preachers of one religion criticizing another religion in an offensive way. Once, a speaker in the middle of his lecture, began a tirade against another religion. Nalwadi sternly told the speaker to espouse and expound only the tenets of his religion, he may leave the other religion to adherents of that religion to expound and explain to their satisfaction. Please restrain your lecture to your religion only. He believed that the core beliefs of all religions had a similar and common ideology. He did not see the contradiction in their universal message. He studied Western philosophers and often compared them to eastern thinkers.

Nalwadi had made an in-depth study of various religious tenets and also the six schools of Indian philosophy (*Shad Darashana*). He donated large sums of money to temples outside the state and also to churches and mosques. He once built a masjid for his Muslim bodyguards. When Roman Catholics were building St. Philomina Church, he gave them generous donations. In one speech, the Maharaja said, "In the matter of basic tenets and ritualistic worship of God, the various religions differ in their practices. People address God with different names, but all our humble prayers reach the one almighty Lord. We may tread different paths, but only to realize the eternal truth and to purify our minds and hearts. One path may take us to our goals quickly and another path may delay the journey. The final realization through all religions amount to the same spiritual experience." Nalwadi always practised what he preached.

When the Maharaja visited Ajmer city, he paid his respects to the great Saint Hazrat Khwaja Kamaluddin Allama Chishti by laying a Chador on the tomb. He prayed there for the welfare of his subjects and his relatives.

The Jain citizens of Mysore city built a temple for Jain Tirthankar Parswanatha. The Maharaja was invited to inaugurate the shrine. He went there and offered his prayers. He twice attended the once-in-twelve-years *Mahamastakabhisheka* of Sri Gomateshwara during his reign. He openly displayed his devotion for the Jain saints.

Sir Mirza M. Ismail, Dewan of Mysore State, in his public address on 4th January 1940, said, "Our Monarch has justly earned the title of "Raja Rishi" (Sage-king). He has earned the love and respect of his subjects.

He is known for his austerities and simple lifestyle. The remarkable reputation he has earned brings magnificent credit to his dedication and hard work."

An aristocratic lady belonging to a reputed royal family and wife of a ruler of a princely state made this statement – "In India or in any other foreign country, we do not experience the same vibrations that we feel as one enters Mysore State. Mysore State is empowered by a spiritual force of its Raja Rishi Sri Nalwadi Krishnaraja Wodeyar."

Chapter 13

Recent Developments in the State

******

"*yatha kaastancha kaastancha Sameyaathaam mahodadou|
Samethya cha vypeyaatham tadvadbhutha samaagamah||*"
"*yathobayudaya ne Sreyasa Siddih sa dharmah|*"

******

In the ocean, one driftwood and another driftwood come together and a little later, they drift away from each other. Similarly, multitudinous lives come together at a confluence of rivers of life.

What is "Dharma?"

That action which brings forth prosperity and well-being of an individual,

From that action, which brings forth transcendental knowledge and wisdom shall be described as true "Dharma."

A portrait of the Queen Regent Sri Vani Vilasa Sannidhana

Mother's Death

Sri Vanivilasa Sanniddhana did not enjoy good health during 1932 and 1933. Hence, Nalwadi avoided travelling outside the state. He had immense respect and undying love for his mother. During Rameshwaram pilgrimage, he always sent his mother in a palanquin, whereas he walked beside his mother's palanquin. He always took the blessings of his mother, before ascending the throne to sit upon it in the Darbar hall. He did not make any major decisions affecting the state without consulting his mother. Any official could do business with him only after reporting to the Queen-mother. All affairs of the palace were conducted only after obtaining Mathushree's permission. Once the queen-mother said, "In ancient times, Sri Rama was known for his obedience and complete loyalty to his parents. But in the present age, our son Ayyaji is known for his allegiance to his mother. His devotion and love for his mother makes him an ideal son."

During the illness of Queen mother, Nalwadi served her day and night, foregoing food and sleep. He showered extraordinary care upon his mother. Special poojas were performed in temples. He also did a lot of charitable acts by donating money, clothes and food to the poor. When the queen-mother became wheelchair-bound, the Maharaja built special ramps by destroying even marble steps to facilitate her movement to pooja room, bathroom, drawing room, bedroom and dining hall.

At 12 o'clock in the morning, a cannon was fired from the gun house to announce the time of the day. Nalwadi thought that it disturbed his mother's siesta. So, he ordered the army officers to fire the cannon ball at that time in a faraway place, so as not to disturb his mother's sleep. The Queen mother in her ailing years once said, "I am prepared to embrace death at any moment, but my beloved son is so dedicated and devoted, my death will cause him immense grief. Hence, I wish to live as long as possible."

The queen-mother's health deteriorated greatly and she succumbed to her illness on 7th July 1934. It was a Saturday and *Ekadashi* day in the *Uttarayana* phase of the Sun. She breathed her last in the middle of the night. Soon, the Maharaja, the Yuvaraja and other family members were plunged into immense grief. A royal school classmate of Nalwadi said, "When the Queen-mother passed away, I wept bitterly on that day. I had not wept so much even when I lost my own mother. During our schooldays, she treated us like her own children. I cannot forget her love and affection showered upon us."

All over the state condolence meetings were held by citizens in various towns and cities. Nalwadi performed the final funeral rites for his mother like a commoner. He did not observe royal family conventions. Although hot water was available for bath, before performing rituals Nalwadi preferred to have a cold water bath like ordinary mortals. It was felt by the priests some of the "*Aparakarmas*" (funeral rites) could not be enforced upon a Maharaja. But Nalwadi emphatically told the priests that they ought to forget that he is a Maharaja and in the matter of funeral obsequies, that they must remember that it is a son performing the final rites of his mother and nothing more. He did not want any special privileges as the ruler of the state.

The European Trip of the Mysore Maharaja

During the year 1936, the Maharaja's health went into a decline. This caused a lot of concern amongst his relatives and subjects. He recovered his good health because of Goddess Chamundeshwari's blessings. His personal physicians advised him to go on a trip to Europe to recover his health. Nalwadi agreed to this suggestion given to him by his physicians and also preferred to take his younger brother Yuvaraja Sri Kanteerava Narasimharaja Wodeyar.

The Royal Troupe

The Maharaja decided to take with him the following officials to Europe:
(1) Amin-ul-Mulk Sir Mirza M. Ismail (Dewan of Mysore State)
(2) Prince Capt. Desharaj Urs (Chief of Mysore Army)
(3) Janab Siddiq-ul-Mulk Sri Sadeg Sadd Shaw
(4) Rajaseva Bhushana Lt. Col. A.V. Subramanyaraje Urs
(5) Rajaseva Tilaka Lt. Col. S. Gopal Rao
(6) Lt. Col. B.P. Krishnaraj Urs
(7) Dr. Robinson
(8) D. T. Balakrishna Mudaliar
(9) Maj. M. Nabikhan
(10) Pandit V. Subramanya Aiyya
(11) D.S. Lakshmikanthraje Urs
(12) D.N. Neelakanta Rao
(13) C.V. Subramanyaraje Urs
(14) A. Venkatasubbiah
(15) A.C. Raje Urs
(16) J. Krishne Urs

(17) Veda Brahma Ritwik Ramasastry
(18) Veda Brahma Nanjunda Sastry

This group was accompanied by several cooks, servants and valets. The royal entourage left Mysore on 21st June 1936 in the early hours of the morning by a special train and reached Bangalore. They left by train on 23rd June 1936 and reached the Bombay city. When the Maharaja was in Poona, a telegram was sent to K. Narasimha Iyengar to join the troupe in Bombay. The Yuvaraja with his family members reached Bombay on 26th June 1936. All these travellers boarded the ship that night by the name "*S.S. Ranpura.*"

The Adoration of the Public

On the day of departure in Bombay, several elite Mysoreans like Rajakarya Prasakath Dewan Bahadur Sri K. Ramaswamy, Sri N. N. Iyengar, Sri C. Sitaramaiah, etc., met the Maharaja and the Yuvaraja and wished them bon voyage. Many prominent Bombay citizens also met him and wished the Royal troupe a bon voyage.

A very rich Parsi businessman by the name Sri Cowasjee Jehangir Adenwala sent a "Marconigram" to the ship from Aden inviting the Mysore Royalty to visit Aden City and to do some sightseeing. He put his steam boat and personal cars at the disposal of the royal troupe during their visit. Nalwadi sent a "Marconigram" to Sir Cowasjee accepting his gracious offer. The ship anchored at Aden Harbour on 2nd July 1936 in the afternoon at 4:30 PM. They went ashore as planned, did some sightseeing and returned to their ship. The ship began its voyage at 9:30 PM. The co-passengers were very much impressed by the regal bearing, simplicity and friendly nature of the royal personages. The Yuvaraja took the other members of the troupe on a guided tour of the ship. Whereas, the Maharaja in his cabin was listening to a reading of Hindu religious text by Sri. V. Subramanya Aiyya and discussing the finer points of philosophy.

Maharaja and Dewan being received by dignitaries at Victoria Railway Station, London.

At Croydon Airport. The Maharaja on the steps of Aeroplane
L – R: D. N. Nilakanta Rao, D. S. Lakshmi Kantharaja Urs, Rajasena Bhushana
A. V. Subramanya Raje Urs, Maj. M. Nabhi Khan, Amin – ul – mulk,
Sir Mirza. M. Ismail, K. C. I. E, O. B. E, Rajkumar Capt. C. Desharaja Urs,
Lt. Col. B. P. Krishne Urs, Raja Sena Tilaka Lt. Col. S. Gopala Rao,
Siddiq-ul-mulk Sadegh Sad Shaw and Dr. T. Balakrishna Mudaliar.

Arrival at London

The Maharaja's private cabin had been modified at his request to suit his religious needs. He had a special pooja room adorned with a gold statue of Goddess Chamundeshwari. He had a special bathroom attached to his bedroom. He also had a private dining room.

They had carried with them on the ship big containers containing River Ganga water. This water was used for cooking and drinking by the whole party. The ship crossed the Red Sea and continued its journey via the Suez Canal on 6th July 1936. The ship sailed through the Suez Canal in the early hours of the morning. They saw the full moon shining upon the sea and within a few hours, they saw the beautiful sunrise. This unforgettable scene was enjoyed by the whole troupe in the company of the Yuvaraja.

On 10th July 1936, around 10 P.M, the ship reached the port city of Marseilles in France. The next morning, the royal troupe visited Marseilles and stayed in an expensive hotel. The cooks and servants had already gone there to prepare breakfast and lunch for the royal troupe. After lunch, the Yuvaraja took the troupe on a city tour. They visited magnificent cathedrals and museums in the city. The next morning, they took a train at 11.30 A.M to reach the capital city, Paris. They travelled 700 miles from Marseilles to Paris and reached the capital city at 10:55 PM.

The beautiful city of Paris impressed the visitors. They were in Paris city until 15th July 1936. They visited the Eiffel Tower, Versailles Palace, Louvre Museum and various parks. They left Paris on 16th July 1936 by train and reached London's Victoria Railway station at 6:55 PM. The Maharaja of Mysore was received by British dignitaries such as Lord and Lady Goschen, Major General Frederick Sykes, Sir Harcourt Butler, Sir Stuart Milford Fraser, Mr. Kneigh(?), Mr. A. R. Banerjee, India State Secretary's representative Col. Sir Neil William Barton, Raja Jagannath Rao, Sri Bhandarkar, and many ladies and gentlemen were there with bouquets of flowers. Some one hundred and fifty Indian students had come to Victoria railway station to welcome the Maharaja to Britain. Nalwadi took half an hour to wade through the crowds. The Maharaja, Yuvaraja and some high-ranking dignitaries of Mysore State stayed in a luxury hotel called "Dorchester Hotel." The other members of the royal entourage stayed in Kensington Mansion.

A Sensation in London

The arrival of the Maharaja of Mysore caused a huge sensation in London. He was already famous as a modern reformist ruler of a progressive princely state. The next day, one morning daily newspaper reported that the drab lacklustre Victoria Railway Station Platform No. 8 was transformed into a magical wonderland by his visit. When the Mysore Maharaja stepped on to the red carpet welcome, it looked as if a rainbow had appeared in the bright blue sky.[4] He was also received with a lot of fanfare at Dover Docks. He was already famous as a very wealthy Maharaja of a large princely state, which was bigger in size than many European countries.

"East and West met and mingled – waiting for Dover Train to bring the Maharaja of Mysore, one of the richest princes in the world on his first visit to England.

In the crowds, diamonds flashed from nose and ear; red and gold and green gleamed silken saris. The platform was scented like a florist's shop with perfume from garlands brought in accordance with the Indian custom of welcome"- *Daily Sketch*, July 17, 1936.

Nalwadi Sri Krishnaraja Wodeyar was dressed in a long black close-collar coat. He wore a silk Mysore turban. He had worn diamond ear studs, which flashed brilliantly. He had in his coat pocket a gold watch tied with a chain. In the expensive luxury Dorchester Hotel in his suite, he had a special pooja room, where a gold statue of Goddess Chamundeshwari had been installed and worshipped daily. The British society was astounded by the secular practices of the Maharaja. The Dewan of Mysore State was a Muslim gentleman, the Huzoor Secretary was an Indian Christian and a British Protestant Christian was his private secretary. It was well known to the public that the Maharaja and the Yuvaraja had received the best of Western education. But still, the Maharaja had remained a vegetarian in his food habits. He had brought with him Indian cooks to prepare Indian meals for the contingent. The Maharaja of Mysore threw a Grand gala banquet for his friends in London. The invited guests were served with the choicest wine list. Whereas the Maharaja raised a toast to everyone with "Ganga Jal" (water of the holy river Ganga).

The British public admired the virtuous qualities of the Maharaja, such as his humility and simplicity. He was kept busy in the Hotel by a stream of

---

[4]. "No. 8 Platform of grey prosy Victoria Station last night looked for half an hour like a place where the rainbow ends."

V.I.P. visitors of the British society. The who-is-who of the aristocratic British elite society called upon him. He did not go out of the hotel for several days to do any sightseeing.

The Maharaja of Mysore was one of the wealthiest persons in the world. But he did not hesitate to visit the poorer quarter of London city. Whenever he got an opportunity to visit the cottage of a farmer or the house of a factory worker, he willingly entered their houses to see their economic conditions. He compared them with the poor people of his state. If any improvements could be effected to the conditions of the poor in his own state, he wanted to learn from these random visits.

> "The Maharaja's main purpose was to discover how the poor English man lives in comparison with the poor of his own state. He took every opportunity during his stay here to see this for himself. For instance, on the Isle of Wight, which he also visited, he toured the farms and entered labourers' homes. Several aspects revealed by his visit will be considered in relation to improvements in his own country."
>
> - *Evening Standard*, August 19, 1936.

The newspapers and magazines of Great Britain ran special editions with articles praising Nalwadi and published photographs of public appearances of the same. The Star Newspaper dated 17th July 1936 reported thus-

> "Talking to him makes one realize that he is one of the gentler spirits in any country or of any generation."
>
> - The Star, Friday, July 17, 1936.

London Impresses Mysoreans Greatly

The visitors from India were greatly impressed by the magnificent buildings, palaces and parks of London. At that time, the city of London had a larger population than the total population of Mysore State. The underground tube train of London fascinated the visitors. They were impressed by the punctuality and efficiency of its citizens. In big shops, the goods were displayed with fixed price tags. The customers bargaining with the salesperson was unheard of in daily life. The London bus and car drivers followed the traffic rules implicitly, even when there was no traffic police officer in sight.

At that time, many artefacts of Tipu Sultan were displayed in Windsor Castle. Tipu Sultan, the Usurper of Mysore State used to sit on a gold throne. The four legs were shaped like the face of four tigers. The golden throne had a white umbrella canopy, with a Golden "Huma bird" studded with diamonds and gems (Huma bird is a mythical bird of paradise). The officials had displayed the sword of Tipu Sultan and his personal horse saddle, stirrups, decorative head ornaments, etc. The Windsor Castle also had a collection of antique clock collection of King George the third numbering 391. They went and saw at Hampton Court belonging to King Henry the Eighth, a grape vine aged 250 years. It still bore very fine-quality grapes in the 20th century.

They also took city bus rides in London. The red buses had state-of-the-art features and each one cost 1,800 pounds (Rs. 27,000.00).

The Maharaja's Travel in Great Britain

The Maharaja of Mysore received a Royal invitation to call upon His Highness Emperor Edward the Eighth in Buckingham Palace on 22nd July 1936 (Thursday). Nalwadi met the British Queen Mary on 27th July 1936. The Maharaja gave a banquet to his well-wishers and friends three weeks after his arrival in London. On 3rd August 1936, he left Dorchester Hotel and then, visited Oakley court a glorious western mansion set in the countryside on the banks of a river. Here, he participated in the "*Upakarma* ritual." All upper caste Hindus change their sacred thread on an auspicious day depending on their adherence to a particular veda. This dharmic ritual was performed by the Maharaja without any embarrassment. Perhaps, this was performed in Britain for the first time in its long history. The Englishmen were astonished by the conservative religious habits of the Maharaja of Mysore. It was a well-known fact that rich Indian princes went to Europe for fun and frolic.

Nalwadi left by a special train to do sight-seeing in parts of Northern England and Scotland. This special train with the royal entourage left Portsmouth city on 9th August 1936 at 8 AM and reached Torque town by noon. From here, the special train took them to Keswick Town in Cumbria. After alighting from the train, the royal entourage travelled by a coach to famous lakes such as Ullswater, Brothers water and Windermere and also took lake cruises. The lake district in Northern England is also home to famous romantic poets. They saw a rock near Windermere Lake upon which the famous poet William Wordsworth (1770-1850) used to sit and compose poems. They travelled from here to Oban town in Scotland. They visited Inverness Town, which is close to the famous lake Lochness, home of an underwater monster. After visiting many famous places in Scotland, the royal entourage reached the capital city of Edinburgh on 15th August 1936. The railway company, in a magnanimous gesture, had attached a steam engine named "Mysore." But they had christened it many years ago. Nalwadi appreciated this kind gesture of the railway company. He showered flower petals upon the engine before the journey. The Maharaja was warmly received by the dignitaries and citizens at Edinburgh railway station. Col. Locke and his wife received Nalwadi with a bouquet of roses and a big basket full of homegrown vegetables. In a sightseeing coach, they visited all the important places in Edinburgh. They also visited a famous tourist spot called firth of forth, which is the estuary leading to the North Sea. Several Scottish rivers including the River Forth meet the North Sea here. It is eight miles from Edinburgh. Here, they have built a massive railway bridge at a cost of 30 lakh pounds (Rs. 4.5 crores). From a distance, the railway train plying on the bridge looks like a toy train.

The Maharaja of Mysore visited the Edinburgh Zoo. In 1914, he had gifted a baby elephant called "Sundara" (beautiful) and a few leopard cubs to this zoo. All these animals had grown to full size and they were in good health. They visited the famous Edinburgh Castle. Here, they saw the nursery of King James, where his mother Queen-Mother Mary had nurtured him. They had preserved the nursery in the same condition as it once existed some 360 years ago.

The Edinburgh castle has a special collection of Tippu Sultan's swords, shields, guns, amulets, silk overcoats, horse saddles, etc. They also saw the portraits of General Sir David Baird and Tipu Sultan. The whole royal party returned from Scotland by a special train to London on 16th August 1936.

Later after consulting his private secretary and other officials, the Maharaja decided to visit Germany by an Aeroplane. They travelled to Croydon International Airport to catch a flight to Germany on 19th August 1936 at 12 PM. They travelled by Royal Dutch Airliner to Amsterdam, Holland via Rotterdam. They spent a few hours in Amsterdam doing a brief sightseeing excursion in the capital city. Their aeroplane took them from Amsterdam and landed in Berlin. The rest of the contingent travelled by train to a harbour in England and reached Germany by ship. The Maharaja of Mysore was received by German foreign office officials and by prominent German Citizens. The Maharaja stayed in Adlon Hotel, Berlin, which is a luxury hotel of repute.

During one of their sightseeing trips, the general public and children mistook a turbaned Indian gentleman for a Maharaja. They wanted a group photo with this individual. Later, they learnt he wasn't the Maharaja.

The Tour of Germany

The Maharaja with his group of travellers visited the Kaiser's palace (Berliner Schloss). Then, they visited the famous Berlin Zoo with its collection of 4,000 exotic animals. They also visited Wintergarten Theater. Here, circus acrobats, gymnasts and trained chimpanzees performed before spectators. They travelled to Dresden City on 24th August 1936 and saw the museum located in the royal palace (Dresden Castle). In this 400-year-old castle, rare paintings and marble statues are preserved. They saw a six-foot-high an old master painting of Virgin Mary with Child Christ. They travelled from Dresden to Budapest, Hungary. Here, the Maharaja was received by high-ranking dignitaries of the Hungarian government. The President of Hungary loaned his private railway train for the personal use of the Maharaja and his royal entourage. They travelled from Budapest to Vienna, Austria.

Instructions to horse trainers in Mysore in such events as "dressage," "show jumping," "show hunters," "eventing" and "English pleasure" had been imparted by an Austrian Horse trainer. Each horse of the Spanish riding school was worth at least Rs. 10,000.00. This horse-riding school was part of the building of the old palace. This was a semi-circular indoor theatre. In the large well inside, the white horses danced to the accompaniment of a musical band. Above the well all round the theatre, there were thousands of two-tier seats for the spectators. There was an inner indoor horse training circular arena.

One historic incident made the Maharaja of Mysore very popular with the common people of Germany. It is a well-known fact that Mysore State Cavalry and army fought bravely in Palestine during the I World War (1914-1918) on the side of the British allies. The Mysore Army under Lt. Col B.P. Krishne Urs succeeded in driving out the German army from Haifa Port. One war time German painter by name Robert Stopmann had to leave behind his pictures and sketches before fleeing. They fell into the hands of Lt. Col. B.P. Krishne Urs. When the Mysore Army returned to Mysore, these paintings were given to the Maharaja as war trophies. But Nalwadi realized the importance of these art works to the artist. In Berlin, he met some high ranking army officials and handed these paintings to them. He requested them to trace the painter and return it to him. The army officials traced the artist and returned his paintings to him with compliments from the Maharaja. This magnanimous gesture of the Maharaja was reported in German press widely. Even "Daily Herald" of London reported this kind gesture of the Maharaja. So, the ordinary people of Germany mobbed him, wherever he went and showered affection on him. After his return to Mysore city, he received few complimentary paintings from the grateful artist Robert Stopmann and also a thank you letter..

A Trip to Switzerland

The Maharaja and his troupe travelled from Germany to Vienna, Austria. They travelled from here to the city of Lucerne in Switzerland and reached it on 5th September 1936. Switzerland is a small mountainous country blessed by nature with places of green scenic beauty, lakes, rivers and snow-covered Alpine mountains. They produce a lot of electricity through a number of hydroelectric projects. Though they have no coal, still they have managed to generate surplus electric power. This has helped Switzerland to become an industrialized nation. Their mountain trains travel on electric power and they have laid railway tracks through mountain tunnels. They have tarred mountain express highways running through the length and breadth of the country. On either side of the highway, we can see apple and pear orchards. Millions of tourists visit Switzerland throughout the year during all the four seasons. A small Swiss village with fifty cottages boasts of twenty-five hotels.

The Maharaja did sightseeing in Lucerne and took a boat cruise on Lake Lucerne. They also visited Zurich and Berne cities. They travelled from Switzerland to Milan, Italy. After a sightseeing trip of Milan and Genoa, they reached Nice city in France. Later, they left for the port city of Marseille on 17th September 1936. The Maharaja worshipped Lord Ganesha on 18th September 1936 as it was the holy festival day of "Varasiddi *Vinayaka Vrata*." They travelled by the passenger ship "*S.S. Strathmore*" from Marseille and reached Bombay city on 29th September 1936. The Maharaja and his entourage were received by Prince Sri Jayachamaraja Wodeyar, Sir M. Vishweswariah, Rajamantra Praveena S.P. Rajagopalacharya, Rajakarya Prasakta Dewan Bahadur K. Ramaswamy and many others with garlands and bouquets. The Maharaja reached Bangalore city on 2nd October 1936 and then travelled to the capital city of Mysore. The citizens of Mysore gave a warm welcome and thanked Goddess Chamundeshwari for his safe return.

The Dewan Sir Mirza M. Ismail delivered a speech in Mysore Representative Assembly (lower house) on 26th October 1936, explaining the beneficial aspects of the Maharaja's European tour. The main purpose of the tour was to recover his health and to study and learn the recent developments in science and technology from Europe for the industrialization of Mysore State. Similarly, many innovative measures were adopted by the state to improve the public transport system, public park development and starting of new industries. The state government was importing a special variety of copper to be used for decorative and artistic purposes. The artists were using it in bas-relief works. So, Nalwadi made arrangements for local production of the same quality copper here. This import substitution was well appreciated by the public.

The 9th World Congress of Philosophy was held at Paris, France from 31st July to 6th August 1937. The Maharaja sent from India Sri. V. Subramanya Iyer and Paul Brunton as delegates to this World Philosophical Congress with a special message. The Maharaja wanted world peace and harmony and he reiterated the vedantic message - *"Sarve Jana Sukinobavanthu"* (Let everyone be happy). The delegates took note of the Maharaja's message and placed on record his valuable opinion. They thanked him formally for this noble gesture. This message of the Maharaja received wide publicity in English and French press.

Prince Sri Jayachamarajendra Wodeyar after the initiation ceremony

Sri Jayachamaraja Wodeyar's Trip to Japan

The Maharaja and the Yuvaraja jointly agreed to send the young prince Sri Jayachamaraja Wodeyar on an educational tour of Japan in April 1937. It would enlarge his heart and widen the horizon of his mind. It was decided that the young prince would be escorted by the Government Surgeon Dr. S. Subba Rao, Sri A. Venkata Subbiah and a few others.

The young Prince studied in the "Royal School" until S.S.L.C. along with a few other students (Kannada novelist "Chaduranga" Subramanyaraje Urs was one of them – Translator). Later, he studied a two-year intermediate course in the Yuvaraja College, Mysore. From 1936-1938 he pursued B.A degree course at Maharaja College, Mysore. (The translator's father Dr. S. Srikanta Sastri taught History to the young prince)

During the voyage, the ship anchored at Shanghai, China. The Prince wanted to do sight-seeing in China, but he could not land, because of civil unrest. He continued his journey to Japan. He impressed a lot of people with his refined manners. He was a connoisseur of classical Indian and Western music. He loved literature, painting and historical monuments. He visited many cities and museums in Japan. He returned to Mysore city in July 1937. He passed his B.A degree in 1938 with good grades.

Nalwadi again with the intention of bringing forth legislative reforms in the state appointed a committee under the Chairmanship of Raja Sabha Bhushna Dewan Bahadur Sri K.R. Srinivasa Iyengar. This reformation committee began to function on 1st April 1938. The Maharaja conveyed a message to the committee on the occasion

"Our sole aim is to bring about all-round development of state and initiate welfare programmes meant for people belonging to different religions and communities. It is also our desire that any development and improvement in conditions of living of people of Mysore should be qualitative and quantitative contribution to the National economic development of India as one nation. Your constructive recommendations in this regard for the development of state ought to take note of democratic changes taking place in western countries and also, it must rest on a foundation of such Indian values as truth (Sathya) and righteous action (Dharma). I pray to God to bless you with harmonious feelings and desire for peace and prosperity." (Translation from Kannada extract – not a verbatim report.)

Maharaja Sri Jayachamarajendra Wodeyar and Maharani Sri Satya Premadevi during marriage "urutane" (floral ball rolling game) ceremony

Prince Sri Jayachamaraja Wodeyar's Marriage

Yuvaraja Sri Kanteerva Narasimharaja Wodeyar had performed the Upanayanam (initiation ceremony) for his son Prince Jayachamaraja Wodeyar in 1931. His marriage took place on 15th May 1938 with Princess Sou. Sathyaprema Kumari sister of the ruler of Charkhari State, Central Province. The ruler of the State, Maharajadhiraja Shifadhar-ul-Mulk Arimardhan Singh Judev Bhadur gave his younger sister in marriage to the Prince Sri Jayachamaraja Wodeyar of Mysore State. The wedding was celebrated on a grand scale. This marriage was sanctified by the presence of the Maharaja.

The royal wedding was attended by the princely aristocracy of India like Maharaja of Bikaner, Prince of Hyderabad State and son of Nizam, Maharaja of Jigni State, Bundelkhand, dignitaries from Madras State and V.V.I.Ps from eight districts of Mysore State. On the fifth day, after marriage, the newly married couple were taken in a procession on the elephant through the streets of Mysore in the evening. Thousands of citizens of Mysore cheered the newlyweds, who made progress on a caparisoned elephant in a colourful procession lead by soldiers in uniform and a musical band.

Two Great Annual Festivals of Mysore

The Mysore state under the Maharaja celebrated two great festivals every year on a grand scale. One was the coronation day of the Maharaja and the other was 9 days Dasara festival concluding on the 10th day with the Vijayadashmi "Jambu Savari" procession through the important streets of Mysore. Every year, the State Government officials made sincere attempts to improvise the various arrangements made for those festivities. The state was visited by Indian and Foreign tourists on these occasions in large numbers.

Maharaja's birth anniversary ceremony procession on horses
L to R: Maharaja, Yuvaraja, Prince Sri Jayachamarajendra Wodeyar

The birth anniversary of the Maharaja ceremony
L to R: Maharaja, Prince and Yuvaraja on horses

Coronation Anniversary

This anniversary was celebrated on *Jesta Shuddha Ekadasi* day as per Hindu calendar. Early in the morning, the Maharaja would take an auspicious bath on that day. He would perform Sandhyavandana and pooja. He would participate in *Ayshuya Homa* for long life. Afterwards, he would enter the Darbar Hall wearing a silk dhoti, silk vest and a long silk coat. The Darbar Hall would be filled with relatives of the royal family and palace officials. On this occasion, young girls belonging to Devadasi community gave a performance of Bharatanatyam to the accompaniment of music in front of His Highness. Then, the Chief Pontiff of Sri Brahmatantra Parakala Mutt would enter the Darbar Hall with his disciples. The Maharaja would offer him a special golden square shaped seating platform. The Swamiji would bless the Maharaja on the coronation anniversary day. The Maharaja, the Yuvaraja and the young Prince would wash the holy feet of Swamiji with Ganga water. They would offer their respectful *pranams* to the Swamiji by prostrating before him. Some visiting princes from far away states were surprised to see this devotion to the royal family guru. The swamiji would honour all the three male members of the ruling family by giving them garlands, coconuts, fruits and later, sanctified rice grain would be sprinkled upon their heads. They were also honoured with expensive shawls given in pairs to each of them. After obtaining permission from the pontiff of the mutt, the Maharaja would ascend the golden throne. The palace officials would signal the royal artillery to fire cannon balls from the ramparts of the fort, when Nalwadi sat upon the throne. They normally fired the exact number of cannon balls signifying his present age. The well-known artists would sing Carnatic classical music compositions to the accompaniment of musical instruments. The courtiers came one by one to the Maharaja and offered "Nazar" (some silver coins on a hand kerchief were offered to be touched by the ruler). The vedic pandits recited veda mantras on this occasion and blessed the ruler with long life and good health. They also presented him with coconuts, fruits, flowers and sanctified rice grain as a mark of their benediction. The assembled guests were given attar, flower garland and tambula (pan leaves with areca nuts) at the end of the Darbar. The Maharaja signalling the end of the Darbar would descend from the throne. The Maharaja, the Yuvaraja and the young Prince would walk back to their private quarters. The invited guests would also leave the Darbar hall in an orderly fashion.

In the evening, the Maharaja, the Yuvaraja and the Rajakumara would travel from the palace on their horses in a procession to the parade grounds of the government guest house through the streets of Mysore. This Royal procession was led by an Army contingent, the high ranking officials, the cavalry, the music band and the courtiers in formal attire on foot would accompany the Maharaja. This was a grand spectacle for the pubic of Mysore. The royal artillery would fire the cannons 21 times to declare that the ruler of Mysore was entitled to this honour as it was sanctioned by the British Emperor. At the government house, they would change their riding dress and wear more formal attire for the evening function. They also had an afternoon high tea with guests. The parade ground was decorated with colourful electric lights. The cavalry regiment presented an equestrian show before the Maharaja. The palace Carnatic and Western music bands played music. The evening function concluded with a show of fireworks. A large gathering of Mysore citizens enjoyed the evening programme and cheered the royalty. The royal group returned to the palace in an electric car after the conclusion of the sound and light show. When the party reached the palace, the artillery fired another 21 gun salute to His Highness. The next morning, the Maharaja had a lunch with relatives and guests at 11 AM. The author states, "I can predict in the coming years the present ruler Sri Jayachamaraja Wodeyar's coronation anniversary will be celebrated in the same manner."

The Maharaja worships the Holy Cow During Dasara

The Maharaja performs Puja to the Royal Horse

Navratri Celebrations:

The Mysore city throbs with life during nine days of Dasara festivities. It begins every year on *Ashwayuja Shuddha Padiyami* day and concludes on the 10th day with "Vijaya Dashami procession." Nalwadi managed to put Mysore city on the global tourist map, because of these festivities.

The Maharaja, on the first day of Dasara, would wake up early in the morning and take an auspicious bath (Mangala Snana). The palace priests would administer "Diksha" mantras to his highness that he would abide by the religious restrictions during the Navaratri (Nine nights dedicated to various poojas). He would begin the day's activities by performing Sri Ganesha puja and Sri Chamundeshwari puja. Nalwadi would undergo "Kankana Dharana ceremony." The auspicious sacred thread would be tied around his right wrist. He would take an oath stating that he would be observing and performing all the austerities as per the dharma sastras during the Navaratri.

The Maharaja, the Yuvaraja and the Rajakumar would be escorted by the Sardars of the Ursu community to the Darbar Hall at 10 AM. The royal sword of honour decorated with flowers would be carried by a nobleman. The royalty would be received by Rajakumar Sri Desharaje Urs, Nalwadi's brother-in-law and the Dewan of the State, the high ranking officials, the aristocratic courtiers of the Ursu community, the prominent citizens of Mysore, priests, vedic pandits and Dharmadikaris in attendance. Before ascending the throne, the Maharaja would perform *Navagraha* puja (pacification of nine planets puja) and "*Kalasha* puja"- a silver vessel containing Ganga water, mango and pan leaves with a whole coconut placed on top which would be worshipped. Then, he would perform puja to the golden throne as per "*Kalika puranokta*" ritualistic procedure. Then, he would wave a sacred flame in a clockwise manner in front of the throne, offering his utmost respect to the family throne. He would circumambulate thrice around the throne. Next, the Maharaja would climb the steps of the throne by holding the hand of his bodyguard. The traditional nadaswaram music would be played on this occasion. The large crowd of people and the army soldiers would cheer the Maharaja. Nalwadi would accept their spirited adulation of the audience and after doing a Namaskara, he would grace the throne. The official carrying the royal sword would place it on the throne next to His Highness. Then, the Vedic scholars would recite "*Ashirvachana mantras*" in front of the Maharaja. They would offer him flowers and fruits as prasadam. They would also sprinkle sanctified rice grain upon the head of the Maharaja. After this, the noble men, officials, citizens and relatives would offer "Nazar" to the Maharaja. After this ceremony, all the invitees were given attar, flowers and thambula.

The designated royal elephant and the royal horse would march towards the palace Darbar Hall in a procession. The guards carried flagpoles and royal standards, and a musical troupe lead the procession. The royal standards depicted Krishna's wheel, conch, "Sharaba" (a mythical animal - part lion and part bird with eight feet), "Salva" (Falcon bird) and Ghandabherunda (mythical twin headed eagle), which is the royal family crest. The royal elephant stood at the ground level and after trumpeting, it paid respect to the Maharaja by picking up flowers and sprinkling it at his feet and throne. The Maharaja sat in the Darbar Hall in first floor facing the open parade ground. Similarly, the royal horse showed its respect by kneeling on its forelegs. The palace band, at the conclusion of the day time Darbar, would play the state anthem "Kayou Sri Gauri" (May Goddess Gauri, wife of Shiva, protect the Maharaja and the royal family). Then, the Maharaja would descend from the throne with the help of his bodyguards. He would retire to his private quarters.

On all the nine nights, the Maharaja conducted Darbar in a similar manner. But in the evenings, the palace was illuminated with thousands of electric bulbs. From one electric pole to another electric pole a string of colourful lights would be hung and all this attracted the visitors to come in droves. The spectators watched wrestling bouts, fencing matches, torch light parades and acrobatic exercises, which were performed. The cavalry regiment displayed their horse-riding skills like tent pegging, etc. The folk dance troupes performed before the Maharaja. The various comic characters appeared before the king wearing masks and costumes. A funny figure walking on wooden stilts and dwarfs in funny costumes and artists wearing outlandish masks kept spectators in splits. Everyone enjoyed Indian and Western classical music, military bands, folk music and wind instruments ensemble.

Nalwadi worshipped the goddess of learning Saraswathi on the designated day and Durga puja on Durgashtami day. On Mahanavami day, the royal elephant, the royal horse and weaponry and chariots were worshipped in a ritualistic manner.

On the ninth day evening (Mahanavami Day), the Darbar was called European Darbar. During Nalwadi's rule, the British Resident of Mysore State along with other European guests would attend the Darbar. The British Resident, in formal attire, would make entry from one end of the Darbar Hall and the Maharaja from the other end would simultaneously enter the hall.

All the European guests would sit down after the Maharaja sat on the golden throne. The Dewan of the State presented the British Resident with attar (perfume) and a garland of flowers. When the resident entered and exited, 13-gun salute was offered in his honour. The elite European gentlemen and ladies offered their salutations to the Maharaja. The ladies were given flower bouquets by palace officials.

Every evening, the Maharaja was offered in a golden plate one flower garland, perfume in an ornate gold cup with precious gems embedded upon it and tambula (pan leaves) on a silver plate at the time of ascension to the throne. Then, the Dewan of the state offered his salutations to the Maharaja and received a garland from the king. He also thanked His Highness formally for granting him audience. The assembled courtiers offered salutations before the start of the Darbar and again at the end of the Darbar in batches. The Maharaja acknowledged these salutations from each group by reciprocating it in a similar manner. On Vijayadashmi day, in the morning, some religious rituals were performed. The "*Vajra Mushti Kalaga*" was staged in the boxing ring. The wrestlers staged a very violent form of wrestling matches. The wrestlers dashed their heads against each other, often resulting in bloodshed.

The grand Dasara procession began in the afternoon. The Maharaja, the Yuvaraja and the Rajakumar would go in a procession on an elephant carrying "Ambari." They would be seated in a golden howdah. The Dasara procession was led by an army contingent, cavalry, scouts and guides, caparisoned elephants, horses and camels. The procession would be accompanied by the palace Carnatic and Western music bands playing music. There would be tableaus (Floats) showcasing the state's development and heritage. This procession took two hours to pass by in front of assembled spectators on the pavements. This procession reached "Banni Mantap" in the evening. There, the royal family members worshipped the Banni tree (*Prosopis cineraria*) as per Hindu custom. After having refreshments, the Maharaja and others witnessed the torch parade and gymnastics. The Dasara procession returned to the palace through the brightly decorated lighted streets of Mysore. On the 10th day, Vijayadashami procession every year attracts lakhs of Indian and foreign tourists

The Maharaja performs puja to the royal elephant

Vijyadashmi day procession on "Ambari" in Golden Howda Nalwadi seated, and Prince Sri Jayachamarajendra Wodeyar climbing the steps.

Vijayadashami Day Procession on "Ambari" in Golden Howdah.
L – R: The Maharaja and the Yuvaraja

The Mysore State Golden Throne

Many historians believe that the golden throne of Vijayanagar Empire fell into the hands of *palegar* Sri Rangaraya of Sri Rangapattanam after the fall of Vijayanagar Empire. Later, the King Raja Wodeyar of Yadu Dynasty came to possess it. Since then, during "Navratri Utsav" the throne was ascended by successive kings. It became a tradition to allow public to visit the palace on the eleventh day of Dasara to view the golden throne from close quarters.

The golden throne is decorated with precious gems like rubies, emeralds, jade, etc. The most expensive silk cushions are placed on the seat of the throne. At the back, a tall golden bent tube rises to a height to support an umbrella. The strings of pearls dangle from this umbrella. After the public viewing on the eleventh day, the throne is transported to its safe room and locked up for one year. It is taken out whenever a new king has to undergo coronation ceremony. It was taken out on 8th September 1940 for the coronation of Sri Jayachamaraja Wodeyar.

The umbrella staff of the golden throne is engraved with a lengthy benediction Shloka in Sanskrit meant to protect the occupant king from various evil forces.

Sanskrit Version

"*Brahma Vishnur Maheshascha sva sva Shakti Samanvithah|*
Rathna Simhasanroodam rakshanthu tvamaharnisham||
Vani Vaghaikarim dadya Lakshmi Sampad moorjithaam|
Mangalani Sada Dadyabhavethe sarva Mangala||
Pratapam tava pushnatu Lokachakkashurgbastiman|
Nirmalaam Chandramah Keerthim mangalani Mahisutah||
Saumyathamindujo dadyathraprgnthvam Suradesikaha|
Suneetham Kaviraddhadytasukam shaniranuttamam||
Rahurbahubalam dadaytheketusatva Kulonnattim|
Sarve grahasnakshatrah Suprasanna bavantu te||
Durgadevi Ganeshascha Kshetrapalo bayankarah|
Vasthoshppattih prasannathama Sarve rakshantu Sarvathaha||

....

"*Iravatham Samaasthaya vajrahastah purandarha|*
Tanothu sampadaam Vriddhim Tava Rajayam prasnaasathah||
Mesharuda saptha hastassurkrurs vaadyaaudonalah|
Tejasvitam pradadyaathe simha pitadhirohinnah||
Dandaadhi Kayudopethu Mahishopari samstitah|
Dharmarajah prasannasthe dadyadarme matim sthiraam||
Nararudo gadapaniryaathudaana Ganeshvarah|
Dustagraha bayam Chindaayattava prithvi prashasatah||
Prachetana karmarudah paashaadayuda samyutaha|
Dadyaathraprasanna Chittatvam Shuchitvam Sada Tava||
Bibrachhorpam mrugaarudah prananameshwaro marut|
Arogyam bala Sampattim Dadyaattava Niranttaram||
Ashwarudah Khadgahasto Raja Rajo Mahaayashah|
Dadyddnardhimakashyyaam tyage Sathyapi boorishah||
Tungam pungavamaarudah Shoolaadaayudhajaalabruth|
Deva Devo Maheshano Dadaadayushyamoorjitham||
Dilipasagaro Ramo Harishchandro Nalasthatha|
Yam Dharmamanvartantham Dharmamanupalay||"

....

English Translation

May the combined strength of Brahma, Vishnu and Maheshwara protect the occupant of this throne. May Goddess Saraswathi bless the occupant with rich and intelligent oratory skills. May Goddess Lakshmi grant the occupant of this throne with external wealth. May Goddess Parvathi (Sarva Mangala Devi) grant the occupant of the throne with auspicious gifts.

May the eye of this universe, God Suryadeva, promote your courage and strength. May the God Chandra, son of earth protect your fame and give you many auspicious boons. May the son of Chandra, the Budha, a divine Guru, grant the occupant with supreme knowledge, humility and gentleness.

May Shukracharya grant you statesmanship virtues,
May Shanaishcchara grant you bliss,
May Rahu grant you great strength to your arms,
May ketu grant your dynasty every prosperity and progress in the coming ages.

May the nine grahas (planets) and stars be pleased with your general rule.

May the God of Gods Indra holding vajrayudha in his hand and sitting on his white elephant Iravatha grant you immeasurable wealth.

May God Agni who sits on "Mesha" (Ram) with seven hands holding ladles and spoons (Agheyastra) grant you "Tejas" – illumination and valour.

May the God of Justice Dharmaraya, who sits on a water buffalo holding the staff of justice and a sword in the other hand grant you equanimity of mind, while dispensing justice.

May the God Niruthi, who rides a human being and leader of "rakshasi ganas" (demons) (personifying death, decay and sorrow) drive away from you the fear of cruel planets.

May God Varuna, who rides a crocodile and holds in his hands such weapons as noose, varunasthra and Gandiva grant you pure consciousness.

May the God Vayu, who sits upon his antelope and possess four arms, grant you health, strength and wealth eternally. He holds a lance in one hand and a powerful goad (ankusa) in another hand. His other two hands are held in Abhayamudra and Varadamudra (Hand Signs). He also has a wind weapon called vayvayastra.

May the God of wealth Kubera, who rides a horse and holds a sword in one hand grant you inexhaustible wealth to you, so that you can indulge in endless charity.

May the God Maheshwara who rides a bull (nandi) holding in his hand a trident grant you good health, a strong body and long life.

You rule your country in a Dharmic way like the great kings Dilipa, Sagara, Rama, Harischandra and Nala.

During the ten days of Dasara, people enjoy the pomp and show in the palace immensely. But the hero of our story, Nalwadi Sri Krishnaraja Wodeyar, had to go through a lot of tribulation, adherence to religious rules and regulations, long hours of puja and fasting as per dharma sastras.

Every day during Dasara, Nalwadi woke up from bed early in the morning. He took a bath, performed puja and gave food articles and alms to deserving Brahmins in charity. Afterwards, he performed puja to a holy cow and then washed his mother's feet with water and offered his prayers. This holy washed water he would sprinkle on his head. He would do "Japa" (recitation of God's name) till 3 PM for the welfare of his subjects. Later, he would drink a cup of sweet "payasa" with raisins and almonds. He did not consume any other dish until dinner. Then, he would visit the Darbar Hall to supervise the final seating arrangements for the evening Darbar.

On the first day of Dasara, Sri Nalwadi would install the statue of Goddess Chamundeshwari in the mirror courtyard or in a hall of the palace. The palace priests would perform puja to the Goddess from 8 AM to 11 AM. Afterwards, one priest would recite any one of these sacred texts like *chaturveda parayana* (4 vedas), Devi Bhagavatha, Bhagavatha, Sri Ramayana, Sri Mahabharata and Navagraha japa.

Nalwadi even during Navaratri attended to official files between 12:00 P.M and 5:30 P.M. He would pass relevant orders on various issues, even in the midst of Dasara festivities. He would go to his private rooms to get dressed in formal regal dress for the evening Darbar. He was not normally fond of wearing expensive jewellery. But during the nine days, he had to wear the crown and various other jewels like pearl necklaces, gold and diamond rings, etc.

After the Darbar, Nalwadi would visit Amba Vilas and stand on a wooden plank. The ladies of the Ursu community would wash his feet with water and they would shower flowers on his head. They performed an "Arati" to him. They would wave a lighted lamp set in a golden plate in a clockwise manner around his face. He would give generous monetary gifts to these ladies.

Nalwadi went to his private quarters to have his evening shower. After dressing up, he would perform evening "Sandhyavandana" culminating in Shiva puja and Rajarajeshwari mantra japa. From here, he would go to the mirror court hall to attend to the "Sahasranamarchane" (one thousand names of Sri Chamundeshwari recited by priests.) He stood in full devotion till the end, when "Maha Mangala Aarti" was performed. On Durga Ashtami day, his religious duties increased by many folds. So, he was more exhausted and tired at the end of the day.

During Navaratri, Nalwadi's day started at 4 AM. and he went to bed at 11 PM. His supper consisted of rice, sugar and milk served to him at night time. After the 10th day of Vijayadashami, the next day was "Ekadashi" the Hindu day of fasting, Nalwadi spent the whole Ekadashi day in prayers and consumed only liquid diet. On the "Dwadashi day," after doing puja, he shared a grand formal lunch in the company of his relatives and friends. This grand luncheon party was conducted in Amba Vilas Thotti (hall). The Ursu community courtiers, who recited Sanskrit shlokas were honoured later with expensive double shawls per individual.

"Ekadashi" and "Dwadashi" Darbars

On these two days, the private Darbar took place in the kalyana mantapa. The Maharaja would sit on an ornate chair and he would accept "Nazar" and "Muzare" from high ranking officials and private individuals. He would confer honorary titles and bestow upon them garlands, fruits and shawls. On the second day, he would honour exceptional civilians involved in social service with gold medals. Lastly, the students of Mysore and Bangalore Sanskrit patashalas, who had passed the Vidwath examination, would receive graduation certificates. Exceptional students received cash awards and gold medals.

Viceroy's Visit to Mysore State

The Governor-General of India and Viceroy of India, the most Honourable the Marquess of Linlithgow, his wife and his daughter visited the Princely State of Mysore. They arrived in Bangalore on 13th January 1939 and on the same day, they left for Mysore.

In the period before the arrival of the Viceroy, the Yuvaraja had caught pneumonia during a visit to Madras. This caused great anxiety to the Maharaja and to Yuvaraja's wife and others. They all travelled to see the Yuvaraja. When his family members called upon him, he had recovered his health. They returned to Bangalore on 10th January 1939 and from here, they travelled to Mysore.

The Viceroy, his wife and daughter received a grand reception at Bangalore and Mysore. During a Banquet given to the visiting Viceroy at Lalitha Mahal Palace, Marquess Linlithgow praised the progress made by the Mysore State under the rule of Nalwadi.

A special Khedda operation had been organized at Kharapur for the visiting dignitaries. Many important guests like Maharaja of Bikaner, the Governor of Madras and the Dewan of Mysore State were all there to see the Khedda operation. They were all seated under a canopy on the banks of Kapila River. They witnessed 2,000 Shikars herding tuskers, elephant cows and baby elephants towards the Khedda enclosure. It was a grand sight to watch herds of elephants crossing the river and entering the forest on the other bank. Many wild elephants with their young ones got trapped in this Khedda operation. The Maharaja posed for photographs with the visiting dignitaries and other Khedda officials. The Viceroy killed two wild bisons during the hunt. The Viceroy's family enjoyed their stay in Mysore State and thanked His Highness for the hospitality. They returned to Delhi after a memorable stay in Mysore and Bangalore.

The Sharavathi River Hydro-electric Project

The pride of Mysore State is a natural wonder called "Gersoppa Falls" of Sharavathi River at Shimoga District. The Sharavathi River here gets segmented into four divisions called Raja, Rani, Roarer and Rocket and plunges from a height of 830 ft into the gorge.

Nalwadi realized that with the water of Sharavathi, hydro-electricity could be generated for the benefit of Mysore and Bombay states. Hence, he allotted 1 Crore and 50 thousand rupees from the same budget for the project. A foundation stone was laid on 5th February 1939 by the Maharaja.

Before Yuvaraja's European trip with his family
L to R: Princess Sri Jayachamundammanni, Yuvarani Sri Kempuchaluvajammanni, Princess Sri Sujayakanthammanni, Yuvraja Sri Kanteerava Narasimharaja Wodeyar, Princess Sri Vijayalakshammanni, Rajakumari Sri Sathyapremadeavi, Rajakumar Sri Jayachamarajendra Wodeyar

Yuvaraja's Trip to Europe

The Yuvaraja, with his wife, son, daughter-in-law, daughters, palace officials, servants, cooks and a troupe of musicians on 13th July 1939 left Bombay by ship to Europe. The Yuvaraja had an audience with the head of the Roman Caholic Church Pope Pius XII. The musicians from Mysore performed before the pope and Carnatic classical music appealed to the pontiff. He made enquiries about the Maharaja and other Royal family members. These eminent musicians performed in various European cities and even performed on Radio. All the Royal family members returned to Mysore to celebrate Navarathri festivities. The Yuvaraja stayed back in Europe for some more time to recover his health after a bout of pneumonia at Madras. The safe return of the royal family members to India by flight relieved the Maharaja as dark clouds of the IInd World War were looming large over Europe.

Political Reforms

The political reforms committee submitted its report to His Highness on 24th August 1939. After studying the recommendations suggested by the committee, the Maharaja approved many of them and on 6th November 1939, gave orders for the proclamation of the new Act through a government gazette notification. The Maharaja wanted a larger number of citizens of repute participating in public administration, although Mysore Representative Assembly and Legislative Council functioned under two different Acts. Henceforth, they will be governed by one single Act. Members of both houses enjoyed freedom of speech, they enjoyed protection from any possible arrest from agencies of law and their tenure was increased from three years to four years. In the representative assembly, the members' right to be consulted on important bills and to heed their advice continued unhindered. The total strength of the representative assembly was increased from 275 to 310 to accommodate members from minority groups, captains of industry and business and more representation to women was provided. The total number of members of the Legislative council was increased from 50 to 68. According to the new Act, in the legislative council, out of 68 members, some 44 members were elected to the house through direct elections. In the newly constituted house, the Chairman of the Legislative council was nominated by the Maharaja during the first term of four years. Afterwards, in the coming years, the house would elect its own elected member as a Chairman. At present, Dewan was appointed as chairman of the legislative council by virtue of his office. In the future, the chairman's post was not the preserve of government officials. A civilian elected member would officiate as a chairman. Even the Vice-chairman was elected from 44 members, who were all civilians. The two houses in the future would enjoy more powers in enacting laws and debate and suggest recommendations to the budget proposal.

In the future, the representative assembly members can submit any number of petitions, questions and also they were free to take decisions. In the past, there were caps on all these things. The Maharaja also made a decision to lower the bar for eligibility to vote in elections. So, it was decided to lower the income tax ceiling as a criterion for voting and it was also decided to lower the educational qualification to qualify as a legitimate voter. The number of working days of the Assembly was increased. The state government also made special provisions to minority groups and "special purpose" groups to cast vote in general elections.

It was also ordained that the Executive council must accommodate four ministers along with the Dewan as chairperson. Out of four ministers, two must be selected either from Assembly or Council by the Maharaja. These nominated ministers could hold any portfolio and conduct official business accordingly.

A Tour of Chitradurga District

The Maharaja had planned an official tour of Chitradurga District on 31st January 1940. But his sister's daughter Princess Srimathi Doddamanni became ill. So, he postponed his official trip. A little later, Srimathi Doddamanni succumbed to her illness. This untimely death plunged the royal family into infinite grief.

The Maharaja, Prince Sri Jayachamaraja Wodeyar, the Dewan and government officials visited Davanagere town on 22nd February 1940. In a grand civic reception, the leading citizens of the town honoured him and presented him with a memorandum. Nalwadi made a fine speech after receiving honours. Lakhs of people had come from these far away towns like Kolhapur, Sangali, Ranibennur, Hubli, Karwar, etc.

The Maharaja visited Chitradurga town on 23rd February 1940. The people of Chitradurga gave him a rapturous welcome. Here too, the Maharaja delivered an eloquent speech. That evening, he switched on the electricity lights of the town. The next morning, he travelled to Kallodi to inaugurate Sri Krishnarajendra Bridge.

Mahamastabhisheka of Sri Gomateshwara

The Maharaja visited Sravanabelogola on 26th February 1940 to attend this rare event, which attracts Jain pilgrims from all over India. He offered flowers to Sri Gomateshwara idol and performed puja. He also participated in the All India Jain conference as a special guest. In his informative speech, he expressed his admiration for the Jain religion. He also possessed a deep understanding of Jain philosophy.

The Death of the Yuvaraja

The Yuvaraja Sri Kanteerava Narasimharaja Wodeyar returned from his European tour to Bombay on 9th March 1940. Here he contracted pneumonia infection and succumbed to it on 11th March 1940 (Monday) at 2:30 A.M. This tragic news plunged the whole state into deep mourning. In many towns and cities, condolence meetings were held. The Maharaja received tributes and condolence messages from all over the world. His funeral was conducted in Bombay as per the customs of the Royal family. His ashes were brought to Mysore city by a special train. The mortal remains were taken in a procession through the crowded streets of Mysore city to Madhuvan. The last rites of the Yuvaraja were performed by His Highness Sri Nalwadi Krishnaraja Wodeyar.

Prince Jayachamaraja Wodeyar becomes Yuvaraja

Prince was anointed as the Yuvaraja of Mysore State on 28th March 1940. A special Gazette notification proclaimed this news to the world. In many towns, various organizations conducted special meetings to express their happiness over the elevation of Prince Jayachamaraja Wodeyar to act as the next Yuvaraja. The Maharaja began to give him various official duties, so he would take over the reins of the administration.

The Silver Jubilee Celebration of Kannada Sahityaparishat

The Silver Jubilee Celebration of Kannada Sahityaparishat was a very important literary event in Bangalore. It took place on 30th June 1940.

It was attended by the Maharaja and the Yuvaraja. They were received warmly by the cheering crowds. They arrived at 9 AM by car. They were welcomed by the government officials, palace officials, male and female members of parishath, invitees, delegates from all over the state and litterateurs. The poets had composed several poems in honour of the Maharaja and the

Yuvaraja. They were recited before the audience. Rajasevasaktha Prof. B.M. Srikantiah, Vice-President of Kannada Sahityaparishath gave a memorandum in a silver rotund casket to the Maharaja. The chief guests were garlanded and were given bouquets by the organizers. The Maharaja, in his speech, mentioned how much he adored Kannada language and literature. A large number of public speeches delivered by the Maharaja on different occasions were in Kannada language. He also noticed the absence of a well-known Kannada intellectual and writer of books. He made enquiries about his health. Later, when he met him in person, he wanted to know the reason for his absence during this august function.

This attractive corner plot on the main road was allotted by the then Dewan Sir Mirza M. Ismail to the parishath. A grand building was constructed with the help of a generous donation of cash by the Yuvaraja Sri Kanteerava Narasimharaja Wodeyar and Late Rajasevadhurina Sardar. M. Kantharaja Urs. The present Yuvaraja readily agreed to become the chief patron of the Kannada Sahityaparishath following the royal family tradition. Sadly, this was the last public appearance of the Maharaja. The ruler belonged to the proud lineage of glorious Vijayanagar Dynasty. He had preserved and propagated the best cultural and Dharmic traditions of the three hundred years old Vijayanagar Empire founded by Sage Vidyaranya. He had also inherited the sacred gold throne of the Vijayanagar Dynasty. His famous last words on a public platform were "*Siri Kannadam Gelge*" (May the rich Kannada Language and Culture be victorious).

Au Revoir

The Maharaja returned to Bangalore in July second week from Mysore. After a few days, on 21st July 1940 (Sunday) morning the Maharaja went for a ride on his favourite horse. The weather was cloudy and cool. He always enjoyed a brisk ride through the Bangalore Palace grounds. He returned from a long ride and he dismounted from the horse. Soon, he complained of severe chest pain to the bystanders. Many doctors who were on duty rushed to his aid. They diagnosed it as a severe heart ailment and perhaps, he had suffered a heart attack. A few days later, the Maharaja appeared to be making a recovery. The Queen Sri Lakshmi Vilas Sannidhana arrived from Rajkot on 1st August 1940 (Thursday) by train. She was overjoyed to see the Maharaja making a good recovery. On the same day, she left for Mysore and on Friday special pujas were performed to Sri Chamundeshwari to save the life of the

Maharaja. On Friday night, Nalwadi slept well. Even the physicians rejoiced at the improvement in the health of the Maharaja. On the next morning, he told his private secretary to fetch the blueprints of some civil construction projects at Mysore. He studied these plans and estimates thoroughly. The Maharaja dictated his orders to the private secretary, so as to enhance the budgetary allocation and execute the civil construction projects in quick time. But after lunch time, the heart began to ache again. In one or two hours, Nalwadi's condition again became critical. The Yuvaraja, the British resident, the Dewan, the Huzur secretary and many other officials were present in the next room. The Maharani returned from Mysore and she was plunged into grief. The Maharaja's near relatives, men and women were sorrowful at the turn of events. When the Maharani saw the pitiable condition of the Maharaja, she fainted and remained inconsolable.

The Maharaja Sri Nalwadi Krishnaraja Wodeyar died on 3rd August (Saturday) 1940 at 9:05 PM. His close relatives, officials, citizens and admirers from India and abroad were drowned in sorrow hearing this tragic news. Sir Mirza M. Ismail, Dewan of Mysore state exclaimed, "We have lost a rare gem."

Many dignitaries of Bangalore City including Poorna Raghavendra Rao visited the Bangalore Palace to pay last respects. The Maharaja's cortege with a flag flying upon the hearse began its final journey to Mysore. Some fifteen cars with relatives, officials and friends followed the cortege. The next morning, the newspapers announced the demise of the Maharaja to the state population. Everyone felt sad, because the state had lost both the Yuvaraja and the Maharaja within a span of six months.

The body of Nalwadi in regal royal dress was kept in the palace Kalyana Mantapa Hall for public to pay respect. The Maharani and other Ursu ladies came there to pay their respects. The cloth curtains were set up on all four sides of the platform, where the dead body was lying in state, so that the ladies of the royal family could mourn in privacy. The menfolk who were standing outside the hall heard the loud wailing of these ladies. They felt this kind of misfortune should not have befallen upon Mysore State. A huge gathering of mourners had assembled before the Darbar Hall. They all felt sad that they would not see their beloved Maharaja in his formal attire and jewels standing upon the throne once again.

Many grief-stricken high-ranking officials came to the hall at 8:45 AM. The Dewan was crying inconsolably. All the other officials like Rajasabhabhushana Sri. Thumboo Chetty, Rajasevasaktha Sri. M. Rama

Rao, Sidiq-ul-Mulk Janab Sadeg Sadd Shaw, Rajasenabhushana Sri A.V. Subramanyaraja Urs, Sri M.P.D. Srikanta Lakshmikantharaja Urs and Sri. C.V. Subramanyaraja Urs were involved in making funeral arrangements.

The Maharaja's dead body was brought from the hall and kept in front of the elephant gate. A flower decked palanquin was placed on a platform and the Maharaja's body was laid on a bed of flowers. Nalwadi was dressed in a red silk turban and green coat. He still wore diamond finger rings and other jewellery. The Maharaja appeared to the mourners as if he was in a deep sleep. There was no shadow of death cast upon his calm face. When the palace band began to play the state anthem the pall bearers lifted the palanquin. The formal procession which was a mile long began to move towards the cremation ground lead by the Yuvaraja Sri Jayachamaraja Wodeyar carrying in earthen pot "Mantragni." While walking, he was tottering because of extreme sorrow. A close relative, Sri. M.P. Subramanyaraja Urs often supported him physically by holding his arms. The procession was led by a contingent of palace army marching slowly. The music band was playing direful music. The spectators were throwing flowers, coins and pan leaves upon the dead body as a mark of respect. The funeral procession exited by Varaha Gate and began to wind its way to the cremation ground upon the Doddakere tank bund road. Many villagers wept loudly crying "Oh, Our Lord have you left us," and "Oh! I wish I were dead instead of you." Many people fell at the feet of the Yuvaraja and bemoaned the loss.

The cortege was lowered on to a platform in Madhuvana and various dignitaries such as the British resident, Dewan, Chief Justice, ministers and other officials paid their last respects. The funeral pyre was constructed next to the "Brindavana" (a memorial) of his mother Sri Vanivilasa Sannidhana. The priests covered Nalwadi's dead body with Sandalwood logs. A cloth curtain was erected on all the four sides of the funeral pyre so that the Yuvaraja could perform the last religious rites of the Maharaja in total privacy. He sprinkled rice grain into the mouth of Nalwadi. Afterwards, the curtain was withdrawn. The dignitaries such as Sir Mirza M. Ismail, Rajasabhabhushana Sri T. Thumboo Chetty, Rajamantrapraveena Sri K. V. Anantha Raman and Sir Darcy Reilly sprinkled rice grain into the mouth of the dead person with tears in their eyes as per the orthodox Hindu custom. Even the British Resident of Mysore State paid his respects to the departed Maharaja with folded hands (Namaskara). The infantry soldiers of the Mysore Army fired bullets into the air, three times as a mark of respect for the departed soul.

The nadhaswara musicians played sad and melancholic music in the honour of the departed Maharaja. The Yuvaraja Sri Jayachamaraja Wodeyar at 12:15 P.M lit the funeral pyre of the late Maharaja. Soon, his body was consumed in "Agnideva" (Fire God) and merged in "Panchabhuthas" (the five primordial elements: *prithvi* (earth), *apas* (water), *agni* (fire), *vayu* (air) and *akasha* (space/ether).

There were heart rending scenes like a ninety year old man, who was weeping inconsolably and the Dewan tried to calm him with soothing words, but to no avail. But these kind words of the Dewan made the old man and bystanders weep much more uncontrollably. The Maharaja had earned the love, respect and admiration of millions of people. His soul after receiving everyone's love and respect departed to his eternal abode of bliss to merge with the maker "Sarveshwara."

The state mourned the Maharaja's death in a sombre manner. The army men fired cannons at 12:15 P.M in Mysore and Bangalore 56 times at one minute intervals signifying his age of 56 years and showed their respect to the departed soul. A special gazette notification was proclaimed that all State Government departments shall hoist the state flag at half mast for twelve days. The administration declared a complete holiday for thirteen days to government offices, schools and colleges.

The Yuvaraja performed obsequies of Sri Nalwadi Krishnaraja Wodeyar during the twelve days of mourning as per Hindu custom. On the 13th day, (*Vaikunta Samaradhane* day) the Yuvaraja released Rs. 73,000 to distribute clothes and food to the public. So many rich merchants in the state spent money to feed the poor on the 13th day. In Bangalore city, a large portrait of the late Maharaja was taken in a procession through major roads of the city. The Bangalore citizens paid respects to their beloved Maharaja.

Obituary Notification and Condolence messages from all over the World

The untimely death of Sri Nalwadi Krishnaraja Wodeyar plunged the admirers in great sorrow. They mourned his death in Mysore State and all over India including in British ruled presidencies and condolence meetings were conducted in Australia, Africa, America and in European countries. The Mysore State government received condolence letters and telegrams from all over the world. They expressed their grief to the royal family members, such as the Yuvaraja, Yuvarani, Mathushree Kempa Chaluvajammani and to the Maharani of Mysore.

The telegrams were sent by the King Emperor George the Sixth, from the Viceroy of India, from various Maharajas and Nawabs, from many public men and women from several reputed institutions and from eminent political leaders of the world.

Mahatma Gandhi wrote, "A great statesman and an able administrator has left this world." Sri Madan Mohan Malviya wept bitterly in the condolence meeting and praised the noble qualities and achievements of the Maharaja. In a condolence meeting held in London, the former Viceroy of India Lord Wellington expressed his whole hearted admiration for the Mysore Maharaja and expressed his deep regret over his sudden death.

The Right Honourable V.S. Srinivasa Sastri delivered a radio speech on 4th August 1940 and summed up his impressions of the Maharaja,

"The sudden death of Sri Nalwadi Krishnaraja Wodeyar is not only a loss to Mysore State or to political establishment, but it is an irretrievable loss to whole of India. The Maharaja was handsome and always strode in an erect manner wearing a silk (Jarathari) gold embroidered turban, which made him look taller than he actually was. He had a genial smiling, beautiful face. He was a man of few words and remained dignified even under stress. He did not show off his regal qualities in his everyday interaction with other people."

"The Maharaja was a generous patron of fine arts and music. All the great actors, painters, sculptors and musicians of India and abroad have been his generous beneficiaries. He was a generous patron to artists throughout his life. It is an established fact that modern Mysore State was ahead of other states in India in the area of rural development, education, healthcare and industrialization. So, the princely state of Mysore became the most progressive state in all spheres." (Not a verbatim report- only a translation from Kannada).

This is what Dr. Cousins said about Nalwadi, "The generosity and kindness of the Maharaja was not constrained by religion or caste. He did not distinguish between rich and poor. He believed that the whole world was his family. He treated his subjects as his children. Hence, his subjects had become orphan."

In a condolence meeting held in Bangalore Cantonment, the British Resident stated, "The death of the ruler of Mysore State is a great loss to the people, who loved and respected him. The Maharaja had only one aim during his rule that is all-round wellbeing of his subjects. He set very high standards in this regard for us to emulate. The Maharaja remains an everlasting inspiration to all of us." (Not a verbatim report – a translation). In a condolence meeting held at Mysore, the Reverend G.D.W. Sawday said, "In our deep sorrow, we feel that an individual, who is equal to our late Maharaja, may not be born again."

In another condolence meeting held in Bangalore, Rajadharma Praveena Dewan Bahudur Sri Chandrashekara Iyer said, "The Maharaja of Mysore Sri Nalwadi Krishnaraja Wodeyar Bahudur was truly a great person. When you evaluate him either by ancient dharmic code or by modern day standards, he comes out as a public servant par excellence possessing all the virtues of a good ruler."

The condolence meeting was held in Madras, Mumbai, Kashi, London, etc. In a condolence meeting held in Bombay, which was presided by Sri M. Vishweshwaraiah, he remarked, "During the late Maharaja's rule in Mysore great strides of progress were made, which ought to be recorded in golden letters. He had earned universal love and respect from the rich and the poor, from scholars and ignoramus, from people belonging to different castes and religions and this no exaggeration.

The Maharaja marched with changing times in the matter of political ideology, social customs and in religious practices. The Maharaja was a man of few words. He was never hasty in action and did not use either harsh or rude language. He exhibited immense patience and did not yield to anger. While debating contentious issues, he exhibited patience. The Maharaja did not stand on dignity and excessive pride."

In a condolence meeting held at London by the Christian congregation, Lord Samuel praised the late Maharaja of Mysore and compared him to Emperor Ashoka.

The newspapers and magazines published all over the world came out with great tributes in their obituary notices, praising the Maharaja of Mysore as a great ruler with modern vision. The newspaper from Bombay called "*Commerce*" wrote, "The Maharaja of Mysore worked relentlessly for 38 years with great enthusiasm and energy to make Mysore State a modern state. It was not only a model state for other princely states, but also to the other British presidencies." The *National Herald* of Lucknow wrote in its editorial, "Maharaja with human failings are rare to come across. A Maharaja who is cultured, blemish-less and fit to be called "Raja Rishi" (A sage ruler) is a rarity in this world. The Maharaja Sri Nalwadi Krishnaraja Wodeyar was one such exceptional ruler." The *Statesman* newspaper from Calcutta wrote, "The whole of Mysore State is a grand memorial that stands as a witness to the achievements of the enlightened ruler. The Mysore State government is a model of perfect governance." "*The Sind Observer,*" a newspaper from Karachi, in its editorial wrote, "The Maharaja was not only a maker of modern Mysore, but also a maker of modern India." "*The Amrit Bazar*" newspaper described the Maharaja as "A personification of the best of Indian and Western culture." "*The Hindu*" and "*The Madras Mail*" praised the Maharaja's character, his love for his subjects, statesmanship in administration, his wisdom and his other worldly preoccupation. His selfless nature was a remarkable trait in his character.

"*The Times*" London journalist wrote, "The untimely death of the Maharaja of Mysore is a great loss to India and the British government has lost a good friend. He was an extraordinarily good administrator. The Maharaja Sri Nalwadi Krishnaraja Wodeyar and his father Maharaja Sri Chamaraja Wodeyar ushered in political reforms that lead to universal education, application of modern science and technology to improve agriculture and industry. Mysore State was not only a model to other princely states but also to the British administered states of India."

The Princely state of Travancore, Baroda, Bhavanagar, Kolhapur, Kapurtala, Bikaner, Sangli and many other states declared a few days of mourning. They closed government offices and schools during this period of mourning. In these states, flags were hoisted at half-mast and condolence meetings were conducted.

In 1940, October, the legislative assembly of representatives met to conduct the business. They mourned the death of Nalwadi and passed a resolution recording his remarkable contribution to the Mysore State during his 38 years reign. The assembly session was called off as a mark of respect to the departed soul.

State of Mysore's Contribution to the British Government's War Effort

The Second World War, which began in 1939 engulfed the whole of Europe and spread to the rest of the world. The Maharaja Sri Krishnaraja Wodeyar again rose to the occasion and helped the British Government greatly. The present ruler Maharaja Sri Jayachamaraja Wodeyar is continuing generous contribution of men and material for the war effort. The State of Mysore contributed Rs. 10 lakhs to the Royal Air force. The Right Honourable Lord Beaverbrook in charge Minister of Aircraft production sent a telegram to the Mysore State government acknowledging the generous contribution made for war effort. No one else has shown this magnanimity by making a generous contribution. The British government and people are grateful to the Mysore government.

The state government established a war committee and also several subcommittees to augment resources for the war effort. Many high-ranking government officials are involved in this project. Recently, the present Maharaja has contributed Rs. 6 lakhs to the war fund. This has been appreciated by Honourable Lord Beaverbrook and the Viceroy of India. The British public is grateful for the help rendered by Mysore State.

Chapter 14

Praiseworthy Noble Qualities of the Maharaja Sri Nalwadi Krishnaraja Wodeyar

******

"Kalasya karanam Raja kalo va rajkaaranam|
Ethi te Samshayo maaboodrajaa kalasya karanam||"
"Bhima kantyanurpaguneyassa babuvopajivinaam|
Adrushayashaschabigamyashascha yadoratney revaarnvaha||
Gnanemaunam kshama shaktau tyage Shlagaa viparyayah|
Guna Gunanu bandittvattasya saprasava eva||"

******

Whether a king shapes an age or an age shapes the king? Let there be no doubt, it is the king, who shapes an age.

A king must instil fear in his subjects, he must have a dignified and calm composure. He must personify noble qualities. He should appear like a tumultuous sea with great precious gems strewn on the seabed all the while instilling fear in the onlookers. He must be easily accessible to his citizens.

The noble king must possess two virtuous qualities. One is boundless knowledge and the other is a golden rule of silence. He is brave and courageous when faced with challenges. He was also tolerant and forgiving when the occasion required it. The generous king was not averse to making sacrifices. He never succumbed to flattery and praise. In this manner, the good king was complimented by one quality with another. His virtuous qualities had become his obedient children of sorts.

The author has reiterated in this narrative, time and again the noble inborn qualities of Nalwadi Sri Krishnaraja Wodeyar. The purpose of this chapter is to elaborate on this aspect of the Maharaja. He showed remarkable virtuous qualities in his childhood.

The motto of the Indian culture is embodied in the vedic quotation, "*Mathrudevobhava, pithrudevobhava, Acharyadevobhava.*" The mother is supreme, the father is supreme and the guru is supreme. All three are divine figures fit to be worshipped. Throughout his life, Nalwadi practised these precepts and became a model for others.

The Maharaja's bedroom had a painting of Goddess Sri Chamundeshwari, photos of his parents and a picture of Sacchidananda Shivabhinava Nrusimha Bharati Mahaswami (1872-1912) of Sringeri mutt and he never went to bed without offering his pranams to these figures. I have already described how on his coronation day, he would wash the feet of the chief pontiff of Brahmatantra Swatantra Parakala Mutt swamiji before ascending the golden throne. The visiting Maharajas of other princely states were surprised to see him prostrating before the family guru on coronation day.

The Maharaja had immense respect for his guru Vidyanidhi Brahmasri Virupaksha Sastri, who later took sanyasa and came to be known by the new name Sri Madbinava Valukeshwara Bharati Swamiji. Nalwadi also respected and expressed devotion to the monks of Sri Ramakrishna Mission.

The Maharaja always showed great devotion to the heads of the religious mutts. He treated the heads of all mutts with equal respect.

Once, a sanyasi told the Maharaja that he had no rich gifts to bestow upon him. He could only transfer his accumulated fruits of tapas acquired from seven years of continuous Shiva puja to His Highness. These profound words left Nalwadi speechless and he shed tears of gratitude on that occasion.

The head of one mutt had presented him with a pearl necklace adorned with two emerald stones. While visiting this swamiji, he always wore this necklace. Once, a palace official suggested to the Maharaja that the two emerald stones could be replaced with stones of superior quality from the family treasury. But the Maharaja rejected this suggestion saying that the original pearl necklace with two emerald stones were blessed by the swamiji and hence, more precious and more valuable.

Once, he came across an elderly old guru, who was his own guru's guruji. He pleaded with this very old man to accept some money from his disciple's disciple. But he had a very humble request. He told the Maharaja during morning puja that he must remember the motto "*Sarvejana sukino bavantu*"

(May everyone be happy) and offer on behalf of this old guru a handful of flowers to God. The old guru was also equally concerned about the welfare of people. Nalwadi wept silently at these words of wisdom. The old guru cared very little for the filthy lucre and hence, refused to accept money.

Once, Nalwadi was informed about the illness of an old guru, who was a mentor to his father, Sri Chamaraja Wodeyar. He called upon him and assisted him by giving him medicine orally. He also sliced an apple and fed him the pieces.

The Maharaja came to know that his Guru was ill and could not access proper medical care at home. He was shifted to the palace hospital for better medical treatment. He was treated by palace doctors and nursing staff in the first-floor special room. He always showered his mother with great affection and love. Many friends and companions of his father received from Maharaja love and respect at all times. The Maharaja regularly climbed the one thousand steps of Chamundi Hill to offer his prayers to Goddess Chamundeshwari. If the group had very old infirm devotee, he would send them up in "Thamjan Chairs" (chair attached to two poles) carried by four servants. He would walk beside these carriers during his climb.

Servant's Welfare

The Mysore palace had hundreds of male and female servants. The Maharaja was especially fond of retired old servants. Some thirty years ago, the Maharaja had travelled to North India with his entourage. A retainer who had worked from the time of Sri Chamaraja Wodeyar was immersed in a private conversation with other servants. In the palace, he worked for a department called "*Dustina Bokkasa*" (Ceremonial dresses for the nobility and decorative articles used for elephants, horses, cows and camels during festivals were stored in a storeroom). This old servant, out of familiarity with Nalwadi, while discussing the noble qualities of the ruler, he was addressing him in the singular pronoun "he," which is derogatory. The servant did not know he was being overheard by the Maharaja. Then, the Maharaja appeared before them and they were ashamed of their faux pas. Nalwadi did not show his ill temper, instead, he was smiling, cordial and more affectionate towards them. He had the presence of mind to show his magnanimity and tolerance on that occasion.

Once, an old servant who had served the palace from the time of Sri Chamaraja Wodeyar was going to retire. Nalwadi was very much pleased with his loyal service. Hence, he asked the servant whether he wanted anything from the palace. The poor servant requested the Maharaja to grant him some permanent source of income. Nalwadi conceded to his request by purchasing 14 acres of agricultural land with his personal funds and gifted it to the old servant. Whenever the Maharaja heard one of the old servants was ailing, he would send money and medical assistance. Every year, he spent thousands of rupees on such charitable acts from his private funds.

The Maharaja was equally affectionate towards exceptional servants as well as run-of-the-mill servants. He did not discriminate between them. These servants could approach the Maharaja round the clock without any hesitation. He was available to them day and night. These dependents received generous help from the Maharaja in the form of funds for the construction of houses, writing off debts, small amounts of money was given to tide over a financial crisis or robes of honour or gown (khilat) on special occasions.

One reputed scholar wrote a valuable Sanskrit work. The Maharaja was so impressed by the book that the venerated scholar was gifted with 50 acres of fertile agricultural lands near Hanasoge village in Krishnarajanagara Taluk, Mysore district.

Whenever the Maharaja set out on any official tour or hunting expedition, he would give strict instructions to cooks that they should serve the same food to all the staff without any distinction. Once in Hassan town, the cooks faced a shortage of homemade pure ghee. They purchased some ghee from a local grocery shop. They served pure homemade ghee to the Maharaja and others, the staff were served with market ghee. When Nalwadi came to know of it, he was upset by this discrimination. He told the cooks that they should have also served him with market ghee. It is highly unlikely in the whole of India, that we may come across any other ruler like him who treats everyone equally under all circumstances.

Whenever in the house of a music vidwan or mahavidwan or a Ursu gentleman, a wedding or "upanayanam" (initiation) ceremony was organised, the Maharaja would send what is described as "Palace honour." Nalwadi would send an "open" (convertible) car for procession, assistance in the form of cash, jewels and ceremonial dresses was given to the intended person. When a high-ranking palace official's daughter got married, the Maharaja sent all these gifts plus Sri Chamundeshwari Goddess prasada and garland. During his visit to Bombay in 1939, he was met by an ex-palace official. The Maharaja told his private secretary to buy a white cashmere shawl and this was sent as a gift to the mother of the ex-official. For those attendants, who put in extra hours of work either in the kitchen or in some other department, Nalwadi would give them gifts in recognition of their hard work. One palace official was a good calligraphist. He was often given assignment to copy Sanskrit shlokas. He was rewarded with costly gifts. Once a "Dafedar" of the palace army fell sick and got hospitalised. The Maharaja, to everyone's surprise, called on the patient in the hospital and enquired about his health. Nalwadi gave him some money before leaving the hospital.

Once in Bangalore palace, a lowly worker fell sick. The Maharaja noticed that this worker was not turning up for work. When he came to know that the worker was down with some illness, he personally visited the servants' quarters to see the worker. He also instructed that doctors must treat him well and ordered palace cooks to prepare a special diet for this worker's consumption.

The Maharaja had introduced a new service rule, wherein the official or worker celebrating "upanayanam" or the marriage of his son or daughter could draw three months' salary from the palace office. This advance amount paid to the worker was recovered in equal monthly instalments over a period of time. If a palace worker died in service, his children's education was taken care of by the Maharaja. The family would receive educational assistance on a monthly basis.

Once, the Maharaja was proceeding in his car towards Vasanth Mahal palace. A palace worker was coming from the opposite direction on a bicycle. The nervous worker got down from the bicycle and offered his pranams to His Highness. The Maharaja stopped his car and told the worker henceforth he should not alight from the bicycle to offer pranams. If per chance the worker suffered a fall and received injuries, then Maharaja would be blamed for this mishap.

After his return from the Kailash-Manasarovar trip, Nalwadi happened to meet the mother of a palace official. He profusely thanked the mother, who had sent her son on such a hazardous journey. He admired her courage and sacrifice in risking the life of her son. Whenever he noticed that a worker or official was doing exceptional service to the palace, he would commend the official or worker immediately without any delay.

During the 1928 Dasara Vijayadashmi procession, the Maharaja noticed that a concerned official had made very good arrangements in the conduct of the tenth-day festivities. He told his Huzur Secretary that since the time of Dalwai Sri Devaraja Urs, no other official had made such wonderful arrangements. Dalwai Sri Devaraja Urs had a great talent for organising the

Vijayadashmi procession on a grand scale. A palace official was immediately despatched to the residence of the concerned official late in the night at 10:30 PM to convey the Maharaja's satisfaction and appreciation for the good work done by this individual.

Once in Dasara evening "Darbar," some pink diamonds from the necklace worn by the Maharaja had fallen to the ground. They were found by one of the bystanders. They were very valuable diamonds. But the finder returned them to the Maharaja promptly. The finder was rewarded generously by the Maharaja, who said "This is not an adequate compensation for his honesty."

In the olden days, the Maharaja and other officials would travel to Ootachamund in a four-in-hand coach. This coach was drawn by four horses. Those were the days before motorcars had made their appearance on Indian roads. Some forty years ago, the Maharaja, Darbar surgeon Col. Smith and a few others were travelling from Ootachamund to Mysore. Nalwadi held the reins in his hand and a whip in the other much to the amusement of everyone, he was driving the coach. One servant lost his balance and fell on the highway. The first person to jump from the coach was the Maharaja and he rushed to the help of the injured servant. Later Col. Smith the palace surgeon rushed to the help of the injured attendant. Everyone admired the Maharaja's quick response in an emergency. Recently, the Maharaja was travelling in his car from Bangalore to Mysore. He found a poor woodcutter, who had fallen from a tree branch and he had suffered a few fractures. The Maharaja stopped his car and rushed to the help of the injured villager. After giving him first aid, he was taken in a car to Mysore hospital. There, the Maharaja ensured that the poor villager received the best medical attention. If this was the case with a total stranger, you can very well imagine how he treated his own employees.

Whenever the Maharaja travelled by train, his retinue followed him. At railway stations, the fruit vendors approached His Highness to buy fruits. Nalwadi purchased good quality fruits in large quantities such as oranges, figs and grapes, so that his whole retinue could relish it. Nalwadi also supplied expensive vegetables like green peas or cauliflower, which are prohibitively expensive in India to the households of servants. He often treated his attendants to expensive exotic rare sweet dishes, etc.

During tours, Nalwadi occupied only one room in the traveller's bungalow. It was his puja room, drawing room, bedroom and dressing room. This, he did to enable others to occupy those remaining rooms in Dak bungalows. He did not want his servants to sleep in the corridors and verandas, which are inhospitable places during winter. The servants were given warm woollen sweaters and bedrolls in Ootachamund, which is a hill station. Those attendants, who looked after him in his childhood, received later good dresses and monthly pensions. They were remembered with great affection during coronation day and ten days of Navratri festival

Nalwadi had instructed his cooks that they must serve the same food to tribals, officials and invited guests during a hunt in Kharapur forest. This tradition of treating everyone on equal terms during a hunting expedition is continued by the present Highness Sri Jayachamaraja Wodeyar. The palace guards were served a proper breakfast early in the morning. Those garden workers, who worked in hot sun were given straw hats for protection.

Once in an absent-minded mood, Nalwadi forgot to have his breakfast. He was proceeding towards his car and then he remembered he had missed his breakfast. So, he returned to his private quarters only to find a servant consuming his breakfast. He patiently waited outside, so that the servant could finish the breakfast. Then, he entered the dining hall and the servant was taken aback. The nervous shivering servant profusely apologised for his transgression and he informed that he thought the Maharaja was not returning to have his breakfast. He assumed that it was leftover food. Nalwadi did not lose his temper and did not raise his voice to berate him. Instead, he told the servant calmly that he should not repeat his mistake. The Maharaja instructed the kitchen staff to prepare the same breakfast for his personal attendants every morning. He often took the trouble of verifying whether the same quality food was being served to others as well.

The Maharaja left the palace in the early morning hours while going on official and pilgrimage tours. He was followed by officials and his retinue in other vehicles. The palace cars carried the early morning breakfast, coffee in a thermos flask and drinking water. After two hours of driving, the Maharaja would stop the vehicles on the highway under big trees for breakfast. Everyone would have breakfast and coffee. Nalwadi treated this kind of stop over as also a break up for smokers. He knew many people in his entourage were smokers. But they would never smoke in front of the Maharaja out of respect for him. Hence, the Maharaja would go out for a walk in the countryside leaving others behind. It was a signal for them that they could indulge in smoking. He would return to the same location after half an hour's break. He treated his staff as if they were his own children.

Once in Kashi, the Maharaja of Mysore was staying in "Nandeshwar Koti Palace" which was lent to him by the Maharaja of Kashi. He would wake up at 4 AM to go to ghats for his ritual bath and puja. He did not want to wake up his servants at 4 AM. Hence, he tiptoed out without his shoes and carrying clothes in another hand. He came down the staircase without making the slightest sound. He walked to Hanuman Ghat with his chief priest pandit Sastri a distance of three and a half miles. Later in Royal camp, his retinue woke up much later. They were all under the impression that the Maharaja was still sleeping in his bedroom. Hence, they were speaking in hushed tones. When Nalwadi and the priest returned from the temple, they were surprised that the duo had left the palace in the early hours of morning for bathing and pooja without waking up anyone. The Maharaja always showed his concern and compassion for others comfort and wellbeing.

The Maharaja of Mysore with his troupe went on a pilgrimage tour to Kedarnath. This holy site is situated in Himalayas at a height of 11,755 ft from the sea level. It gets very cold and it receives snowfall. Some of the party members had not seen Badrinath temple. So, the Maharaja organised a trip for these devotees. The Maharaja continued to stay in Kedarnath with his retinue for a few more days. The pilgrims from Badrinath did not turn up on the expected date. So, the Maharaja got worried about their safe return. He even climbed a rocky mountain to take a look at the road from Badrinath to Kedarnath to see through a pair of binoculars whether the travellers were returning to the camp or not. Sometime later, they all returned to camp safely.

Some thirteen years ago, in the Bandipur forest, a tribesman was killed by a man-eating tiger. His poor wife and children became destitute overnight. He had taken a loan from a greedy landlord after pledging his two children as bonded labourers. When Maharaja came to know of the misfortunes of this tribal family, he decided to help the surviving family members. The Maharaja cleared the debts of this tribal person. His house which was pledged with a money lender was released and his two children were freed, after loans were repaid with interest by the Maharaja. This family received a new pucca house built by the Maharaja's engineers and they also received cows and oxen as gifts. A few acres of fertile farmland was given to the wife and children. The poor tribal family was given Rs. 750 in cash to tide over their hardship until they were able to harvest their first crop. The widow and her children were supplied with free ration on a monthly basis.

Some twelve years ago, the small pox epidemic ravaged Mysore city. Even the Maharaja was afflicted with the disease. Instead of being worried about his health, he showed extraordinary concern for others. He told visitors, who had not been infected by the smallpox disease not to come near him. He advised the state population to get themselves inoculated as early as possible. Before his European tour, he was bedridden with some affliction. After his recovery of strength, these are the words spoken by him, "I must have given all of you a lot of trouble. My sleeping pattern and food intake became erratic. So, you were all forced to work at odd and inconvenient hours because of my ailment."

Once Dewan Sir Mirza M. Ismail quoted a quotation of Thomas Carlyle, "A man must indeed be a hero to appear such in the eyes of his valet." But Carlyle had not come across someone like Nalwadi, who was a true hero to his servants. In fact, across all cross sections of the society, he was considered as a virtuous and noble ruler, a true hero to everyone.

The Maharaja truly cared for the members of his Ursu community. The boys and girls of the Ursu community had their free hostel. But he did not shower any special favours upon them in job recruitment or matters of promotion. Once, a young engineering graduate belonging to the Ursu community approached him for a job in the state government. Nalwadi told the young man, he heartily assisted Ursu students in their pursuit of higher education, but when it came to jobs, there was a state government agency. He did not want to bypass the regular procedure of recruitment. He could easily provide him with a job, but if a more meritorious candidate was there in the line, he will be denied his rightful opportunity. Moreover, he did not want to appropriate the authority of these officials in the matter of recruitment. But Nalwadi had one genuine fear that a Ursu official might misuse his caste links with the ruling family. Such an official might grow into an incompetent, arrogant and complacent administrator. Once, a young graduate managed to secure an official position in the government service on the basis of his merit. He came to meet the Maharaja and take his blessings. Nalwdi gave him a piece of valuable advice, "If you do good or bad, the people will judge you based on your caste links. Please remember that your action either brings good name to our community or a bad name. May Goddess Chamundeswari bless you."

Adulation of His Subjects

Once while passing through a village, he noticed a farmer lying near his farm rolling on the ground with chest pain. He was immediately taken in his car to

Mysore hospital for medical treatment. On the same day, a messenger was sent to the village to convey to the family members this news of medical emergency.

On another occasion, Nalwadi was passing through Chikkaballapur Taluq in his car. He came across a blind orphan boy. This boy was brought to Mysore and admitted in the government blind school to be trained as a violinist. He was given every financial help to receive musical training. He later became a versatile, accomplished violin artist. In a town, he came across a poor Muslim singer of Kannada *"Lavanis"* (Ballads). This balladeer was annually invited to Mysore city during Dasara festival. He would perform before His Highness and hundreds of listeners. He was granted a monthly stipend by His Highness to encourage his talent.

In a village near Sri Kendagannu Swami Gaddige (Tomb of a Saint), the Maharaja had gone on a tiger hunt. He overheard a mentally disturbed youth crying for help as he was being pelted with stones by the village urchins. Strangely, this youth was shouting, "I will complain against you tormentors to the Maharaja himself. He will protect me and punish you fellows by beating you fellows with a stick. Please help me! Please save my life!" At that moment, Nalwadi appeared on the scene and rescued the boy. After making enquiries, he came to know that the young man had been abandoned by his brothers and sister as his own parents were dead. The Maharaja took pity on him and sent him to a mental institution in Mysore for correction.

While driving on a highway, the Maharaja's car engine got heated up. They wanted some water to fill up the radiator. One villager offered to get water from a well one mile away. When he fetched water in a vessel, the Maharaja gave him generous amounts of money for his services. The villager had seen the Maharaja before in Mysore during Dasara. He recognised the ruler of the state and said, "Today, I got an opportunity to serve my king and I am grateful." These words of devotion brought tears to the eyes of the Maharaja.

Nalwadi noticed it in Mysore during evenings a certain old gentleman was taking a walk on a boulevard. He was impeccably dressed and punctual in his evening constitutional walk. The Maharaja sent a teakwood walking stick as a gift to this complete stranger. He could admire good qualities in others silently.

Once, the Maharaja came across a disabled educated gentleman. His legs were short and of stunted growth. The Maharaja placed an order for a special motor vehicle with a foreign firm. They sent a vehicle, which was hand controlled and could be driven by a disabled individual. This greatly helped the concerned individual to earn his living and pursue his profession. Another palace official suffered a paralysis of limbs and became immobilized. The Maharaja ensured that he could attend to his office-work from home. He provided him with all the office facilities at home.

Whenever the Maharaja travelled by car to Ootachamund, the trees lining the highway were painted with white and brown colours around the tree trunks in alternative circles. Once, the Maharaja set out in his car to Ootachamund two days earlier than the notified date of departure. The public works department officials were attending to this beautification work. The Maharaja noticed at one spot an old infirm woman struggling to paint white and brown rings around the tree trunk. Nalwadi approached the old woman, who was cursing under her breath. She worked as a coolie in her old age to make a living. The village patel (chief) had ordered her to do this work as free community service. She complained to Nalwadi, "I do not have the strength and energy to do this work." She did not care for the Maharaja, who traversed the highway. She had not eaten a meal since the previous day. She was weak and hungry. The Maharaja gave her fruits and money to provide her with some relief immediately. He asked her not to attend to this absurd work assigned to her. Later, the Maharaja passed a government order banning this meaningless protocol work supposedly to please His Highness as being unnecessary and wasteful.

The Maharaja visited Krishnarajapet during an official visit. He was staying in the traveller's bungalow. Hundreds of visitors from far away villages had come to see him. But the local Amaldar had kept them at bay. So, Nalwadi called the Amaldar and told him that those villagers had come from far away villages to see him and they all must be allowed to come near him. He patiently enquired about their wellbeing and listened to their problems with a promise of possible rectification.

The Maharaja went on a pilgrimage tour to Mahadeshwara Hill. An old "Lavani" (Balladeer) singer had come from a distant village with the intent of singing before the Maharaja a few ancient ballads. Nalwadi gave him the opportunity to sing before him. This old man was suitably rewarded with cash and sent back to his village in the palace car.

The Maharaja visited one of the districts of the state in 1913. In the district headquarters, an old Brahmin couple called on him. The old vedic pandit pleaded with the Maharaja that he was completing the sighting of "1,000 full moons" during his life time (*Sahasra Chandra Darshana*). He wanted to perform poojas and homas along with his old wife on his eightieth birthday. But he did not possess money. After ascertaining the genuiness of the case, the Maharaja gave the old couple Rs. 500 to perform this ritual. They also received 200 seer of rice (a measurement) and other ingredients for the grand lunch. The old man received 2 shawls, 2 silk dhotis and a long silk coat as gift. His wife received silk saree and blouse cloth. They performed in their village Sahasra Chandra Homa according to the sastras. Later, the old couple took out a procession through the streets of the village, in which they carried a garlanded photograph of the Maharaja. The villagers took the old couple also in a procession accompanied by the nadaswaram musicians.

During a trip to Hassan district, Nalwadi was approached by a poor village woman near Santhenahalli. She was very poor and in dire straits. He listened to her woes patiently. Later, she was given financial help to tide over her poverty. He loved his subjects immensely and he was ready to help total strangers.

Forgiving Nature of the Maharaja

The Maharaja appreciated honest and hardworking individuals. If perchance they erred in their duty, he would forgive them wholeheartedly. One efficient honest high ranking official had earned the wrath of jealous petty officials. Hence, he was worried that he may be framed up in a case under false charges. Nalwadi sensed his innermost fears and apprehensions. He called that official and told him not to worry about the future calamity. The Maharaja told him your superior officer has a good opinion about you and I am satisfied with your work. Please dispel your worries."

The official expressed his heartfelt thanks to the Maharaja and asked him to forgive his future trespasses. Nalwadi replied, "You have not committed any crime now. If you are going to commit one in the future why apologise for it in advance? To err is human and please do not commit any crime. Please go on working without any trepidation."

One servant who worked in the royal bathhouses dropped a "basin" (an enamel big bowl) of very pleasant colour to ground and damaged it. It was a favourite wash basin of the Maharaja. The supervisor noticed it and questioned the servant in-charge. The shivering servant confessed to the act of damaging the beautiful basin. This was reported to the Maharaja. The Maharaja made one remark that the poor servant had owned it up, even when there were no eyewitnesses. Nalwadi pardoned the servant and gave him a small reward. He was appreciated because he did not put the blame on others.

Once, the Maharaja imported special bulbs for the Ooty palace from a foreign country. These electric bulbs lit up on a low voltage and emitted considerable heat to warm up the room. One illiterate servant without any technological knowledge switched on the high voltage current switches. All the imported expensive bulbs got damaged. He was shivering with untold fear and had assumed that he would be fired from his job. The servant pleaded with the Maharaja for forgiveness as he had committed a grave crime out of sheer ignorance. Nalwadi pardoned him and told him to act with greater responsibility in the future. He reprimanded him in a gentle manner. Once again, a fresh order for these electric bulbs were placed with the foreign company.

The Maharaja often condoned the mistakes or lapses on the part of an official doing his regular duty. If someone caused a severe disappointment, he expressed his displeasure or disapproval silently. Once, an official caused immense mental agony to the Maharaja. The reaction of Nalwadi was remarkable, he did not give an audience to the concerned official for three months. Then, this official pleaded for forgiveness and apologised profusely for his misdemeanour with Nalwadi. This official was once again in the good books of the Maharaja after a while. He was kind to officials who were diligent in their work, but if they made any mistake inadvertently, they were forgiven. The Maharaja, before extending a hand of friendship to an Indian or a European official, he would test them on several counts, before embracing them as friends. Once he trusted them, there was no question of letting go of their friendship.

His Highness was never harsh upon criminals. But he did not forgive repeat offenders. One servant was a repeat offender. He was warned and requested to mend his ways. But he did not relent. Nalwadi was left with no option, but to dismiss him from service. As he had not put in the required number of years of service to be eligible for pension, he would have gone home empty handed. But the Maharaja was the personification of compassion, though the State Government rules did not permit it, this individual was granted half his pension on humanitarian grounds.

Once, the Maharaja had gone to Paschimavahini Ghats to take a holy bath in Cauvery. He wanted to perform his *"Ahnika"* (Any religious rite or duty, which is to be performed at a fixed hour like mid-day Sndhyavandana).

He entered a room to squat and do his afternoon Sandhyavandana ritual. He noticed a dead frog behind the door. He did not lose his temper and scold the concerned servants. Instead, he calmly reprimanded them and advised them to be more diligent in their performance of duty.

This incident happened in Ooty palace. The Maharaja after a purification bath was proceeding towards the puja room. He was wearing a freshly washed dhoti and upper cloth. A servant coming from the opposite direction in a hurry, bumped against the Maharaja. This caused an unforgivable religious pollution to the Maharaja. He did not shout angrily at the irresponsible servant. The servant was stupefied with fear. But, Nalwadi told him, "Do not be scared. You committed this mistake inadvertently. In the future, do not commit a mistake like this. The Maharaja went back to his bathroom to take a purification bath again. He had to make all the necessary preparations like changing his clothes, etc. His regular puja could resume after a delay caused by this unpleasant interruption.

Once, the Maharaja was performing "Shraddha" (Death anniversary or memorial service) of his father Late Sri Chamarajendra Wodeyar. During a Shraddha ritual oblation is offered to father, grandfather and great-grandfather. The Hindu priests recite vedic mantras, which pleads with the departed ancestors to come and accept the oblation offered to them. The priest chanting the mantra, due to a slip of the tongue inserted his father's name instead of Late Maharaja Sri Chamarajendra Wodeyar's name. This is a serious breach of protocol. But Nalwadi gravely asked the priest, "Are you performing the Shraddha of my father or yours?" Any other person would have taken the erring priest to task and he would have punished him with outright dismissal. Even under utmost provocation, Nalwadi could control his temper and remain cool.

One day, the Maharaja was coming down the hill in his car from the Chamundi temple. When he took a "U" turn on the hilly road, he noticed a sanyasi sleeping in the middle of the road. Nalwadi could stop the car with great difficulty. Otherwise, he would have run over this sanyasi lying across the road. The Maharaja got down from the car and walked up to this man. When he was questioned for this irrational behaviour. He informed them that he did this to earn some money. Nalwadi angrily questioned him, "You are insulting the ochre robes of a sanyasi. You are faking a suicide on the highway for a few coins. Have you really renounced this world?" Nalwadi gave him a good piece of advice and before leaving gave him some coins.

Nalwadi did not encourage either sycophancy or gossip mongering. But sometimes, people expressed their prejudices based upon caste or religion, even in those circumstances, he would neither join them or reprimand them. But with infinite patience, he would pacify these detractors. When the renowned civil engineer Sir M. Vishweshwariah became Dewan of Mysore State, he welcomed visitors and he could be approached by the public more easily. This was not relished by other bureaucrats. One Deputy Commissioner complained to the Maharaja that usually supplicants waited outside their houses or offices for hours, just to meet them and give a petition. They were official representatives of the Maharaja. Now, the new Dewan not only welcomes these supplicants, but offers them a chair in his office. The Maharaja told the bureaucrat that we are here to serve our subjects. Please remember that times are changing and we must change accordingly. In other words, he told the official to be more democratic in his functioning.

The Maharaja had invited Mr. Dutta an economic advisor to improve the fiscal policy of the state. Mr. Dutta was requested to go through the state revenue accounts and its expenditure on viable state projects. The Maharaja wanted to improve revenue collection and plug loopholes in taxation. An elderly high-ranking official of the revenue department told Nalwadi, "We have invited an outside auditor to check our state accounts. He will find fault with our financial management. Is it not a shameful situation?" Nalwadi replied, "Let our people come to know about our tax revenue and expenditure. I am all for transparency in financial transactions. We are spending on various schemes to improve the quality of life. Let it be exposed by an impartial outside auditor."

During meetings, when people disagreed with each other, he would remain calm and pacify them with proper explanation. He had given lower rung officials absolute freedom to operate. But he did not endorse their opinions all the time. Often, he disagreed with these adamant officials politely.

Many years ago, the State was going through a political and financial crisis. The then Dewan of the state sent his report to His Highness with several suggestions and recommendations. When Nalwadi went through the report, he told his private secretary, "These are not well thought out suggestions. He has studied the problem seriously. But his recommendations are not practicable. Please keep this report on the shelf for a few days, the Dewan may send fresh suggestions" As per the prediction of the Maharaja, the Dewan sent a telegram asking for the file back. The Maharaja told the private secretary that he was expecting this and the file with all the relevant papers was sent back to him.

An elderly retired official, who had seen Nalwadi since his younger days remembered that the ruler never lost his temper under any duress. Nalwadi's true nature was to remain calm and cool under all circumstances. But he had taken a vow in his youth to control his anger. Once, Nalwadi was returning to palace on his horse. One stranger on the pavement loudly pleaded with him for some relief from injustice. He was shouting loudly in a rude manner, "Please ride your horse upon my body and get rid of me." Even repeated requests to clarify the matter did not produce any result. Nalwadi, with great difficulty, managed to collect his name and residential address. That troubled and perturbed individual went on insisting that he must be run over. He moved forward to drag the horse by its reins. This would have scared the horse and it would have pranced up. Nalwadi carried a horsewhip with him and he gave this rude person a blow. This sudden attack on the abrasive individual, prevented Nalwadi from falling off from the horse. He rode back to the palace and informed his mother about the incident. He was upset because, he had hit this man in anger. The Maharaja sent a messenger to this individual's house to fetch him. Later, the man was able to report his problem to the ruler. Nalwadi gave him some money to overcome his immediate crisis and he also found a remedy to his vexing problem.

Love for Children

The Maharaja was fond of children. He had immense love for his younger brother Yuvaraja's children. He loved to play and watch the pranks of Prince Sri Jayachamarajendra Wodeyar and his sisters. He carried them in his arms and listened to their lisping childish babble. He regularly presented them with toys. He enjoyed their mischief and games.

When he went to Kharapura with his hunting party, he did not forget to carry toys and sweets for tribal children. He would personally meet theses tribal children and give them laddus and jilebis. He gave them toys and trumpets. He shared their joy and happiness immensely. The poor Soliga parents could not believe their eyes that the all-powerful Maharaja was playing with these poor tribal children of the forest. They often prostrated at his feet with tears in their eyes and offered their gratitude to him.

One year, during Dasara Vijayadashmi procession, Nalwadi observed from the elephant Howda, a lot of mothers standing in the hot sun holding their young babies. It pained him greatly because he was sitting under a golden canopy in comfort upon an elephant. The next year, he ordered the officials to erect a shamiana for women and children. This gave them protection from rain and sun.

Sometimes, Nalwadi would visit a village school in plain clothes. Neither the villagers nor the children knew his identity. He would talk, joke and test their learning abilities. Later, he would send fruits and sweets to the children of that school. These people would learn later that they were visited by the Maharaja only after they received his gifts from the palace officials.

One morning, Nalwadi visited an English school. The students were making a lot of noise. The school teacher had not turned up till then. Nalwadi entered a classroom and the students stood up to receive him. The students assumed that a school inspector had come to meet them. Nalwadi asked a number of questions. He was pleased with their answers. He asked the students, "Do you know who I am?" They all replied in unison that he was a school inspector. A smiling Nalwadi pointed at the portrait of the ruler on the classroom wall and asked, "Do you recognize me?" All of them joyfully shouted "Our Maharaja, Our Maharaja." The smiling Maharaja left the school and the village very quietly without waiting for honours from its residents.

On 16th July 1938, the Maharaja visited a village called Hanumanthapura near Hassan town. He enjoyed the visit to the village school. Here, the teacher was asked to give a demonstration lecture. The teacher asked several questions after the lecture. Nalwadi was immensely pleased with the answers given by the boys and girls.

Whenever the Maharaja was invited to a town to inaugurate a newly constructed building, he would make arrangements for distribution of laddus to children at his own cost. At Kemmangundi mining village, he got a children's park built for miner's children. This park had a slide, a see-saw and swings. A few months before his death during a visit to the town, he told officials to distribute thousands of laddus to children at his cost. He also gave them "jubbas" (long shirts) free of cost to all the children. A group photograph was taken and this found a cherished place on the mantel piece in the palace drawing room.

Compassion for Animals

Nalwadi loved animals and birds very much. The Mysore zoo with a good collection of animals and birds was founded by his father Sri Chamarajendra Wodeyar. It was rated as one of the best zoos in India. Nalwadi made further improvements in living conditions of wild animals. Some wild animals were provided with more open space reminiscent of its wilder habitat. Now, tigers were not confined to cages, they were kept in open grounds with a moat running around it. At present, this kind of free environment is provided in Sydney Zoo and in one another zoo in Europe. Now, the tigers in Mysore Zoo can climb trees and sleep on branches.

The Maharaja made a serious study of wild animals by reading several books written by experts. Nalwadi instructed the zoo staff to feed, as far as possible, the food relished by these animals. He often paid surprise visits to the zoo to see whether the caretakers were looking after animals properly or not. The Maharaja read in one of the books that the bears loved to eat butter. Hence, butter was supplied to bears. But Nalwadi discovered that the caretaker was also equally fond of butter. He caught him stealing the butter. The poor man confessed to his crime and sought forgiveness. Nalwadi possessed a generous heart, so he sent the bear keeper a double ration of butter for human and bear consumption. But he warned the caretaker not to deny the bears their due share of butter. The palace cooks used to send boiled oats to horses in royal stables. One horse caretaker began to appropriate half of the boiled oats and began to smuggle it to his home. He was caught red handed and brought before the Maharaja. He owned up his crime and informed the Maharaja that he was a poor man with a large family. He could feed his brood with the stolen boiled oats. He also begged for forgiveness. But the kind-hearted Maharaja gave him a generous hike in salary and gave him permission to take the extra ration of boiled oats home.

The Maharaja conducted his own experiments on wild animals in the zoo. He had trained a chimpanzee to ride a tricycle. They were trained to share food among themselves amiably and not fight over food. He wanted to find out whether tigers and lions could live together. Nalwadi succeeded in making a tiger and a lion live in the same enclosure in a friendly manner. These two experiments achieved their goals. In fact, the zoo animals were maintained with the palace funds.

The Maharaja wanted everyone to treat the domesticated animals with utmost kindness. The palace had many oxen to pull the carts. These oxen had to be shoed frequently. The normal practice was to tie the front and hind legs of the ox with ropes. They would make them to lie on the hard ground. Then, the ox shoes were nailed to the hoofs. This caused considerable pain. So Nalwadi got a big pit dug up and it was filled with soft sand. Later, oxen were trained to lie down on the sand pit to a command of "Bait, bait." A huge pillow was placed beneath its head. Then, farriers would nail the ox shoes to its hoofs. He had told the palace servants not to overload the carts with excess goods. The oxen and the horses were branded with hot iron to make identification easy. He stopped this practice of numbering oxen, which was painful to the animals. The animal caretakers were told to use indelible coloured ink to mark the animals.

Once, stone slabs were being transported by hired ox carts up the Chamundi hill. These owners of hired carts were loading two stone slabs per cart. The Maharaja noticed this overloading and told the cart owners to ship only one granite stone slab at a time. The additional transport cost was borne by the Maharaja from his personal funds.

Whenever the Maharaja and his friends planned a hunting expedition, he would send the tamed elephants from Mysore to Kharapura. But "Howdahs" were sent separately by lorries. He did not want these tamed elephants to carry heavy "howdahs" on their backs over a long distance. If he was taking pet dogs on a long trip in his car, he would spread soft cotton quilts upon the car seat, so the dogs could lie comfortably.

The Maharaja often climbed the one thousand steps of Chamundi Hill to pray at the temple. He encouraged old men and women to ride a pony to reach the top of the hill. He told caretakers to give horses a break after an hour ride. He would allow these horses to graze grass to their heart's content. While coming down, these old people were asked to walk down slowly. He did not want horses to slip and fall, while coming down with riders on their saddle.

Once, in Nilgiri hill station, he came across a bleeding puppy. Someone had inflicted injuries upon this pup. Nalwadi personally carried it to the palace, where he treated the dog with utmost care, applied ointment and bandaged its wounds. He took care of the pup until it recovered its good health.

During Dasara, some of the rich Ursu families used to organise ram fights and bull fights. Nalwadi put an end to these bloody sports, by requesting these Ursu family heads to abandon violent sports.

The Maharaja had imported wild horses from Australia. While training them, the horse trainers were using horse whip with nails, which was causing bleeding wounds. Instead, Nalwadi introduced new methods, which were less painful to the animal during training.

This is a lesser-known fact of history. The horse carriages were a common sight in Indian towns. But most of these carriages were badly designed. They were uncomfortable to travellers. The horse tied to the cart also suffered because 5 or 6 people used to sit in the cart. The poor horse had to pull these travellers on a metalled road. Nalwadi designed a new type of horse cart called "*Shah Pasand* cart." The carriage and wheels were well balanced. The two passengers could climb into the back portion of the cart easily. The two passengers could sit in the front. The horse took this balanced weight comfortably. In some cities, the wheels were too big for the carriage and ended up being a heavy load on horse. Many of these "Shah pasand carriages"[5] were built in palace stables and sold to cart drivers at manufacturing cost. Whatever money was earned from this enterprise was ploughed back to build low cost houses for cart owners.

Whenever horses were purchased for the palace, the Maharaja was concerned about the mouth gear called a "bit," the part of bridle that is inserted into a horse's mouth. He wanted that to be comfortable and compatible to the horse. Sometimes, the metallic mouthpiece called "Mullen," a straight bar with a slight curve to accommodate the horse's tongue caused pain and soreness in the mouth of the horse. There was another egg-shaped metallic bar called "snaffle bit," which connected the mouth piece and the bit ring, which hurt the lips if it was too tight. Once, a rich European gentleman purchased an expensive horse. But it behaved always in an unruly manner. He decided to sell it cheap, but there were no takers. So, he decided to put the horse to sleep by pumping a bullet into it. The Maharaja was informed about this horse and he decided to buy it and save its life. He examined this whole head gear called a "bit" and found out that it was causing immense pain. The Maharaja changed the whole contraption to ease the pain. Ultimately, the horse became a docile and gentle animal. It also became a favourite horse of the Maharaja.

Once, in Mysore city, the Maharaja saw a horse carriage being pulled by a thin horse with open sores on the body. Moreover, the driver was beating the poor horse to make it run. He stopped the horse carriage and examined the horse. He informed the driver to send it to the Royal stables for medical treatment. It received good fodder and the vets treated the wounded horse with ointment, etc. Soon, it became normal. During the interim period, the horse owner's family received a monthly allowance of money from the

---

[5.] Reza Shah Pahlavi (1878 – 1944) the ruler of Iran visited Mysore State. He took a ride in the newly designed horse carriage in Mysore. He loved the horse drawn carriage very much. That's why the new horse carriage came to be called "Shah Pasand" (Shah's choice).

palace to make both ends meet. This kind act of Nalwadi received all-round praise.

Nalwadi loved horses and horse riding was a favourite pastime. When he entered the palace stables, the horses would neigh loudly and greet him. If he called a horse by name, that particular horse would come running to him. He always carried with him jaggery, carrots and greens to feed the horses. During his trip to Europe, he had observed how farriers shoed the horses. Our Indian practice was too cruel to the horses. Hence, the European method was adopted to ease the pain of the horses. He loved his pet dogs and played with them. He worshipped the cow as a sacred animal. Every morning at 10 AM, he would perform pooja to the holy cow, so nominated by priests (*pattada Hasu*). He would feed this cow with special Nanjangud dwarf bananas.

On Vijayadashami day, the palace elephant was made to lie on the ground. The workers tied the Golden Ambari on to its back with thick ropes. This caused a lot of suffering to the elephant. The Maharaja, on the advice of the engineers, purchased a crane. The workers would tie the golden Ambari to the dangling hook of the crane. This was hoisted on to the back of a standing elephant. They would fasten it to the back of the elephant with thick ropes. He also ordered the Golden Ambari to be lifted by crane and placed on the ground at Bannimantap during puja ceremony. The puja and torch light lasted three hours. During this period, the elephant was made to relax without the heavy Ambari on its back.

The Maharaja drove the car at moderate speed, so as to avoid accidents. One of the palace officials drove his car at breakneck speed during a long trip. Nalwadi asked him sarcastically, "How many chickens and sheep did you kill today? Did you also kill a human being also? Now onwards drive slowly and spare life, for heaven's sake."

The Maharaja had taken his mother Sri Vanivilasa Sannidhana to witness a tiger hunt in the forest near Kendagannu Swamy Gaddige in 1924. While returning from the hunt, on the highway, he noticed a bullock cart carrying huge logs of timber blocking his path. It was an uphill journey for the oxen. Nalwadi stopped his car, removed his turban and coat, before confronting the cart driver. He questioned him why he was not giving way despite honking several times. The car driver mistook the Maharaja for a commoner and said, "It is easy for you to reprimand me. Look at my oxen. They are struggling to heave this heavy load up the hill. They are already out of breath. Who is there to help me by pushing and manoeuvring the wheel so that I can give way to a motorist, who intends to overtake my cart? How can you human beings understand the agony and suffering of these dumb animals?" This tirade made the Maharaja to call his bodyguards for help. All of them including the Maharaja pushed the wheels of the cart until it climbed the hill. Then, the Maharaja went back to his car and continued his journey. A little distance away, there was a police station on the highway. Nalwadi stopped the car and went into the police station. He requested the police officer to pass on Rs. 10 to the bullock cart driver, who was coming with a heavy load of timber.

The dowager Queen-mother had sent a closed carriage to fetch an aristocratic lady relative to the palace. In those days, these closed carriages were drawn by oxen. This lady guest arrived at the palace and went inside. The driver of the carriage did not unharness the oxen from the yoke. Nalwadi was observing this from the third floor of the palace and came down and admonished the carriage driver. He told him to give some respite to the oxen by freeing them during the waiting period.

This incident took place when the Maharaja paid a visit to Kemmangundi in 1940. On that day, it was raining heavily in the morning. The Maharaja was walking towards the traveller's bungalow holding an umbrella. He noticed a dog and its two puppies getting drenched in the rain beneath some rocks. The dog had sought protection from the rain under a huge stone. The two puppies were on the rock getting drenched in rain. The dog was howling loudly. He told the servants to pick up the puppies and bring it to the bungalow. The dog also followed the Maharaja. In the verandah of the bungalow, the puppies found shelter. They were able to rest on a makeshift bed of gunny bags. The dog and the puppies were fed with warm milk and rice.

Love of Discipline

Even from his boyhood days, Nalwadi was obsessed with discipline and order. Everything he did, small or big tasks, were done with utmost concentration and application of mind. He had a good aesthetic sense while arranging furniture in a study room. Even in the classroom, he arranged writing tables and chairs in a proper order. He did not approve of classmates standing on tables and chairs.

One day, in front of the Ooty palace, the uniformed cavalrymen had lined up on either side of the driveway. An ochre robed sanyasi asked the

Maharaja himself, "Who is coming to the palace?" Nalwadi replied "Today, Huzoor Sannidhana is visiting the palace." The queen-mother Sri Vanivilasa Sannidhana was always addressed by her former title "Huzoor Sannidhana" (Queen Dowager) Nalwadi, even after becoming the monarch of the State, did not withdraw any of the privileges of his queen-mother. As per protocol, she was still treated as a dowager queen.

After taking the reins of power, the Maharaja visited "Ursu Boarding School" in Mysore. Nalwadi asked the school superintendent a simple question, "How many boys are studying in the school?" The superintendent was overwhelmed by the presence of the Maharaja. He was a nervous wreck. He replied that each room had two students. Nalwadi repeated the question three times. He got the same incorrect reply. A respectable Ursu gentleman, who stood beside the superintendent said, "The hostel has 16 rooms and totally, 32 students are residing. Now the Maharaja sternly told the elderly gentleman, "The question must be answered by the Superintendent as per etiquette. I want him to answer my question." Now the Superintendent realised his mistake and blurted out an apology, "Your honour, we have 32 students in 16 rooms. I was overcome by my nervousness, please forgive me." That evening, the Maharaja sent a memento to the hostel superintendent with a note "This gift is given to boost your courage to give relevant replies to questions."

The Maharaja with his Queen-mother visited Sri Vanivilasa Sagar dam. They were staying in the traveller's bungalow. In plain clothes and unescorted by bodyguards, Nalwadi went out for a stroll. When he returned, the police constable at the gate was a different constable, who had come on duty. He had not seen the Maharaja during his lifetime. He stopped Nalwadi at the gate and refused to allow this "Stranger" into the Bungalow. He told that His Highness and Queen-mother were residing in the guesthouse, hence he was ordered not to allow strangers into the compound. At this moment, an official shouted at the police constable not to stop the visitor. The palace constable said, "I took you for a stranger. My orders were not to allow any loiterers. The official inside is ordering me to allow you sir. Please walk into the bungalow. After a while, the Maharaja sent a handsome reward (inam) to the police constable who did his duty in an exemplary manner.

In 1920, the viceroy of India, Lord Reading, visited Mysore state. The Maharaja had organised an elephant trapping Khedda operation at Kharapura. The viceroy was staying in a hunting lodge. The Mysore state police had made strict security arrangements around the lodge. Entry into the bungalow was restricted to a few high-ranking dignitaries, who were given numbered metal tokens. The security guards allowed a person only after verifying these tokens. One high-ranking official went to the hunting lodge to meet the Viceroy in the evening. The guards knew by sight, who this official was, but still in Hindustani language, the guard refused the entry on the grounds of want of a token. The high-ranking official returned to his tent to fetch the token. Nalwadi was watching the incident from his tent. The bemused Maharaja approached the lodge without his token. The Muslim guard again barred the entry to the Maharaja. Nalwadi asked him whether he recognised his own ruler or not, the guard replied in Hindustani that he recognised the Maharaja, who had ordered this security measure. Although he was servant of the Maharaja, he was only obeying orders given to him by his superior. Now, the Maharaja told him in Hindustani jocularly that he was rescinding his own orders. He refused entry into the lodge to anyone without token including the Maharaja. The next morning, the Maharaja sent an official to present the guard with a monetary award of Rs. 50 and an official letter acknowledging his exemplary sense of duty. The guard also received an official message that his salary had been hiked with a special increment. The guard who had spent sleepless night felt elated at the turn of events.

The Maharaja and his entourage were travelling in their cars to their destination. They were stopped at a railway crossing as the gates had been locked. Nalwadi sent his driver with this message to the railway guard that the Maharaja should be allowed to continue his journey as the train was going to pass on the tracks after 10 minutes. Nalwadi was only testing the integrity of the guard. The Mysore State Railway functioned in the princely state as one of the departments under the Maharaja. The guard joked with the chauffer, while on his duty the railway train was more important than the Maharaja. He only obeyed the rules and regulations of the railway department. After the train passed by, the guard came to the Maharaja's car and with folded hands informed him that he was only performing his duty. The Maharaja praised the honest guard for performing his official duty and gave him Rs. 30 as "inam" (reward).

The Maharaja insisted that all state functions like religious festivals, chariot festivals, floats on lake with Chamundi idol, evening Darbars and felicitation functions ought to be organised as per strict protocol. In the evening Darbar, the Maharaja noticed that the courtiers on either side sat in clusters or singly in a disorderly fashion. In the next Darbar, green numbered cardboard tokens were placed on the carpet in an orderly manner for the courtiers to sit. The people who honoured the Maharaja during functions were told in advance what type of garlands and bouquets to be presented to him. He did not like oversized gaudy garlands or very big bouquets to be presented to him. Even the palace priests and vedic pandits had a dress code to be followed during religious functions. They had to sport turbans and shawls in accordance with ceremonial customs. The Maharaja always insisted that the functions must start on time. He cared for punctuality and expected all the others to comply with it.

Nalwadi's Civility

The Maharaja not only expressed kindness and compassion to animals, but also extended it to all human beings. When he received an invitation to visit the summer capital of India, Shimla, from the viceroy, he travelled by train. It was a common practice in Shimla, which is a hill station to travel by rickshaws pulled by coolies. The Maharaja refused to be transported by the rickshaw pulled by the poor coolies. A rickshaw puller was waiting outside his hotel. Nalwadi refused this mode of transportation and preferred to walk instead. But he gave a sumptuous amount to the rickshaw puller, before resuming his walk. But the other rickshaw pullers did not appreciate his compassion and kindness, they were only concerned with loss of business to them.

Once, the Maharaja went to Kemannagundi to hunt tigers in the Shola forest. The forest officials had engaged hundreds of tribals to drive the tiger to Maharaja's "Maatchan" (a platform built on a tree for the hunter). The poor tribals had to endure the leeches in the forest. These leeches liked to suck the blood of tribals. The Maharaja cancelled tiger hunts in this area in the future to avoid inconvenience to tribals. He did not relish the idea of sitting in the "Matchan" cosily and killing a tiger driven by these unfortunate tribals. In this trip, Nalwadi killed a tiger at the ground level braving all odds.

During Dasara festival, on the ninth day of Dasara, the wrestling bouts were fought in front of the palace in the traditional manner. The raised wrestling pit was designed with mechanical parts to part in the middle and two halves would move away. This had intricate machinery with wheels, axles and gears. Some ten workers would turn the wheels to make each half of the pit move sideways on rails. They worked in sweltering and suffocating heat and darkness. It was done manually. During a Darbar when the royal elephant, holy cow and sacred horse were brought for puja, this wrestling platform had to be separated to make way for the animals. Nalwdi did not like ten workers toiling with the heavy machinery in the darkness. So, he decided to go in for motors, which would separate the two halves and join them. Once during the evening Darbar, the electrical machinery failed to function. When engineers tested it in the evening at 5 PM, the contraption had worked smoothly. That particular evening, when the holy cow, sacred horse and the royal elephant came to the palace, the wrestling platform did not part for them. They had to circumambulate the wrestling arena. Every evening, the elephant garlanded His Highness and showered flowers upon him during Dasara. The palace officials apologised for this inconvenience. They told the Maharaja that the earlier manually-operated machinery was more dependable. But Nalwadi disagreed with them and told them any day, electrical machinery spared the toiling workers from unnecessary labour. Even in the future, if the machinery failed to work, the animals could go around the wrestling pit to greet His Highness on the throne.

The Maharaja did not want to give the villagers any trouble in organising a civil reception for him during an official visit. During an official visit to Solur village in Magadi Taluq, he strongly objected to the erection of a stage and a temporary shelter (*pandal* or *pergola*) covered with coconut palm fronds. They often felled Areca nut palm trees for its slender lengthy trunks. These poles were used as cross beams to erect a pandal. All this meant extra-expenditure to the local residents. They also gave a bouquet and fruits to the Maharaja. They would honour him with flower garlands.

Nalwadi decided to visit the holy town of Tirumakudalu Narasipura for a dip in the "Sangam." Here, the Kaveri and Kabini rivers join with a mythical spring or lake called Spatika Sarovara. This was going to be a private visit on an auspicious day. He gave Rs. 100 to the chief priest Panditratnam Kankanahalli Narayana Sastri and requested him to make all the necessary arrangements for the ritual bath. Pandit Narayana Sastri was in a dilemma, because local government officials like Amaldar would ask him about the visit of a very important unnamed guest. The Maharaja told the pandit to inform the questioners that a high ranking Ursu nobleman was coming there for a ritual bath and puja. The whole visit of the Maharaja was a low-key affair without any publicity. Later, Pandit Narayana Sastri told the Maharaja, he was blamed by the officials and the citizens of T. Narasipura for denying an opportunity to welcome the Maharaja in a formal manner. Naalwadi told the pandit, it was a private visit and not an official visit. He did not want the towns people to spend huge sums of money on a grand reception. It was a private visit made on religious grounds.

The Maharaja did not smoke, drink or eat non-vegetarian food. He had adopted a Spartan and simple lifestyle. But he knew other human beings had their own frailties. Some of his officials smoked cigarettes and brahmin priests had a weakness for snuff (Tobacco finely ground into powder). Nalwadi did not sit upon them in moral judgement. He never lectured anyone against smoking or drinking or eating meat.

Once, Nalwadi saw an official smoking a cigarette from a distance. He admired and respected this official. So, he took a different path and avoided an embarrassing encounter. After four or five days, this particular official had an appointment with His Highness. During the meeting, the Maharaja showed him a gold cigarette case and asked him whether it was good. The official examined it and said it was very good. Nalwadi, to his surprise, told him it was a gift to him. The official began to stammer in his nervousness and informed His Highness that he was not a smoker. But Nalwadi told the official, the gold cigarette case embossed with the double headed eagle (Gandabherunda) is a work of art, which will tempt even a non-smoker to become a smoker. You can keep it as a memento without causing any harm to anybody. It is absolutely useless to me. So, you can keep it. The concerned official, who was a confirmed smoker liked the gift very much.

On another occasion, a well-known Asthana Vidwan pandit_____ Sastri was climbing the staircase in palace to reach the upper floor, where he was expected to deliver a lecture on one of the "puranas" (epics). This pandit had the habit of inhaling snuff. He joyfully stuffed his nostrils with the snuff powder which brought about a loud sneeze. At that moment, the Maharaja was descending the steps and he suppressed a laughter and told the pandit, "Take it slowly, take it easy, no need to hurry up." He smiled at the pandit in a friendly way and moved on. The next morning, the Maharaja sent a gold snuff box to this pandit as a gift through a messenger. This gold snuffbox was a royal heirloom. In another incident, a priest who was reciting "Japa mantras" took a break and he covered his face with his shawl only to stuff his nose with snuff powder. This act was observed by the Maharaja. The next day, he presented the priest with a silver snuff box and told him to consume snuff powder without covering his face with a shawl. One can compare Nalwadi's civility with similar exemplary behaviour exhibited by famous American president Abraham Lincoln during his lifetime.

Compassion Incarnated

The Maharaja decided to take food after the cooks, attendants and servants had consumed their lunch. This decision was prompted by a freak incident. The Maharaja always dined in the company of his queen mother and younger brother the Yuvaraja. One morning, his mother was indisposed and she was reluctant to have a regular meal. Perhaps, her physician had advised her to consume a restricted diet. His younger brother, the Yuvaraja, on that day, was out of town. Nalwadi sent in a word that he was not going to have his lunch. His mother made anxious enquiries why he had refused to take his lunch. He did not divulge the real reason for refusing the food. He told his mother that he was not hungry at all. But he made a startling proposal to his mother that let the kitchen staff consume food first and then the royal family could sit for lunch. He told his mother that the servants and cooks worked for long hours. They had a better appetite than the royal family members. These hardworking individuals were exposed to the smell of various tasty dishes which tempted them. They also saw with their eyes the delicious dishes being prepared by expert chefs. Naturally, their hunger increased by many fold, because they could only eat after the royalty had consumed their lunch. Nalwadi did not want these servants to go hungry for a long period. Nalwadi did not want these servants to serve food on an empty stomach. The queen mother appreciated the sensitivity and compassion showed by her beloved son. She readily agreed to have food after the servants and cooks had eaten. Some two months later, after the protocol was adapted, one morning, Nalwadi revealed his real reason for declining food on that day. The cook had placed his lunch in a gold plate on the table. This plate would normally be covered with a plantain leaf. Because the Royal family members came for lunch after a delay of 5 or 10 minutes. The gold plate had several small cups with different tasty dishes. He noticed the servant take a tasty ingredient in a spoon and consume from one or two cups. This was an extremely provocative and undignified act on the part of the servant. This sight would have enraged any normal human being. Of course, the Maharaja could not have consumed this leftover food. If he reported the matter to his mother, she would have dismissed this truant servant immediately. So, he remained silent, but made a decision not to consume food before others consumed it. He kept up this practice in Mysore, Bangalore and other towns during his official tours also for the rest of his life.

The Maharaja visited a town in 1915. In the evenings, he went out for a walk. The nearby villagers came to this town to see the Maharaja take a walk in the evenings. They would line up on either side of the road and cheer him. Once, a blind man came to this road to feel the presence of the Maharaja. He was heard shouting, "Welcome to our Maharaja. I have been told that he is a very good man. I would like to see him." The gathered crowd made fun of the blind person. They questioned him, "How can you see the Maharaja when you are born blind?" They also shouted to him to make way for the Maharaja. Nalwadi, on hearing this, went in search of the blind man. He met him and identified himself as the Maharaja. He asked the blind man, how he could see the king. The blind man said that his sight has been denied by God, but he can touch human beings and feel them. When Nalwadi heard his statement, he shed tears for this blind man. He held his hands and told him to feel his face and body. The blind man lovingly ran his hand over the face and chest of the Maharaja. He blurted emotionally "Oh! You are our king! You are our ruler!" Then, he fell to the ground and touched the feet of the Maharaja with great reverence.

Later, Nalwadi asked a close confidant, how can I recompense this blind person's love and reverence for his ruler? This blind man was granted a disability pension for life. Every month, he spent thousands of rupees from his own pocket to help needy poor people and orphans. Some poor people, including a blind boy, were given special permission to dine in the palace's common kitchen every day. One day, he called the blind boy and asked him how he was being treated by the palace staff. He told the blind boy that during dinner, he should ask the person serving ghee (clarified butter) to put it on his palm for they may deny him his share of ghee as he was sightless. He not only readily helped the poor, but also took the trouble of supervising its execution to perfection. The Maharaja's charitable acts are numberless. He never ever hesitated to assist and help these unfortunate individuals. He was a true Samaritan.

The Phenomenal Memory of the Maharaja

Nalwadi possessed a phenomenal memory and powers of concentration of mind. According to one gentleman, the Maharaja could vividly remember what coloured coat and turban he was wearing during a viceroy's visit some twenty years ago.

During a visit to "Maari Kanive" in Chitradurga district (Vani Vilasa Sagar Dam). His Highness was being introduced to the district board members by the District Commissioner and one member by the name Sri Nadiga Siddaramanna was introduced. The Maharaja immediately said, "Five years ago, I was travelling in my car from Hollalkere to Chitradurga, you gave me a civic reception on that day near Shivagange village, isn't it?" Nalwadi visited Shimoga town in February 1901. A huge crowd had lined up on either side of the main thoroughfare to welcome the Maharaja. Amongst the crowd, he noticed a retired official Shekadhar Shyamrao standing. Nalwadi had visited Jog falls some nineteen years ago (1901). Shyamrao had taken him to the waterfall and had acted as a local guide. Now in retirement, he was residing in a nearby town called Channagiri. He told the private secretary to fetch this gentleman. The Maharaja was glad to receive Shyamrao. Nalwadi honoured him with two shawls and a long overcoat. When the Maharaja visited Sakaleshapura town in 1921, he had honoured a vedic scholar and a purana reciter named pandit Suryanarayana Sastri aged 70 years, who had called upon him with fruits and tamboola. On the eve of the Silver Jubilee Celebration, he had sent an invitation to pandit Suryanarayan Sastri. During the celebration, he did not see pandit Suryanarayan Sastri in the Darbar hall. The Maharaja told his private secretary to find out why this vedic pandit did not come to the celebration.

In 1938, the Maharaja and his hunting troupe were trekking through the forest. The Maharaja saw a tribal fellow at a distance. He identified him as Javara whom he had met in 1917. But others disagreed with his identification. So, Nalwaadi called him and asked him whether his name was Javara. The tribal fellow assented to this query. Then, the Maharaja asked him, "Why are you not wearing your ear studs?" He replied that they were damaged due to wear and tear. This demonstration of the phenomenal memory of Maharaja always surprised everyone. When he read a book or a few pages of a report, he never forgot the contents. He possessed immense powers of concentration. His memory retention power was proverbial.

Power of Observation

During the evening Darbar, the invitees were honoured with a garland of jasmine flowers. Some palace officials had been entrusted with this chore.

The Maharaja was sitting on the throne. He noticed that the officials missed out on one guest. He sent a word to these officials, that one invitee had not been garlanded. He saw to it that this lapse was made up by the forgetful official.

During Dasara, the gold throne was decorated with flowers. The decorators normally used white water lilies. But one evening, the Maharaja found red water lilies used in the decoration of the throne instead of the white variety. Later, he enquired with the officials about the reason for the change.

During Darbar, an elderly Ursu courtier approached the throne to offer Nazar. At that moment, the Maharaja observed that one foot was swollen and he was limping. After the Darbar, he sent a messenger to the residence of this elderly courtier to enquire about the swollen foot. The Maharaja wanted to know what medical treatment was being administered to hasten the healing process. The elderly courtier was overcome with emotion and described the medical treatment to the messenger. One evening, during the Darbar, the Maharaja noticed a newly tamed elephant standing in front of the palace and it was refusing to eat jaggery cubes wrapped in green grass. Nalwadi sent in a word to the Mahut to know whether the elephant was not eating out of fear or because of indigestion. Once he observed an elephant standing before the palace was not flapping its ears and its tail had become stiff and arched. So, he wanted to know the type of ailment, which had impacted its normal behaviour.

In 1930, the Maharaja of Mysore was on a tour of North India. In one city, he visited a pharmaceutical company. After the inspection tour, the director of the company asked Maharaja whether he was satisfied with the hygiene and modern procedure adopted by the company to produce drugs. The bottles with medicines were being inserted with cork pieces by a "crown corking machine." At this final stage, a worker was loading cork pieces onto the machine with his dirty hands. When this was brought to the notice of the director, he praised the keen observational skills of the Maharaja and thanked him profusely for the valuable suggestion.

Spirit of Adventure

In the earlier part of this biography, we have discussed the adventurous spirit of Nalwadi during his childhood and youth. In the course of time, this spirit got crystalised. While driving the car, he demonstrated his love for speed and dexterity. One European gentleman remarked, "His Highness drives with Nerve and Knowledge."

Once Nalwadi was galloping on his horse and the saddle strap tied to the underbelly of the horse got snapped. He fell to the ground immediately and hurt his knee. The bodyguards riding behind him stopped their horses and were about to unmount and help him. But Nalwadi got up from the ground and limped back to his horse. He ordered the bodyguards to remain on their horses. He temporarily fixed the saddle by using the other straps to hold it together. The Maharaja had expertise in breaking down unruly and truant horses. He often took risks while taming these horses. He had trained some horses to prance when the rider was still seated on the saddle. It would jump up in the air and clear hedges and obstacles during show jumping. He was also an expert coach driver. He would drive a chaise with four horses and sometimes with five horses with great skill. He also drove a tandem coach with great dexterity. In this chaise, 2 or 3 horses would be harnessed in a single file one behind the other. The Maharaja handled these horses like an expert coachman. One expert remarked that Nalwadi as a horse rider was riveted to the saddle.

The director of the Spanish horse-riding school of Vienna, who was on a visit to Mysore could not believe his eyes that in India one came across a fine horse rider like Nalwadi. Mr. Soorustha (?) said, "My countrymen will not believe that such a skilled horse rider lived in India. I can only convince them by taking photographs of Nalwadi in action. I will also take photos and I want the palace photographer to take some photos of Nalwadi demonstrating his riding skills." Once, Nalwadi was riding a huge Russian horse, the horse got frightened and began to misbehave with the rider still seated on the saddle. The bystanders, including Mr. Soorustha, feared for the safety of the Maharaja. But Nalwadi brought this frightened horse under control. Later, Mr. Soorustha exclaimed, "It is difficult to believe what one has seen with one's eyes."

The Maharaja trekked boldly inside the tiger reserve forest. On a few occasions, when a tiger jumped from a bush and took everyone by surprise, Nalwadi would stand boldly with his double-barrelled gun and fire at it. He has killed a few tigers at point-blank range. Once, he saw the British governor's son drowning in the lake in Nilgiri and Nalwadi jumped into the lake and rescued him, risking his own life.

The Kailash Manasa Sarovar trekking expedition was fraught with several risks. Some of the mountain paths were narrow and steep. The trekker had to be very cautious. If the climber slipped, he would fall into a deep gorge and die. Many pilgrims literally crawled on their fours, but even in these places, Nalwadi boldly walked in an upright position. These pilgrims had to cross the furious fast flowing river with strong currents by a swinging rope bridge. This swinging rope bridge made the individual crossing the river giddy. Some crossed the bridge by holding the hands of others and their eyes closed. Some crawled on all fours to cross the river over the bridge. But the Maharaja walked across the bridge without any nervousness. He, in fact, enjoyed the fast-flowing Kali river in flood and admired the skills of the engineers, who had constructed it.

Pain Tolerance

Since childhood days, Nalwadi had a high degree of pain tolerance. This was seen during his illness. This tolerance for pain caused immense wonder in the doctors. In 1928, he was down with small pox. Although he suffered from a high fever, he did not flinch even once. In 1929, the Maharaja and a few others went on a trekking expedition in the Nilgiri Hills. They covered a distance of 32 miles during this trek. They did a lot of climbing and trekking in the Shola forest area. Nalwadi only carried with him a flask of drinking water. When they returned from the trekking, the Maharaja still looked quite energetic. Once during Dasara festival, before climbing the Golden throne, he removed his gold footwear and was circumambulating the Golden throne three times as part of the religious ritual. A sharp pin pierced his heel causing excruciating pain. But he did not divulge it to anyone. He quietly climbed the steps of the throne and occupied his seat. The evening Darbar lasted two hours. He conducted the Darbar in a regular formal manner though experiencing unbearable pain. He revealed this to his attendants only after returning to his private quarters.

Nalwadi had a small inflammatory swelling on his back. The surgeons decided to remove it surgically. During the surgery, Nalwadi sat in an erect posture reciting Sanskrit hymns. He did not show any symptoms of pain during its removal.

Simplicity and Modesty

If someone is simple and modest, that individual is a blessed soul. These are not only rare virtues to possess, but they are difficult to imbibe and practice in everyday life. It proves that the said individual has overcome his ego. This is difficult to achieve in one's lifetime. Anyone who has conquered his ego is a spiritually evolved human being. The Maharaja was one such person.

In 1908, the Maharaja of Mysore visited the birthplace of Sri Adi Shankaracharya at Kaladi in Kerala. The Dharmadhikari of palace Vidhya Visharadha Veda Brahma Kunigal Ramasastry alias Veda Brahma Krishna Sastri had made elaborate arrangements for his stay. It was too luxurious and opulent. Nalwadi did not relish these arrangements and asked the Dharmadhikari why they had gone to such lengths to make his stay comfortable. The Dharmadhikari replied that His Highness could use whatever comforts he wanted. He had made all these elaborate arrangements, which were fit for the Mysore Maharaja. The local population of 40,000 had turned up to see him. They had immense respect and admiration for him. Hence, these arrangements had been made keeping in mind his rank and status, so as to impress the Cochin state's Citizens. Nalwadi only smiled and kept quiet. It was obvious that he did not relish any of these luxuries.

Once, the Maharaja was travelling from Poona to Bombay. He noticed that Sir Cowasji Jehangir, 2nd Baronet, GCE, KCIE, (1879-1962) a prominent member of the Parsi community was travelling to Bombay in the next carriage. He sent a messenger and requested him to come to his private railway carriage for a tete-a-tete. He did not stand on excessive formality or protocol. They travelled together to Bombay.

Like the fairytale Kings, Nalwadi visited remote hinterland villages in plainclothes. He often travelled by bullock carts incognito in the company of farmers and questioned them on many subjects like,

"What is your opinion of the Maharaja?"
"Is the local Amaldar helpful or unhelpful?"
"Are you burdened by the land taxes?"
"How can the government officials help you in marketing your produce?"
"How much do you earn annually?"

These secret visits were an eye-opening experience for the ruler. The Maharaja was able to attend to their several problems later.

During a trip to Ootachamund with his officials, one court official made fun of poor people, who consumed ragi balls and horse gram Sambar (curry). This joke did not go well with the Maharaja. He ordered the palace chefs to prepare only ragi balls and horse gram sambar for a week. Everyone including His Highness consumed it for a week without a murmur. This was an unforgettable lesson for the arrogant official, who made fun of the diet of the poor. The Maharaja came across a poor man on Chamundi Hill. He was carrying with him ragi gruel. Nalwadi wanted to know how this gruel was prepared. The poor man gave the simple recipe of the ragi gruel. He observed that some members of the royal party smirking. Nalwadi did not like their condescending ways. He told them to look at this poor old man, who was so healthy. He has maintained his health on a diet of ragi gruel. See how unhealthy we are in comparison? That day, the whole royal party was served with ragi gruel during luncheon as an act of retribution.

Flattery and Sycophancy

The Maharaja disliked people praising him excessively. He discouraged sycophancy of any kind. He also did not lend his ears to gossip mongers.

During the month of July 1938, there was a Hindustani classical music concert. The North Indian vocalist was singing his own composition. The song praised the Mysore Maharaja to the skies. This went on for twenty minutes, abruptly the Maharaja got up from his seat and walked out. He showed his resentment to this panegyric composition.

One of the confidants of Nalwadi an old friend was describing the artistic skills of old timers, who were good at building kites. They would fly these kites in open fields after Makara Sankranti. He went overboard and began to praise old timers excessively. Nalwadi sarcastically remarked laughingly, "Yes, I agree with you. Yes, we do not have the good breeze of olden times. The moon and sun of today are different. Everything has changed for good. How can present-day people build such kites?"

In 1924, the members of the royal family went on a sight-seeing trip to Kemmannagundi in a bus. After enjoying the mountain scenery, they decided to return to their camp. The mountainous road was narrow and precarious. So, Nalwadi took over the job of a driver. He drove the bus skilfully and brought everyone to the camp safely.

On another occasion, a government official took over the responsibility of driving the car. But he drove the vehicle in a reckless manner. Nalwadi joked with other co-passengers, "Keep your hand on the door handle, to jump out of the car in case of an accident. As far as I am concerned, I am sitting here like a solid rock." After the driver covered one or two miles of distance, Nalwadi gave a lecture to him, pointing to his faulty driving skills.

Once, the Maharaja was driving his car from Kunigal to Bangalore. Some of his friends were also travelling with him. One passenger from the back seat took undue liberties with the Maharaja. He humorously commented, "What a fine driver we have here? How dignified he looks? We are lucky to have such a driver without remuneration." Although the Maharaja was lost in thought, those irresponsible comments did not escape his notice. He kept a dignified silence. In a short while, one car wheel tyre suffered a puncture (flat tyre). The Maharaja parked his car on the wayside and got down. Another palace car was following his car and it came to the rescue of the Maharaja. Before getting into the other car, he sarcastically commented to his co-passengers. "Your driver's job is only to drive the car. Now your job is to get the car tyre repaired and replaced. You can all follow me at your leisure." So saying, he continued his journey in the other car leaving the others behind.

On another occasion, Nalwadi was travelling by car with some officials from Oootacamund to Mysore. Perhaps, he felt hungry and asked the gentleman seated next to him, whether he had any snacks. That gentleman replied in the negative. Maharaja exclaimed, "Oh! Only Kutchha bandobast!" When the car was passing through Gundelpet town he joked, "Now, we have here pucca bandobast in the wayside hotel. He asked whether they wanted to go there and buy some snacks?" So saying, he laughed loudly and others joined him.

Maharaja of Mysore (Dark Coat and Turban) with the Indian Hockey Team on their way to the Berlin Olympics on the ship deck during the voyage to Marseilles Port

Love for Home State

The modern state of Mysore is a memorial to the vision, dream and aspirations of the Maharaja Sri Nalwadi Krishnaraja Wodeyar. Mysore State embodies his valuable and inestimable contribution to the development and progress of the state. His love and patriotism for the land nurtured and ruled by his ancestors for centuries dating back to 1399 A. D. knew no bounds. He worked day and night tirelessly for the development of Mysore State. He not only loved his state, but he had an equal commitment to the concept of the Indian Nation. During a convocation address delivered during the graduation ceremony of Benaras Hindu University, he said, "We must all remember that we are Indians first and then we belong to a particular region, religion and language. We must strive for the development of the Indian Nation." As far as the Maharaja was concerned, he practised what he preached.

Whenever a famous person visited Mysore city from any corner of India, he or she was invited to palace for an audience with the king. He also contributed funds generously to various organizations functioning in different parts of India. This incident happened some 22 years ago. A gentleman from another state had come to Mysore. He was a Kannadiga of Mysore origin. He wanted to meet the monarch personally. But he could not get an interview through formal channels. So, he hit upon a risky plan. Nalwadi was returning to palace in his car after performing a puja at Chamundeshwari temple. This gentleman knew about it and he spread his *uttariya* on the ghat section road and decided to lie down on the road, so that he could stop the car. Of course, the Maharaja noticed a person lying on the road and stopped the car. He wanted to know the reason for this unique style of protest. When he came to know a Kannadiga from another state badly wanted to meet him, he extended an invitation to him to visit him in the palace. When they met in the palace, Maharaja treated him to refreshments and gave him Sri Chamundeshwari prasadam. This gentleman was very much elated by the one-to-one meeting with His Highness. Nalwadi had a soft corner for Kannadigas living in other states.

When Maharaja was travelling to Europe in 1936, he came across the Indian hockey team travelling to Berlin on the same ship. The Indian Hockey team was going to Germany to participate in the Berlin Olympics of 1936. Nalwadi sent many rare Indian vegetarian dishes to the hockey players from his private kitchen. The Yuvaraja, who was on the ship was especially fond of sportsmen so he sent them Indian sweets, savouries and buttermilk (yoghurt). The Royal entourage was parting their company at the French port of Marseilles. The Indian Hockey team wanted a group photograph with the Maharaja. Nalwadi obliged them with the request. Later, they won the gold medal at the Berlin Olympics. The players attributed their success to the encouragement given by the Maharaja of Mysore. Their only regret was that they were not fortunate to be his subjects.

The Maharaja was blessed with lofty ideals. He was worried about the welfare of his subjects round the clock. He cared for their happiness, well-being and comfort. He wanted them to be physically healthy and well educated. He wanted his citizens to generate wealth. He did not look down on industrialists and businessmen. At the same time, he stressed that the subjects must lead a righteous life. They must be God fearing and they must endorse universal brotherhood. Nalwadi was eager to see his Mysore State achieve prosperity. He wanted to see its fame spread far and wide. After his visit to European countries, he wanted to emulate the best practices of these advanced countries.

During the construction of the present Darbar hall, the Maharaja was advised to engage artists from other states to paint various subjects from Indian epics on the ceiling. But the Maharaja told them he wanted painters from Mysore State to execute these works. He wanted to encourage the local artists because they could also earn some income. It has been already mentioned how copper plates imported from Germany was substituted through indigenous manufacturing innovations.

Once, he went to inspect a newly constructed state highway. He was disappointed to see the patch work of asphalting done by civil engineers. The road did not appear to be a seamless one. He said to them with great pain, "We must make better highways than Europeans. If we cannot improve upon it, at least we must equal it. We have intelligent and trained technical personnel in our country. Any shoddy work done by Indians will give the country a bad name. We can only develop and progress through honest hard work." He recently said, "We must give better facilities to the people. We must deliver latest inventions and discoveries to our people so that their quality of life improves. Our lifespan is short and time is running out." These words were quoted by a high-ranking courtier with tears in his eyes.

Humility

The Maharaja possessed many noble qualities such as wisdom, knowledge, scholarship and musical talent. He was pious, dignified and reserved in his conduct, but the crown of his achievement was humility. This caused immense wonder and amazement in Indian and International visitors.

The famous British chronicler, Col. James. L. Sleeman, C.B, C.M.G, C.B.E, M.V.O, M.A, J.P said he was fortunate to have had a long interview with the Maharaja. He was impressed by the Maharaja's erudition, generosity and humility. Col. Sleeman thought that he was honoured to have met such a great person in his lifetime. Many individuals who were reticent in praising others indulged in wholesome praise after a meeting with the Maharaja.

Nalwadi had acquired a mature intellectual outlook by a lifelong study of books, through reflection and by meditating on important dilemmas of life by resorting to philosophical analysis and contemplation. When Lord Lothian received the news of Nalwadi's death, he exclaimed, "Such a decent gentleman endowed with great humility is rare in today's world. We may not see such a great personality again."

The Maharaja of Mysore was a good talent scout. He selected his Dewans and other high-ranking officials on the basis of merit. It did not matter to him, where the individual hailed from or his caste or religion or even his race. The Maharaja of Mysore was a generous patron to sanyasis, ascetics, patriots, political scientists, sculptors, painters, musicians, preachers, vedic scholars, fine arts craftsmen, scientists, reciters of Hindu epics, bhajan singers, comic actors and any achiever who had made a mark in public life was welcomed with open arms. They were given plenty of encouragement and they were rewarded generously with gold medals, shawls and money. His younger brother, the Yuvaraja Sri Kanteerava Narasimharaja Wodeyar was equally a great patron of writers, poets, artists, sportsmen and musicians. Even today, these recipients, who are spread all over India remember the royal patronage with great fondness.

The Maharaja Nalwadi Sri Krishnaraja Wodeyar was an *"Ajaathashatru"* (one without enemies), humble, wealthy and moreover a ruler adored by his subjects. He was a model ruler. Even today, people remember his good deeds, generosity and kindness. His immortal fame and popularity will live for ever.

Huzoor Secretary to the
Maharaja Rajasabha Bhushana Sri. T. Thumboo Chetty, B. A., O. B. E

Chapter 15

The Present Ruler Sri Jayachamarajendra Wodeyar

******

"Aakaara sadrusha pragnah pragnaya sadrushaagamah|
Aagamaisadrusharambah praramba Sadrushodayah||"
"Raja prajnaam praanam vy"
"chiramabivardhatam yadu Santana srih"

******

"The ruler possesses an awareness and consciousness suited to his personality. His genius lies in having scholarship in received traditional knowledge (*Agama*). His actions are guided by dharmasastras. He has developed qualities, which enable him to accomplish any project undertaken by him. "The monarch is the life-breath of his subjects. May Goddess bless the Yadu dynasty with plentiful progenies in the coming centuries."

The Royal Proclamation Darbar

The King-Emperor George VI of Great Britain proclaimed through an official proclamation that Sri Jayachamaraja Wodeyar is officially nominated as the successor to the throne of Mysore State after the death of the Maharaja Sri Nalwadi Krishnaraja Wodeyar. The Viceroy of India, Lord Linlithgow, conveyed this official proclamation to the British Resident. Sri Jayachamaraja Wodeyar was proclaimed on 29th August 1940 as the Maharaja of Mysore State by the British Resident in the Darbar Hall. The Viceroy of India had sent a pearl necklace and a ceremonial dress for the occasion. In turn, expensive robes were given to the British Viceroy of India by the royal family and they were conveyed through the resident. This special Darbar was attended by the Dewan, two cabinet ministers, Chief Justice, Huzoor Secretary, chief secretary and many other dignitaries. The British resident in his speech praised the rule of the previous Maharaja and his administrative acumen. He also lauded the noble qualities of the successor and wished that his rule will also be equally remarkable and beneficial to the state. The whole cabinet of ministers and officials, who had worked under Nalwadi stood beside Sri Jayachamaraja Wodeyar, when he took the oath of office. They had declared their allegiance to the new Maharaja.

The State government administrative machinery is run by the following officials:

(1) Amin-ul-Mulk Sir Mirza M. Ismail Dewan of Mysore State
(2) First Cabinet Minister: Rajamantra Praveena Sri N. Madhava Rao
(3) Second Cabinet Minister Rajamantra Praveena Sri K.V. Anantharaman
(4) Palace administration: Huzoor Secretary Raja Sabaha Bhushana Sri T. Thumboo Chetty O.B.E
(5) Private Secretary: Sir Charles Todd Hunter, K.C.S.I.

In my opinion, this cabinet will make any state in India proud. From next June, as per political reforms the Maharaja will be assisted by two more Cabinet Ministers and by a chairperson of Legislative council. The present Maharaja has been striving hard to make the lives of common people better. He is blessed with talent and scholarship. He wants Mysore State to progress further and hence, he is working round the clock without rest.

The queen-mother Sri Maharanai Sri Lakshmi Vilasa Sannidhana (wife of Nalwadi) gave her consent to her Godson (nephew) to ascend the gold throne on 8th September 1940 (As per Hindu calendar *Vikramanama Samvatsara bhadrapada Shuddha Saptami*). The formal invitations were printed and they were sent to dignitaries and guests.

Many religious rituals were performed on 7th September 1940. It also happened to be the day of Sri Chamundeshwari Devi Kalasa and Sri Utthanahalli Jwalamukhi Devi Kalasa were consecrated. Yuvaraja Sri Jayachamaraja Wodeyar Bahadur underwent holy ritual bath, Diksha Vastradharana and Kankana dharana rituals were performed.

All over the Mysore State, 9000 homa and havanas were performed for the well-being of the new Maharaja. The State government declared 7th, 8th, 9th and 10th September 1940 as public holidays, because of the coronation ceremony through a gazette notification.

The capital city of Mysore wore a festive look. The streets were decorated with colourful bunting flags. On top of every government building, the Mysore State red flag with "Gandaberunda" (double headed eagle) figure was flying on flag poles. People had flocked to Mysore from distant towns and villages to witness the coronation ceremony. The uniformed soldiers, guards and cavalry riders put up an impressive show. The palace was decorated with plantain stalks and mango leaves. The elephants, horses and camels took part in the procession.

On 8th September 1940, preparations began in Mysore palace for the coronation ceremony early in the morning. The Yuvaraja and his wife arrived at Lakshmivilasa Thotti in Mysore palace at 5:30 AM. Seven married women applied holy oil on their heads. They were given a sacred ritual bath with waters of Ganga, Yamuna, Cauvery and Kapila rivers. They were given a special bath with perfumed water. After this auspicious bath, the Yuvaraja and Yuvarani wore ceremonial dresses and jewellery for the occasion. Early in the morning from the ramparts of the Mysore fort the infantry men fired 21 guns in honour of the new Maharaja.

Sri Jayachamaraja Wodeyar arrived at Kalyana Mantapa holding a bow and arrow at 7:30 AM. He performed puja to "Kalasha" (holy silver vessel with Ganga water, coconut and pan leaves) dedicated to favourite Gods. He circumambulated the "Homa Kunda" (worship of fire god Agni) three times. Then, he sat on a low wooden stool placed on a tiger skin facing east. Then sixteen brahmin priests, who had performed homa and yagna on the previous day gave a holy ritual purification bath. They chanted veda mantras from all the four vedas. A golden ring with nine precious stones embedded in it was held on his head and water from sacred rivers were poured on him. This is how Sri Jayachamaraja Wodeyar was anointed and elevated to the status of a new Maharaja (*pattabhisheka*). A few auspicious married women tied a gold headband on the Yuvarani Sri Satyaprema Devi and performed upgradation rite. The Royal couple donated different types of gifts to brahmin priests and to auspicious married women such things as holy cow gift, gold coins, nine kinds of cereals, clothes, gold and silver statues of Hindu Gods and Goddesses. Afterwards, the Maharaja and Maharani performed "*Acharya puja*" and "*Bruhspathi puja.*" Then, the Maharaja was given "*Gorochana*"[6] for

---

[6.] "Gorochana" is a valuable holy medicine obtained from the forehead of an "ox." It appears like yellowish wax during its collection and then it becomes hard and reddish brown in colour.

consumption. Then, the priests applied twelve scented holy oils to different parts of Maharaja's body. From there, the royal couple went to the ladies' quarters to take the blessings of former Maharani and Yuvarani (mother of Sri Jayachamaraja Wodeyar). The Maharaja at 10 A:M on "Akashavani" (Radio) delivered his inaugural speech. In his speech made in English and Kannada assured the citizens of Mysore State that he intends to give a just and fair administration. He wants to continue the good work done by his uncle the previous Maharaja Sri Nalwadi Krishnaraja Wodeyar.

The printed copies of the inaugural speech were circulated among press corpus and Government departments. In full ceremonial regalia with the crown on his head, Sri Jayachamaraja Wodeyar Bahadur ascended the golden throne to the musical rendition of the state anthem.

The people in various cities and towns organized gala functions to celebrate the coronation of the new Maharaja. The whole population of Mysore State was thrilled by the spirited inaugural speech of Sri Jayachamaraja Wodeyar. Here is the gist of his speech.

"Today, I have taken a vow to dedicate my whole life to the development, progress and prosperity of the State of Mysore, while ascending the throne of my illustrious ancestors, who have ruled the state for several centuries. This objective cannot be achieved by one individual alone, it calls for your wholehearted help, co-operation, trust and love in good measure." These words of Sri Jayachamaraja Wodeyar touched the hearts of the state population. It raised immense hope and expectation in the mind of the common man.

The coronation ceremony took place in the Kalyana Mantapa. The gold throne of antiquity was placed on a tiger skin with its head facing east. All the government officials and courtiers had assembled in the hall. In the courtyard, the nadaswara musicians were playing auspicious music. All the spectators in the gallery were eagerly looking forward to the arrival of the Maharaja. In the foreground of the palace, four caparisoned elephants and four decorated sacred bulls stood in waiting. Along with these animals, the holy cow, the royal elephant and the royal horse waited for the Maharaja. The guards carried the royal family standards and the auspicious white umbrella into the coronation hall.

Sri Jayachamaraja Wodeyar, after doing puja to Sri Vigneshwara arrived in Kalyana Mantapa at 10:15 AM with his bodyguards. The court criers proclaimed the titles and honours of the new Maharaja. The Maharaja looked grand in his elegant formal dress and he was bejewelled with gold, diamonds and pearls. Sri Jayachamarajendra Wodeyar stood before the gold throne facing north and with bowed head performed puja as per the "Kalpokta" procedure. While Gana paatis were chanting veda mantras, Sri Jayachamaraja Wodeyar climbed the steps of the throne by holding the right hand of his maternal uncle, Sri Srikanta Lakshmikantaraja Urs during "vyraja" muhurta and took his seat. At that moment, a 21-gun salute was given in honour of the new Maharaja. The palace musicians played classical music on the occasion. Sixteen Brahmin priests sprinkled holy water from silver vessels with mango leaves on all the assembled people. The holy cow, elephant and horse were worshipped by the priests by sprinkling holy water upon them. These dignitaries Dewan Sir Mirza M. Ismail, Chief-of-Army A. V. Subramanyaraja Urs and State Treasurer Sri T. Thumboo Chetty sprinkled holy water with mango leaves upon the new Maharaja. Then, the Darbarbakshi Sri H. L. Devaraja Urs recited the Wodeyar Royal Family "*Vamsavali*" (Genealogy) in Kannada. He was honoured with a ceremonial coat by the Maharaja. He bowed before the Highness and thanked him for the honour of serving him. The Dewan of Mysore leading eleven other noblemen offered "Nazar" to the Maharaja. The Maharaja received coconuts, fruits and sacred rice grain that had been sent by famous temples and religious mutts of the Mysore State. Many royal courtiers and dignitaries offered "Nazar" to the Maharaja.

A well-known dancer performed Bharatanatyam before His Highness. The coronation ceremony concluded with a Carnatic classical music concert by the vocalist Gayaka Shikamani Sri Mutthaiah Bhagavatar. Then, the Maharaja retired to the private quarters to receive the blessings of the former Maharani and Yuvarani. The women performed "Aarati" to him. The guests in the Darbar Hall were garlanded and given "Tamboola" (pan leaves with areca nuts). The Maharaja conducted Darbar on the next two evenings. On the 9th of September 1940 (Monday) evening, the Maharaja travelled in a silver chariot drawn by oxen to the temples on the palace grounds. This procession was watched by thousands of Mysoreans with great joy.

First Cabinet Minister Rajamantra Praveena Sri N. Madhava Rao

Second Cabinet Minister Rajamantra Praveena Sri K. V. Anantharaman

Significance of New Changeover

The coronation ceremony of Maharaja Sri Jayachamaraja Wodeyar took place on the auspicious day of *Shuddha Saptami* (Sunday) in *Bhadrapada* month of Sri *Vikramanama Samvatsara*. This coronation day has gone into the annals of Mysore State history as a red letter day. This new phase in our history heralds a new era of progress. The new ruler's name starts with the word "Jaya," which means victory. So, we all wish our Maharaja victory in every endeavour, he takes up in the coming days.

At present, our Maharaja is only twenty-one years old. However, he has acquired immense knowledge and earned valuable experience through his interaction with the public. He excelled academically during his student days at the royal school and at Mysore University. His love for fine arts like painting and music blossomed forth in his early childhood days. When he was a young babe in the cradle, he responded enthusiastically to gramophone records and loved music. During his youth, he received music lessons in piano and classical Carnatic music.

He became a favourite student of his teachers by displaying remarkable memory. He was modest and well-mannered in his behaviour. God has blessed Sri Jayachamaraja Wodeyar with handsome looks, a charismatic personality, sharp intelligence and noble qualities, which have endeared him to everybody.

The Maharaja has displayed from childhood a remarkable penchant for discipline and punctuality. He followed a strict schedule with regard to studies and sports. Even when enjoying a jolly good conversation, he would stand up suddenly and excuse himself by saying he had to attend to evening sandhyavandana or puja. He showed a remarkable degree of mental maturity at a young age.

Sri Jayachamaraja Wodeyar was fluent in English at the age of five. He was fond of listening to stories, especially from puranas (epics) and he was also a good storyteller. Some playwrights wrote short plays for the royal school children. In these plays, Sri Jayachamaraja Wodeyar took often a lead role and enacted plays before the family members, much to their delight. In his childhood, he dreamt of a railway connection to every village and wanted to provide free train ride to all the villagers. Such was his generous bent of mind. Once the young prince was asked what he would do with huge sums of money if it was given to him. He naively replied he would distribute it amongst the poor. Like Nalwadi Krishnaraja Wodeyar, Prince Jayachamaraja Wodeyar had instructed the cooks not to make any distinction between him and the royal school students while serving food. He gave financial assistance to many of his middle-class friends, who needed help to tide over problems at home. If someone was sick, he would organize medical assistance for such needy persons. If he saw a bruised horse or ox harnessed to a cart, he could not bear the sight of it. He would order the cart driver to unharness these animals from the cart. Once, he saw his teacher getting drenched in the pouring rain. He gave his personal umbrella to him, though the teacher was reluctant to accept it. The young prince opted to get drenched in the rain instead of the teacher. Whenever the prince visited Ooty with his sisters, it was a common sight to see him pull the buggy cart himself with his three sisters in it. His simple affable lifestyle had a great appeal to the public.

The present Maharaja as a youth gets up every day at 5 AM. He takes music lessons, Hindi language lessons and horse-riding lessons before breakfast. Before going to the royal school, he would memorize lessons. Because of Nalwadi and Yuvaraja's influence during his college days, he mixed with his classmates easily and he was informal in his behaviour. He was a diligent scholar and learnt piano and other musical instruments. As far as outdoor sports activities are concerned he was fond of horse riding, "racquets" (squash), tennis and gymnastics.

The chief instructor in the royal school was J. T. Turner, who taught the Prince from 1930. Sri Jayachamaraja Wodeyar had developed a great passion for reading books. If he found any new book that appeared in the bookshops, he would procure one for his library. He has a formidable collection of books in his private library worth thousands of rupees. He has remained an avid reader of books.

Coronation of Maharaja Sri Jayachamarajendra Wodeyar Bhadur

Sri Jayachamaraja Wodeyar graduated from Mysore University in 1938. He secured a high first class in B.A course. He had secured the highest marks in his optional subjects. He was awarded five gold medals in the university convocation from his paternal uncle Sri Nalwadi Krishnaraja Wodeyar the chancellor of Mysore University. This gladdened the hearts of the admirers, who were present in the auditorium. Whenever any charitable collection was made in the college, Prince Jayachamaraja Wodeyar would be the last contributor. He did not want to embarrass his classmates by making a big contribution at the beginning of the collection drive.

Prince Jayachamarja Wodeyar did not study books during his student days only to score good grades in the examination. Often, he studied several books on the same topic to gain in-depth knowledge. In history class, he would ask his professor such questions as:

(i) What are the reasons for a war between the two countries?
(ii) Why peace is not a better option?
(iii) Why permanent peace cannot be established globally?

These penetrating questions expose the rational thinking of the Maharaja. He had immense compassion and concern for the poor. Once, he asked his teacher to take him to the poorer quarters of the city. He dressed in plain clothes, he went incognito to these slums with his teacher. When he saw the grinding poverty in these slums, his heart melted with compassion.

His study of economics did not restrict him to only theories. He was a practical man with a realistic outlook on life. His extensive travels within the country and his trips to Europe and Japan gave him rich experience, which had an added advantage to his received education.

Sri Jayachamaraja Wodeyar travelled to Japan via Saigon by ship. The Indian community in Saigon gave a grand gala banquet. This trip to Japan was made after his marriage. In Japan, an American tourist met him. They had a long conversation. After the meeting, the American exclaimed, "This young Indian Prince is better educated than our senators. I am astounded by his knowledge of international affairs, global economic trends and political conflicts much better than our university professors. I had harboured the stereotype image of an Indian Maharaja as an indolent person languishing in luxury and going about his capital on an elephant. After meeting the Mysore Maharaja, I realized I was dead wrong."

This incident took place in the lobby of a Tokyo Hotel. A Gujarati businessman was also staying in the same hotel. He saw the Maharaja in informal dress studying a world map on the wall in the lobby. The businessman asked him whether he belonged to the royal entourage. The Maharaja nodded his head. The businessman asked him how he could get an interview with the Maharaja. What formal dress must he wear? How he should address the Maharaja? In the end, Sri Jayachamaraja Wodeyar informed him laughingly that he was talking all the while with the Maharaja of Mysore. This was a great surprise to the businessman. He was overwhelmed by the unassuming simple behaviour of the Maharaja. He profusely apologized for his informal and casual behaviour with the Maharaja.

As Yuvaraja of Mysore State, Sri Jayachamaraja Wodeyar was invited as a chief guest to grace several functions. On 14th May 1938, Kannada Sahitya Parishat invited him to address *"Vasantha Sahitya Utsav"* (Spring literary festival). He delivered an impressive speech in Kannada. He gained experience in administration by visiting various government departments and by studying the functioning of the secretariat. The Yuvaraja was helped by Mr. Elwin and Janab Mekhri Saheb. Sri Jayachamaraja Wodeyar loved Kannada language and literature. He was the chief patron and president of Kannada Sahitya parishat. He felt that the citizens of Mysore State were the children of one mother. They should develop a feeling of brotherhood and must develop a feeling of oneness, because of Kannada language and culture. He has enjoyed the love, affection and respect of his subjects from his childhood days. In a public gathering at K. R. Nagara, where thousands of villagers had come from faraway villages, they all felt thrilled and happy, when Dewan Mirza M. Ismail announced in the presence of Prince Sri Jayachamaraja Wodeyar that he was going to be their new Yuvaraja in 1940.

After the coronation ceremony in October 1940 and after Dasara festival, the Bangalore Municipal Corporation invited him for a civic reception. A public function was organized on 4th November 1940 at Town Hall and a memorandum was presented to him. In his reply, he expressed his great love and commitment to the welfare of his subjects. When he came in the procession, Bangalore city's businessmen and rich citizens had erected pandals, victory arches, welcome banners and bunting flags. Several thousands of citizens had lined up the streets on either side. He was cheered and flower garlands were offered to him. He was overcome with emotion and shed tears of joy seeing the love and affection of his people. A large number of people had come from different towns of Mysore State.

Sri Jayachamaraja Woeyar had an adventurous spirit from his childhood days. When he was twelve years old, he would ride a horse doing all kinds of stunts. This show riding amazed even grown-up experienced riders. Later, he developed a penchant for the Tiger hunt. In the month of November 1940, he hunted a few tigers. A lone tusker (leader of a group of elephants) had strayed away and it was running amok and causing immense damage to standing crops and had damaged a few houses in the village as well. The Maharaja killed this rogue elephant in January 1941. It requires great courage to confront a rogue elephant on foot in the forest and kill it. The Maharaja has not shown any fear in such a situation till now.

Sri Jayachamaraja Wodeyar is blessed with noble hereditary qualities, strength of mind and administrative skills. He has received a good education and developed a sharp intellect with incessant reading of books and his extensive travels in India and abroad which has enriched his experiences. This well-thought-out opinion of Dewan Sir Mirza M. Ismail is a valid and valuable statement, "The onerous responsibility shouldered by our Maharaja is nothing new to him. He is well-equipped and qualified to carry out the tasks assigned to him by the divine force. He is competent to carry out these duties with ease and comfort. He is going to fulfil all our expectations in this regard though young in age. He occupies the throne, on which his great predecessor Sri Nalwadi Krishnaraja Wodeyar reigned for 38 years. Similarly, the present ruler will strive to live up to the expectations of all of us. He will work hard for the economic development and progress of Mysore State unflinchingly. We are all confident that his rule will be a successful and productive rule." These words of the Dewan are no exaggeration.

Prince Sri Jayachamarajendra Wodeyar after graduation ceremony with a B.A Degree from Mysore University

Sri Jayachamaraja Wodeyar on 26th December 1940 inaugurated a "Scout Rally" in Bangalore. He visited the tents of scouts, who had come from different states of India. He made enquiries about their health and well-being. The Maharaja's simple unassuming ways impressed all India delegates. Again, on 28th December 1940 in Mysore city, he inaugurated the All India Conference of Economists and Political Scientists. His inaugural speech astounded the Indian delegates with its contents and critical outlook. Even the experts were awe-struck by the in-depth scholarship of the Maharaja in the field of economics and political science. They had not expected such a profound speech to come from a young Maharaja.

Prince Sri Jayachamarajendra Wodeyar on a pony

The Maharaja went on an official tour from 9th February 1941 to 19th February 1941 and visited Shimoga, Kadur and Hassan districts. His official visit entailed him to lay the foundation stone for various projects. He did not complain about the physical strain or discomfort that had to be endured. His speeches and courteous behaviour won the hearts of the population. He killed two man-eating tigers during this visit. He also allotted Rs. 2 lakhs to the Malnad development fund. He donated vast sums of money to various organizations in this region. He visited the hydroelectric project site at Jog, the Bhadravathi Iron and Steel plant and the Belur temple built in the Hoysala style of architecture. In many places, he gave money for free distribution of "laddus" (sweets) to children. He gave a press interview to ten journalists. Each journalist received a wristwatch as a gift. The speeches delivered by the Maharaja during his official tour reflect his staunch patriotism, love for his subjects, future vision, noble ideals and goals for the modernization of Mysore State.

The humble author concludes this biography with an ardent prayer to Goddess Chamundeshwari. May our present Maharaja follow the steps of his predecessor Sri Nalwadi Krishnaraja Wodeyar who was an ideal ruler and "Raja Rishi". Nalwadi was a leading light among Yaduvamsha rulers, a lover of classical music and literature. May our present ruler treat his subjects as his own children. Sri Jayachamaraja Wodeyar must emulate the previous ruler and become a source of pride to the Mysoreans. He must become an apple of the eye of his subjects. The new ruler must become a beacon of light to the world. He must propagate Indian philosophy and culture through his state policies. May his rule be a long and fruitful one. The Maharaja must make the Modern State of Mysore more famous and progressive in the coming years.

Om Shanthi! Om Shanthi! Om Shanthi!

The Royal couple: Maharaja Sri Jayachamarajendra Wodeyar Bahadur and Maharani Sri Satyapremadevi

www.ingramcontent.com/pod-product-compliance
Ingram Content Group UK Ltd.
Pitfield, Milton Keynes, MK11 3LW, UK
UKHW020245240426
12048UKWH00026B/1618